CULTURE AND CONTRADICTION

Dialectics of Wealth, Power, and Symbol

Hermine G. De Soto

EMTexts
San Francisco

Library of Congress Cataloging-in-Publication Data

Culture and contradiction: dialectics of wealth, power, and symbol /
  edited by Hermine G. De Soto.
      p. cm.
    Festschrift in honor of Aidan Southall.
    Includes bibliographical references.
    ISBN 0-7734-1938-1
      1. Ethnology--Methodology. 2. Ethnology--Philosophy.
    3. Southall, Aidan William. I. De Soto, Hermine G.
    GN33.C85 1992
    306--dc20   92-24002
                                                               CIP

Editorial Inquiries:

Mellen Research University Press
534 Pacific Avenue
San Francisco
CA 94133

Order Fulfillment:

The Edwin Mellen Press
P.O. Box 450
Lewiston, NY 14092
USA

Printed in the United States of America

FOR AIDAN SOUTHALL

TABLE OF CONTENTS

IV. **SYMBOLIC MANIFESTATIONS: KINSHIP, IDEOLOGY**
AND TEXTUALITY

LIST OF ILLUSTRATIONS

ACKNOWLEDGEMENTS

From the beginning to the end of preparing and editing the Festschrift, two special persons--David John De Soto, and Bernelda Roberts--receive my deepest appreciation and thanks for their tireless emotional support, solidarity, commitment and assistance without which the final work would have been considerably delayed. Naturally, both of my friendly critics should not be held in any way accountable for the final versions of this text, which are wholly my responsibility.

Additionally, I acknowledge with great appreciation the institutional support of the Women's Studies Research Center of the University of Wisconsin-Madison. My special thanks are extended to Cyrena Pondrom for her continuous and enthusiastic encouragement.

I am also grateful to the international contributors for their participation. Without them, this Festschrift would not have come to fruition. Finally, it is my sincere hope that I have done no injustice in the process of transmitting the contributors' ideas and gratitude to this book honoring Aidan Southall.

I. INTRODUCTION

Hermine G. De Soto, Assistant Scientist
University of Wisconsin-Madison, United States

To honor a scholar of such magnitude as Aidan Southall is an intimidating task. Nevertheless, as one of Professor Southall's last students, and while I was teaching in the department of anthropology at the University of Wisconsin-Madison during the spring of 1990, I began to carry out this challenging thought by communicating with several of Aidan Southall's former students, friends, and colleagues-- who then were in areas of Africa, Asia, Europe, North America, and in New Zealand--about the possibility of paying homage to this very distinguished scholar who markedly and fundamentally influenced anthropological research and theory in various subfields of social and cultural anthropology.

There was enthusiastic response to the invitation for Festschrift articles by contributors from various parts of the world. I learned not only about the many lives Dr. Southall has touched in his long and productive career as an anthropologist, but also that my earlier-held perception of Aidan Southall as an authentic global anthropologist, before "globalism" had become fashionable, was confirmed even more.

In his global vision Professor Southall also stressed a comparative perspective, a view which I think over the years allowed him to become an intellectual cultural critic of the rarest kind, a producer of cultural knowledge who challenged most profoundly--yet professionally--any form of mystification wherever he encountered it in the presentations of the political, economic and symbolic realm in the development of human history. With this commitment, Dr. Southall untiringly drew attention in anthropology to the reproduction of poverty, social and economic injustices and to the struggles of marginalized peoples whether in rural or urban environments around the globe. It is in this intellectual context that Aidan Southall's former students, friends and colleagues express their gratitude and respond in *Culture and Contradiction: Dialectics of Wealth, Power and Symbol* to a prominent scholar's life in anthropology.

Although I have organized this Festschrift with chapter titles, this does not mean that these essay groupings necessarily need to be read together. Instead, each contribution is original, offering the reader new cultural insights on an individual basis. The affiliation line and the country of residence for each author, as presented under each article's title, is current as of the last communication prior to publication of this volume.

Since I began editing the Festschrift, several marked changes have occurred which directly or in some ways relate to the progess of the volume. For example, while I was successful in communicating on the progress of the volume with almost all of the contributors, I am not certain if Professor Ruan Xihu in Beijing, Peoples Republic of China, ever received the correspondence that I sent to him. On the other hand, the outbreak of the civil war in Zaire sadly interrupted my correspondence with Professor Mukohya Vwakyanakazi of Shaba University, a former student of Aidan Southall. Even though Dr.

Vwakyanakazi still was able to send his article to me, my letters to him were returned unopened via Brussels, Belgium. My thoughts go to Dr. Vwakyanakazi during these troubled times.

The second major change, the collapse of the socialist rational redistributive regimes in eastern Europe, affected me in that I had to reorganize my timelines and therefore the progression of the Festschrift. Part of the work was completed in east Berlin where I have been engaged in fieldwork since the collapse of the "iron curtain."

The last change, however, was Aidan Southall's retirement in 1990 from the department of anthropology in Madison, Wisconsin. While this Festschrift for Dr. Southall goes to press, he is in Uganda revisiting the Alur society, the place from where he began his journey in anthropology.

May his new research continue to inspire and to motivate us to build further upon the solid anthropological groundwork he initiated for all of us.

II. ECONOMIC RELATIONS: GENDER, CLASS, AND POVERTY

Gender Power and Marital Options for Low-Income Women In Nairobi

Nici Nelson, Professor
University of London, United Kingdom

In the 1960s, when I completed by master's degree at Columbia, two important factors came to bear on my choice of topic for my doctoral research. The first was my realization of how androcentric anthropological research is (though, of course, I would not have expressed it that way then)--a realization that had its origins in my search for substantive data on women when writing my master's library thesis on Islam and the role of women in West Africa. The second was Aidan Southall's edited volume, *Social Change in Modern Africa* (1961). Determined as I was to do my research in Africa, this volume confirmed my inarticulate feeling that real and exciting work was waiting to be done in Africa's cities, and in my case, on women in Africa's cities. I must thank Aidan Southall for more than the initial inspiration to do an urban rather than a rural study.

In 1973, I was fortunate to meet him in Nairobi in the middle of my fieldwork. Due to the collapse of Makerere University during the early years of Amin's regime, I had virtually no supervision during my research period. His insightful and generous informal supervision at that time encouraged me to analyze where I was going, focus my data gathering, and finish my research. His practical advice at this crisis in my postgraduate career also helped me to find another department in which to finish writing my thesis and complete my degree. From inception to final write-up, it is no exaggeration to say that my research would not have been done without the inspiration and advice of Aidan Southall. So it was that in 1971 I first entered Mathare Valley (a large shanty town in Nairobi) to begin my work on female beer brewers. In subsequent years, I have maintained contact with many of my original informants and their daughters; some of them stayed in Mathare and some scattered to other parts of Nairobi.

Between 1971 and 1974, I carried out research in one "village" of a large shanty town, Mathare Valley. It was an extended piece of participant observation that included life history interviews with some eighty women, and other extended, open-ended interviews on various topics. Four subsequent visits of varying duration (one to three months) were made in which I did research of a more or less formal nature. My latest visit was a three-month period of research in early 1990. In the original research my understanding and knowledge was greatly enhanced by the intelligent and committed assistance of Veronica Nyambura wa Njoroge. In my revisits, my ability to find and recontact my previous informants, as well as to come to grips with the changing world of Kenyan politics and society, would have been difficult without the dedication and inspiration of David Irungu.

Until the 1970s, African anthropology viewed marriage as a clearly defined institution with accepted structures and functions.

The British Structural-Functionalists defined marriage as the institution creating the elementary family, the building blocks of the unilineal descent system. The consensus model of society did not allow for much variation and flexibility in these so-called "institutions." Recent reexamination of old and new ethnographies reveals that this has been a fault of the old analysis. Gough's reassessment of Evans-Pritchard's own data (1940) showed there was a statistically significant incidence of uxorilocal marriage, woman-to-woman marriage, unmarried daughters staying in their father's camp, and the possibility of tracing connections to a high status clan through the female line; enough for him to assume the unchallenged hegemony of patriliny in the organization of marriage and kinship (1978). Amadiume's (1984) study of Igbo kinship and gender politics demonstrates clearly that there have always been variants of marriage in a context of a surprisingly flexible definition of gender. Daughters, for example, could be declared "sons" in order to give a sonless father an heir. The female "sons" stayed in their fathers' compounds and produced descendants for the lineage. Obbo (1980) traced many of her Luo informants from their Kampala residence to their rural homes, and found that in these rural compounds there were significant numbers of unmarried daughters/sisters living with their fathers/brothers.

The French Structuralists' interest in marriage was in its role of forging and maintaining alliances among male descent groups. Neo-Marxists saw marriage as part of the structure of exploitation and inequality with kin groups. Levi-Strauss's Alliance Theory has been criticized as treating women as objects of exchange, mere pawns in men's power games. This type of analysis abstracts the analysis of marriage from any empirical process of choice and negotiation (Rubin 1975). Meillassoux (1975) treats marriage so cursorially that he seems to assume that elders' control of marriage is both unproblematical and unchallengeable by either young men or women.

Bordieu contends that an overemphasis on "rule" in anthropological theory ends with a mechanical model that provides no insights into the choices and nonchoices existing for the actors (1977). This heavy emphasis on "models and rules" reifies abstractions which then are treated as realities endowed with social efficacy. The living, breathing actors (female actors even more than male) in this social drama are rarely dealt with in a meaningful way. Burnham's suggestion seems a constructive way to redress the balance.

> It seems analytically valuable to consider all forms of conjugal relations, from consensual unions to "ordinance" or "church" marriages, as representing bundles of interactional possibilities with associated political, economic, legal and other implications. How these interactional possibilities are utilized by male and female actors is a central, if very complex, question for future research (1987, 50).

What marital options were open (and closed) to low-income Highland Bantu (Gikuyu, Meru, Embu) women of Mathare and Eastlands of Nairobi? And what are the implications of the patterns of choices observed?

Connell, in his exploration of gender relations, has proposed that gender relations be examined within three "structures of relationship between men and women": first, labor (both productive and reproductive labor); second, power, such as authority, control, and coercion (including state, institutional, and personal violence and sexual regulation); and third, cathexis (or the patterning of desire and sexuality). These are the structures within which the practice of gender relations take place. They are the constraints within which the gender negotiate relations (1987, chap. 5). I will show that within the constraints operating on them and choices available to them, these women try to improve their position in the asymmetrical gender power system of Kenya today by manipulating conjugal and sexual relationships with men.

Kenya is an East African country that, before colonization, was occupied by decentralized, patrilineal pastoralists and shifting horticulturalists. From 1900 onward these people were increasingly incorporated into a colonial state, which also sustained an influx of settlers. The Gikuyu were the most severely dislocated in this process.

At independence, the future looked bright for Kenya: good agricultural prospects, an increasingly well-educated populace, a central position in the East African Federation (both literally and metaphorically), a moderate, populist political leadership that seemed ready to make use of the skills and resources of the remaining Europeans in the development process, rather than to take revenge for the years of exploitation and war.

At the time of the research, that promise seemed to be bearing fruit. Kenya was a relatively stable, prosperous, mixed-capitalist country with a largely rural population of eleven million and attracted a great deal of Western foreign aid and multinational investment. Even at this time, however, the authorities could not cope with the rapid rural-urban migration taking place, and the Informal Sector (both in housing and in jobs) was expanding enormously. Mathare Valley was part of this expansion. The picture in 1990 is less optimistic. The oil crisis of 1974 brought about a recession in Kenya, as elsewhere, from which it only partially recovered. After a decade and a half of one of the highest population growths in the world (4.2 percent), growing unemployment, and increasing class differentiation with accompanying corruption at all levels, the economy is stagnant and the government increasingly centralized and dictatorial.

Changing Aspects of Gikuyu Marriage

Marriage and gender power relations in precolonial society

This brief survey is based on Leakey (1977), Kenyatta (1938), and Cagnolo (1933). Marriage in precolonial Gikuyu seems to have been a personal affair where the young people made their choices at dances and in closely supervised, limited sexual experimentation. To marry, the couple had to obtain both parents' permission. In general, the Gikuyu seemed to take the sensible view that to force a marriage only ended in the girl running away in the end.

Unions were formalized by a lengthy series of visits and exchanges of beer and goats, but the bridewealth did not seem to be excessive or difficult to raise. A young man could raise his own, if his father refused.

Pregnancy before marriage was only a minor disgrace, especially if the genitor married the girl. If there was no marriage, the boy paid a fine to the elders, after which the girl was free to marry someone else. The child belonged to her subsequent husband's lineage. The serious shame was for an uncircumcised girl to become pregnant.

The Gikuyu woman-to-woman marriage allowed a barren woman to "marry" a woman by paying her bridewealth and then keeping the subsequent children as hers.

Divorce was probably relatively frequent in the early stages of the marriage, but rare after several children were born. Both men and women could institute divorce proceedings on a wide variety of grounds including barrenness (for the man) refusal to fulfill conjugal duties, ill treatment, and impotence (for the woman). Bridewealth was only repaid if the woman had borne fewer than two children. A woman's family would try to persuade a woman to return to her husband to avoid repayment. A woman who was divorced before the harvest lost her standing crops. Children could remain with their mother until their adolescence. Polygyny was permitted. The levirate was practiced. Adultery was treated seriously but not severely.

Gikuyu marriage took place within a gender power system that might be characterized as a limited form of dual sex system (Okonjo 1976). The gender division of labor was such that women were farmers, child carers, and reproducers, while men were long-distance traders, politicians, and religious specialists. Men controlled the major resources of the Gikuyu: the land and the cattle. Land was allocated only to men by the elders of the residential sublineage. Men could pioneer new land as well. Women only had use rights to land through either fathers or husbands but their rights were well protected by custom.

Women were largely autonomous farmers who controlled their own labor process, managed their farms, and traded surplus crops for small stock (a woman's currency for saving). Their control, however, was limited by their responsibility to provide surplus grain for their husbands' beer production for hospitality and work parties. Conversely it can be seen that a man's capacity to become a "big man" in community affairs was limited by his wife's or wives' capacity or willingness to produce surplus grain to further his political ambitions.

Children were the source of a woman's status and her security in old age. "The social status of a woman increased with the number of children she was able to bear to her husband. The barren woman had no prestige" (Molnos 1968, 55), but a good worker would not necessarily be divorced. Women expected to be cared for in their old age by their sons, which is why a woman-to-woman marriage was an important option for a barren woman.

The political organization of the Gikuyu was based on patrilineal clans and lineages, and a system of male age grades where the "big men" of the youngest elder grade made decisions for the group (usually a residential group based on the sublineage), settled disputes, and made policy. Women had their own age grades, a simplified system made up of two grades that dealt with women's affairs only.

In sum, it might be said that the Gikuyu had a limited form of dual sex system. A "dual sex system" because women and men had separate domains in which they were relatively autonomous, "limited" because in the last analysis women's domain was subordinate to that of men's.

Changes in Gikuyu marriage during colonial era

Scholars considering gender relations under colonialism generally agree that women found their power and autonomy eroded (Etienne and Leacock 1980; Obbo 1980). For the Gikuyu the most significant changes during this period were the introduction of the cash economy, land registration, and Christianity. Young Gikuyu men were forced into the cash economy through the mechanisms of taxes and land alienation. Jobs were the province of men who were seen as the "natural" wage earners, and the early provision of education for boys alone reinforced this trend. Later in the century, cash crops were introduced to male farmers. Increasingly during the colonial period, men migrated away to seek work, leaving their wives working harder on the family farm to extract declining yields from ever smaller plots. Thus, during the colonial era, men established control over the new resources of cash and education, and through outmigration came more and more into contact with the outside world, while their wives worked harder for fewer returns. They continued to be responsible for supporting their children in a system that increasingly necessitated cash.

During the Emergency, land registration was introduced, largely as a measure to control the freedom fighters (Sorrenson 1967). One of the by-products of land registration was an erosion of women's well protected rights to land use. Land was registered in the name of the male head of household, and there was no guarantee that a widow would retain the use of her husband's land after his death. By making land a commodity in a market, however, women who had no access to land could now buy land if they could accumulate the capital.

Christianity introduced a new morality, which rejected polygyny. Though it was not immediately successful among the Gikuyu, the long-term impact of this new morality has been the institutionalization of a national legal code (based on the British legal code), which makes monogamous civil marriage the only legitimate form of marriage. A wife married by civil contract will take legal precedence in inheritance or child support matters over an earlier wife married by custom (Kuria 1987). The missionaries insisted on a higher age of marriage for girls, in order to encourage education for girls. This also led to an increase in premarital pregnancy for girls, since the local residential group relinquished active supervision of the sexual morals of the young (Worthman and Whiting 1987). Ironically an increasingly moralistic attitude meant that unmarried mothers were largely unmarriageable.

Gikuyu marriage in the postindependence era

A number of trends have been observable in Gikuyu marriage in the 1960s, 1970s, and on through the 1980s: (1) The continuance of the split family in middle levels of the society. (2) Polygyny has declined. Certainly it has happened more quickly among the Gikuyu than among other Christianized groups in Kenya (Parkin 1978). The result of this is that barren women and even women who bear only daughters are almost inevitably divorced. (3) With the exception of some deeply committed Christian couples or certain elite couples (Obbo 1987), most Kenyans have so far not developed in their marriages what literature has referred to as "couple mentality." While "romantic love" is very popular among young people, marriages have a strong segregation of the social roles of the couple. Women work (in the formal sector, informal sector, or farm) and then stay at home in the evening with their children. Men are deeply involved in the "bar culture" where they seek the sexual adventure so tied up with male identity and social power (Schoepf n.d.). It is not an exaggeration to say that in many (if not most) low-income urban marriages, neither spouse trusts the other (Jansen describes in detail such marital suspicion and tension in Algerian towns (1987, chap. 8). The deepening economic crisis makes it increasingly difficult for men to fulfill their economic obligations to their wives and families. Children have become an economic drain. As a result, there would seem to be an increase in child abuse and marital instability (Kilbride and Kilbride 1990). When I began this longitudinal research in the early 1970s, single heads of household seemed a small category of the Kenyan population. In 1990, the forthcoming census will show that female headed households make up at least forty percent of urban and thirty-five percent of national households (Edward Mburugu, personal communication).

Gender power relations are still unequal. Men control the economy, especially the formal employment sector. The "feminization of poverty" has certainly occurred in Nairobi since the early 1970s. Although women have full political rights, few women are actively involved in politics, and there is a sense that women "do not count" politically. In the middle 1970s, MP's voted out an affiliation law (according to local wits, because the MP's could not afford to keep up the payments on the numerous affiliation orders brought against them). Oddly enough, there seems to have been no agitation by local feminists to change this situation. When a recent female academic criticized the government's plans to build a high-rise building in a centrally located park, the president furiously denounced her in Parliament, demanding by what right did a *woman* contradict men! In the last two years, a national women's organization (an independent NGO) the Mandeleo ya Wanawake was co-opted into the one national party, KANU, on the pretext that it will become more politically active as a woman's wing of KANU. Kenyan feminist cynics maintain that this merger will effectively suppress any challenge it might mount to the current gender power relations.

Marital options of low-income urban women

Civil marriage was and is still rare in the low-income areas of Mathare and the other low-income neighborhoods of Eastlands. None of my original informants had been married in this mode and more recently none of their daughters had either. Civil marriage seems to be the monopoly of the educated elite. Even my well-educated and relatively sophisticated ex-research assistant had not legally married her "customary" husband with whom she had four children. She was surprised when I described the risks involved in this type of marriage.

Religious marriages were also relatively rare in Mathare and its environs. A few devout Christians married in a religious service. A belief prevails, however, that such a form of marriage must be accompanied by an attendant civil marriage and a lot of expensive ceremony. Likewise, most of my Islamized Gikuyu friends had not bothered to be married in the orthodox Islamic manner with a signed contract and an agreed *mehir* (payment to be made at the time of divorce).

Customary Gikuyu marriage continues in varying forms. For better off families, very high bridewealth can be exchanged. Poor urban couples carry out shortened and cheaper versions of the original ceremonies, but the two sets of parents are consulted and subsequently meet to share honey beer, goat meat, and special black bean dishes. Some minimal bridewealth, even if it is only beer and a goat, is expected. This type of conjugal relationship allows a man to claim the children at the breakup of a marriage. In the early 1970s this would certainly have been the case. It also gives the husband greater control over his wife. For example, the local KANU committee elders or the police would not intervene in a dispute between husband and wife (short of preventing murder, or very serious injury) as they would between other less orthodoxly constituted couples. One Mathare KANU leader initiated a system of checking men's claims that they were "married" to the women they abused. If the KANU Youth Wing interfered in a couple's quarrel, the man usually claimed immunity from this interference by insisting that they were married by custom. This leader found that most of these claims were false after she checked with parents in the rural areas. When the false claim was uncovered, the KANU "Elders" Council usually found in favor of the woman, who was usually the Mathare resident.

A woman's right to work or accumulate surplus (through business or selling crops) has to be negotiated with her husband, many of whom resent wives working outside the home. Conversely such a marriage gives a wife claim over lands, houses, or resources such as the house he might own, as long as the marriage lasts. She can also appeal to the two sets of parents in case of mistreatment.

Limited polygynous marital options are available among the Gikuyu. Instances that came to my attention occurred in places like the Rift Valley, where Gikuyu men with large farms recruited labor through multiple marriage. Usually only young women who had borne children out of wedlock would agree to being a second wife.

Woman-to-woman marriage still existed in the early 1970s in Mathare and there may have been more than the two cases that I ran across, for the reason that people were embarrassed to reveal this form of union to a *musungu* (European). As women learn to adopt children legally, they no longer need to marry in this way. In 1984 I learned that four barren women informants had adopted children, the first examples I had come across of low-income women adopting children.

Town marriage is an emic category used by Mathare women themselves (in my own translation). This union was characterized by coresidence, economic help from the man for the household, domestic work done by the woman, and an assumption of fidelity on the part of both partners, as in a customary marriage. But there are important differences. First, only the couple is involved in the decision to set up a union. Second, the husband has no claim on the children of the union. In some cases there is hardly an expectation that a man will even be much concerned about his children when he is still living with their mother. (Many Gikuyu women confided to me that they avoided relationships with men from a western province because those men insisted on claiming children from *town marriages* for which no bridewealth had been paid.) This lack of responsibility by the "husband" for his children is symbolized by the naming procedure for children, who will be named only after the mother's relatives (not alternatively father's and mother's relatives as is the case in a customary marriage).

A *town wife* is more economically independent than her counterpart married by custom or perhaps even civil marriage. No *town husband* expects his partner to give up her *biashara* (business) or job. (The result would be that he would have to bear sole support for her and her children and this would be unacceptable to most men and women.) The only business most town wives would not do openly would be commercialized sex work.

In Mathare and Eastland, women control (own or rent) the room(s) the couple live in and each woman has her own economic enterprise. Most significantly, the union can be terminated by either partner at any time. Obviously there is jealousy and possessiveness between partners in such couples, and angry feelings will result from the separations. However, an assumption of impermanence in such unions makes it easier to "divorce." The ease of termination is increased for the woman by the contingent facts that each woman controls her own living arrangements, has her own income-generating enterprise, and does not have to contemplate losing her children.

If such women have their own rooms and incomes, why do they bother to form conjugal unions at all? Most such women cannot afford to live without some economic input from men (who are more likely to have wage jobs). Many women prefer to get the majority of that economic input from town husbands rather than from transitory customers.

Thus when one such union fails, a woman hastens to start another. This leads to a type of "serial polyandry," which may go some way to explain the negative image such women have in the larger Kenyan society. Men are expected to have multiple partners (whether serially or simultaneously) but not women. For women to do so with ease and frequency challenges the proper gender relations of a patriarchal society.

Lover relationships might be considered problematical to include as a form of conjugal relationship. However, in categorizing it thus, I feel that I am doing justice to Mathare women's own view of the relationship. One woman expressed it quite clearly to me:

> I like to love a man, and I need the money that a man gives·me too. But I don't want to be a full wife. I get all the love I need from my "night friends" but at the same time I don't want to have to cook his dinner every night.

Many women saw themselves as acting as a form of wife, though not a full wife. Similar observations have been made for other parts of East Africa. Halpenny describes a Kampala woman with many lovers who "thought of herself as having multiple husbands" as practicing a form of polyandry (1975, 282). White, doing oral history research with women sex workers of the 1930s and 1940s maintains that such women performed many of the reproductive roles characteristic of a wife (1980).

Mathare women did not live with their lovers. A lover could spend the night, ask for food or a shirt to be ironed occasionally, but his residence would be elsewhere (usually with a customary wife). A lover is not *expected* to render her man regular domestic services but does so if she is feeling kindly disposed to her partner. The lover (often referred to colloquially as a *helping bwana*, my translation) is expected to give regular gifts and loans. He does not acknowledge any children born during their union. His right to expect faithfulness is limited; he might demand it and be jealous if he suspects a rival, but no one will blame a woman for having other relationships. Economic realities being what they are, women themselves prefer to have multiple bwana because it increases the income of the household, and with the worsening economic crisis, few women can expect big enough contributions from one lover to get by. The contributions of lovers are undeniably less than those of husbands.

Women themselves frequently preferred to have several lovers because that gave them sex, intimacy, and financial assistance without domestic responsibility. For hardworking women in the informal sector, this was an advantage.

Manipulating marital options

The free women living in Mathare and the areas around it can be viewed as manipulating various options of marital or conjugal relationships with men. They do this to maximize their life chances despite the constraints of action and knowledge within which they operate.

Married women from poor rural areas whose husbands have migrated to town to work, may find the hard, unremitting agricultural work under the eagle eye of a censorious mother-in-law lonely and unrewarding. Such a woman may find it impossible to meet her cash needs. Husbands living away in the expensive city find it difficult or are disinclined to remit enough cash home. Frequently the privation of these rural wives is caused by the fact that their husbands are contributing to town wives. Ironically, if these rural wives chose to divorce and migrate to town to live, they might end by living with town bwana. Thus they would be partly responsible for initiating for other rural women the selfsame process of deprivation leading to divorce and migration to town.

Women may have certain options closed to them by circumstances. A girl who has become pregnant out of wedlock has two choices usually. She can accept status as a second wife of a rich older man, or can come to town to seek her fortune. Few such women have fathers or brothers generous enough (or well off enough in terms of land holdings) to support an unwed mother for very long. A woman divorced for barrenness will not be able to remarry. A widow with small children who has lost her rights to her husband's land to a greedy relative will have a hard time surviving in the rural area. A woman without access to land through father, brother, or husband has a very hard time of it in rural Gikuyuland.

The women I knew in Mathare professed not wanting to be married again or at all (if they had never married). These statements must of course not be accepted uncritically under the circumstances. Some of the younger women would sigh when they were particularly fed up with struggling for money and say that they would love to be taken care of by a caring husband. These girls are the type Ilsa Schuster refers to as "transitionals," the ones who still dream of a stable and loving relationship with a man (1979, 95). However, they would always end by commenting wryly that since there were almost bound to be no such "caring" husbands, it was not worth the trouble to marry. Mathare women and their daughters are very cynical about the possibilities of a loving, caring, and trusting marriage. It is not even that such women never receive an offer of marriage. I knew a number of cases where men literally begged or tried to bribe their lovers or town wives to marry them according to custom. But in vain in most cases. Women felt that having learned the joys of freedom, it would be impossible to submit to the authority of a husband again. Or others would opine that supportive loving relationships between men and women were too short lived to bother to institutionalize them with a ceremony of marriage that just made terminating the relationship more difficult. In all the time I did research in Mathare, only one free woman chose to become a wife (in this case by Christian marriage). An older, barren woman was asked by a widower with five young children to marry him, and she accepted. It was interesting to note her friends' derisive and critical comments on what they saw as her sellout. Most felt that she had only accepted his proposal because she yearned so much for children. All thought that she was risking a lot because he took over the running of her lucrative maize meal wholesaling business and her rental houses in Mathare.

Many women in Mathare opted for the briefer and less constricting form of conjugal union, which allowed the woman more freedom and more rights to control her own economic life: the *town marriage*. In fact, these free women deny that there are any longer any practical advantages to customary marriage. In the course of the marriage, a wife is more under the control of the husband, especially if she lives and works on his farm. If the marriage proves unsatisfactory it is harder to divorce (for all the practical reasons listed earlier). Without a concept of community property after divorce, a wife stands the chance of losing her children, her house, and her farm. Even if she does keep the children (and she usually would keep the younger ones), she doesn't have a clearly defined or easily accessible option of claiming support for them in the courts, as she could if she were married by civil contract. As the economic situation worsens, many men are failing to keep up their responsibilities for maintaining their children by previous marriages. As far as I could ascertain, the practical advantage the women of Eastlands saw in customary marriage was respectability. Women trade off respectability and relative certainty of customary marriage for economic autonomy and free choice of town marriage.

One of the problems may be that customary marriage is less certain now; in other words, the limited certainty is not worth the loss of freedom. As Gikuyus become more mobile and extended family ties weaken, the customary marriage may seem less and less to be a guarantee of support for a woman and her children, either during or after marriage. In the early 1970s there were disturbing signs that children are less and less valued by their father, and parents find it more difficult to enforce any norms of proper filial obligations on their children. My impressionistic observations during my visits of the 1970s and 1980s indicate that these trends have grown more pronounced throughout the decade, as do statements made to me by local scholars and a recent book on women and children at risk (Kilbride and Kilbride, 1990). Further research focused on this issue is necessary to confirm or refine this hypothesis. It would seem that with increasingly lower income, urban Gikuyu men provide no support for or show little interest in their children once their customary marriages are terminated. My interviews with the women of Eastlands, as well as conversations with friends and fellow academics, indicated that this is increasingly the case.

A woman who chooses to leave a customary marriage, or who is forced by circumstances (such as barrenness) to leave one, may then choose to go to town and find lovers or town bwana. They involve themselves in informal forms of serial polygyny or polyandry in order to maximize their economic returns and freedom. A woman might choose to operate a number of relationships simultaneously. A woman with a town bwana might have lovers on the side secretly so that if things didn't work with her town bwana she could get rid of him and choose a successor. As already explained, some women eschew even the minimal ties of a town bwana relationship in favor of having a number of lovers.

The option of a woman-to-woman marriage was in operation in the early to middle 1970s in Mathare. I doubt that it happens much now. Even then younger informants found it embarrassing to discuss and found it a thing of *zamani* (long ago). Barren women can now choose to adopt children. Perhaps the number of abandoned and orphaned children has increased as expanded family ties have weakened (Kilbride and Kilbride 1990) thus creating a pool of available children for barren women who still see investing in children as an answer to their old age. They no longer have to seek the old-fashioned alternative of a woman-to-woman marriage to attain the goal of someone to care for them in their old age. Thus in a situation of a declining economy, it seems that both men and women are increasingly disengaging themselves from long-term ties with the opposite sex. In this equation, men have the advantage. One young woman, doing sex work in 1990 to support herself and three children after having been abandoned by her customary husband, put it succinctly, "Each time a man divorces or leaves a woman, he leaves everything behind and starts fresh. Each time a woman divorces or leaves a man, she is left with the remains of the last marriage." Women's responsibility for their children means that they cannot "start afresh." The other advantage men have over women in general is that more men than women are employed in the formal sector. Women are relegated to the lower echelons of formal employment or to the informal self-employed sector (my informants were bar girls, house girls, sweepers for city council, hawkers, beer brewers, or sex workers) enforce a form of redistribution of men's wealth by means of a series of more or less short-term multiple relationships. I described this previously as a form of unrecognized polygyny for men operating simultaneously with a form of unrecognized polyandry for free women. As the economic crisis deepens, it becomes more difficult for men to regularly fulfill their complete economic responsibilities to their partners, while at the same time continuing their participation in the "bar culture." For many men, the psychological pressure is unacceptable and it is probably easier to move on when the complaints become too loud.

Often the process of disengagement is accompanied by a high degree of domestic violence. Urban East African marriage was accompanied by a high degree of domestic violence though it is a subject which has attracted little research. Schuster's work on Zambia is probably one of the few works that addresses male violence against women. Every woman I knew in Eastlands (and if the rumors one constantly heard circulating among middle-class Kenyans are true, a number of elite Kenyans as well) had been beaten by their partners. The degree of acceptance was striking; many would not believe that my husband did not beat me. But if the level of violence must be contained and if it reaches too high a level, then the woman is forced to leave. One young woman I interviewed in 1990 finally left her customary husband when he broke her jaw and arm in a quarrel (he had been staying out every night with a new girl friend. If the noticeable increase in coverage of child beatings in Kenyan newspapers in the late 1980s means anything, then there is also a higher level of child risk present in low-income Kenyan society as well. This is the thesis that Kilbride and Kilbride (1990) address in their new work on East African families.

Women (both married and free) find it harder and harder, for a number of reasons, to stay permanently with one man and so must have multiple partners (simultaneously or serially) to survive in an ever more difficult urban environment. Men make decisions about their multiple relationships for reasons of comfort, sex, convenience, children, emotional satisfaction, and ego aggrandizement. Women make converse choices for similar motives with very important differences. They make these decisions with economic survival and the personal safety of themselves and their children as goals. I have indicated the economic advantage of the choices they are making.

Another advantage men have in this urban practice of changing partners is that for men this game is expected and can even confer social power and prestige in the eyes of their peers (though admittedly the extent to which this is true must be investigated systematically. For women to participate in this type of game threatens the social order. As I have written elsewhere, "such women posed a threat to the normative Kikuyu marriage where women reproduce the lineage" (1987, 237). However, many women consider that loss of respectability and good name is an acceptable price to pay for greater economic and sexual freedom, greater economic flexibility, wider choice of partners, and increased capacity to end relationships when they prove a liability.

Conclusion

Connell, in his exploration of gender relations, has proposed that gender relations be examined within three "structures of relationship between men and women": first, the division of labor (both productive and reproductive labor); second, the system of authority, control, and coercion (including state, institutional, and personal violence and sexual regulation); and third, what he chooses to call cathexis (or the patterning of desire and sexuality). These are the structures within which the practice of gender relations take place. I have discussed mainly the first two, though elsewhere (1987), I have examined aspects of the last. It is clear that in the present situation of high population growth, rapid urbanization, and a depressed economic situation, the structures of gender relations have altered in a way that mitigates against marriage and makes temporary town marriages or lover relationships more reasonable choices for poor urban Gikuyu women.

In the division of labor, poor Gikuyu women are increasingly at a disadvantage. Village relationships and customary marriage do not protect their land rights. With increased male outmigration, women's work loads have increased. When women migrate to town they are relegated to the informal sector or the low-paid areas of the formal economy. The previous division of labor in which women were largely responsible for day-to-day reproductive labor continues to prevail in the urban area, except that men are increasingly unwilling and/or unable to contribute to the reproduction of their own households. The rural Gikuyu concept of a mother being the provider for her children was never replaced by the concept of the urban male wage earner using his family wage to support his wife and children. Thus many men view their salaries as theirs by right to spend on their own concerns. Yet at the same time it becomes increasingly difficult for women to provide for their children's needs. In a desperate attempt to fulfill these responsibilities, poor urban (or semi-rural) Gikuyu women turn to sex work or form multiple, short-term relationships to maximize economic support.

In the twentieth century, the structures of control and coercion have altered in ways that have sometimes disadvantaged women, especially poor women. Previously these structures, while operated by the male lineage elders, would have operated for women by settling serious marital disputes and protecting women's rights to land and support. In the twentieth century, political power was transferred to the state. In many ways the new legal codes were designed to assist women (e.g., equal pay and maternity leave). However, they discriminated against poor rural and urban women in the area of customary marriages, inheritance, divorce, and paternity laws. The new codes have not adequately addressed the issue of marital violence, which has undoubtedly always existed. In the village, however, the violence of men against women would have been controlled and limited by the presence of women's relatives. In the urban area, this is no longer the case, and low-income women suffer a high level of violence.

The current cathexis among the Gikuyu supports the view that men have the right and perhaps even the necessity of multiple sexual partners. In the popular view, men are "by nature polygynous." It is also thought that celibacy is not possible for men. However, women are expected by men to be faithful to their husbands and celibate if their husbands are away. Women who have had multiple partners are thought to be "spoiled," they will never be able to settle down to one man ever again.

References

Bordieu,P.
1977   *Outline of a theory of practice.* Cambridge: Cambridge University Press.

Burnham,P.
1987   The analysis of African marriage. In *Transformation of African marriage,* edited by D.Parkin. Manchester: Manchester University Press.

Cagnolo,C.
1933   *The Akikuyu: Their customs, traditions, folklore.* Nyeri, Kenya: Mission Printing School.

Connell,R.W.
1987   *Gender and power.* Cambridge: Polity Press.

Etiene,M., and E.Leacock
1980   *Women and colonization.* New York: Praeger.

Evans-Pritchard,E.
1940   *The Nuer.* London: Oxford University Press.

Gough,K.
1978   Nuer kinship. In *Translation of culture,* edited by T.O.Beidelman. London: Tavistock Publications.

Halpenny,P.
1975   Three styles of ethnic migration. In *Town and country in central and eastern Africa,* edited by D.Parkin. London: Oxford University Press.

Jansens,W.
1987   *Women without men: Gender and marginality in an Algerian town.* Leiden: J. Brill Press.

Kenyatta,J.
1938   *Facing Mount Kenya.* London: Mercury Books.

Kilbride,P., and J.Kilbride
1990   *Changing family life in E. Africa: women and children at risk.* University Park: Pennsylvania State University Press.

30

Kitching,G.
1980   *Class and economic change in Kenya.* New Haven,
            Conn.: Yale University Press.

Kuria,G.
1987   The African or customary marriage in Kenyan law today.
            In *Transformations of African marriage,* edited by
            D.Parkin. Manchester: Manchester University Press.

Leakey,L.S.B.
1977   *The southern Kikuyu before 1903.* New York:
            Academic Press.

Lévi-Strauss,C.
1949   *Les structures élémentaires de la parenté.* Paris:
            Presses Universitaires de France.

Leys,C.
1975   *Underdevelopment in Kenya.* London: Heineman
            Press.

Meillassoux,C.
1975   *Femmes, greniers et capitaux.* Paris: Maspero.

Molnos,A.
1968   *Attitudes to family planning in East Africa.* New
            York: C. Hurst.

Nelson,N.
1978   Women must help each other. In *Women united:
            Women divided.* London: Tavistock Publications.
1979   How men and women get by: Gender division of labour
            in Mathare valley. In *Casual poor in Third World
            cities,* edited by C.Gerry. New York: John Wiley and
            Sons, Inc.
1987   Selling her kiosk: Kikuyu notions of sexuality. In *The
            cultural construction of sexuality,* edited by
            P.Caplan. London: Tavistock Publications.

Obbo,C.
1980   *African women: Their struggle for economic
            independence.* London: Zed Press.
1987   The old and the new in East African elite marriage. In
            Transformations in African marriage, edited by

D.Parkin and D.Nyamwaya. Manchester: Manchester University Press for the International African Institute.

Okonjo,K.
1976 Dual-sex system political system in operation: Igbo women in Midwestern Nigeria. In *Women in Africa*, edited by N.Hafkin and E.Bay. Stanford, California: Stanford University Press.

Parkin,D.
1978 *Cultural definition of political response*. London: Academic Press.

Radcliffe-Brown,A., and D.Forde (eds.)
1950 *African systems of kinship and marriage*. Oxford: Oxford University Press.

Ross,M.
1973 *The political integration of urban squatters*. Evanston, Illinois: Northwestern University Press.

Rubin,G.
1975 The traffic in women. In *Toward an anthropology of women*, edited by R.Reiter. New York: Monthly Review Press.

Schoepf,B.
n.d. AIDS, sex and condoms in Zaire. In *Medical anthropology*. Forthcoming.

Schuster,I.
1979 *New women of Lusaka*. Palo Alto, California: Mayfield Publishing Co.

Sorrenson,M.
1967 *Land reform in the Kikuyu country*. London: Oxford University Press.

Southall,A.W.
1957 *Townsmen in the making: Kampala and its suburbs*. East African Studies no. 9. Kampala: East African Institute of Social Research.
1961 *Social change in modern Africa*, edited by A.W.Southall. London: Oxford University Press.

32

1967   *The city in modern Africa.* New York: Praeger.

White,L.
1980   Women domestic labour in colonial Kenya: Prostitution
            in Nairobi from 1909 to 1950. African Studies Center,
            Boston University.

Worthman,C., and J.Whiting
1987   Social change in adolescent sexual behaviour, mate
            selections and premarital pregnancy among the Kikuyu.
            Ethos 15(2): 145-165.

The Holy Woman and the Homeless Men of East Harlem: a Brief Look at the Underclass Concept

Anna Lou Dehavenon, Founder and Director
Action Research Project on Hunger,
Homelessness, and Family Health
New York, United States

Introduction

Deindustrialization (Newman 1985) and disinvestment (Dehavenon 1982; Maxwell 1988) in the people, housing, and community-based institutions in the low-income areas of American cities after the early 1970s resulted in the dramatically worsened urban poverty conditions of the 1980s and 1990s. Much of the subsequent academic and journalistic discussion of the causes of this "new poverty" (e.g., "new" as contrasted with that presumably ameliorated by the "War on Poverty" of the 1960s) is based on the concept of a hypothesized "underclass," thought of generally as a group of the poor whose "dysfunctional" behaviors and values permanently preclude their participation in mainstream social and economic activity (Auletta 1982; Wilson 1978).

Simultaneous discussion of the material causes of the more recent poverty conditions, including the widespread hunger and homelessness of the 1980s and 1990s, is much less frequent; that is, of the expansion of United States manufacturing overseas in the 1970s into countries with low wage policies where there are no trade unions (Nash 1987), the decreased status of the United States in the world economy, federal tax cuts and the large proportion of the gross national product spent on financing the national debt, and the persistent priority given the defense budget in shaping domestic and foreign policies, even after the demise of the Soviet Union. The result was a serious erosion in public funding for education, housing, and other social programs, occurring at the same time that inflation was eroding the purchasing power of family income including the minimum wage, Public Assistance grants, and housing costs. Finally, the federal response to the AIDS (Acquired Immune Deficiency Syndrome) and drug epidemics of the 1980s and 1990s, which threaten poor urban areas disproportionately, has been only minimal at best.

The behaviors and values ascribed to the hypothesized "underclass" echo those proposed by Oscar Lewis (1968) and Daniel P. Moynihan (1965) in their concepts of a "culture" or "cycle" of poverty, respectively: high rates of male unemployment and abandonment of women and children, female-headed households, transgenerational poverty, Public Assistance participation, and crime (Maxwell 1989). Furthermore, many "underclass" descriptions echo Marx's tone (1977, 219) when he described the lumpenproletariat as the group:

> which in all big towns forms a mass sharply differentiated from the industrial proletariat, a recruiting ground for thieves and criminals of all kinds, living on the crumbs of society, people without a definite trade, vagabonds, *gens sans feu et sans aveu.*

This essay examines the experiences of some of the people living in 1989 in a low-income East Harlem block, which would surely be labelled "underclass" by those who use the term, and where all the material causes of the "new poverty" of the 1980s and 1990s are manifest. Observations are made, interviews are done, and the data are used to analyze the degree to which these experiences conform with the findings of Mincy, Sawhill, and Wolf (1990) who use certain logical operations and U.S. census data to measure the hypothesized underclass in an article published in one of America's most respected scientific journals. The goal here is to use the same operations to preliminarily test the underclass hypothesis with data collected expressly for that purpose rather than census data that is secondary.

The place and the people

Little Mount Calvary Whosoever Comes Pentecostal Church stands in the East Harlem block where since the early 1970s I have conducted research and observed the processes of abandonment and disinvestment, which culminated in New York City's current low-income housing crisis. At the local level, these included particularly the conjunction of the rent control laws first enacted during World War II and the high rates of inflation which after the mid-East oil embargo of 1974 raised fuel costs while steadily decreasing the purchasing power of the Public Assistance shelter allowance. Thousands of landlords stopped paying taxes and making the necessary repairs on buildings they no longer found profitable, and many finally abandoned or set fire to their properties in order to collect the insurance.

In the middle 1970s, New York City was on the verge of bankruptcy and did not undertake to maintain the thousands of buildings of which it became the owner of last resort through landlord tax default. Eventually, many were destroyed as safety hazards while others were renovated as permanent housing for homeless families. During the 1980s, most of those located near wealthy neighborhoods were sold to real estate speculators for redevelopment. In the poorest areas, others remain unoccupied until today.

Beginning in 1973, these same processes led to the razing to the ground of eighteen of the forty-one building lots in the block where the Little Mount Calvary Church stands. By 1989, the buildings on only six of the remaining seventeen lots were occupied, and of eleven others, four were vacant and six--plus an abandoned elementary school--were being renovated as condominiums by the new owners who had bought them from the City. Because of the earlier, massive loss of habitable housing, the block's population had dropped to twenty percent its former size, and while most of the people still referred to themselves as African American or Puerto Rican, the more recent arrivals included individuals and families who were of other Hispanic, Asian, and White origin.

Since 1977, the church has rented the small, storefront space on the ground floor of one of the occupied buildings where the rituals and other activities of its missionizing pentecostal faith are performed. Pentecostalism is one of the numerous small fundamentalist protestant groups growing out of the holiness movement which, beginning in the early twentieth century in the United States, emphasized a perfectionist doctrine of holiness. Among its practices are baptism by the Holy Ghost, religious excitement accompanied by possession trance, glossalia or "speaking in tongues," faith healing, and a belief in the impending second coming of Christ. Writing on the relationship between possession states, social movements, and social stress, Erika Bourguinon (1991, 55) describes traditional, lower-class, Protestant Pentecostalism as follows:

> "There is also a positive side of possession belief in Christianity, namely the idea of being "filled" with the Holy Spirit. It is based...on the account of the Pentecost (Acts 2) when according to the text the Holy Ghost descended on the apostles and bestowed on them the gift of tongues. That is, they preached to a multitude in languages they themselves did not know... Pentecostal cults are religions of salvation, with dramatic conversions, spiritual healing, group participation in

ritual, singing and music, sometimes dancing, but generally a broad range of motor behavior... It is a characteristically American phenomenon; it developed among both black and white poor, in relatively isolated rural areas.

According to Bourguinon, the types of needs satisfied through Pentecostal ritual practice relate specifically to the "healing of physical illness in societies where medical care is inadequate and where the stresses of life lead to a number of psychosomatic disorders."

Approximately seventy members regularly attend Little Mount Calvary's first service of the week which begins each Sunday at 11:00 A.M. and concludes toward the end of the afternoon. Throughout the ritual, a queue of eighty or more persons forms on the sidewalk outside the front door. Most of them are young, African American and Hispanic males who live in a large city shelter for single homeless men located fifteen minutes away by foot on an island in the East River. They will wait all afternoon to be served the substantial meal for which the final preparations are now being made in the minuscule kitchen behind the church altar.

According to one of the informants who previously stood on the line, many of these men have just been on "a crack mission." "They smoke crack, snort cocaine and don't eat or sleep for two or three days. Or, they only eat a 'crack meal' consisting of a 25-cent package of crackers and a 25-cent juice. They sleep in the subway, on top of a building, or on a park bench. This is the first good solid meal they have had in days--sometimes weeks."

When the regular ritual is finally over, the ushers lead in the men on the line in shifts of twenty-five and seat them in the chairs the church members have just vacated. Each shift participates in a short version of the ritual and then eats. As Pastor Roundtree observes, "First you feed them. Then you clothe them. Then you save them for the Lord."

Methodology

Since December 1988, I have done participant observation of many of the church's activities. The data used here was collected in the in-depth interviews I completed with four men who now live in the church after being homeless, standing on the line, and being "saved" to participate regularly in its rituals and other activities. To test Mincy, Sawhill, and Wolf's method for identifying and measuring an "underclass," I asked each one where they were born, whether or not their parents had lived together most of the time they were growing up, and what their parents' principal income sources had been. I also asked about their own schooling, work histories, income sources, and lives with their spouses and children. Finally, I asked how they became homeless and what their hopes for the future were. Using the methods of "reflexive" anthropology, I transcribed and word processed the responses. I then showed each one his own transcript for further suggestions before including them here as individual case studies.

Case study 1: Brother Paul

I was born forty years ago in upstate New York. I am an only child. My parents were very strict. They always lived together. They had their own house in Westchester and were never on Public Assistance. My mother taught elementary school, and like his father, my father was a pastor. My mother was a paraplegic, and my father died of a heart attack when I was fourteen. When I was small, they sent me to live with my great-grandmother in a small town in North Carolina. They were trying to get themselves educated and wanted me to get a southern training. My great-grandmother was an ex-slave who remembered the day Lincoln was killed. I read the Bible to her because she couldn't read or write, and I lived with her until she died. I came back to New York when I was eleven.

I majored in theology at a black southern college where I completed four years. But, I still had to go through all this and come here to Mother Roundtree's to become a minister. I have never been on Public Assistance. I worked as a case aide in probation, the director of a youth center in a small town in New York, and the assistant director of a program for adolescent girls in residential treatment. All I've ever done is work with kids.

About my own family, my wife and I separated when I was just out of college. We had a kid but did not get married. Ten months after our son died of pneumonia, she committed suicide. I had a second son in another relationship. He is now twenty years old, and I helped raise him even though his mother and I never really lived together. We had separate apartments, but we had a common ground--our son. He would come to my office and stay with me until she got home from work. If there was a problem in school, or when he was a teenager, I would go help. He came to me on weekends, and I contributed to his financial support. To the best of my knowledge, his mother was never on Public Assistance.

Later I also lost my grandmother. I pushed all these losses aside and drank. I became an alcoholic/workaholic. There were no drugs in high school and college. I didn't use cocaine until I was twenty-nine. After that I sniffed both heroin and cocaine. I only used crack for one year. Crack is the most seductive drug there is. It fools you. Heroin and cocaine you can stop, but crack is a physical and a mental addiction. All I did was think about crack. When I hadn't eaten in three days and there was food in the kitchen and crack in the bedroom, I went to the bedroom. My grandmother's death was the straw that broke the camel's back. I did not even go to her funeral. The day of her burial, I was smoking crack in a motel in Yonkers.

Soon after I left my job and went on another "mission." I stayed at a motel in Manhattan. After a while everything was used up. I was too embarrassed to call my mother, my friends or my job. I just didn't go back. I was sleeping in the subway, abandoned buildings or cars. One Saturday morning, this woman took me to Reverend Ronald's for breakfast. He's another Pastor in this neighborhood who provides food and spiritual guidance to the homeless.

The next day, Sunday, I was here at Mother Roundtree's standing on the line. Four or five days later the Volunteers of America brought me to the shelter. The food there is not like Mother's--not the warmth, the woman's touch, the seasonings. The shelter gives you small portions--not enough. One of the first things I heard there was that if you want good, home-cooked, soul food, you go to Mother Roundtree's. She's a holy woman, our spiritual mother who's going to get us to the next world. I have a biological mother who brought me into this world, but she's my spiritual mother.

My parents were Baptist, but after my father died I went to the Christ's Temple Holiness Church near my home. There they beat the drums and spoke in tongues just like here. I was thirteen, and my mother said I could make up my own mind where I wanted to go. Now I want to be a pastor in an inner-city church or a street ministry that will reach young people and the down-trodden, like Mother's.

Case study 2: Brother Brendan

I'm thirty. I was born in Newark, and my mother raised me. There were eight children. My father wasn't around. When I was thirteen, he died of diabetes. My mother used to take me to see him toward the end. She worked as a home attendant and then in a nursing home. When I was small, she was on Public Assistance. I remember I had to hide certain appliances when the woman came. After my father died, there was Social Security for her and me as long as I was in school.

I went through the ninth grade, but I had an attendance problem in high school--thinking I was a man. I wanted to experience this and that--girls you know. I dropped out but got my General Equivalency Diploma later when I was twenty-four.

Once someone shows me something, I pick it up. I managed a fast food restaurant. I wanted to have my own business, a restaurant. I also worked in a mailroom, as a messenger and as an orderly in a nursing home. After I was homeless, I received Home Relief, the Public Assistance for adults without children, but I failed to show up at my work site and they closed my case. Now I only have Medicaid to fix my teeth and Food Stamps.

I don't have any family of my own. I had my first child when I was fifteen, a son who is now sixteen. I saw him two years ago at my aunt's funeral. The next year, I had another son. He died when he was five in a hit and run accident. His mother and I were both incarcerated at the time--for different things. Now there's my daughter who is seven. The last time I saw her was some time after Christmas. Her mother goes to the Baptist Church. She's supposed to get married in September. She won't let me see my daughter even though she smoked crack herself and knows what it is to be strung out.

Why I became homeless goes back to when my mother passed away. She was heart broken after one of my sisters was killed and had a cerebral hemorrhage when she was only fifty. I was seventeen at the time and in trouble with the law. But, I didn't hurt anyone. My mother died when I was incarcerated. That was a blow! I felt like it was my fault. They gave me parole the next day, but I felt very guilty. My other sister took me in, but I picked up the vibes that I was a burden there. I was young, dependent, not working, and on Social Security.

I went to work in a nursing home, feeding people, doing arts and crafts. I saw this woman who reminded me of my mother--the same age category. I first started drugs at fifteen, but then I really started with pills. I left the job. I would be working and something always came along--the deaths in my family and losing my son zapped me. Then when I started really using drugs, my sister told me I had to go get work. Someone brought me here on a Thanksgiving Day a while ago. Later I was in the shelter. One day this guy said, "I want to hear the Word." The Salvation Army was too crowded, so I told him, "We can go to Mother Roundtree's." The more I read the Word, the more I hear the Word, the more I'm around Mother, the more I'm strong. I feel like Mother's my mother. The more I draw close, the more I listen, the more it seems like I always knew her.

My mother cooked the same food. When we didn't have meat, she'd get back there cooking so it smelt like there was meat in the whole building. She did rent parties sometimes to raise the rent for people. She would cook chittlin's. She only cooked 'em for parties, not for us. I remember the mens fighting over the juice in the pot. I tasted it for the first time here--pots that smelled familiar, hog maws, chittlin's, black-eyed peas, and kidney beans. Certain dishes I can do real good myself.

Case study 3: Brother Ethan

I was born in Rockland County, New York. I am twenty-eight years old. My parents lived together all the time. I was the third oldest of seven kids and the oldest boy. My father worked as a mechanic and a school janitor. They owned their own house and were never on Public Assistance. I was adopted.

When I was around seven or eight, I discovered my real brother in the same class in school. We recognized each other, because we looked so much alike. He lived with our parents, and I lived with mine. I never knew why, and I always thought it was strange they never told me.

I graduated from high school and went to community college for a year and a half. I studied business, but I didn't know what I really wanted to do, so I went in the army. Afterwards, I worked in restaurants as a cook, a second cook, and the manager of one. I'm trying to get back into it now. I just graduated from a hotel/restaurant school in March. I did really good. I surprised myself! I have a job interview tomorrow. Two weeks ago I was laid off as a cook in a drug/alcohol program. They're cutting back because things are really slow. I have never been on Public Assistance.

About a year-and-a-half ago, I got married and my wife became pregnant. Our baby was born at the same time I was at the cooking school. She's my heart! Unfortunately, we're separated now, and I don't know why. I think I let her make a lot of decisions, which is not always good. But I try to bring her in on things. She likes to decide. She's already given me the divorce papers. I don't understand it, particularly when she's spending a lot of time with my side of the family. She put me out of my own place, and I went to the shelter. I was using drugs, and she had stopped when she got pregnant.

Even with my wife, I was still lonely and looking for satisfaction. I was tired of dealing with this and that. I was looking for something that wasn't there to begin with. I don't even drink. When I was young, I was smoking reefer, but that's all. Then I started

with cocaine. I learned from someone in the shelter to come to
Mother's to get something to eat. The shelter food wasn't so great.
But, it was Mother's attitude, the way she was as a person--something
about her that is positive, her individuality and power. She doesn't
pull no punches. She lets you know what's what from the beginning.
She's for real. She doesn't play. I knew about church but not like
this, nothing close to what I've learned here.

Now I live in the church and help out. I would have to earn at
least $20,000 a year to have my own place. A black man has a really
hard time today. You have to be that much better. It's not that I'm
prejudiced, I'm not because I went to an all white high school.

Case study 4: Brother Harold

I was born fifty years ago in South Carolina, thirty-two miles
from Charleston. I was delivered by a midwife who did not read or
write. The county supplied care, but if you went to the hospital you
had to work off the bill. My father did not marry my mother, but I
knew him and his family. I used my grandmother's maiden name. My
mother worked six days a week as a cook in a restaurant. It was open
on Saturday and Sunday and closed only on Monday. She earned $25
a week but was never on Public Assistance. We also grew vegetables
and raised chicken.

During the war, my mother worked as a welder in a shipyard in
California. There she married my stepfather who was in the armed
forces. He helped support her, but he did not adopt me. My mother
sent money back and my grandmother raised me. We stood out
because everything depended on how you carried yourself. I knew my
father's family, and I was close with my siblings. He gave me a dollar
every Christmas. How I waited for that dollar!

We were Baptists. There were holiness churches but we didn't go to them. My cousin from New York went to one, and my family would talk about how she talked out in church when she came to visit. I was only exposed to the holiness church later on.

I finished the twelfth grade in school and came here in 1960. I worked at a large private New York City hospital. I tried to experience that hospital day and night. I also could have worked at another hospital. For twenty-seven years, I had one job as a warehouse picker. I put orders onto a truck and took them to various locations. On my days off, I worked as a private duty home attendant. That was moonlighting.

I can't work now because I had a broken ankle, but I can go back any time and they will give me a sit down job. I'd like to do something different and be a supervisor of catering. I'd like to go to France and learn how to cook with wine. I'm very creative.

My wife and I had four sons and one daughter. We separated for incompatibility twenty-one years ago, but we have a very close relationship. I took care of the kids, and we remained friends for the rest of our lives. She no longer wanted marriage. I was stunned, and I still haven't accepted it. I go there two or three times a week to eat. We don't have sex. It's like a dream. It's twenty-two years and I still think we might get back together.

I don't drink, but when I got on drugs, I lost everything I had on crack. At forty-seven, I ended up in a men's shelter. I didn't know where to turn to. I was still limping with my leg. Once at the shelter checkout point, someone told that me they serve a very good meal at the Whosoever Comes Church where there's a lady they call "Mother." They told me I needed someone to look to. When I went, Mother told me, "Welcome, son. You're at the right place."

I give God a blessing for becoming homeless. I learned to live with eight hundred guys and to stand in food lines. I'm baptized and

I've traveled. I'm not speaking in tongues yet. That's what I'm working for. I've felt the Holy Ghost, but when the speaking in tongues comes, that's my salvation.

This has really taught me something. Hustling food lines, I've learned whatever situation you're in, you can do it. Coming to God helps. When Mother brought us out of that shelter to the Church, I wept, and she wept too. Now I'm the coordinator here. We interview homeless guys when they're ready. We take them in when they're drug-free, born again Christian and wanting to get their lives together.

Discussion

Mincy, Sawhill, and Wolf (1990, 450) define one "persistence-based" measure for identifying and quantifying an underclass as a subset of the poor with "chronically low incomes" which can in the extreme "extend for a lifetime or even across generations, leading to a total lack of social mobility." Applying this criterion to our four cases, the parents in all four had been at least intermittently employed while they were growing up: those in three at entry-level jobs, and both the mother and father of Brother Paul at jobs requiring a higher level of education (e.g., as a pastor and a teacher). Only Brother Brendan's mother had been on Public Assistance, and then only briefly before her deceased husband's Social Security payments came through for herself and her son.

As for themselves, all four informants were working at the time they became homeless: the two younger ones, Brothers Brendan and Ethan at a low-paying, entry-level jobs; the two older ones, Brothers Paul and Harold, at better paying work as the assistant director of a social program and in a hospital. Only one of the four had ever been on Public Assistance--and then only after becoming homeless. While the income of both generations in all four families was modest, these work histories do not suggest the cross-generational syndrome of lack of aspiration and effort, chronic unemployment, and Public Assistance participation generally associated with the term underclass. Furthermore, Mincy, Sawhill and Wolf acknowledge that the data for measuring the extent of lifetime poverty do not exist and that the size of a persistence-based underclass can therefore only be estimated.

The "behavior-based" measures these authors use to try to identify and quantify an underclass are (1) not completing high school, (2) not delaying childbearing until the offspring can be supported, (3) not working, and (4) not abiding by the law. All four of our informants completed high school; one also completed one-and-one-half--and another four--years of college. All of them had also worked and had children of their own: with Brother Ethan and Brother Harold marrying--and Brother Paul and Brother Brendan not marrying--the mothers of their children. Before becoming homeless, all but Brother Brendan had continued to see and contribute to the support of their children. Only Brother Brendan had fathered a child in adolescence, and only he had been incarcerated--briefly at age seventeen.

Another "behavior-based" measure these authors propose is receiving "socially unacceptable" forms of income from "crime, Public Assistance or private charity." At the time they were interviewed, all four informants were receiving the church's charity and had previously stayed in the City's public shelter system. Only Brother Brendan had been on Public Assistance, and none of them reported ever receiving income from crime. However, all four reported having used hard drugs. In order to be able to measure the size of a "behavior-based" underclass, Mincy, Sawhill, and Wolf propose empirically estimating the probabilities of congeries of these kinds of behavior, and of their inhibiting effect on intergenerational mobility, since "the longitudinal data needed to define someone as a member of the underclass do not exist."

These authors' "location-based" measure of an underclass is based primarily on the proportion of an area's population that is poor and has certain behavioral characteristics. These include high rates of school dropouts, single parents on Public Assistance, unemployed males, and racial segregation. At the time they were interviewed, all four of our informants lived in what would be identified as an underclass neighborhood on the basis of these criteria. However, only Brother Brendan had grown up in the black/Puerto Rican ghetto of one of the large Northeastern cities where "underclass neighborhoods are somewhat disproportionately concentrated." To conclude, Mincy, Sawhill, and Wolf's estimates of an American underclass of approximately two to three million persons are based almost entirely on the relative proportion of poor people living in low-income, "behaviorally bad" or "ghetto" neighborhoods as defined by tracts with boundaries chosen by the Census Bureau.

Conclusion

The complexities in the lives presented in our four case studies suggest that in order to draw valid conclusions about the "underclass" status of individuals living in low-income neighborhoods, much more needs to be known about their individual life histories than is documented for only a single point in time in self-reported census data. Trying to quantify a hypothetical underclass primarily on the basis of where you live on a certain date, and of a set of specific behaviors which may or may not be your own is scientifically and humanly irresponsible. Notwithstanding, the informants in our four case studies do have three important experiences in common: (1) the early loss of one or more close family members through separation, premature illness, or violent death, (2) a stress-related addiction--particularly, to the crack cocaine which precipitated their homelessness and current residence in a very low-income neighborhood--, and (3) having found an indigenous cultural resource with which "to be healed" in order to try to rebuild their lives.

50

References

Auletta,K.
1982   *The underclass.* New York: Random House.

Bourguinon,E.
1991   *Possession.* Prospect Heights, Illinois: Waveland Press.

Dehavenon,A.
1982   Planning for people and housing in the North Sector.
            Report prepared for the Metro-North Association.

Lewis,O.
1959   *Five families: Mexican case studies in the culture
            of poverty.* New York: Basic Books.
1968   The Culture of Poverty. In *On understanding poverty:
            perspectives from the social sciences,* edited by
            D.P. Moynihan. New York: Basic Books.

Marx,K., and F.Engels
1969, 1973, 1976, 1977
            Selected Works, vol. 1. Moscow: Progress Publishers.

Maxwell,A.
1988   The anthropology of poverty in black communities; a
            critique and systems alternative. In *Urban
            anthropology and studies of cultural systems and
            world economic development* 17(2-3).
1989   The myth of underclass culture. Papers presented in
            symposium on Culture and Poverty Reconsidered, the
            88th Annual Meetings of the American Anthropological
            Association. Washington, D.C.

Mincy,R., I.Sawhill, and D.Wolf
1990   The underclass: Definition and measurement. *Science*
            248:450-453.

Moynihan,D.P.
1965   *The Negro family: The case for national action.*
            Washington, D.C.: U.S. Department of Labor.

Newman,K., ed.
1985   Declining fortunes: anthropological perspectives on
            deindustrialization. In *Urban anthropology* 14(1-3).

Nash,J.
1987   Corporate hegemony and industrial restructuring in a New England industrial city. In *Perspectives in U.S. Marxist anthropology*, edited by D.Hakken and Hanna Lessinger. Boulder, Colorado: Westview Press.

Wilson,W.J.
1978   *The declining significance of race.* Chicago: University of Chicago Press.
1987   *The truly disadvantaged.* Chicago: University of Chicago Press.

African Workers: Are They Really Out There?

Peter Gutkind, Professor
University of Warwick, Coventry, United Kingdom

In his book, *An Economic History of West Africa,*
A.G.Hopkins (1973, 164) observes that "Trade first brought the
Europeans to Africa in the fifteenth century, and trade remained the
basis of their relations with the continent from then onwards."

Perhaps this is a slight exaggeration as curiosity also played a
part during the Age of Discovery in the fifteenth and sixteenth
centuries, as did the drive to transplant Christianity. As the nation
states of Europe thought it vital to consolidate their might, expansion
beyond their borders contributed to extensive explorations. However,
the spirit of adventure was no doubt fueled by economic objectives.

If this established the pattern of Western relations with Africa,
we should pay particular attention to those whose labor, then as now,
facilitated production and trade. If we view labor as central to all
production, then African workers have been, and continue to be, a
central feature of the continent. I would go a step further and suggest
that the study of labor, particularly labor subsumed by capital, moves
us to the very essence of history, history as experience and not mere
narrative history; not a history of a chronology of events but the
history of production (particularly surplus production) trade, and
exchange. To concentrate on the history of productive labor of men
and women stands in strong contrast to imperial history, the history
of the colonizers, their alleged achievements and benefactions, which
has dominated the Eurocentric historiography of Africa: Africa has
no history--at least not until European penetration--and even then it
used to be argued that African history is merely an extension of

European history. After all, history is made by the "great" and "famous." Thus Professor Charles Kingsley expressed the following view in his inaugural lecture at Cambridge University in 1861 (Jones 1973, 98):

> The new science of little men can be no science at all; because the average man is not the normal man and never has been; because the great man is rather the normal man, as approaching more nearly than his fellows the true "norma" and the standard of a complete human character . . . to turn to the mob for your theory of humanity is (I think) about as wise as to ignore Apollo and the Theseus, and to determine the proportions of the human figure from a crowd of dwarfs and cripples. The object of history is to find out what great men did with the various aspects of public-life in which they were involved.

In contrast, I rather share the view of that great Irish republican socialist, James Connolly, who expressed the opposite when he said in 1916: "The cause of labour is the cause of Ireland, the cause of Ireland is the cause of labour." But let us not dwell on the matter as this kind of language on either side of the divide might be viewed by many as rhetoric.

My interest in African workers has always been part of my concentration on African urbanization and urbanism, on migrancy and the migrant, the evolution of class structure, and the rise of class and political consciousness among various segments of the urban population. I think that I was perhaps the first social anthropologist, twenty-five years ago, whose interest focused on the unemployed; today they comprise an ever larger portion particularly of the African urban population (Gutkind 1968). At that time I did not ask myself how that unemployment had come about, I merely recorded that many migrants, or urban born, could not find work and that they often expressed quite radical sentiments which I expressed in the title of an article: "From the Energy of Despair to the Anger of Despair" (Gutkind 1973). Somewhat later I wrote a little monograph with the title *The Emergent African Urban Proletariat* (1974). I concentrated on archival materials of the 1920s and 1930s in order to obtain some insight into two questions: How did the British administrators view the African worker and urbanite, and how did the African workers view themselves? I looked for evidence of strikes and other manifestations of labor unrest in West and East Africa; I read petitions produced by African workers raising a wide range of complaints, demanding better pay and working conditions; I studied the correspondence between Colonial Office officials and British administrators who frequently expressed fear of the "urban mob" and also cast African workers, correctly, as a distinct class with a distinct consciousness.

I believe it was this background that led me to concentrate on early precolonial African labor history. In particular I have become interested in the history of the canoemen of southern Ghana. I hope that this study will turn out to be a modest contribution to establish the field of early precolonial African labor studies and by doing so reveal the continuity of the forces, the structures, and the responses of African workers when they began to be influenced by the complex processes of incorporation into new structures of accumulation, labor processes, production, and trade.

This excursion into the past is still experimental, particularly the attempt to apply the approaches of social history, an intellectually adventurous yet still somewhat amorphous field. Because social anthropologists are not adequately trained in the methods of historical research (Cohen 1987), they do not always recognize how the past may help us understand the present. Incredulity is the likely response to my declared objective of tracing evidence for, and the evolution of, political and class consciousness among a group of workers whose labor under early Western capitalism began in 1482. To have been stimulated by, and to use as a possible point of reference E.P. Thompson, E.Hobsbawm, and F.Braudel (all viewed as social historians), will surely elicit a reaction of benevolent indulgence, of a flight of fancy, of overinterpretation, of an ideological determinism in face of the thinnest of evidence, particularly in the African case. Yet I received some encouragement for my own flights of fancy when I read some of the papers presented at a conference at Rutgers University in 1983 devoted to the theme, "Proletarianization Past and Present." I noted that David Levine read a paper on "Production, Reproduction and the Proletarian Family in England, 1500-1850" and Catharina Lis spoke about "Policing the Early Modern Proletariat, 1500-1850." The argument was made by a number of participants that "long before urbanization and large factories were dominant, capitalism had gripped the countryside and turned much of the peasantry into part or full-time workers" (Radtke 1983, 81). Evidently early cottage industry generated large proletarian households, which collectively revealed their power of protest fueled by a proletarian consciousness that can be traced directly to the relations of production. This consciousness provided E.P.Thompson with the often quoted view that "class is a relationship and not a thing." If this is so, "then a necessary condition for the historical treatment of working people must be an awareness of the changing content of the labour process and those being proletarianized" (Radtke 1983, 83). Whether a precolonial labor history of Africa is possible remains to be seen, but initial results give me some hope that careful archival digging will provide testimony for the proposition that Africa's labor history has substantial roots and does not commence only when a "proper" working class is established.

These few introductory and discursive comments lead me to the objective of my contribution in honor of Aidan Southall--a friend and colleague for almost forty years--namely, a few controversial reflections on African workers. The title of the paper (taken from a conversation with an economist with conservative inclinations) will allow me to raise some issues, mostly still unresolved, and certainly often controversial (Gutkind 1983, 1988).

The literature on the "African worker" has grown rapidly and no longer lags behind labor studies in India and Latin America. Three years ago, Bill Freund published his *The African Worker* (1988), which contains a twenty-nine-page bibliography. To Freund's important contribution must be added John Iliffe's study of *The African Poor: A History of the African Working Class*. This reformulation is not designed to invoke romantic images of the burden, past and present, borne by African workers (and Third World workers, and what remains of the working class in the West--and I do believe that such still exists despite assertions to the contrary). It is not my view that the working class has been and always will be "the salt of the earth," yet their importance in a timeless sense cannot be denied. It is risky to make predictions, but I suggest that the voice of the African working class will be heard more frequently as it consolidates its position. African workers face a struggle because the obstacles to a better life seem as remote as ever, as inequality crystallizes, and migration intensifies along with unemployment. African workers are now exposed to structures and struggles, which come with the New International Division of Labour (Timberlake 1985), and the policies of the IMF and the World Bank (Castells 1989; Research Working Group on World Labour 1986; and Walton 1987).

On the first page of Freund's book, he tells us that "the African has always been an economic person." This is a safe assertion and can be said about anybody. Even if we do not like it, work--economic activity--is central to our existence. Needs are unequally defined and distributed as access to meet these needs is not open to all. All this quite apart from the inequalities of gender, age, ability, and other structures that divide the socioeconomic and political order. Structure and agency articulate in a complex interface, the fortuitous and the calculated, the consciousness of being, and the consciousness of class. But how do we identify African workers? Workers anywhere?

I think the starting point is "labor." I think it quite wrong to suggest that there were no African workers until the onset of colonialism and wage labor, an extension of the view that African economies were primitive (precapitalist) prior to European hegemony. If "the African has always been an economic person," then it follows that African workers have a long history. My work on the history of the canoemen of Ghana, whose labor for the Portuguese began in the late fifteenth century, serves as an instructive case (Gutkind 1985, 1986, 1989). What is quite clear is that these workers were "waged," that they went on "strike," that labor legislation was applied to them, and that they revealed a distinct consciousness. They labored for others (as well as their household and kin), and as free canoemen (there were also slave canoemen), they sold their labor. They frequently demanded better terms (from the Europeans who established trading stations along the coast) and when these were refused, they simply withdrew their labor, and that is exactly what workers do today.

Historians of Africa, particularly economic historians, have generally defined workers and labor according to categories and conditions primarily identified with industrial society (Peil 1970). That, surely, is too narrow an approach. We insist that the economies of "precapitalist" societies have been very different, perhaps even classless, despite obvious divisions and specializations of labor. Labor, we are told, has been cemented in kinship. While the so-called "decentralized" systems revealed such a feature, those we have come to label "centralized" and "hierarchical" also appear to have been minus real workers, or if we did identify workers who labored for others, they were few in number and not at all like those in the West.

In common usage we claim that we are all workers. But the workers we are talking about are producers within a particular system of production, exchange, distribution, and merchandising, and an economy which for at least three hundred years has spanned the globe. But even prior to that, labor was not restricted to social reproduction, the production for the household. The appropriation of surplus production was also in place in many small-scale societies. So perhaps what we should attempt is to periodize what I will call the evolution of the African working class. No doubt regional differences will be marked, perhaps West Africa was ahead in some respect, but a distinct strata was in place, prior to European penetration, in many societies. I think that we can go a step further and identify a political community with its own organizational order, and a consciousness that revealed itself in a variety of manifestations. I believe that the time will come when we will be able to show that craft guilds and various associations of workers came into being to protect and advance their standing long before colonialism. This is not an assertion that elevates ideology over careful research; rather we look for social relations that spring from a specific system of production.

This approach raises an avalanche of issues and controversies. For example, we must ask: Does surplus-value production and appropriation invariably create a working class, a proletariat? Are commodity production, economic-political hierarchy, and a capitalist labor process central to working class formation? Is "waged" work in preindustrial societies the same as wages in industrial societies? (Here, as an aside, I suggest that other areas than Europe independently developed forms of capitalism, and that labor-capital confrontation, and mechanisms to control labor, were an integral part of societies engaged in production, which almost always centralized control over resources and the labor market.) Remuneration can vary from in-kind to a monetary wage. Is the former more abstract than the latter? Why are monetarized economies a central feature of wage labor? Surely, the antecedents of capital accumulation are not just its "primitive" and early forms, which by stages grew into mature capitalism, but a great variety of labor processes and capital formation. And what of the even more complex issue of the consciousness of workers as a class? Process and structure vary over time and respond variously to hierarchy, power, and control (Katznelson and Zolberg 1986). Has it not been said often that the working class is the child of the industrial revolution; that the African working class, if there is one, is not a proletariat as it has not been severed completely from the ownership or access to the means of production. Shivji (1986, 242) recently suggested that the weakness of the Tanzanian working class is due to "the absence of its own proletarian organization." If that is vital, there is clearly no proper working class in the United States of America, as this class has never spawned a party of labor. It is clear that the transition to mature Western industrial capitalism in Third World countries has generated an underclass, a vast labor reserve, which has yet to transform itself into a "proper" working class.

If we were to adopt, experimentally, the approach of social history; that is, the analysis of socioeconomic and political organization, such as the protoproletariat, technology, the labor process, and class formation "from below," then we might accept more readily the view that working class formation, consciousness, ideology, and action existed long before contemporary capitalism. Ancient societies, urbanization, the state, all created workers who created surplus value; workers who protested, deserted, destroyed, and created self-defense organizations; and in some cases unions of the poor. A central issue of interest to social historians is this: what is and has been the historical process whereby labor was and is subsumed to capital?

I have no hesitation to suggest that African workers very early moved to center stage. They certainly did so beginning with the immediate precolonial era when a waged labor force, defined in a more conventional sense, was certainly moving in place (Coquery-Vidrovitch 1988, 215-268). How important these workers were is constantly revealed during the colonial era (let us say from 1870-1950) because of the constant concern about "the labour question," often a euphemism for the urban mob (generally feared by the colonial administrators (Gutkind 1974), a proletariat, and a working class. We have documented the rise and fall of African peasantry but have made little effort to explore the rise of the African working class (in a "crippled state" in Marxian terms), nourished by forced labor, labor recruitment, migration, and urbanization. Nor should we ignore the rise of a rural-based working class such as agricultural workers (Swindell 1985) and public works labor. Freund (1988, 46) has pointed out that "generally speaking, the classic processes of proletarianization are occurring in rural Africa but [these] Africans do not confront a powerful or effective indigenously based capitalism anxious to make use of their labour." As far as I know, no study has been made of that famous colonial institution, the Public Works Department. We had better leave the controversial issue of whether we can identify a working class as far back as precolonial Africa.

Turning to the present, the issues are just as controversial and, as I indicated earlier, still largely unresolved. The debate is still very much alive: namely, can we identify a "proper" African working class, and the even more controversial issue of political and class consciousness (Sandbrook 1981). I am afraid that I take an oversimplified view: namely, where there are producers of surplus value--products they do not price and market but must leave to others--there is a working class however embryonic, even if partly tied to land, that consciousness and activism will be manifest, yet retreat can be as marked as agitation (Goldberg 1981). Those who insist that there is no African working class should explain the actions of African workers when they withdraw their labor, or why covert forms of protest and resistance (Cohen 1980) are less conscious than organized manifestations such as strike action. Why is working class consciousness always so directly linked to industrialization, and not to the development of various types of capital in preindustrial societies? Why is it argued that true class consciousness is different in degree, if not in kind, from incomplete and sporadic manifestations of class awareness; that class is weak but ethnicity is strong; that the patron-client relationship reveals a false consciousness; and that economism is a conscious reformism and not a desire for systemic change. I suspect that all these are features of the African working class. Peter Waterman (1976, 159-184; 1975, 57-73) has indicated a strong conservative streak among Nigerian waterfront workers. Sandbrook and Arn (1977) and Peter Lloyd (1982) have questioned the existence of class--at least as conventionally defined--while Lloyd has suggested that urban Africans perceive society to be relatively open, that luck and misfortune determine success, that it is important to create a network of patrons and a strong belief in individual economic achievement. Class consciousness and actions do not exclude personal perceptions of how the individual fits into a socioeconomic and political order; agency and structure can be symbiotic or antagonistic. But African workers are viewed quite differently: they do not perceive inequality, injustices, employment relations, and working conditions as debilitating as do Western workers. Different layers of occupations do not, somehow, reveal some sort of corporate identity that might at least approximate class consciousness. But why is this so, if it is so? Why are African workers, as workers, so different? It is often argued that only those Africans in certain occupations such as dockworkers, miners, and railway workers approximate the Western model of a blue collar worker. For others, kinship and ethnicity will always pull the African worker back into a condition loosely labeled as primordiality. What clearer evidence exists, we are told, but that South African workers, as often as they show solidarity, equally often fight and kill one another. And of course, workers organizations are weak, rent with corruption, and often run on ethnic lines. Unions are only successful if they set limited objectives. Political unionism, as an instrument of systemic transformation, requires skilled leadership, a sophisticated ideology, and strategy. It is never explained why it is that African workers do not understand (worse yet, not interested in knowing) what a capitalist system of production is, particularly a colonial/neocolonial system, and how such a market system operates. While it may well have been true in early colonial times that the "degree of consciousness among African workers was [not] sufficiently intense for the working class to become the 'general representatives' of their societies" (Shivji 1986, 240), in more recent times this assertion is worth testing very widely. I think most African governments know what a working class looks like (Gutkind 1974), but why do so many scholars have such difficulty (Gutkind 1983)?

Research on the more recent economic history of Africa has revealed the structures that gave rise to the African working class, and matured it. Capitalist penetration created the migrant, was labor intensive and export oriented, and few benefits found their way back to the African worker, a condition no different today. It is the economic history of the continent that has determined the history of the African worker, but semantic contests wipe away clarity of vision. The historical record indicates that the African working class has stabilized rapidly, and has increased in number. Thus Silver (1978, 83), writing about Ghanaian miners, suggests that they are "a highly stabilized social category [and] reproducing itself as evidenced by the growing number of second generation mineworkers." It may well be unevenly proletarianized (as is the working class in the West), but this is surely due to the so-called underdeveloped colonial/neocolonial capitalism to which it has been exposed. The tempo of economic activity has steadily increased, and the "laws" of the labor market are well in place but also reflect particular African conditions--a dialectic as true today as in the past. Merchant, finance, and industrial capital created conditions that reflected back on African workers and created relations of production. Whatever the forms of capitalism and how they confront workers, the objective is always the same: how to extract from the worker the amount of labor both to pay wages and to make a profit, the difference between the two being the amount of surplus value the worker creates. This is exactly what African rulers, merchants, and various entrepreneurs sought long before colonialism engaged the continent (Kea 1982). Why is it doubtful that African workers had something to say in the past about a system that used their labor but rarely allowed them a fair share of the wealth they created? I sometimes suspect that a subliminal racism clouds our understanding of non-Western societies and their history.

I have not touched on what might be the most controversial question: What is the political position of the African working class (Cohen and Michael 1973; Gerold-Scheepers 1978; Sandbrook 1981)? Does it have the potential to force systemic change? Has it shown such potential in the past? Have African workers, past and present, seen themselves as agents of their own empowerment both politically and economically (Sandbrook 1977)? I think the short answer is yes at times, but as with workers everywhere, this empowerment is not always continuous or successful; periods of activism are followed by quietude, retreat, consolidation, and even reverses of "deskilling" (forcing workers into low productive labor), which can give rise to new collective solidarity. Today as in the past, the African working class is not homogeneous but layered; the unskilled and casual workers struggle at the bottom (and women workers particularly), while the artisan and the skilled command more influence. The waged have progressively transformed themselves into a proletariat that is more attuned to the industrial and commercial ethos, which they have challenged by means of membership in unions and new social movements (Freyhold 1987; Newsletter of International Labour Studies 1987, 1987a) such as ecological concerns, or the rights of women workers, who are no longer "outside the typical working categories" (Silver 1978, 48). Such developments do not offer certainty that the African working class is destined to be revolutionary or conservative. Freund (1988, 25), for example, concluded that "the radical African nation-state is no longer assumed to be the object of working class struggle." Urban discontent (Wiseman 1986) and peasant boycotts or revolts can explode in many different directions and seek a variety of objectives. False consciousness is often more evident than an explicit class consciousness (the British working class has certainly been influenced by Thatcherism). But I do not see ambiguity, contradictions, and a lack of consistency as evidence that seriously challenges the assertion that an African working class has been in place for a reasonable time, and is conscious of its existence and its place in the bodies politic and economic. What African country has been without strikes whatever their frequency and the skill of those who organize these manifestations? What African countries are without labor legislation, particularly antistrike legislation? Why such legislation if the African working class is an epiphenomenon, a mere protoproletariat, and class consciousness that begins at the level of the bourgeoisie? Or is it the case that the African working class is so manipulable and so chameleonlike that it can go in any direction (Peace 1976; Levine 1973; Cohen and Michael 1973)? Is it all a case of "now you see it, now you don't?" Were all this so, then African workers have been and continue to be so different from their comrades elsewhere that we need a new vocabulary to identify the unit of our interest. For all the doubters, it seems so much easier to label a group as "peasants" or "elites" and describe their ideology (Ranger 1985) than to recognize an African worker. We can identify the poor (Gutkind 1968; Iliffe 1987), although that took us a considerable time, but we still have some doubt whether we should really speak about unemployment in Africa.

Does working class consciousness find true expression in knowing who its class enemies are, or in a show of violence? The state knows who its supporters and enemies are. Why would ordinary workers be less perceptive? The consciousness of African workers may be radical, utopian, and visionary; more often consciousness and struggle are expressions of breaking down barriers to opportunity and mobility. Perhaps their vision of the future is "a lucky break," a hope some would treat as evidence of false consciousness. But should we argue that only industrial workers have so far shown signs of class and political radicalism, a true proletariat, while most African workers are marginal? I think it more correct to suggest that African workers have always had an important stake in the economy. If that is so, then it would seem rather more realistic to suggest that African workers understand the particular niche they occupy. It is their actual work experience that fertilizes the seeds of class consciousness, authentic or distorted (and the latter is consciousness and not some mental aberration). This is surely obvious when we listen to workers tell their own stories. Here social history might come to our aid, perhaps in the manner of work by the late Ruth First (1983) and Walter Rodney (1981), or the work of Van Onselen (1976), Peace (1979), and Crisp (1984).

The title of this paper is in the form of a question: Are they really out there? To this we could add many other questions such as What is the political future of the African working class (Sandbrook 1977)? How will it respond to the shift from a labor- to a capital-intensive economy? How will it respond to increasing polarization? The African worker, and collectively the African working class, is potentially revolutionary if only perhaps because it is viewed as such (the fear of the urban mob) by a weak bourgeoisie whose political power is fragile if not backed by state repression.

I end with a quotation from Ousmane Sembene (1970, 74):

> And so the strike came to Thies. An unlimited strike, which, for many was a time for suffering, but for many was also a time for thought. When the smoke from the trains no longer drifted above the savanna, they realized that an age had ended - an age their elders had told them about, when all Africa was just a garden for food. Now the machine rules over their lands, and when they forced every machine within a thousand miles to halt they

became conscious of their strength, but conscious also of their dependence. They began to understand that the machine was making of them a whole new breed of men. It did not belong to them; it was they who belonged to it. When it stopped, it taught them that lesson.

References

Castells,M.
1989   High technology and the new international division of labour. *Labour and society* 14:7-41.

Cohen,B.S.
1987   *An anthropologist among the historians and other essays.* Oxford: Oxford University Press.

Cohen,R.
1980   Resistance and hidden forms of consciousness among African workers. *Review of African political economy* 19:8-22.

Cohen,R., and D.Michael
1973   The revolutionary potential of the African lumpenproletariat: A skeptical view. *Bulletin Institute of Development Studies* 5:31-42.

Coquery-Vidrovitch,C.
1988   *Africa: Endurance and change south of the Sahara,* translated by D. Maisel. Berkeley: University of California Press.

Crisp,J.
1984   *The story of an African working class: Ghanaian miners' struggles, 1870-1980.* London: Zed.

First,R.
1983   *Black gold: The Mozambican miner, proletarian and peasant.* Brighton: Harvester Press.

Freund,B.
1988   *The African worker.* Cambridge: Cambridge University Press.

Freyhold,M.
1987   Labour movements or popular struggles in Africa. *Review of African political economy* 39 (September):23-32.

Gerold-Scheepers,T.J.
1978   The political consciousness of African urban workers: A review of recent publications. *African perspectives* 2:83-98.

Goldberg,M.
1981   Formulating worker consciousness. *Social dynamics* 7:32-41.

Gutkind,P.C.W.
1968   The poor in urban Africa. In *Power, poverty and urban policy*, edited by W.Bloomberg and H.Schmandt, 355-396. Beverly Hills: Sage Publications.
1974   The emergent African urban proletariat. Occasional paper 8. Montreal: McGill University, Centre for Developing Area Studies.
1983   Workers are workers and Marxist intellectuals are mere intellectuals (said Alice). *Contemporary Marxism* 7-184-193.
1985   Trade and labor in early pre-colonial African history: The canoemen of southern Ghana. In *The workers of African trade*, edited by P.Lovejoy and C.Coquery-Vidrovitch, 25-49. Beverly Hills: Sage Publications.
1986   The boatmen of Ghana: The possibilities of a pre-colonial African labour history. In *Confrontation, class consciousness and the labour process: Studies in proletarian class formation*, edited by C.Stephenson and M.Hanagan, 123-166. Westport, Conn.: Greenwood.
1988   Are socio-historical studies of the labour process central to Third World studies? *Journal of Asian and African studies* 23:5-20.
1989   The canoemen of the Gold Coast (Ghana): A survey and exploration in pre-colonial African labour. *Cahier d'études africaines* 29:3-4. In press.

Hopkins,A.G.
1973   *An economic history of West Africa.* New York: Columbia University Press.

Iliffe,J.
1987   *The African poor: A history.* Cambridge: Cambridge University Press.

70

Jones,G.S.
1973   History: The poverty of empiricism. In *Ideology in Social Science*, edited by R.Blackburn, 98. New York: Random House.

Katznelson,I, and A.R.Zolberg, eds.
1986   *Working-class formation: Nineteenth century patterns in Western Europe and the United States.* Princeton: Princeton University Press.

Kea,R.A.
1982   *Settlements, trade and polities in the seventeenth-century Gold Coast.* Baltimore: Johns Hopkins University Press.

Levine,N.
1973   The revolutionary non-potential of the "Lumpen": Essence or technical deficiency? *Bulletin Institute of Development Studies* 5:43-52.

Lloyd,P.
1982   *A Third World proletariat?* London: Allen and Unwin.

NILS (Newsletter of International Labour Studies)
1987   32-33.
1987a   34.

Peace,A.
1976   The Lagos proletariat: Labour aristocrats or populist militants. In *The development of an African working class*, edited by R.Sandbrook and R.Cohen, 281-302. Toronto: University of Toronto Press.
1979   *Choice, class and conflict: A study of southern Nigerian factory workers.* Brighton: Harvester Press.

Peil,M.
1970   *The Ghanaian factory worker.* Cambridge: Cambridge University Press.

Radtke,T.
1983   Proletarianization past and present. *International labour and working class history* 24:81-83.

Ranger,T.O.
1985   *Peasant consciousness and guerilla war in Zimbabwe*. London: Currey.

Research Working Group on World Labour
1986   Global patterns of labor movements in historical perspective. *Review* 10:137-155.

Rodney,W.
1981   *A history of the Guyanese working people, 1881-1905*. London: Heinemann.

Sandbrook,R.
1977   The political potential of African workers. *Canadian Journal of African Studies/Revue canadienne des études africaines* 11:411-433.
1981   Worker consciousness and populist protest in tropical Africa. *Research in the sociology of work* 1:1-36.

Sandbrook,R., and J.Arn
1977   *The labouring poor and urban class formation: the case of greater Accra*. Montreal: Centre for Developing-Area Studies, McGill University.

Sembene,O.
1970   *God's bits of wood, (Les bouts de bois de dieu)*, translated by Francis Price. New York: Doubleday.

Shivji,I.G.
1986   *Law, state and the working class in Tanzania c. 1920-1964*. London: Currey, Heinemann.

Silver,J.
1978   Class struggles in Ghana's mining industry. *Review of African political economy* 12:67-86.

Swindell,K.
1985   *Farm labour*. London: Cambridge University Press.

Timberlake,M., ed.
1985   *Urbanization in the world economy*. London: Academic Press.

72

Walton,J.
1987   Urban protest and global political economy: The IMF
              riots. In *The capitalist city: Global restructuring
              and community politics*, edited by M.P.Smith and
              J.R.Feagin, 364-386. Oxford: Blackwell.

Waterman,P.
1976   Conservatism among Nigeria's workers. In *Nigeria:
              Economy and society*, edited by G.Williams, 159-184.
              London: Collings.
1975   The "Labour Aristocracy" in Africa: Introduction to a
              Debate. *Development and change* 6:57-73.

Van Onselen,C.
1976   *Chibaro.   African mine labour in southern
              Rhodesia,1900-1933*. London: Pluto.

Wiseman,J.
1986   Urban riots in West Africa, 1977-1985. *Journal of
              modern African studies* 24:509-518.

Fishing in the Luapula River in Southeastern Zaire:
The Contradictions of the Second Economy

Mukohya Vwakyanakazi, Professor
University of Lubumbashi
Shaba, Zaire

Professor Aidan William Southall, to whom I dedicate this short essay, is an intellectual giant. Witnesses of this are his many former graduate students, now widespread throughout the world, and the Alur people of western Uganda and northeastern Zaire, to whom he devoted the most remarkable piece of his wide academic work (Southall 1956).

Professor Southall, however, left in his notes a great many open questions and mistrusted unfounded generalizations. I remember his joy when I informed him about the Bambuba being a small ethnic group neighboring the Banande of eastern Zaire. Alur mythology indeed sometimes mentioned these people, but Professor Southall had never been able to locate them geographically. I also remember him complaining about some of my comments during graduate seminars. In some cases he found them a little bit exaggerated.

The story I want to tell is neither on the Alur people nor exaggerated. It is an ethnographic piece on fishing in a Zairean rural area. It raises the question of contradictions within a society in socioeconomic crisis and tells the hardships of an African people involved in second economy activities. More precisely, my question is, Does involvement in second economy activities lead to successful fending-for-oneself (J.MacGaffey 1983, 351-356, 1986, 141-155)?

The concept of "second economy" is getting greater acceptance in academic circles of the social sciences. It refers to all kinds of underground production, distribution, and exchange activities. It also includes the social relations between people, institutions, and organizations on this occasion. These activities and social relations are said to be "underground" because they are in essence illegal. They escape government control and recognition. In this they may be contrasted with those of the economy of the "day" or legal economy, be they formal, official, and structured or informal, unofficial, and unstructured.

Second economy as well as informal economy have so far been considered an urban phenomenon characterizing Third World societies in socioeconomic crisis. Some population members are said to operate in this sector because they feel marginalized from the mainstream economy and are confronted with survival difficulties. But they have to comply with sets of informal rules, the content of which is increasingly being specified and structured. At the extreme limit, entire national communities such as Zaire, Uganda, or Ethiopia may gradually be transformed into "second" societies with second economy as the predominant production, distribution, and exchange system (J.MacGaffey 1987, 23-25, 111, and bibliography).

Empirical evidence to help refine the concept of second economy has in most cases been drawn from studies on big and small urban centers of developing countries. Second economy activities are, on the one hand, said to be highly destructive of the official economies because they include anarchic production, distribution, and exchange of scarce resources. They are, on the other hand, considered as an avenue toward improving the standards of living of the involved population because they provide employment to the jobless and supplementary revenues to household budgets.

Some scholars, like Janet MacGaffey, find in the second economy an efficient instrument for self-defense and for class struggle on the part of the most marginalized population members of the Third World countries (J.McGaffey 1983, 1987). But careful research is still to be undertaken in rural areas in order to determine the extent of this type of economy and its impact on the involved rural masses.

This short essay on fishing in the Luapula River is aimed to test further the preceding hypothesis. It results from the observation of fishing activities in the field during trips to the Luapula area, the last of which took place between 27 March and 18 April of 1990. It also brings in further personal thought on the second economy activities. It shows that present-day fishing in the Luapula River is a second economy activity but less on the level of production than on that of distribution of fish. Because of the presence of unequal social forces involved in fish production and trade, fishing becomes in the area an arena of conflict and contradictions. It enriches the already rich and impoverishes the already poor. By so doing, it little helps the rural people to fend for themselves.

Fishing in the Luapula River

The Luapula River constitutes the official border between Zaire and Zambia to the southeast about three hundred fifty kilometers (see map of the Republic of Zaire on the following page). It flows from Lake Bengwelo in Zambia to Lake Moero shared by Zaire and Zambia. It is recognized to shelter plenty of the fish on which people mostly live on either bank. Fishing, which I observed especially between Kasenga, Kashobwe, and Kilwa in Zaire, occupies about sixty percent of the Bemba border population. It is far more important than agriculture or hunting. It impinges on the pattern of space occupation and exploitation. People along both riverbanks are settled in dispersed habitats in a savanna environment and in small rounded, straw houses. The straw villages, which local people call "fishing

Map of the Republic of Zaire
(M. Vwakyanakazi)

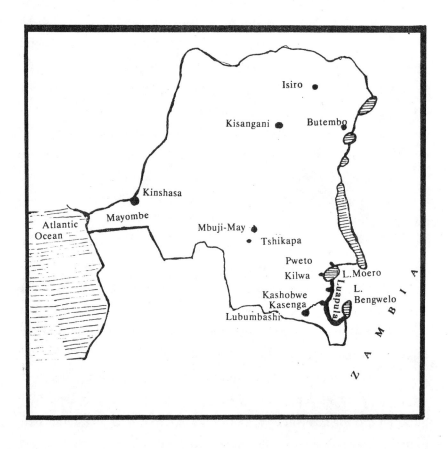

camps," shelter from five to twenty families linked by kin relations. They assemble kinsmen grouped in small matrilineages under the rule of local chiefs depending, themselves, upon higher-ranking chiefs. In traditional Bembaland these lineages constitute the basic unit of production (Richards 1969, 23-26). The occupation of space is denser on the Zambian than on the Zairean bank of the Luapula River. This is likely the result of better available medical care in Zambia than in Zaire where the health of people is a matter of little concern on the part of the government--with only two percent of the national annual budget devoted to medical care as against fifteen percent in Zambia. The Luapula geographical area is indeed infested by enemies such as malaria, smallpox, tuberculosis, and leprosy.

In some geographical areas of the Luapula riverside, the Zambian government has initiated an integrated scheme of space occupation with the regrouping of people into big villages of about ten thousand inhabitants. This policy has helped make available to the rural people amenities such as running water, electric lights, schools, dispensaries, and houses roofed with corrugated iron, which are not frequently seen on the Zairean riverbank.

Unlike the situation among fishermen of the Zaire River between Kisangani and Kinshasa, ownership of fishing territories is not recognized. People fish freely on both riverbanks of Luapula. The political frontier, which arbitrarily cuts the same Bemba people into two parts between the two countries, is not recognized. This geographical mobility for fishing is facilitated by people along both riverbanks pertaining to the same Bemba ethnic group, often to the same lineages and families and sharing the same local culture, especially the language. So in the eyes of the inhabitants of the left riverbank, for example, there is nothing illegal about fishing on the right riverbank and vice versa, although colonial as well as postcolonial governments maintained that it was unlawful. This view gives grounds for a great deal of misunderstanding and conflict between frontier people and the governments. The administered do not always understand the modern notion and conception of frontier. Wyatt MacGaffey noted this fact as early as 1970. When studying Lower Congo custom and government, he pointed out that the Kongo people, pertaining to three different political communities (Zaire, Congo, and Angola), did not in fact understand the notion of a political entity based on territory. They still conceived kinship as the only basis of polity (W.MacGaffey 1970, 263). They were also, of course, economically organized on the basis of what Southall called, in a recent study, "the kinship mode of production" (1988, 184-188). On the part of the African people and governments, this results in conflicting attitudes toward the second economy activities, with the governments striving to regulate or sanction them whereas people, in the final analysis, see no reason for regulation or sanctioning.

The consequence of communal exploitation of the fishing territory is the minimization of taxes on fishing for the elders and the headmen of villages. The Bemba political system is made of scattered chiefdoms composed of matrilineal lineages. These share and exploit a territory as a communal property. Rights over the lineage land are recognized but usufruct is individual or collective, depending on labor invested in the productive activities (Richards 1969, 245-246). Where, by contrast, political systems are like those among the Lokele of Haut-Zaire, more centralized and collective fishing is emphasized, taxes on fishing in alien territories may be heavy and absorb as much as one-third of the fish catch or take the form of large amounts of foodstuffs (Baruti 1972).

The techniques of fishing, carefully studied by A.I.Richards as early as 1939, remain rudimentary (Richards 1969, 329-342). A fishing canoe is made of a wood trunk and owned by an individual or by a work team whose number varies from three to five individuals. The most successful fishermen may own a larger fishing canoe. This kind of canoe is manufactured by the Kashobwe technical school students at the price of 80,000 Z. the unit. (In Zaire the national currency is also called "Zaire" (Z.). It suffers from rampant inflation. In 1970, 1 Z. was worth $2.00. Today $1.00 is exchanged for 600 Z. in the official exchange market.) Fishing nets, whose size and meshes vary, are also locally made but with the use of commercial thread. Wicker traps of varied sizes are made of local materials. A fishhook is rather rarely used except by young children. No mechanical fishing has been observed on the Luapula River, as sometimes is the case on Zairean lakes such as Moero, Tanganyika, or Mobutu. Likewise no locally made sophisticated fishing equipment is encountered there as it is among the Lokele and neighboring fishermen of the Zaire River in Haut-Zaire. In Haut-Zaire fishermen have come to devise highly technical fishing equipment made of local wood. These include scaffolding and other machinery destined to bar parts of the river or to slow down the speed of the water stream. One would, however, not contend that the Lokele, in the matter of fishing technology, prove more imaginative than do the Bemba of the Luapula riversides. The difference is likely accounted for by differing natural environments to which people strive to adapt. The Haut-Zaire tropical rain forest contains large amounts of wood while the southeastern savannas are made up of only grasslands and rare woodlands. The latter are, furthermore, increasingly depleted by the inhabitants little concerned with rational use of natural resources.

The techniques of fish conservation also vary. For lack of refrigeration facilities, except for a single big Lubumbashi businessman owning some refrigerated trucks, fresh fish is sold at the very riverbank for domestic consumption. Salted fish is also prepared. But its conservation is not altogether satisfactory because, in order to save on the quantity of salt used, salting is superficial. As a consequence, rotted fish is often delivered to consumers. Smoking fish is a more usual technique. Fish treated this way is then assembled in baskets of from ten to twenty kilograms in weight.

While individuals or small work teams may fish for themselves, well-off persons such as urban or local traders, local government employees, traditional chiefs, and local religious leaders usually hire fishermen who send them the entire fish catch in exchange of generally low salaries (ten thousand to fifteen thousand Zaire per month).

Fishing, more on the Zairean side than on the Zambian riverside, is a matter of state regulations. The Zairean regulations authorize fishing from 25 March to 25 December and forbids it the remaining months of the year. This enables fish to multiply during the breeding season. As a matter of fact, one may note among the fishermen as well as among the local authorities a propensity to fish anarchically. As a consequence, the aquatic fauna thought available in inexhaustive quantities by rural people ignorant of environmental problems is systematically destroyed. Since noncompliance with the local state regulations forbidding fishing during some months of the year is the rule among fishermen as well as among the local authorities, many incidents and conflicts occur in this period between people and local authorities. These vary from pursuits, fines, and arrests to the confiscation of the fish catch. All such harassment is purposely intended and used to lubricate the machinery of the second economy in the geographical areas.

The quality and quantity of fish caught vary depending on the seasons and the fishing techniques. But it is recognized that the

Luapula River shelters more fish than does Lake Moero of which it is a tributary. Its water is fresher than that of the neighboring lakes. Likewise, its depth is such that fishermen can catch considerable amounts of fish without having to use any sophisticated equipment especially in dry seasons.

Something noteworthy in the area is the high geographical mobility of fishermen. As we have already pointed out, these fish freely on both riverbanks without worrying about the political frontier between Zaire and Zambia. The fishing territory has never been a problem. If in the past, especially in 1984 to 1986, conflicts arose among the inhabitants of the fishing villages of both riverbanks, up to having houses and some family belongings burned, it was because armed confrontation was taking place between Zaire and Zambia at the southern border on the one hand, and on the other hand because the respective national media had exaggeratedly reported the incident, while at the same time urging the nationals to protect themselves against exterior aggression.

Finally, let me point out that in contrast to what happens, for example, in the basin area of Zaire and among some river fishermen of West Africa, Luapula River fishing is an economic activity for men in the traditional division of labor. Because of harsh work and because of the many risks involved, women do not take part in fishing. They may, however, contribute to complementary tasks such as cleaning of fish, the preparation of wood and its transport for smoking fish, the fish smoking itself, the transport of fish to the village, and the care of it until it will be either consumed or commercialized.

In sum, Luapula River fishing as a productive activity is still traditional. It is no more than traditional gathering with minimized conflicts over the ownership of fishing territories and fishing equipment. As for the production relations among fishermen, they remain tempered because of communal ethnic links and collective exploitation of fishing territories.

Fish trade on the Luapula River

Fish trade on the Luapula River takes different but not mutually exclusive forms:

Fish trade on the very bank of the river. The exchange takes place between the fisher, coming back from his fishing activities, and the consumer. It is made usually, but not exclusively, in small quantities and mostly for domestic consumption. The kind and quantities of fish sold vary depending on the buyer's level of personal wealth. In many cases, the best fish product is left to the buyers, while fishermen keep the low-quality fish product for domestic consumption.

Fish trade at home. Buyers purchase fish at the fishermen's homes. To this end, correct information about the quality and quantity of the fish catch is needed. In case of salted or smoked fish, the buyer will have to wait until salting or smoking has been completed.

Fish peddling. The fisherman, and especially some of his dependents (wife and children), peddle part of their fish catch from house to house. This trade method is mostly used during periods of plentiful fishing (April and May).

Fish trade on board passing steamboats. This method is mostly used for selling important fish quantities. Fishermen catch their own fish, salt or smoke it, and deliver it to passing steamboats.

The owners of the steamboats constitute an actual social force in the Luapula rural area, the impact of which is felt by local fishermen and rural dwellers. About fifteen steamboats sail on the Luapula River. Boat traffic is heavy between Kasenga and Pweto almost every day, Sundays excepted. Tuesdays and Fridays remain, however, the busiest days with three or four steamboats on average up- and downstream.

Most steamboaters are Greek families living in Lubumbashi but with hired Greek or mulatto middlemen established in Kasenga. Kasenga (twenty-five thousand inhabitants) is a rural administrative and business center at the Zairean Luapula riverbank two hundred kilometers from Lubumbashi. It serves as the nodal point of the second economy activities in the area. It has already been noted that second economy activities take as a focus a central place from which they expand to the neighboring small centers and rural hinterlands. This is the case of Butembo in North Kivu, of Mbuji-Mayi in Kasai-Oriental, of Kisangani and Isiro in Haut-Zaire, and of Kasenga in southeastern Shaba. This enables the researcher to recognize second economy areas in a given country. About six such second economy areas in Zaire have been recognized and will be studied carefully in the future (Vwakyanakazi 1986, 13-20).

Some Zairean nationals from Kasai also take part in transport activity as steamboaters and owners. But they are few in number. No native of the area owning a steamboat has been mentioned, except two mulatto families with expatriate fathers and Bemba mothers. One must emphasize here that beliefs in sorcery are deep-rooted in the area and that economic and social success stirs up jealousy and leads local people to use often violent mechanisms for leveling personal wealth. As a consequence, native entrepreneurs find it is better to attempt their business ventures in town or in different ethnic milieus (Vwakyanakazi 1988a, 91-92).

The steamboat traffic is linked to Lubumbashi by a truck fleet. Trucks carry the fish product from steamboats to warehouses in Lubumbashi before it can be sold to urban consumers. They can be counted daily in numbers of about twenty either coming or going on the Lubumbashi-Kasenga road axis, which unfortunately is ill-kept by the National Road Office.

The total tonnage of salted and, more especially, of smoked fish, collected and traded in this traffic is huge. A steamboater estimated the total fish quantity carried by a single steamboat to amount to a load worth four full trucks or 4 million Zaires of net profit (i.e., after deducting the expenses for handling, labor, transport, and taxes). This suggests that the steamboaters accumulate considerable wealth at low cost.

Let us emphasize here that this traffic pertains as a characteristic of the second economy. To begin with, the price of fish is arbitrarily stated by the buyers and steamboaters to the greatest disadvantage of sellers. It varies, depending on the fishing seasons, between 4,000 and 6,000 Zaires per ten or twenty kilogram basket as against 25 thousand Zaires for the same quantity delivered in Lubumbashi, and between 1,500 and 3,000 Zaires per bunch of three or four kilograms of salted fish as against 3,000 or 4,000 Zaires in Lubumbashi. In addition, fish collecting is indistinctively made by the steamboaters on the Zairean as well as on the Zambian bank of the Luapula River. In this latter case, to avoid illegal accounting problems, the steamboat simply stops in the middle of the river water. Zambian fishermen bring along with them in fishing canoes all that they may have to sell. They constitute actual fleets around the steamboat. In addition to fish, the major commodity traded, I noted among the collected goods large numbers of sacks of corn flour, sugar, vegetable oil for cooking, Zambia-manufactured cigarettes (Peter Stuyvesant), soft drinks, car spare parts (tires, inner tubes, jacks, spark plugs . . .), cement sacks, gas and oil cans, and barrels. The USAID is still occupied with studying legal as well as illegal traffic of corn flour from Zambia to Zaire. According to a student's undergraduate thesis in 1988, five hundred tons of corn flour illegally entered Zaire from Zambia through the southern Kasumbalesa entry alone. Corn agriculture in Zambia is more profitable than it is in Zaire because it is subsidized and public authorities are more concerned about its production.

It is also worth mentioning that food for sale (corn paste *bukari*, fish, sweet potatoes) is cooked by male permanent travelers on the platform top of the steamboat. Willing passengers may buy some of this food if food offered at either riverbank does not please them. This means that the Luapula River is the scene of tremendously variable second economy activities that bring together big owners, peddlers, travelers, local government officials, and the local population.

Furthermore, this traffic evades paying taxes to the state. A noteworthy fact is that many government services have been established in the area: the Zone, the Collectivity, the Constabulary, the Police, the Customs Office, the Office for River and Lake Traffic, and the Health Care Service. In Zaire the Zone and the Collectivity are, respectively, the third and fourth levels of the local administration. Because salaries are not paid on time and are far below the required minimum for living, the personnel of these administrative services rely for survival on the Luapula River traffic. This accounts for the fact that most collected taxes do not enter the state coffers. Or they are simply evaded under the complicity between the traffickers and the representatives of public powers.

Finally, as in the matter of fish production, fish exchange and distribution bring about in the area an atmosphere of insecurity. The pursuits, fines, arbitrary arrests, confiscation of fish and other commodities mentioned earlier also take place during fish trade.

They provide local gossip and are considered among the major local social happenings.

On the Zambian Luapula riverside, however, no similar boat or truck traffic takes place. It is likely because here fishing and agriculture are better balanced among rural masses, which, in addition, are of more concern to state authorities.

Fishing and the standards of living

Fish production and trade as undertaken today in the Luapula River region bear an impact on the standards of living of the local population. The first and certainly most important impact is that less food is available for the local population's subsistence. Since the entire productive labor is mostly involved in fishing, the result is the marginalization of agriculture, especially of maize and cassava. As a consequence, the local population absolutely depends on Zambia for corn, the basic subsistence means of the region, and also for basic commodities such as sugar, salt, soap, and vegetable oil for cooking. Likewise, fish for domestic consumption noticeably becomes rare in the area. In the rural Kashobwe center (five thousand inhabitants), no salted or smoked fish can be seen in the local market. Fishing is mostly done for the steamboaters. As these buy the fish product at low prices, local fishermen cannot by means of their low revenues supply themselves with the basic manufactured goods and with what supplements agricultural activity would have provided them.

This rarity of food and fish rich in protein directly impinges on the health of the local population and especially of the young children. According to the Kashobwe dispensary records, sixty-five percent of children presented at the local dispensary show the symptoms of chronic malnutrition as do fifty percent of school children enrolled in the first degree of the local elementary school.

In addition, anarchic fish trade bears a strong impact on the local habitat. Except for the rural Kashobwe center where petty traders, teachers, local government and health employees live, the dwellings of the Luapula River fishermen remain traditional. The "fishing camps" mentioned earlier are no more than disorganized assemblages of small rounded huts covered with straw from top to bottom, without windows or recognized family spaces. Such a mode of space occupation is indicative of the low level of living conditions in the local population and of its propensity toward nomadism. It impinges on the health of households, which is indeed very poor, and on the education process of children. Children constantly live in such promiscuity with their parents that privacy and authority are made impossible.

Such dwelling conditions are very vulnerable to all kinds of bad weather and unfavorable to an actual psychological development. As a result, inhabitants exist in a chronic traumatic insecurity. At the ideological level, this rampant feeling of insecurity is expressed in an obsessive fear of, and concern with, sorcery. Beliefs in, and mutual accusations of, sorcery are widespread among the local population (Vwakyanakazi 1988a, 91-92). Things go so far as, on the parents' explicit interdiction, children are not allowed to take food outside the family home for fear of being bewitched. Likewise, traditional healers tour villages and small centers of the region in order, as local people put it, to "cleanse" them, meaning to clear and protect them from whatever evil forces and persons they might shelter. They have a greater audience than do the local state officials and the Christian preachers of all kind established in the area.

A further impact of fish production and trade is felt on the level of the school and of the youth. It is striking that most people canoeing on the Luapula River and on Lake Moero are youngsters of school age: either their school attendance is on a part-time basis, they are school-leavers, or they have never been schooled. The major aspiration of these young, like that of their counterparts elsewhere, is to enter adulthood with the implements useful for making it agreeable and happy. To the young of the Luapula region, it is through the avenue of fishing and aquatic activities that they think they will be able to suitably attain such an objective. This belief is reinforced by the past example of some elders like schoolteachers or local government employees who abandoned their salaried jobs for fishing. Consequently, among the young the actual rush toward fishing and river trafficking is remarkable. The resulting effect of this situation is the drastic reduction (in contrast to the prevalent scramble for places in schools elsewhere in Zaire (Bandundu, Bas-Zaire, and Kivu) in school attendance in terminal classes of local elementary schools (fifth and sixth grades especially)). In a similar way, the only secondary school of the Kashobwe center, though state-approved, does not in practice function for lack of students, teachers, and adequate infrastructure. It was only in 1988 that the first two girls of the Luapula collectivity completed their secondary school cycle but outside their administrative entity. One of the two came back to work as a schoolteacher, while the other pursued higher education in Lubumbashi. All this is meant to suggest that, despite the quite active fish trade in the Luapula River region, no positive change is noted within the standards of living of the involved local population.

Conclusion: fishing and local change

From the preceding ethnographic account, it clearly appears that fishing in the Luapula River region, the dominant economic activity, is a focus of social contradictions and tensions. First, it raises a problem of environment and of adaptation to it. To the extent that Luapula people do not succeed in adequately coping with the conditions of their living environment in a way to harmoniously satisfy their basic needs in food, health, education, housing, and saving, one may speak of an actual maladjustment to this environment. As L. Goffin rightly remarks, environment is neither a mere matter of conservation of nature nor a concern with pollution and wastes. It is rather

> a dynamic system of interrelations between human populations and their living environment. . . . This environment includes the renewable and unrenewable resources on the one hand . . . and on the other hand the space, i.e. the topographical distribution of these resources and the specific management of the activities of the social groups (1989-1990, 106 (translation mine).

Second, fishing in the Luapula River region, an economic activity pertaining to the social field of second economy, is bringing about in the region a negative social change. By this I mean to say that it contributes little to local government. It neither contributes to the transformation of the local landscape nor improves the standards of living of the local population. This means that for the involved people, second economy in the Luapula River region does not prove to be an efficient instrument for fending-for-themselves as it has been in some other geographical areas of Zaire such as North-Kivu (J.MacGaffey 1987, chap. 6; Vwakyanakazi n.d., chap. 2; Kasai-Oriental (see case studies on the illegal traffic of diamonds in Kasai in national journals such as *Zaire Afrique, Annales de l'ISP-Kananga, Ujuvi* (ISP-Bunia), and so forth); Haut-Zaire (J.MacGaffey 1987, chap. 5); or Bas-Zaire (see works by P.Dupriez (1962; 1968) on the illegal trade of palm oil). Some of the conditions, which favored the success of the second economy elsewhere, are seemingly still to be met:

(1) The nature of social forces present during second economy activities. To the extent that the negotiating power of the local population with the powerful groups (government, big traders, traditional chiefs, religious leaders) remains limited, local entrepreneurship in the matter of the second economy will by the same token remain ineffective. This seems to be the case in the Luapula River region in contrast, for example, with North-Kivu, Kasai-Oriental, or Haut Zaire. Here second economy has been a game with the local population and the powerful groups as players. In the Luapula region, by contrast, fishing remains an economic activity through which the powerful groups siphon local resources out for themselves at the expense of the local population.

(2) For the second economy to bear a positive impact in a given geographical area, the contribution of the local elite is inescapable. In Butembo, Mbuji-Mayi, and Kisangani, for example, members of the local commercial elite not only learned the trade techniques and relations from the expatriates, but also finally united to overcome competition from them and took an active part in the local productive and distributive activities. Ironically, in the Luapula River area, the successful natives do not want to take part in the local activities or to invest back home some of their resources accumulated outside their native milieu. As a consequence, economic activities in their native land are still taking the form of savage gathering during which outsiders, especially expatriates, siphon most resources out to their own advantage.

(3) Fish, the basic resource on which the second economy rests in the Luapula River region, is a rather fragile commodity. This situation can be contrasted with that which prevails elsewhere. In North-Kivu, Haut-Zaire, Kasai-Oriental, and Bas-Zaire, as J.MacGaffey and Vwakyanakazi showed, second economy activities

have been successfully concentrated since the beginning on a few valuable commodities like gold, diamonds, coffee, tea, and palm oil before they were extended to other resources available for production and sale in the local environment (J.MacGaffey 1987; Vwakyanakazi 1988b, 115). This confirmed the process of wealth accumulation and diversified the range of business ventures because of quite satisfactory prices and revenues offered to local entrepreneurs. In the Luapula River area, fish, the basic commodity in the second economy, by contrast, is badly sold. The local population cannot expect from this sale either wealth accumulation or improvement of revenues and living conditions.

Therefore, second economy, though attracting large numbers of the population, should not be considered a magic tool. People would be better off to think about exerting pressure on the powerful groups in order to, little by little, plan and implement, together, regular economies, the rules of which, despite a part of what Southall calls "hegemonic mystification" (1988b, 2) have proved successful elsewhere in the world. That is the moral of my story on the Luapula River fishing.

References

Baruti,L.
1972   Structure   et   fonctionnement   des   institutions
                traditionelles chez les Lokele. *Cahiers du CEDAF* 8:
                series 2.

MacGaffey,J.
1983   How to survive and get rich amidst devastation: The
                second economy in Zaire. *African Affairs* 82:351-366.
1986   Fending-for-yourself: The organization of the second
                economy in Zaire. In *The crisis in Zaire: Myths and
                realities*, edited by Nzongola Ntalaja, 141-155. Trenton,
                New Jersey: African World Press.
1987   *Entrepreneurs and parasites: The struggle for
                indigenous capitalism in Zaire.* Cambridge:
                Cambridge University Press.

MacGaffey, W.
1970   *Custom and government in the lower Congo.*
                Berkeley: University of California Press.

Goffin,L.
1990   Les   fondements   éthiques   de   l'éducation   á
                l'environnement. *Humanités chrétiennes* 2 (December
                1989-February 1990):106.

Richards, A.
1969   *Land, labour and diet in northern Rhodesia: An
                economic study of the Bemba tribe*, 1st ed. London:
                Oxford University Press.

Southall, A.W.
1956   *Alur society.* Cambridge: W. Heffer and Sons.
1988a   On mode of production theory: The foraging mode of
                production and the kinship mode of production.
                Dialectical anthropology 12:184-88.
1988b   The rain fell on its own: The Alur theory of development
                and its western counterparts. *African studies review*
                31(2):2.

Vwakyanakazi,M.
n.d.   Import and export in the second economy in North-Kivu.
                In *System D: The second economy in Zaire*, edited

by J.MacGaffey, chap. 2. London: J. Curry. Forthcoming.

1986   Traders in Butembo revisited: Further reflections on the second economy in Zaire. Paper read at the African Studies Association Conference, Madison, Wisconsin.

1988a   Small urban centers and social change in south-eastern Zaire. *African studies review* 31(3):91-92.

1988b   De l'economie seconde à une société seconde: ou du phénomène de l'émergence d'une société zairoise tripode. *Cahiers zairois d'etudes politiques et sociales* 12 (September):115.

The Creation of an Illegal Urban Occupation:
Street Trading in Nigeria

Lillian Trager, Professor
University of Wisconsin-Parkside
Kenosha, Wisconsin, United States

Street vending is a worldwide urban phenomenon, one which urban authorities everywhere try to regulate, control, and in many cases eliminate. In cities as diverse as Washington, D.C., New York, Hong Kong, Nairobi, and Lagos, street vendors are confronted with a variety of regulations designed, presumably, to keep them off the streets or in designated areas (Clark 1988). Yet in most cases, the regulations are variably enforced and vendors find ways to continue in their occupations, although often at considerable risk.

In most countries, policies regulating street vending have long been in existence. Nigeria represents an interesting exception in that, while there were some regulations, they were rarely enforced, and it is only since the middle 1980s that regulation and enforcement have become a high priority of urban and other government authorities. In the case of Nigeria, then, we are able to examine the rather recent *creation* of street vending as an illegal urban occupation.

The case of Nigeria is even more interesting in that strict regulatory policies governing street vending (as well as various other urban informal sector occupations) have been developed nearly simultaneously with an increasing concern by the government with

An earlier version of this paper was presented at the 12th International Congress of Anthropological and Ethnological Sciences in Zagreb, Yugoslavia in July 1988, in the session on Extra-Legal but Organized Urban Occupations.

unemployment and with developing policies to assist in employment generation. Employment generation policies have particularly emphasized the role of self-employment and of the informal sector as a source of employment. Thus we find the simultaneous development and enforcement of constraining regulatory policy with attempts to assist and support informal sector occupations.

Efforts at "development" of the informal sector are not of course limited to Nigeria. They are part of a much broader concern in development circles to promote private enterprise and especially those enterprises now termed "microenterprises" (e.g., Levitsky 1989). Street trading has been among the occupations to which some attention has been paid in urban development efforts (Cohen 1986; Tinker 1987).

These contradictory policy efforts--advocating, on the one hand, support for informal sector small enterprises, and on the other hand, seeking to regulate and eliminate at least one set of such enterprises-- suggest a need for the examination of the process of urban policy development and implementation as we seek to understand urban development, urban economic activities, and the relationship between the state and urban residents seeking to survive through a variety of economic strategies. It is clear that enforcement is variable and relatively ineffective, although it tenders some pay-offs both for government and for those individuals who act as agents of government. It is clear as well that there is a dynamic relationship involving authorities at various levels of government, traders, and others, and that the situation at any one time is the outcome of actions and reactions by various members of these groups. The data for this paper derive from observations, discussions, and newspaper articles collected during visits to Nigeria in 1983, 1984, and 1988 and residence there from 1985-1987.

Regulation of street trading in Nigeria

As Eades has pointed out, state regulation of trade in West Africa, including Nigeria, typically has involved control through fiscal policies and taxation:

> the types of regulation attempted by the State over trade in West Africa have tended to follow well-defined patterns: indirect control through fiscal policy, import regulation and price control; direct control through licensing and market fees; and increasing State intervention in the market and restriction of the activities of non-nationals.... *There has been little systematic attempt to regulate where traders may or may not operate, and the streets in many towns are literally lined with traders* (1985, 210 (italics added)).

Although Eades is mainly describing policies toward marketplace trade here, what he says was generally true for street vending, as well as for other roadside informal sector activities such as mechanics. Some laws on the books, mainly deriving from the colonial era and largely concerned with sanitation, were not enforced. Instead, regulatory efforts and conflicts mainly centered on taxation, which led to some of the well-known confrontations between women market traders and the state (see Mba 1982 for discussion of several protests over taxation policy). Taxation of market traders continues to be an important issue, leading to conflict between traders and authorities, as Eames' paper on Ondo traders (1988) and newspaper articles show.

However, attempts to tax traders are quite different from policies that declare certain trade activities illegal. Prior to 1984, government authorities basically attempted to control and regulate trade through taxation and other fiscal policy. They did not, however, regulate the location of trade activities or make illegal those activities that took place outside of designated market places.

In contrast, beginning in 1984, a variety of attempts have been made by Nigerian government authorities not only to regulate and control trade, but also to make certain categories of trade illegal. They have done this through a variety of mechanisms, the net result of which has been to declare that trade in certain locations is illegal. As in other regions of the world where street vending is illegal, discretionary enforcement results (Bromley 1985, 186), but such enforcement patterns nevertheless have serious implications for the vendors.

Three basic mechanisms have been used by Nigerian government authorities in their effort to regulate street vending. One has been the reactivation and enforcement of old (mainly colonial era) laws; the second has been overall policy declarations, especially the policies known as the War Against Indiscipline (WAI) and accompanying environmental sanitation laws; and the third has been the enactment of specific new laws and decrees directed toward street trading. All levels of government have been involved in one way or another with these efforts, including the federal government, state governments, and local governments, although the initial impetus came from declarations of the Federal Military Government.

On New Year's Eve 1983, a military coup overthrew the civilian government of Nigeria and a military regime headed by General Buhari was installed. During the first six months of 1984, this regime declared a number of new policies, all of which came under what was called the War Against Indiscipline; these were inaugurated in several stages and included both practical and symbolic efforts, such as declaring that everyone must learn the Nigerian national anthem; that people should stand in line at bus stops; and that the environment must be kept clean and orderly. This last became a major emphasis, with a number of pronouncements concerning "environmental sanitation," which included cleaning up garbage in urban areas, and clearing of what were termed "illegal structures" from the roadside.

Although the Buhari regime was itself overthrown in mid-1985 and the rhetoric of WAI was considerably toned down under the new head of state, Major-General Ibrahim Babangida, concern with environmental sanitation took on a life of its own, especially at the state and local government levels. Laws and decrees were enacted in a number of different locales, and their enforcement has continued up to the present.

Street vendors were first affected by the reactivation of old laws as part of the environmental sanitation efforts under Buhari. In July and August of 1984, military authorities ordered the removal of "illegal structures" from roadsides in all major cities. In Oyo State, for example, authorities reactivated an old public health law that makes it illegal to erect any structure within a certain distance of the center of major roads. This led to the demolition of many food vending stalls along major roads in the state's urban areas and their environs (see Kujore, Pearce, and Agbok, n.d., for details on this process in the city of Ile-Ife). Not surprisingly, although this removed the structures, it did not remove the vendors, who continued to operate without sheds. Even in this initial, harshest stage, there was variable enforcement. For example, in another city in Oyo State, a local official charged with the responsibility to carry out the destruction of sheds and stalls simply decided not to give the order to do so.

Subsequently, state and local governments began to enact new laws and decrees that were more specifically directed toward the policies they wanted to effect. Again, to take Oyo State as an example, a Ministry of Information publication announced that "the Oyo State Government has enacted an edict titled 'Environmental Sanitation Miscellaneous Enforcement Provisions Edict No. 4, 1986'." The announcement continues, "It becomes operative as from *1st*

September 1986 and it is published in the Oyo State Gazette No. 10, Volume 11 of 6th March 1986" (Oyo State Ministry of Information, n.d.a., 87 (italics added)). The edict establishes an Environmental Sanitation Committee that has responsibility to maintain "the cleanliness and beautification of the environment" (Oyo State Ministry of Information n.d.a, 87), followed by a long list of specific areas of responsibility, including several that concern street trade and markets:

> (j) to enforce and ensure observation of all rules and regulations relating to street-trading, erection of structures, street-begging and to rid the streets of corpses, carcasses, destitutes and other undesirable things;...
>
> (p) to ensure that the Local Governments and other appropriate authorities erect fences around all existing and new market sites with a view to eradicating street trading and hawking;...
>
> (r) to enforce all existing regulations relating to food and meat hygiene and ensure that food and meat vendors display their wares in specially constructed model boxes.... (Oyo State Ministry of Information n.d.a, 88).

The state did not limit itself to such general pronouncements, however. In addition, according to a speech made by the governor in November 1985, specific laws concerning street trading in Ibadan, the state's capital and largest city, had been enacted. These laws designated three streets where trading was allowed on a daily basis, and four others with one day per week trading. Trading by minors below the age of sixteen was also prohibited. In announcing these regulations, the governor commented that

> It should be noted that anyone caught erecting illegal structures on these streets will be prosecuted. Similarly, anybody trading on these streets other than on the days indicated will be prosecuted. And all areas not

earmarked for street trading must be kept free for flow of traffic.... Finally, it must be noted that the concession of street trading will last as long as people do not abuse this privilege (Oyo State Ministry of Information n.d.b, 8).

This process was not by any means limited to Oyo State. It has probably been carried furthest in Lagos State, where an edict was published in April 1984 prohibiting street trading and illegal markets. This edict not only defines illegal street trading and declares that any goods being sold illegally may be seized by authorities and forfeited to the state, but it also lists all the streets and areas affected by the edict (Lagos State of Nigeria Gazette 1984). This edict also prohibited the *buying* of goods from street traders, and an amendment in January 1985 included a form for a receipt to be issued to those who paid on-the-spot fines for violating the edict (Lagos State of Nigeria 1985).

In other states, new laws took the form of regulations regarding permits and fees rather than prohibiting street trading outright. For example, Kwara State published Hawkers Bye-Laws in 1984, which require all street hawkers to have a permit (Kwara State 1984) and Bendel State published a list of fees to be paid by all types of traders, including hawkers and street traders (Bendel State Gazette 1985). In some areas, these laws were enacted at the local government level. For example, in Ondo State, the Ekiti Local Government published market bye-laws which included the prohibition of construction of "unauthorized structures" within or near the markets (Ondo State Gazette 1985, 22). Although the previous examples come from states in the southern part of the country, the same processes occurred throughout the country; newspaper articles from the same time period refer to laws prohibiting and/or regulating street trading in eastern states such as Imo and Rivers and northern states such as Kaduna.

Overall, the various laws have had the effect of creating a set of illegal activities out of pursuits that were previously accepted as part of the local scene. In some cases, requirements have been established for permits; in others, the structures where the activities take place have been deemed illegal; and in still others, all buying and selling in specific locales have been declared illegal. In Lagos, this includes essentially all major streets and bus stops where vendors are likely to find customers.

Implementation and impact

The creation of street trading as an illegal occupation has had a number of effects over the past several years. Not surprisingly, it has created problems for vendors and has led to conflict between vendors and authorities. It has also generated revenue for local and state governments, and less obviously but almost certainly, for their agents. In addition, it has led to considerable public commentary and controversy over the role of street trading in the society.

As in other countries where street trading is illegal, enforcement of regulations is carried out irregularly and on a discretionary basis (Bromley 1985); it is hard to see how it could be otherwise. Nevertheless, the varying laws and their enforcement have had considerable impact on the vendors. In those situations where sheds and stalls were destroyed, traders immediately lost their selling sites. A newspaper article describing the destruction of a popular *suya* (grilled meat) selling area in Kaduna, a major northern city, states that as a result "the economic life of [that section] of the state capital has been paralyzed with the whole area looking like a ghost town" (*Daily Times*, 13 November 1985). Investigation by O.O.Kujore and others of street food vendors in Ile-Ife immediately after the 1984 destruction of stalls there showed that all felt they had been adversely affected--they had lost customers, their profits had decreased, and they were now forced to either sell in the open or sell from inside their houses. All interviewed continued to sell, however, stating that this was their sole source of income (Kujore, Pearce, and Agbok, n.d.).

Newspaper headlines and articles convey a sense of the conflicts that have emerged between traders and urban authorities. Some describe raids, such as one at a major Lagos bus stop, which led to the arrest of about one hundred fifty hawkers, the destruction of several local government vehicles, and which "brought commercial activities to a temporary halt" *The Guardian*, 28 December 1985). Others describe protests by groups of traders, such as a protest by those selling in the vicinity of the airport whose sheds were slated for demolition (*National Concord*, 22 September 1985). In Owerri, the capital of Imo State, street traders organized a protest march to the governor's office. They stated that they began street trading because their shops had been destroyed, and that now police harassment was making it "impossible for them to carry on their business" (Daily Times, 18 September 1985). One and a half years later, traders from another major city in Imo State, Aba, planned a protest march to protest demolition of stalls (*The Guardian*, 23 January 1987). In one case, a group of market traders took out an advertisement in a major newspaper to appeal to the Lagos State Governor about the treatment of traders and to ask that the Local Government not be allowed "to use their just made and back-dated laws on us" (advertisement of Ikorodu Market Men and Women Association, *Daily Times*, 19 December 1986).

Although the government rhetoric regarding the banning of street trading emphasizes the need to clear the streets and make the city more attractive, rather than as an instrument of generating revenue, there is no doubt that enforcement of the new laws has generated considerable revenue. Most states have substantial fines for those arrested (e.g., ₦100 in Bendel State; ₦200 in Lagos). At present exchange rates, approximately \$12 and \$25 but at the time these fines were first imposed, the exchange rate was approximately \$1 = ₦. In a single weekend, the Imo State Environmental Task Force collected over ₦1000 (*National Concord*, 18 November 1985) and between January 1986 and January 1987 the Lagos State Task Force on Environmental Sanitation collected ₦508,997 in fines (The Guardian, 19 February 1987). In addition, the Environmental Task Forces have authority to auction goods seized from traders, generating still more revenue. The head of the Lagos State Task Force told a newspaper reporter that the State had generated more than ₦1 million from auctions, and that in June 1987 alone, sales of seized goods yielded ₦125,000 (*Daily Times*, 2 September 1987).

Less publicly acknowledged but certainly also part of the process is the generation of private revenue for agents of the state. Some of the protests described above refer to attempts by those working for the environmental sanitation authorities and local councils to extract funds. For example, in Rivers State, shop owners sent a protest letter to the commissioner of police stating that law enforcement agents "helped to confiscate or impound shop owners' wares and sold them to their wives, girlfriends, and co-workers" (quoted in *National Concord*, 12 March 1987).

Reaction and debate

During the past several years, Nigeria has moved from a relatively lenient and tolerant position toward street trading activities to the development of a set of regulations making street trading illegal. Despite the variable enforcement of these regulations, their impact has been felt. Women and children, too, are affected (Oloko 1987). Street trading constitutes their source of income. Government efforts have eliminated these activities; rather, they have generated revenue (both for the government and its agents) and have adversely affected the potential incomes of those involved, who now spend time and money avoiding harassment, being arrested, paying fines, and in some cases, spending time in prison.

The development and enforcement of these new laws have not gone unremarked in Nigeria. Public reaction includes newspaper commentaries, letters to the editor, cartoons, and declarations by concerned organizations. Some of these commentaries call for the eradication of street trading. Headlines such as "Problem of Street Trading" (*National Concord*, 30 June 1986); "The Evil that Traders Do" (*National Concord*, 7 July 1987); and photos showing the confusion and disorder of street trading appear with some regularity. A news article, "Street Trading Culture," declared that "In Lagos, the menace of street trading has assumed monstrous dimensions... The street traders with their attendant generation of filth have returned in full force" (*Daily Times*, 16 August 1985). Others call attention to the value of street trading, its importance in the local society, and its role as a source of employment. Letters to the editor have protested the treatment of traders; organizations such as the Lagos State Branch of the National Council of Women Societies and a state bar association have protested aspects of the laws and their enforcement; and several newspapers have published editorials on the issue, one going so far as to call for the legalization of street trading (*The Punch*, 30 January 1986).

Much of the positive commentary makes the point that "street trading is part of our culture" (*The Mail* on Sunday, 3 January 1988).

This article goes on, "From time immemorial it has been a normal thing for any woman to display her wares in front of or beside her house" (*The Mail* on Sunday, 3 January 1988). Other articles note that the eradication of trading is not likely, and usually go on to argue that alternatives should be provided. An editorial published in September 1985, shortly after the change in administration from Buhari to Babangida, called for the rethinking of the environmental sanitation programs, to provide alternative places for those traders whose sheds were being demolished (*The Guardian*, 7 September 1985). Others have called for controlling but not eliminating street trading by, for example, establishing fixed times and locales (*The Punch*, 30 January 1986).

Government officials and former officials seem also to now recognize how problematic their eradication efforts have been. They, too, use the argument that "street trading is part of our culture" and that Nigerian women, in particular, have always been traders. One former official, who was directly involved in the Lagos State edict banning street trading, now argues that this has clearly been unsuccessful and that some other measures should be taken, such as establishing trading sites at major bus stops. In January 1988, I was able to interview Mrs. H.A.Balogun, former attorney general of Lagos State, and to speak briefly with Mrs. Adele Lakanu, chairperson of the Lagos Island Local Government. Both expressed the viewpoint that outright banning of street trading has been unsuccessful and that alternatives are needed. I am grateful to Mrs. Clara Osinulu for providing me the opportunity for these interviews.

These concerns are reflected in some of the recommendations currently being developed by the Lagos-based Working Group on Urban Regulatory Policy toward Informal Sector Employment. This working group, which has brought together academics, past and present government officials, urban planners, and lawyers, as well as participants in the informal sector themselves, has sought to address the conflicts between government authorities and vendors; its report and recommendations are currently being drafted (conversations with Clara Osinulu in June 1987 and January 1988).

Relatively few of the commentators and criticisms note the role of street trading as a source of employment and income, or the apparent contradictions between efforts to eradicate street trading and nearly simultaneous government efforts to encourage employment generation, especially self-employment in the informal sector. Only a trader, quoted in a newspaper article, has pointed out this contradiction. The vendor states, "And since the government is telling everybody to go and establish his or her business, it should not contradict such a policy by continually chasing us all over the place. We are also servicing the economy" (quoted in *New Nigerian*, 3 August 1985).

Conclusion

It is tempting to let the vendor quoted above have the final word. But the question remains, why does this contradiction exist, and why do government authorities not recognize the value of the economic contributions made by street traders? Why, in other words, is there such a concern with regulating and even eliminating vendors, not only in Nigeria, but in most other countries as well?

Clearly, the highly visible nature of street trading activities makes them a natural target for those seeking to control and regulate the informal economy. And as the economic crisis in Africa continues, it is almost certainly the case that the numbers of people involved in street trading is increasing, as this is one arena where people can seek to earn at least minimal income.

The concern with regulating and controlling street trading is not simply a result of the numbers of people involved in it or of its visibility, however. Rather, it involves real political and economic issues, as well as symbolic ones. At the symbolic level, there is a confrontation between the view of street trading as "dirty," and "a menace," and the view of trading as being "part of our culture." One view sees such activities as making the city appear too "third world" instead of "Western" or "modern" and the other sees them as something to be encouraged or at least tolerated. It is not only government authorities who take the former view but also many urban residents, including those in the middle class even though they benefit from the services provided by street traders.

But there are political and economic positions at stake as well. For government, there are issues of control, regulation, and authority; this is especially the case at the local government level, where the ability to control activities in its own domain is important. Furthermore, the revenues gained, even through variable enforcement, can be considerable. It is likewise in the interest of the individual agents of governments to see policies continued that enable them to extract fines and other payments in the process of enforcement.

The struggle over regulation of street trading does not simply involve two monolithic entities--the state and the traders. Traders, and the informal sector more generally, comprise a heterogeneous category involving people with varied interests and economic status (Clark 1988; Trager 1987). Likewise "the state" involves a variety of government authorities as well as the people representing those interests. For example, the effort to "develop" the informal sector and generate employment is a mandate of the Nigerian federal authorities and some state governments, but it is not a basic concern of local governments. Thus, one reason for the contradictory policies noted above is that to some degree they are policies of different authorities with different interests.

What we see at any given point in time is the result of a continuing process of negotiation between those seeking to maintain control and regulate economic activity and those urban residents engaged in earning incomes in activities that have become an increasing focus of regulations. Whereas in an earlier period in Nigeria, there was little regulation or control over street trading, efforts in the middle 1980s sought to enforce strict controls. More recently, there has been some move back from strict regulation to efforts to control without actual elimination of street trading. This process is likely to continue indefinitely, in what Estellie Smith has referred as "only the initial stage of the struggle between the state and those identified as belonging to the informal sector" (1988, 196). Indeed, the effort to "develop" the informal sector and create more self-employment, rather than representing a contradiction to policies seeking to regulate and control street trading, may simply be another mechanism by which government is seeking to gain control over the economy. Rather than eliminate the vendors, the emphasis is to "organize" them and in the long term, presumably make them a part of the formal economy.

References

Bendel State
1985   Local Government Law, 1980, Miscellaneous Revenue (Adoptive Bye-Laws) Order, 1985. *Bendel State of Nigeria Gazette* 22(13), 28 February 1985. Benin City.

Bromley,R., ed.
1985   *Planning for small enterprises in Third World cities.* Oxford: Pergamon Press.

Clark,G., ed.
1988   *Traders versus the state: Anthropological approaches to unofficial economies.* Boulder: Westview.

Cohen,M.
1986   Women and the urban street food trade: Some implications for policy. Gender and Planning Working Paper No. 12, Development Planning Unit, University College, London.

Eades,J. S.
1985   If you can't beat 'em, join 'em. State regulation of small enterprises. In *Planning for small enterprises in Third World cities,* edited by R.Bromley, 203-218. Oxford: Pergamon Press, pp. 203-218.

Eames,E.A.
1988   Why the women went to war: Women and wealth in Ondo town, southwestern Nigeria. In *Traders versus the state: Anthropological approaches to unofficial economies,* edited by G.Clark, 81-97. Boulder: Westview.

Kujore,O.O., T.O.Pearce, and V.A.Agbok
n.d.   Effects of road clearance on the street foods enterprise in Ile-Ife. (Mimeo.)

Kwara State
1986   The environmental sanitation edict, 1984. *Annual volumes of the laws of Kwara State of Nigeria.* Ilorin: Government Printer.

110

Lagos State
1984   Street trading and illegal markets (prohibition) edict,
                1984. Supplement to Lagos State of Nigeria official
                gazette extraordinary, vol. 17, no. 14 of 5th April 1984 -
                Part A.

Lagos State
1985   Street trading and illegal markets (prohibition)
                (amendment) edict, 1985.

Levitsky,J., ed.
1989   *Microenterprises in developing countries.* London:
                Intermediate Technologies.

Mba,N.E.
1982   *Nigerian women mobilized: Women's political
                activity in southern Nigeria.* Berkeley: Institute of
                International Studies, University of California.

Oloko,B.A.
1987   Children's street trading in Nigeria--informal education,
                economic participation, or child abuse? Paper
                presented at Seminar on Self-Reliance for Women,
                Nigerian Institute of International Affairs.

Ondo State
1985   The Ekiti central local government Mmrkets bye-laws,
                1984. *Ondo State of Nigeria official gazette*, vol.
                10, no. 11, 11 April 1985, Akure.

Oyo State Ministry of Information
n.d.a   *Operation keep Oyo State clean.* Ibadan: Oyo State
                Ministry of Information (pamphlet).
n.d.b   *A decade of Oyo State 1976-1986.* Ibadan: Oyo
                State Ministry of Information.

Smith,M.E.
1988   Overview: The informal economy and the state. In
                *Traders versus the state: Anthropological
                approaches to unofficial economies,* edited by
                G.Clark, 189-199.

Tinker,I.
1987   Street foods: Testing assumptions about informal sector
            activity by women and men. *Current Sociology* 35:110.

Trager,L.
1987   A re-examination of the urban informal sector in West
            Africa. *Canadian journal of African studies*
            21:238.

Boomtime in Busolwe: Culture, Trade, and Transformation in a Rural Ugandan Town

Michael A. Whyte, Professor
Susan Reynolds Whyte, Professor
University of Copenhagen

In the years since 1971 Uganda has endured crisis and collapse and, recently, gradual and partial recovery. Yet even today, civil administration is hamstrung by a devastated infrastructure and the inability of government to pay its servants a living wage. The control that central institutions once asserted over the rural economy is a thing of the past. Decentralization has come about willy-nilly and it has brought with it some development opportunities that many Ugandans have been quick to seize. In this paper we look at Busolwe, a rural trading center in Bunyole County, Tororo District, eastern Uganda.

In 1969-1971, we carried out our first fieldwork among the Banyole, a Bantu-speaking people concentrated in the southeastern corner of Uganda. We lived some four kilometers from Busolwe, then as now the largest trading center in Bunyole County. Over the last twenty years we have had a number of opportunities to return to Bunyole and to follow the dramatic changes that have taken place in this part of Uganda--most recently in April 1990. We are grateful to Sylvester Musimami and his family, who have shared with us their views and their home in Busolwe.

In spite of, or perhaps because of, twenty years of political and economic crisis in the country, Busolwe has boomed. Today it boasts a population of two thousand people--a tenfold increase over the town we knew in 1969. No longer merely a center for regional trade and services, Busolwe has come to symbolize regional independence and regeneration for many Banyole. It has become a place in its own right. As a tribute to Aidan Southall, and to his continuing interest in and many contributions to the study of "small towns in African development," we explore what has happened in Busolwe. Our main point, offered in what we hope is a properly Aidan-like spirit of contentious concern, is that the essence of towns such as Busolwe cannot be wholly captured in a matrix of power and capital and political economy. We shall emphasize the cultural significance of a rural town in Uganda today as a center for new ideas from the outside and an arena for the development of a new consciousness of social differences.

Busolwe and Bunyole: roads, cotton, and the colonial system

The Banyole, principal inhabitants of Bunyole County, are a Bantu-speaking group related linguistically to their Ugandan neighbors, the Bagwere, Basamia, and Bagwe, and to the Luyia-speakers of Western Kenya. According to the 1980 census about seventy-four thousand people lived in the county. Banyole have not been labor migrants; most of those not resident in the county were settled cultivators in other parts of eastern Uganda. Although overall population density is high (three hundred sixty-two per square mile) there are no villages in the sense of nucleated residential settlements in the countryside. Banyole live in dispersed homesteads, surrounded by fields and banana groves. The countryside is gently rolling, with seasonal swamps and papyrus-choked rivers.

Bunyole is crosscut by the Uganda railway, but there are no through roads; rivers to the north and west enclose the county and block communication. Busolwe town is located more or less in the middle of the county, on the intersection of the only roads leading "out." The center of Busolwe is the circle where the Mbale road crosses the one from Tororo; neither has ever been paved, and both reflect the years without maintenance. Known as the "kipi lefiti" because of the dilapidated Keep Left sign standing in the weeds, the "roundabout" is seldom disturbed by motor traffic. After the crossroads, the Tororo road continues on to the tiny market center of Busaba, five miles away, passing a Roman Catholic mission two miles beyond Busolwe. The Mbale road becomes the Budumba road, leading on to that subcounty administrative center about seven miles away, and continuing as far as Budumba Station where the train stops, just before it crosses the Mpologoma River on its way to Kampala. Busolwe town thus appears as a classic rural center, positioned in the center of a hinterland which it serves and connects to larger centers; it is on the way to nowhere else of importance.

The founding of Busolwe and the creation of modern Bunyole are both consequences of the "subimperialism" of the great Ganda leader, Semei Kakungulu, who in 1900 settled with his followers at Naboa only about twenty miles to the northeast (Gray 1963; Thomas 1938-1939). Asian, Arab, and Swahili traders moved with him, and when he shifted to Mbale, that town became the third largest trading center in Uganda (Twaddle 1966). In a few years, a Nyole Muslim, Ibrahim Mulogo Byaire, became a subcounty chief at Busolwe with the support of Kakungulu. Ali Bin Nasolo, an Arab trader and teacher of Islam, settled at Busolwe and a mosque was built. In 1904 a road was constructed from Budumba, where canoes crossed the papyrus-choked Mpologoma to Busoga, through Busolwe to Kakungulu's headquarters at Mbale, thirty-five miles from the little trading center. Without a developed Budumba canoe crossing, this road, "suitable for carts and light motors," (Wallis 1920, 316) provided access to and from Mbale. Some twenty years later the Tororo road was built.

In 1910 cotton was introduced in the District (Ker 1967) and, in 1918, a cotton ginnery was built in Busolwe by an Asian businessman; its successor is still in place. It is at this point that the visible, official, colonial economy establishes itself throughout eastern Uganda. From this point on Busolwe becomes a center for the cotton industry in Bunyole, collecting and ginning cotton, bailing lint and bagging seed, and transporting both to the railhead in Tororo. By the late 1920s cotton was the universal cash crop and most Nyole households had a regular cash income.

For about thirty years, the Asians dominated the cotton trade in Busolwe. They hired Nyole agents to buy up cotton, and also sesame and groundnuts, and Nyole farmers spent the proceeds on cloth and other commodities in the Indian shops. With British encouragement, cotton marketing cooperatives were formed in the late 1940s, and the South Bukedi Cooperative Union acquired the ginnery at Busolwe in the 1950s.

Although they lost the cotton trade, the Asians remained important retailers in Busolwe. In 1969, the last year in which they were granted trading licenses, there were fifteen Asian family-run shops; other Asians were employed in the ginnery and one family owned one of the two lorries and the only mill in the region. Customers appreciated their large selection of textiles; *egomasi* (women's gowns) required eight yards of material and the Indians employed local tailors to operate sewing machines on the verandas of their shops.

Trade and cotton processing--both activities dominated by outsiders--thus continued as Busolwe's official economic *raison d'etre* until the general collapse of the Ugandan marketing system in the middle 1970s. However, another economy was also centered at Busolwe, one which until recently was less visible and seldom officially recognized. Muslims (Swahili, Arab, and Banyole) were connected with Busolwe from the beginning. Their trade in peppers, foodstuffs, and hides had earned enough for some to make the pilgrimage to Mecca by the 1930s. As the official cotton economy developed, Muslim businessmen and craftsmen found opportunities at many levels; by 1969 the other lorry owner in Busolwe was a Muslim trader/entrepreneur with a base of operations in a shop in the "African" part of Busolwe, by the "kipi lefiti." This sort of grassroots Muslim business community was common in the region, though largely unrecognized by official Uganda until the Amin years.

In Busolwe, and no doubt in many other centers throughout Uganda, the Muslim presence had a cultural significance, which was also seldom recognized. Unlike the Asian commercial communities, which were connubially endogamous and oriented socially, if not culturally, toward the European/Western world, Muslim communities were open. Nyole Muslims lived in a social world in which important identities, such as clanship, were shared with non-Muslims. An important and perhaps overlooked consequence of this openness was a significant and continuing cultural influence from the Islamic world and its culture. For example, divination with Arabic books, a practice that Ali Bin Nasolo is said to have brought to Busolwe in 1902, became a common alternative to spirit divination, used by Christians and Muslims alike (S. Whyte n.d.b). Ayurvedic medicine made no such inroads.

The period in which the cotton economy dominated Busolwe's history is preserved in what is, as far as we know, the only official map of the town. Dated 1928 and signed by G.M. Gibson, the senior surveyor, the map sums up the role which Busolwe was to play in the official economy. There is a line of numbered plots on the Tororo road (clearly destined for Asians since the much smaller section of plots on the Budumba road is identified as the "native bazaar") marking the "racial" division of economic roles, which persisted until the Amin years in Uganda. The other major feature is the cotton ginnery and, next to it, the clearly labeled labor lines, on the Mbale road. No other industrial role was envisioned and there is, quite literally, no space on the map for locally realized endeavor,

Two events marked an end to this long period in Busolwe's history. One was the 1969 restriction prohibiting noncitizens to trade in small towns. Almost overnight, the Asians left Busolwe, and Ugandans took over their premises. The other event was Amin's coup of January 1971, which ushered in a period of instability that brought the collapse of cotton production. Looking back on the era of cotton and Asian traders in Busolwe, it is evident that the town played what Aidan Southall has called an exploitative role vis à vis its hinterland. It extracted cotton, whose real value was far greater than the price paid to the producer, and it provided commodities upon which traders made a profit. Busolwe was part of a hierarchy of centers, oriented toward the district headquarters at Tororo, which communicated with Kampala. The cotton cooperative system fit precisely into this hierarchy, encapsulating the rural producers and channeling and controlling their contact with the outside world where the market was. The Asian traders avoided government control to some extent, and created their own channels. But their presence inhibited local initiatives to do the same thing. The cultural significance of this system was that it limited relations to the outside world and had the effect of encapsulating local society. Bunyole was a backwater; Busolwe hardly changed from 1928, when the map was drawn, until 1970, when the old map was brought out so that a plan for a rural hospital could be marked in.

Busolwe and the economic transformation of Bunyole

In the two decades between 1971 and 1990, Busolwe grew from a collection of shops and a ginnery with a population of two or three hundred to a town of two thousand people offering urban amenities like a bank, a hospital, a hotel, and a video hall. It was as if local initiatives were unleashed to fill the vacuum left by the Asians and the collapse of cotton. During the chaotic years after Amin's coup, the very isolation of Busolwe may have been its salvation. Trade flourished here, while soldiers terrorized the towns and trading centers on the main roads.

Today Busolwe's five busy mills attest to the importance of grain in the new local economy. Rice has become a major crop, partly because of a Chinese rice scheme in the Doho swamp fifteen miles east of Busolwe on the Mbale road. Local people saw the potential of rice and began to plant swamps on their own. While the Chinese rice is marketed through Mbale, much of the local crop is sold in Busolwe. Rice traders, many of them from Buganda and Busoga, began to frequent the Busolwe mills. During the harvesting season, the mills work until midnight and children white with flour dust glean on the mountains of rice hulls. The largest of the mill enterprises has a fleet of two tractors, two pick-ups, and three lorries, which it rents to producers and buyers. Trucks loaded with rice leave at 4:00 A.M. for Kampala and return the same day. Luganda is the language of the trade and rumor has it that Buganda traders have brought AIDS (Acquired Immune Deficiency Syndrome) to Busolwe.

Important as rice is, many other crops are being marketed in Busolwe today as well. Beans, groundnuts, and millet found a ready market in Uganda's towns, especially as war ravaged other food producing areas. The receptiveness of farmers to new possibilities is seen in the way soya has been taken up as a cash crop. Yet it would be wrong to think of this kind of food marketing as something completely new, created by the demise of cotton. In the early days, the Indians bought up groundnuts, sesame, beans, cowpeas, and peppers as well as cotton. Later, people also sold beans and groundnuts to their cooperative societies. In 1970, truckloads of millet used to be bought up in Busolwe for resale to brewers of *malwa* in Bugisu. Even rice, the new king, was grown on the margins of swamps in Bunyole before the Chinese came. Crop diversity and the willingness to explore marketing possibilities were present all along. It was not merely that they were overshadowed by cotton; they were invisible to the drawers of maps and the agricultural authorities who were primarily interested in cotton, which earned foreign exchange.

From outpost to interface: the Busolwe Hospital

The most dramatic addition to Busolwe since 1971 is the hospital. It has a large outpatient department, one hundred beds, an operating theatre, an x-ray department, a laboratory, and a dental unit. The trained medical staff number nearly a hundred; many live in staff quarters on the hospital grounds. Another two hundred untrained employees live in Busolwe and surrounding communities. Although the present head of the hospital is from Bunyole, many of the medical personnel come from other parts of the country. Sitting around a pot of millet beer in the evening outside the staff houses, one could be anywhere in Uganda.

When construction began in 1971, no one foresaw the breakdown of government health services: the shortage of medicines and staff; lack of supervision, water, and transportation; and least of all did anyone foresee the reversal of position between the salariat and the farmers. In the 1960s, civil servants in rural areas, teachers and extension officers, lived relatively well. Their salaries hired laborers to weed their cotton, paid school fees, and bought radios. By the 1980s, runaway inflation had made civil servant salaries practically meaningless (M.Whyte 1988). Often the salary, meager as it was, failed to come on time. The workers at Busolwe hospital, like other government employees, are forced to "survive" as best they can. At one time, people expected that the staff would buy local goods and services; instead the hospital staff are producing and selling them. Some have borrowed or rented land and at harvest time they fill their staff houses with maize and groundnuts for consumption and sale. Others brew beer, taking turns so that no one's beer "sleeps" because a neighbor is selling on the same day. The good beer of Teso hospital staff is praised by Nyole inhabitants of Busolwe. Most of all the hospital staff sells medicine and health care (S. Whyte n.d.a). Two private clinics and two drug shops have opened in Busolwe, run by medical assistants, nurses, and dressers. In their own homes and in surrounding trading centers, they have gone into private practice, offering an alternative to the government health services with which many people are dissatisfied.

Before the Amin coup in 1971, the elite was part of a national system. Over the past fifteen years, elites have had to come to terms with the collapse of the national structures that supported them. Nonetheless, tasks of many elite men and women (not just provision of health services but also, for example, education) are still desired and, indeed, considered necessary. What has changed is the nature of the relationship between expert and layman. The need to earn a living has lead to privatization; the asymmetry that restricted communication has been replaced by something approaching *mutual* dependence. Health staff in the old structure, even though they dealt intimately with people as nursers and dressers, were still part of the government and its medicine. Nyole patients waited in long queues and accepted what they were given. Now, however, elites have been domesticated. In a very literal sense, they need a house and, above all, land; they need a local household in order to survive. Elites have become dependent on relatives or neighbors who can provide access to land and resources, and on customers who buy or do not buy the services offered. In short, the saga of Busolwe Hospital illustrates the dependence of the elite on the local community, but also the creation of a new social field for cultural exchange. Busolwe town, with its "domesticated" elites has taken the first steps toward a new and more meaningful urbanity. It is no longer an outpost of the national economy. In a sense it is regaining what must have been its original character before the dominance of cotton, when it served both as outpost and as interface with a larger world.

Modern life in Busolwe

Busolwe, always a trading town, got its first government institutions effectively in the 1980s, and they are more under the control of Busolwe itself than of Tororo or Kampala. The hospital, the secondary school, and the new police post were established under conditions in which decentralization had come about by necessity. There is a strong sense of civil interest in Busolwe articulated through the local Resistance Council, which provides a check on the misuse of police powers. The Busolwe Development Committee, comprised of influential businessmen and property owners, also represents the interests of private citizens in Busolwe's affairs.

In terms of transport and communication, Busolwe is worse off today than it was twenty years ago. Then there were morning buses to Mbale and Tororo, which brought passengers back in the evening. One of the buses also made the triangle from Busolwe to Busaba, on to Budumba Station and back to Busolwe. The Tororo bus brought the mail to the Busolwe post office every day. Now there is no bus to Tororo at all. The road has deteriorated badly and the last bus company went under after the owner died. Nor is there any bus service beyond Busolwe; the Busolwe-Busaba road has devolved to a bicycle path. A taxi makes a single run to Tororo each day, but it is expensive; it is very difficult for Busolwe people to conduct business in the district headquarters. The new radio call installed at the Resistance Council office does not compensate for the loss of the daily bus connection and mail delivery.

Yet in another way, Busolwe has acquired new significance as a communication center. In 1984, a new stopping point was established on the railway. Busolwe Station is three miles from Busolwe, and although there is no actual station house, it has become an important extension of Busolwe. A fleet of bicycle taxis (*boarders-boarders*) has established itself under the bus stop tree, an old *mvule* with exposed roots that serve as benches, and these ferry people and goods back and forth to the train. On Fridays, the train brings baskets of smoked fish, and some fresh ones too, and five hundred to a thousand people flock to the station, to meet people home for the weekend, shop at the market at Busolwe Station, and buy up fish to sell next day at the weekly Busolwe market. The train carries charcoal, rice, and other food crops out of Bunyole. Although the train still stops at Budumba as it has since the railway was laid through Bunyole in 1925, that station has been overshadowed by Busolwe, which is a much more important center of activity.

What with the intensification of trade, the hospital, and easier access direct to Jinja and Kampala, Busolwe has become more cosmopolitan in many ways. We have mentioned that during its early days, it was a center for Islam, and it has retained a strong Muslim element. (To this day, no pork is sold in the town; it is available two miles away.) Back when education was in the hands of religious organizations, Busolwe had one of the few Muslim schools in the county. Today the Islamic influence is complemented by important Christian ones in Busolwe. Both a Protestant and a Catholic church have been established; a measure of the more cosmopolitan flavor of Busolwe is that the Catholic service is given in both Luganda and English (many of the people from northern Uganda working at the hospital do not understand Luganda, the language in which Banyole read the Bible). The medical supervisor allows the "saved" Christians *(abalokole)* of Busolwe to meet in a room at the hospital. The Pentecostal churches have made a mark in Uganda's larger towns, and this too is a sign of the times in Busolwe.

One of the striking developments of the last twenty years is the proliferation of schools in the area, despite the political chaos. In 1971, there was one secondary school, Bukedi College at Kachong'a, in Bunyole County. Today there are eleven. Busolwe Secondary School is housed in Shah's old mill, next to the shops; two others are only a couple of miles away from the town at Mulagi and Mugulu. So Busolwe is now an educational center as well; local children do not have to leave to continue their studies.

At the other end of the educational spectrum, two nursery schools have appeared in the town recently. Although the organizers complain that Banyole are backward and do not understand the need of sending children to nursery schools, nonetheless there are children enough to support the schools and this is taken as a mark of Busolwe's increasing sophistication.

"Modern life" is of course more than Pentecostal churches and nursery schools. A disco and video hall has been opened in Busolwe. A piece of blackboard propped up against the bus stop tree shows the day's video: films like *Rambo III* and *Combat Killers*. The Clyde Hotel "offering first class sevice on the Mugulu Road" is nearing completion; already a large refrigerator has been installed so that the bar will be able to serve cold drinks in the courtyard. There has long been a barber who cut men's hair under a tree near the "Keep Left"; now a Hair Saloon in one of the shopfronts has put out a sign showing a picture of a woman's hair "threaded" in a smart style. Two photo studios have appeared as well. "City lights" have come to Busolwe and even though one may regret *Rambo III* as cultural development (see Southall (1988, 4,3) on the aesthetics and morals of soap operas compared to rural rituals and dramatic entertainments), there are jobs and attractions for young people. It is their town too.

Conclusion: inequality, development, and a vision

Almost by definition, towns are places where differences and inequalities among people exist. In their day, the Asian traders were certainly wealthier than the Banyole in and around Busolwe. They were culturally different and segregated themselves socially; their interaction with local people was almost entirely limited to economic transactions. Today's elite has a more multifaceted connection to the rest of the town and its hinterland. Most are Banyole with roots and many relatives in the area surrounding Busolwe. Even those who are not natives of the place form friendships, intermarry, attend church or mosque, and work and relax with local people. Yet there are certainly large wealth differences in Busolwe today and in the recent period of opportunity, those who had resources were able to take advantage of the special conditions of the times. Some had established themselves as successful businessmen even before the Asians left Busolwe. Haji Tanga had a shop and a lorry in 1970, and he was able to obtain rice land as rice began to expand in the late

1970s. Others had or have top level government jobs in Kampala and Entebbe. They are investing in their home town not just out of loyalty, but for security in the face of political instability and because they cannot live on their government salaries. New buildings are going up in the town, and trade is thriving there, while fewer and fewer homes in the country have iron roofs.

On the growing edge of Busolwe, lies a rich commentary on its development. Over several acres of land, long trenches have been dug, punctuated every few meters by pillars of bricks. The builder, said by some to be mad, is both a perfect representative of Busolwe, and a kind of thought provoking jester. He is a Muslim, who worked for a time in Kampala, but came back to where his family was established in Busolwe. Some call him "Coach" because of his enthusiasm and interest in the Busolwe football team. Others call him "Obutu" because he used to hawk fried cassava pieces in the town, calling "*obuto! obuto*!" ("tidbits, tidbits"). He is the town's most diligent builder, collecting bricks from other people's building sites to build his own town, "City Buguna" (the name of his clan). It is a wonderful, totally modern place, with "storied houses," though we others cannot see them because they are underground. He has laid out sports grounds and a landing field for airplanes. In his city, people will not have to work; everything will be done by electricity. Most important, when the day comes for entering his city, we will all go in as equals. Muslims and Christians, Africans and Europeans will be one people. The residents of Busolwe humor this builder; everyone knows "Obutu" and they smile gently at his crazy vision of urban development. In a sense he has captured the hopes of Busolwe for city buildings and modern life with its diversions and freedom from the drudgery of farming. But his idea of equality and sharing is clearly out of place. Those who own the land and bricks which he has appropriated for his vision are the first to point out that "development" is based on the principle of private property.

Obutu's vision is replete with symbols and glosses on basic themes in Nyole culture. That he has named his town after his clan (where all are equal) would seem an attempt to introduce to the modern world a particularly Nyole concept of social person, defined not by status or education but by totemic identification (M. Whyte 1983, S. & M. Whyte 1987). Obutu's city is thus a real attempt to deal with the issues and problems raised in Busolwe today. The modern world is no longer held at bay, and the Banyole are beginning to define themselves in terms of what they produce and what they earn and what they do--and not what they are.

In his writings on small towns, Aidan Southall has emphasized the importance of policies of decentralization for stimulating local activity (Southall 1979, 214) and of a relatively egalitarian class structure to insure that the benefits of growth reach the majority of local people (Southall 1988, 5). Busolwe has two lessons to teach us on these points. The first is that decentralization may well occur by default, rather than as the result of a policy. The virtual collapse of the Ugandan state gave Busolwe the opportunity to create its own solutions, which also meant creating its own lines of contact. The tiered hierarchy of urban centers was far less relevant. The second lesson of Busolwe is that decentralization unleashed petty capitalism and inequalities hitherto held in check. Development meant religious and ethnic differences, differences in education, experience, and skill, and obvious differences in wealth.

Obutu has built a symbolic town on the edge of Busolwe; his piles of bricks and heaps of earth are rich with meaning for him. Because Busolwe itself has economic and institutional functions, it is easy to forget that, like City Buguna for Obutu, it has a symbolic role for those who live there and in the surrounding countryside. Busolwe is "our town" and its growth is an affirmation of local initiative and capability. It shows that Bunyole is a part of the nation, not just a backwater. Busolwe provides models of sectarian, professional and class, as well as ethnic identities. Its cultural role is not to disseminate Rambo films, but to provide a forum in which issues of cultural difference and social inequality are confronted. Consciousness of these issues is created not only for the residents of the town, but for all the rural people who use it.

References

Gray,J.
1963   Kakungulu in Bukedi. *Uganda Journal* 27(1):31-59.

Ker,A.D.R.
1967   Agriculture in Bukedi district.   Arapai Agricultural
            College.

Southall,A.W.
1979   Introduction: results and implications of the preliminary
            enquiry. *Africa* 49(3):213-222.
1988   Small urban centers in rural development: what else is
            development other than helping your own home town?
            African Studies Review 31(3):1-15.

Thomas,H.B.
1938-1939   Capax imperii--the story of Semei Kakungulu. *Uganda
            Journal* 6:125-136.

Thomas,H.B. and R.Scott
1935   *Uganda.* London: Oxford University Press.

Twaddle, M.
1966   The founding of Mbale. *Uganda Journal* 30(1):25-38.

Wallis,H.R.
1920   *A handbook of the Uganda Protectorate.* 2d ed.
            London: His Majesty's Stationery Office.

Whyte,M.A.
1983   Clan versus lineage: notes on the semantics of solidarity
            and conflict among the Ugandan Nyole. *Folk* 25:129-146.
1988   Nyole economic transformation in eastern Uganda. In
            Uganda Now: Between Decay and Development,
            edited by H.B.Hansen and M.Twaddle. London: James
            Currey.

Whyte,S.R.
n.d.a   Medicines and self-help: the privatization of health care
            in eastern Uganda. In *Changing Uganda: The
            dilemmas of structural adjustment and
            revolutionary change,* edited by H.B.Hansen and
            M.Twaddle. London: James Currey. Forthcoming.

n.d.b   Knowledge and power in Nyole divination. In *African systems of divination: Ways of knowing*, edited by P.M.Peek. Bloomington: Indiana University Press. Forthcoming.

Whyte,S, and Whyte,M.
1987   Clans, brides and dancing spirits. *Folk* 29:97-123.

Poverty and the Chimera of Affluence

M. Estellie Smith, Professor
State University of New York-Oswego
United States

Despite a growing concern with poverty at both the global and national levels, it seems reasonable to argue that, (1) an increasing number of people are falling prey to poverty and (2) the ability of policymakers to address and ameliorate the issues(s) in any substantive fashion is declining in proportion to the increase in numbers.

A different way to view the question

One way to define "poverty" is deprivation for some despite affluence for the society as a whole. We do not, after all, refer to some societies where, over a period of two or three years or more, all households have approximately the same quantity and quality of resources, and it is only relative to some external societies that permits us to speak of a society's poverty when all members are deprived of resources, as in a time of drought. Are we perhaps better able to understand poverty and the characteristics which are said to accompany that state of existence if we examine "the culture of affluence" rather than some construct as "the culture of poverty"? It

---

This paper was part of a discussion in a symposium on poverty and culture, organized and chaired by A.L.De Havenon and Delmos Jones, American Anthropological Association annual meeting, 1989. It was refined for presentation in a seminar organized by J.M.Buechler, Hobart and William Smith Colleges, 1990. I thank all three as well as various members of the audience for their comments and queries.

is in societies where, because resources are inequitably distributed, that "the poor" exist as a categorical enclave peopled by those who, relative to others who never "feel the pinch," are chronically under- or unemployed, inadequately housed, undernourished, unable to secure required health care or legal protection, subjected to institutionally based harassment, and in short, those whose lives are a series of rebukes or challenges to what is normally assumed to be a working and workable socioculture. If we are to gain insight into some of the critical assumptions that tend to be ignored but play a powerful role in how we address the issues raised when we discuss poverty, we must address poverty relative to affluence.

In large measure, the affluent determine the existence of poverty in a variety of ways, not the least because they have the wealth and power to define whatever are socioculturally identified as "critical" goods and Good (the latter being those nonmaterial resources valued and sought by most members of most societies (e.g., a voice in decision-making, self-dignity, honor, respect of others, and prestige) and, as well, control the pathways to such resources.

In not a few countries, even nonmarket societies, "The Poor" are not a homogeneous category. Frequently, there is a distinction made between, on the one hand, the "deserving poor," and on the other hand, the "shiftless poor." The former are defined as frugal, polite, clean, respectful to their betters, usually hardworking and always ready to accept any employment for any recompense--in short, deserving of aid because their plight exists despite their best efforts to maintain self-sufficiency. The latter are held to be lazy, profligate wastrels. When resources are available, they are held to live beyond their means, could work if they wanted to, but they have an inflated sense of self-worth that leads them to avoid work (unreasonably considering their needs) they consider demeaning, inadequately rewarding, or too laborious. Finally, it is maintained that these needy do have access to adequate resources to satisfy their needs but they waste those resources obtaining luxury items they really could do without, (i.e., they have expectations unreasonably sited beyond the "legitimate" necessities of those wisely thrifty but economically marginal folk, "the deserving poor." (See Rothman's discussion of "the social work revolution in the United States in the 1920s, in which effort was concentrated on "teaching the lower classes to cope with their situation, to budget more carefully, to emulate those above them." It is, however, the very attempts of the poor to copy that style that still continues to reap the most disdain for attempts "to live beyond their means.")

E. H. Johnson (1973, 156) maintains that, because

> they produce little the community cannot do without, the poor lack collective power....Workers can withdraw their labor...but the poor lack connections with the levers of power to gain a place in bargaining.

I disagree. The visible poor on the streets, in the media, and in our political rhetoric can deprive the affluent of those qualitative rewards--a sense that "things are OK," "are going well and getting better"; they can deprive us a sense of safety and security, of moral certitude, of our senses that we are not required "to walk the mean streets," that we, as individuals or as a society, can believe in the viability and rightness of our way of life. The current cry is that the poor are an affront to and an attack on all this; if poverty breeds crime in the streets, and an omnipresent threat of encountering vandalism, filth, and all that represents "the seamy side of life," then the poor threaten the affluent with the removal of their most valued resources--life, liberty and the pursuit of happiness. This results in what Elman (1966, 281) called an institutionalized poorhouse state, a society that permitted a significant portion of the population to exist in a system of inadequate payments, grudging services, petty rules and tyrannies, and surveillance mechanisms. Why? Perhaps it is a desire to punish for failure, a callous disregard, or residual social Darwinism. But just as likely as any of these, it is because the affluent continue to distinguish between the deserving and undeserving poor and resist being asked to underwrite what they perceive as "freeloaders."

It is important to make an analytical distinction between the poor and the indigent. The former may be poor in that they lack the ability to expand material or nonmaterial resources beyond culturally defined minimal needs levels; the indigent, on the other hand, are those who cannot, even with the utmost frugality, meet the basic needs of themselves or their dependents in one or more areas of housing food, clothing, medical care, or transportation. The phrase "utmost frugality" is important because it addresses the deeply embedded belief that some undeserving poor have squandered or made excessive demands on their resources. Unless we recognize the existence and powerful compulsion of response that such beliefs engender, we will be unable to address and redress the punitive dimension, often inequitable, and frequently institutionalized, that marks certain significant aspects of poverty programs. These programs, as well as the personnel who implement them, are not uncommonly marked by vacillation among the alternative aims of palliation (lessening the pain without curing the disease), punishment, and panacea. Certain categories, such as the abandoned young, the obsolete mature worker, or the battered (legitimate) spouse or offspring, are usually deemed as deserving of palliative care as well as individual/institutionalized panaceas. Many believe that the undeserving poor, those "who can but won't work," "who, in the good times spent rather than saved for a rainy day," "who produced more (or any) children they couldn't afford," or "who drank" [substitute "took drugs," or "gambled,"], "threw their money away on good times" [substitute "extravagant clothes," "high living," "big cars," or "fancy houses,"], are entitled to nothing. The conviction is widely held that "if the taxpayers [substitute "church goers," "social workers," "politicians," or "civil servants,"] now have to take care of such people, then we're neither required to nor do we propose to make it easy for them. See Helen Safa's discussion on the way higher status groups blame the poor for being poor (1974, 105).

One may rail against such thinking but it is prevalent among many, and not only in American society. Rejecting the position as ill-conceived or irrational and raging against or condescending to those who espouse it will not alter either their influence on program funding (or lack of it) or the design of such programs.

Question: If, as argued above, many of the problems of the poor are also problems of the affluent, how do we address those problems when the antidote, while economic, is not monetary--when, in point of fact, poverty may be grounded not simply in deprivation per se but in the extraordinary and insatiable demands an ever-expanding population makes for an ever-higher level of affluence. We are, for example, seeing the emerging distinction made between political refugees and economic migrants. The latter are not a new group; indeed, many of the population movements throughout human history are based on those who would go where opportunities for greater material affluence beckon. It is rare (though not unknown) that people depart for regions where they know it likely they will not achieve at least as abundant a resource base as currently enjoyed. Rather, what lures them is the promise that they or their offspring ultimately will reap greater material benefits. Thus, poverty cannot be defined in terms of the perimeters of a single socioculture but, rather, in terms of what information those of a given population have about the world at large. Villagers ignorant of life in the metropolis will seldom migrate to the city; those of one country do not leave home and hearth unless they see benefits to offset the loss of the familiar and the risk of the unknown. Such shifts, of course, in and of themselves create inequities as well as generate what may result in excessive demands on the resources of the target community--and may even deprive the sending population in such a way that their ability to generate resources declines. Should we, can we amelioratively address this and perhaps separate out these from the "war on poverty" that allows us the luxury of seeing *them* rather than *us* as the problem? Or is every society forced to live in a less than perfect world and are its members required to come to terms with the degree of imperfection, with, relative to benefits, the costs they are "willing to live with" before they assess they are bankrupt?

Question: Let's assume that we have devised an apothecary's scale that distinguishes deserving from undeserving poor: What should we do with the latter--that half million or so that is roughly two percent of America's population and have a disproportionate ability to disrupt the quality of life for the deserving poor among whom they live? Should we send them to "rehabilitation centers"? Or should we maintain them and give them the freedom to live as they will despite cries from both right and left that they are parasites and, worse, seductive corrupters who beckon to others to do likewise? If we establish a minimum income, perhaps we could deprive them of that as punishment for rejecting the shining path of hegemonic social planners and, further, refuse to provide for their needs when they overdose, contract debilitating illnesses, or (old, enfeebled, and rejected even by their own crowd) they litter our space.

Question: Is poverty per se the major concern or does the attention given to the issue wax and wane according to the extent that the affluent are contaminated by their malaise? If all the indigent were "poor but honest," would most (any) pay them any mind? Or do we address the issue (here or in other parts of the world) only when we, the affluent, see poverty as impoverishing *us*, when it invades *our* space, deprives *us* of the freedom to move in pleasant, "nice" surroundings on safe streets, well-kempt neighborhoods, relaxed as to our children's well being--when the poor of the world threaten *our* future political, economic, ecological global environment? If poverty could be seen as much or perhaps more *our* problem than the problem of "the poor," would this alter our cost/benefit analysis?

Question: What can anthropologists contribute?

It is a truism that the kind of cross-cultural, longitudinal, intensive participatory research that anthropologists do has a unique contribution to make in the study of social issues. But truisms become just those because they make important points worth repeating. I can think of no aspect of the debate surrounding poverty that will not benefit from application of the anthropological perspective. Let me list only a few.

I am mightily suspicious of the claim that a significant number of the indigent, especially the homeless, are poor because of mental disabilities and psychiatric problems (figures seem to average out at about thirty percent of the homeless population). I think their behavior is more likely a symptom of their economic disability resulting from hunger, sleeplessness, untreated or grossly treated physical illness, and realistic fears. Some portion of the evaluation may be (following Foucault) the caretakers' evaluation of certain attitudes/behaviors as deranged, unreal, unrealistic because of the way the behavior of their clients violate the caretakers' cognitive view of their socioculture (Cuomo 1983, 78-97, 89). Here is an area where the reemerging field of psychological anthropology could play an invaluable role.

On the other hand, it seems standard to treat the existence of poverty as a *sociocultural* problem but to respond to those who escape as individual (i.e., psychological) success stories. This mixing of levels stifles, I think, our ability to address adequately the structural factors involved in such success stories. What determines how some escape the debilitating and enervating effects of poverty, while some do not? Anthropologists need to formulate more robust, broad-based sociocultural models for limning out the legitimate strategies that worked, when, and how.

The poor identify and define their poverty *as well as* their personal sense of frustration, alienation, and inadequacy in terms of the extent to which they are unable to achieve the consumption patterns, life styles, and goals, of the affluent, knowledge of which is primarily transmitted through the mass media (but, as well, via the schools and contact in work situations).

We should put greater emphasis on exploring what those in the poverty category rank as the more or less critical social indicators of poverty and determine the extent to which this ranking varies according to age, sex, education, or previous condition of life. Relative deprivation emphasizes the cultural nature of poverty since, in important measure, the *sense* of deprivation is generated by acceptance of the macrosystem's functioning and function. A social segment--family, sex/age group, ethnic category, class--feels deprived because others have what they do not and believe it is their right to also have it.

We must find out more about those who work with the poor. What do they see as the major strengths or weaknesses of the programs that address poverty issues? What categories of clients would they identify, by what criteria? What attitudes do they bring to their interaction with clients, and how does this influence their decisions? What recommendations for change would they make? Most of our data on the functioning of institutional gatekeepers in service delivery is anecdotal and we have done little to raise the analytical power of such data. Are there differences, and how do they affect delivery by as varied as, say, newcomers or "old China hands," religious or secular personnel, volunteer versus professional, local, and national representatives? Also relative to these personnel, the programs they implement, and the institutions within which they operate, we need to analytically differentiate their *functioning*--how they operate--with their *function*--what their purpose or goal is.

Anthropologists tend to be suspicious of "number magic," and legitimately so. Our approach is a healthy antidote to the increasing reliance on such a tool. Thus, for example, we can make strong arguments for emphasizing, as Rodman has stressed (1968, 332-337), the need to distinguish between a statistically significant class difference and a class characteristic. It seems obvious that to state, say, that twenty percent of those in the poverty segment have work-inhibiting mental disorders (versus ten percent of the working class) is not the same as saying work-inhibiting mental disorders are a characteristic of those in poverty. Yet the *analyses* of much of the data on poverty populations does just this. An indication of just how dismal is the state of the art may be gained from reading Wilson and Aponte's Appendix (1987, 165-187).

We should also take advantage of the many ethnographic studies of self-help cooperative efforts and begin to analyze these ethnologically, particularly longitudinally, to see the long- as well as the short-term consequences of such efforts. We need studies on the culture of affluence (the culture of consumption?), especially among the new poor, in order to more nearly understand the extent to which that sector defines certain parameters and perimeters of the perception as well as the reality of poverty. We should explore the extent to which the poor identify deprivation with the lack of particular "commodities" such as privacy, leisure goods, lack of access to well-paid (or, for that matter, any) employment, or the inability to provide offspring with fad clothing, toys or jewelry, especially at times such s birthdays or Christmas.

At a more general level, it would help to distinguish between *poverty* issues and *public* issues. We might better deal with the problems of the economically disadvantaged if we remove from the list of "poverty problems" those socially dysfunctional traits that, in point of fact, are not limited to the poor but cross class lines (e.g., substance abuse, vandalism and senseless violence to random strangers, and spouse or child abuse). Perhaps if the general citizenry were made more aware of the extent (even the existence!) of these problems among the affluent, they would be more willing to address the fundamental structural causes--and be willing to pay the costs of implementing programs to bring about necessary change.

Finally, we anthropologists must begin to address these issues with a sense of disciplinary identity and purpose. We should work to make a contribution valuable and unique in its own right, not utilized by policymakers simply as window dressing, or brought in after policy is determined. We must work to assist in implementing programs primarily designed to address the needs of the poor rather than the wants of the affluent.

140

References

Cuomo,M.M.
1983   *Report* of the Governors' Association Task Force on the
            Homeless, the homeless mentally ill. (July).

Elman,R.M.
1966   *The poorhouse state: The American way of life on
            public assistance.* New York: Dell Publishing.

Rodman,H.
1968   Social stratification: Class culture. In *International
            encylopaedia of the social sciences.* New York:
            Crowell, Collier Macmillan.

Rothman,D.
1979   The poor in the Great Depression. In *Historical
            viewpoints 2,* edited by J.A.Garraty, 30. New York:
            Harper and Row.

Safa,Helen
1974   *The urban poor of Puerto Rico.* New York: Holt
            Rinehart Winston.

Wilson,W.J.
1987   *The truly disadvantaged.* Chicago: University of
            Chicago Press.

III. STATE FORMATIONS: POLITY, POWER AND DISSENT

Segmentation of Class

Burton Stein, Professor
University of London
United Kingdom

At the time that I adopted Southall's segmentary state formulation for my monograph on India (Stein 1980), I was insufficiently alert to a discordant theoretical element, which still remains a part of that formulation. This has to do with the relationship between political segmentation or a "segmentary state" and something called "segmentary society." For Richard Fox (1971, 56-57), a fellow debtor at Southall's African bank, this was less a problem because his ruling Rajputs of northern India were organized as segmentary lineages, but even for Fox there was something of a problem since these Rajput lineages do not extend from the bottom to the top of the political order, as Alur lineages do; moreover, the state regimes of Rajput houses have historically nested within larger political orders in which lineage principles were weak, or almost wholly absent--that of the Mughal state and its successors, the Marathas and the British. Southall draws attention to these aspects of Fox's analysis (1988).

Mine was another difference, for I predicated segmentation of a sort altogether different from the segmentary lineages of Southall's Alur or Fox's Rajputs. Still, I did this within Southall's general formulation and particularly his important refinement of pyramidal segmentation. The following definition may be found in Southall 1956, 248-249; Fox 1971, 56; and Stein 1980, 265-285:

> Several levels of subordinate foci may be distinguishable, organized pyramidally in relation to the central authority. The central and peripheral authorities reflect the same model, the latter being reduced images of the former. Similar powers are repeated at each level with decreasing range.

In *Peasant State and Society*, I took the hundreds of local societies called *nādu* in the inscriptions and literature of the ninth to thirteenth centuries as the fundamental, pyramidally organized components of the society; I saw these nādus in the inscriptions as social and political communities and I also saw, and continue to see, the relationship between these hundreds of communities and the state as crucial for an understanding of this Indian, or perhaps other preindustrial societies.

Community must be understood here in its usual English signification of being simultaneously a people and a place, rather than in its limited Indian usage as subcaste or religious group. In short, and in the idiom of things Indian, community is to be understood as *janapada*, not *jati*, and pertains to shared sentiments and values; however, community is also about shared rights or entitlements over human and material resources, and thus in its particularities, pertains to smaller, local spatial entities under conditions of premodern technology. It is because very localized affinities, sentiments, and especially entitlements continued to persist in India until well into contemporary times, together with *the cultural, social, and political means for defending them*, that I have been encouraged to see segmentary political forms as extending well into the last century, thereby giving the concept considerable historiographical reach. Here, I wish to suggest yet another dimension of segmentary, which will enable us to see how community as an element of social segmentation is transformed into class in the guise of the petty bourgeoisie.

For this demonstration, however, ideology must be taken somewhat more seriously than Southall seems to take it. I am taking ideology to pertain to the reasoning of historical subjects about what values they considered of first importance. Partly this is a notion of unexpressed consciousness, but it is also partly an explicitly discursive form. Thus, in a long section of *Peasant State and Society*, I undertook to relate the theory of the segmentary state to elements of consciousness, which were inferred, as well as to moral and political conceptions that were found in normative texts of the age. On the strength of that examination in relationship to premodern, south Indian polity, in part, I have recently reasserted my conviction that the segmentary state form was the only one that fit the evidence we have of the broad pattern of political relations and of the ideology in premodern peninsular India (Stein 1990).

This emphasis on ideology in my application of the segmentary state concept was dictated by the need for a certain kind of historical reasoning about India, not by differences with Southall's revisions of his segmentary state concept along the materialist lines of modes of production (Southall 1988). Though I have difficulties with his adoption of the "Asiatic mode" concept, I do appreciate how his invocation of the structure of productive and property relations is one of the ways of opening a consideration of class, and that an understanding of precapitalist formations of class in India is long overdue.

It is necessary to introduce a better method of class analysis than that practiced by many Indian Marxists, who remain so wedded to a framework of feudal explanations as to contend that even now India awaits capitalist relations! As for non-Marxist scholars of India, including those outside of India, most continue to ignore and even to reject the workings of class and class relations, and until that element of bourgeois social science in and about India is shifted--an urgent knowledge requirement--the essentializing and exceptionalizing effect of caste-centered analyses that are part of Max Weber's legacy remain intact and in place to muddle minds in and about India.

Assessing class and the class situation in precolonial India must commence with a redefinition of class itself. I take it to mean

> a group whose individual members in a market/capitalist order are engaged in similar productive pursuits, with similar relations to the means of production, whether they own and control these or not and whether they are conscious or not of their collective historic interests; a group, moreover, whose members strive to make the most of, or to achieve the best possible balance of, their assets/endowments including their own or others' labor power, property, and culture.

The definition owes much to Jon Elster (1988, 147), but it is different from his in ways other than elegance alone.

This unfamiliar definition of class is intended to focus more clearly on the interaction of the strategies of actors within given institutional frameworks and to better understand how class and state formations have interacted since precolonial times of the seventeenth and eighteenth centuries in India.

The analysis of actors striving to attain individual ends by collective means and within collective contexts during the eighteenth century presupposes that "locality" must occupy a strategic position, whether one is considering India or any other place. "Locality" or "community" may be thought of as the largest arena in which the sort of striving for optimum advantage (proposed in the definition of class given previously) takes place: by individuals against others, within and against other social, rather than abstract collectivities. In times before the electronic closing of enormous distances, such strategic social arenas were spatially miniscule; often they were effectively defined by a face-to-face, *gemeinschaft* dimensionality, where the rules and resources available to individual actors were largely confined to the shared culture and history of particular people and places and to a catchment no more extensive than that capable of being traversed in a day or so by sail craft or burden animals, such a locality as the nādu in medieval Tamil country discussed by Stein (1980, chap. 3). Such entities--localities or communities with their constituent groups--are not merely neglected in scholarship, but are subjected to serious scholarly distortions, as where "community" in the social science usage of and about South Asia inevitably denotes religious or caste groups by even very sophisticated practitioners. In a similar manner, communities are neglected alike in Marxist and conventional bourgeois historiography on capitalist preformations on the dubious presumption that communities and their "rurban" extensions were destined to "wither away" under the twin forces of modernity: unified state organization and a world-centered capitalism. But of course, that has not happened, in part because communities and their culture live on in the massive petty bourgeoisies of what is called the Third World, and in part, they live on because neither unified states nor global capitalism can really make do without these "intermediary classes." Whence Michael Kaleck's conception of "intermediate regimes" of rich peasants and petty bourgeoisie ruling classes, a summary of which and an application to India can be found in Fox (1984, 1985).

Without doubt, states have been key agencies in the transformations of historic collectivities--of communities--but more than that, states have set some of the key conditions under which modern classes came into being. Policies of "absolutist" monarchies of early modern Europe (Bourbon, Hapsburg, Tudor) intended to serve and preserve aristocratic property of ancient feudal nobilities by processing ancient landed wealth into capitalist property. Superior entitlements of private wealth and property gained through state-sponsored legislation were secured by simultaneously conferring police and magisterial powers, while the political power of former feudal nobilities was being enhanced by their incorporation into military and bureaucratic structures of these new states. It was this processual element of European class formation that must have persuaded Perry Anderson to set forth his improbable argument about the persistence of feudal forms until their displacement by industrial capital in his *Lineages of the Absolute State.* In so doing, Anderson ignored the simultaneous and more fundamental formation of a bourgeoisie and its hegemonic society, one that incorporated prior aristocratic strata, produced the world's proletariats, and contained the conditions in which petty bourgeoisies everywhere emerged and flourished, as the older nineteenth century formation commented upon by Marx or the "new" petty bourgeoisie of industrial capitalism.

Though Anderson is often credited with bringing political and economic causation into the same frame of Marxian analysis, it should not be forgotten that Marx and Engels considered class and state formation together in explaining the French and German revolutions of the nineteenth century and the crucial role then of the petty bourgeoisie, a stratum which they defined and contextualized more in political than economic terms.[1] In these first delineations of the petty bourgeoisie, Marx commented on the connection between the politics of that class in his time in relationship to ideology and its makers, the intelligentsia (Marx 1865, vol.2, 27-28,30).

Marx also contributed to the discussion of the dialectic of state and class formation by his brief references to the "mercantile system" in *Capital* in his discussion of money (1957, part 1, chap. 3, sec. 3, 126) and also in a long note there in the Everyman edition (1957). However, it was for his later students of capitalism in Europe and elsewhere to make the concept of "mercantilism" crucial. According to Heckscher's extended essay on the doctrine, originally published over sixty years ago,

> Mercantilism never existed in the sense that Colbert or Cromwell existed. It is only an instrumental concept which, if aptly chosen, should enable us to understand a particular historical period more clearly than we otherwise might. Thus everybody must be free to give the term mercantilism the meaning and more particularly the scope that best harmonize with the special tasks he assigns himself. To this degree there can be no question of the right or wrong use of the word, but only of its greater or less appropriateness (Heckscher 1934).

The vagueness of this definition brought criticism to Heckscher, as did other aspects of his commodious and eclectic gathering of material on the subject from all over Europe, over a course of three centuries. Still, it has been his broad formulation that has rightly constituted the discursive ground for most historians of Europe as it has in subsequent discussions of that bundle of doctrines and practices called "mercantilism."

Consider the differences between Heckscher and the unsigned entry "Mercantile System" in *The Encyclaepedia Britannica* (1911, 148-149). Some of the history of the doctrine during the sixty years since the publication of Heckscher's two-volume work is conveniently found in the set of essays edited by Coleman (1969) with articles by Heckscher, a major critic Jacob Viner, and others.

In an emerging new historiography of the Indian eighteenth century, the suggestion has come that there was an "Indian mercantilism" during late, precolonial times, one concerned, like that of Europe, with the empowering of postmedieval states by increasing their capability to defend their frontiers and their interests against other states and by unifying historically older, segmented political formations under a single state regime. Analyses of state building through the enhancement of wealth available to state regimes gave "mercantilism" its conceptual power for nineteenth century historians of Europe, and the same process has been elaborated in a recent comparative historical account of Muslim postimperial regimes of the eighteenth century (Bayly 1989). In these widely differing places during the seventeenth and eighteenth centuries, what is being spoken of are more or less well-formed circuits of advanced commercialism such as to constitute incipient indigenous capitalisms and modern classes.

Major actors in this order in India included political figures such as petty kings, revenue farmers, and military entrepreneurs; other critical agents were agrarian magnates who ruled the great households and sizeable rural populations through the appropriation of ancient community rights and the privatization of other entitlements gained through state service. Trade, markets, and money were the vital components of authority throughout the eighteenth century and earlier, and these were the essential components of the penetration of the English East India Company in the middle of the century, which was launched from their place in the structure of indigenous capitalism.

Rural communities of eighteenth century India were in some senses coherent and unified entities that stood opposed to the larger political, social, and cultural world but in other senses were not. They were coherent and unified, for example, when their rights or welfare were threatened from without. This could lead to a range of resistance techniques beginning with assemblies of protest (in Maharashta, the *gota*, in Tamil country and Karnataka, *kuttam*; in northern India, the *jatha* or *jhoond*) against what were considered as unjust demands, the withholding of taxes or labor, and finally even armed opposition. Furthermore, rural communities were unified in maintaining the conception that local entitlements of all sorts were shared (however differentially) among members of specific groups according to generally agreed rules of their devisement, and this extended to rights derived from external authorities, such as a king.

Holders of landed privilege during the eighteenth century and later constituted a part of the forming petty bourgeoisie in the sense that they were small landed-property holders often without the productive means to fully exploit their holdings and therefore subordinate to and dependent upon wealthier cultivators to rent their holdings at rates below the usual land tax. These small proprietors for the most part were priests or mullahs, temple and mosque officials, pensioned soldiers, or village servants; they constituted an intermediary class, which required a certain level of capitalist development to attract rich peasants to lease their holdings (and thereby avoid higher, fixed land revenue payments) and also required a certain kind of political regime capable of both protecting their privileges and maintaining a tax demand upon smaller direct producers that provided a modest stream of income for those with landed privilege. Too much capitalism or too strong political regimes could and eventually did threaten such privilege by ending their protection and thrusting many previous beneficiaries of privilege into a land market where they were weak actors compared to others.

Communities were thus internally stratified and divided, according to wealth and the ability of some, but not all, to buy the office of headman or accountant, to freely deploy their domestic resources of land and stock, to hire the labor of others, or to enter into more or less advantageous sharecropping agreements; moreover, it made a difference whether a person or group was considered resident in or foreign to the community.

Delineating class structures that crosscut the contradictory mercantilist structures of economy and the state and the communitarian structures of the eighteenth century is not easy. Nevertheless, we may attempt to specify the context and character of the Indian petty bourgeoisie, who were the inheritors of earlier community rights and ideologies.

A marked feature of the new age and structure was the increase in urbanization, and especially small "rurban" centers. It was in these numerous rurbanities that important elements of the modern classes of India were formed. Administratively, such towns were the precursors of the district and *taluka* headquarters of the nineteenth century Company and Imperial Raj; militarily they were the fortified garrisons of state regimes, where soldiers were supplied and used to maintain order and deployed to assist in the collection of the revenue contracted by an *ijaradar*; economically, they were the nodal points in the massing and distribution of commodities that flowed to and from the coastal ports of high, international commerce; and in cultural and ideological terms, these places harbored the temples, and mosques, sect and cultic centers with their linkages in surrounding villages. But above all, it was in the rurbanities of the eighteenth century that the massive petty bourgeoisie of India was formed and sustained, even as it continues to be now.

Occupationally, this petty bourgeoisie consisted of self-employed craftsmen who combined production of goods with their sale locally and, through other brokers, in distant markets; small shopkeepers; an assortment of economic brokers (*dalal*), that included petty money lenders who often served as agents of big grain merchants, labor recruiters, and contractors of piecework production by the underclass of casual laborers and also therefore linked downward to village producers and upward to major trading groups, and rent collectors. Others of the class were petty office holders and minor commissariat agents provisioning garrisons and the host of minor *religieuse* that served clients in towns and their surrounding villages. The whole of this petty bourgeoisie, not just priests, were linked economically and culturally to villages of a town's hinterland by family ties and through marriage and religious relationships. This petty bourgeois segment of diverse community formations were the major sustainers of local cultural forms, including religious institutions and practices, "proper" caste relationships, and the entitlements related to both.

Not even the most materialistic scholar of early modern India (and many of later times) would dismiss caste and Hinduism as some sort of trivial false consciousness. However, neither do they (nor should they) concede to those peculiarly Indian institutions the centricity which they enjoy among contemporary culturologists, especially American ones.

Happily, Aidan Southall is not of the latter persuasion, and what has been outlined in this brief paper harks back to a formulation of his. For I take his statement and refinements of the segmentary state idea to be more than a proposed type of state form--though that it is and importantly so; I see him as presenting a trajectory from what is an apparently primitive political form into the modern structures with which our contemporary lives are inevitably entwined. In the elaborations upon and perhaps departures from Southall's formulations and reformulations along materialist lines, some of us are exploring cognate structural realms and possibly also expressing the political realm which each of us is.

Note

1. K.Marx and F.Engels, *Selected works*. (Moscow: Progress Publishers, 1969, 3 vols.). Vol. 1, Principles of communism (1847, 95-96); Communist manifesto (1848, 115-116, 119, 129-130); Address to the Central Committee of the Communist League (1850, 175, 177-179); The class struggles in France (1848 to 1850, mostly 1849 but added to by Engels 1895, 228, 281); Revolution and counter-revolution in Germany (1851-52) in *New York daily tribune* by Engels at Marx's request, 304, 380; The eighteenth brumaire of Louis Bonaparte (1852, 423, 447-448, 479); Marx to P.V.Annekov (1846, 527) with more on Proudhon as philosopher and economist of the petty bourgeoisie in vol. 2: 24, 27-28. Vol. 2: The civil war in France (1871, 224); The housing question, Engels (1887, 289).

154

References

Anderson,P.
c.1974   *Lineages of the absolutist state.* London: N.L.B.

Bayly,C.A.
1989   *Imperial meridian; the British empire and the world, 1780-1830.* London: Longman.

Coleman,D.C.
1969   *Revisions in mercantilism.* London; New York: Barnes and Noble.

Elster,J.
1988   Three challenges to class. In *Analytical Marxism,* edited by J.Roemer. Cambridge: University Press.

Encyclopaedia britannica, vol. 18, 11th ed.
1911

Fox,R.G.
1971   *Kin, clan, raja, and rule.* Berkeley: University of California Press.
1984   The genesis of India's intermediate regime. *Modern Asian studies* 18(3): 459-489.
1985   *Lions of the Punjab; culture in the making.* Berkeley: University of California Press.

Heckscher,E.F.
1934[1931] *Mercantilism.* Translated from the Swedish by M.Shapiro, 2 vols. London: George Allen and Unwin.

Marx,K.
1865   On Proudhon. *Selected works,* 3 vols. Moscow: Progress Publishers.
1957   *Capital,* translated by Eden and Cedar Paul. Everyman's Library. London: J.M.Dent.

Marx,K., and Engels,F.
1969   *Selected works.* Moscow: Progress Publishers.

Southall,A.W.
1956   *Alur society.* Cambridge: W.Heffer and Sons.
1988   The segmentary state in Africa and Asia. *Comparative studies in society and history* 30(1):52-82.

Stein,B.

1980 *Peasant state and society in medieval south India.*
Delhi; New York: Oxford University Press.

1990 Section of *Peasant state and society. Purusartha* 13.
Paris: Ecole des Hautes Etudes en Science Sociales.
Forthcoming.

Kingship in the Southern Sudan

W. Arens, Professor
State University of New York-Stony Brook
United States

Kingship is a seductive institution that has not only attracted inordinate attention from anthropology but, as Southall's (1956) pioneering study of the Alur noted, it has also been a beguiling political form for subjects desiring its presumed benefits. My concern here is to reconsider Shilluk and Anuak kingship, which as the result of Evans-Pritchard's interpretations, have come to serve as paradigms for this political arrangement. This exercise is conducted with equal interest in Evans-Pritchard's interpretation of Nilotic society (1948) displayed so clearly in these ethnographic accounts and the messages these reports were meant to convey to interested audiences.

The Shilluk

In addition to their own past, the Shilluk have an interesting academic history, especially in light of their significance, for they have never been properly studied by contemporary research standards in history and social anthropology.[1] Yet they have been the object of constant analysis by scholars with relatively limited fieldwork or alternately studied from archival and literary distance. As might be expected, every possible interpretation has been offered, even though Shilluk kingship is still culturally and politically viable as exemplified by the installation of *Reth* (King) Ayang Aney Kur in 1975.

On a more mundane level, the Shilluk are typical Nilotes now numbering about a quarter of a million, located primarily in a series of patrilineally associated villages strung out in a narrow band along the western bank of the Nile for two hundred miles. Although cattle are of social and cultural significance, the Shilluk are distinguished from their neighbors by their reliance on a mixed economy, which in the past included long-distance trade. More important, the Shilluk are characterized by hierarchical social and political arrangements involving a residentially dispersed royal clan and both local-level and provincial chiefs who have considerable authority in their areas. Both systems culminate at the apex in the office and person of the reth, the presumed direct descendant and spiritual incarnation of Nyikang, their culture hero and first king.

The earliest commentators, beginning in 1760 (Bruce 1905), mention the Shilluk kingship, for apparently even then it was a well-known political office in the Southern Sudan. Likely relying on their own historical experiences and imagery, subsequent authorities up to the Seligmans were much impressed with the assumed political nature of both the office and incumbent, referring to him as an "absolute head--temporal and spiritual--of the state...." (Seligmans 1932, 39).

This impression was effectively dispensed with in 1948 by Evans-Pritchard, fittingly enough on the occasion of the Frazer Lecture. Although he took issue with Frazer's insistence on the ritual slaying of the king, dismissed as unsubstantiated by the evidence (1948, 21), Evans-Pritchard nonetheless revived the classical concern for the mystical and sacred nature of the reth.

Evans-Pritchard admitted that the Shilluk people recognized "a single head, and we can therefore speak of the Shilluk nation and of their king..." (1948, 9). However, he went on to argue that, "we must beware of attempts to define it [kingship] in terms of judicial and administrative functions and view it rather as a ritual office in a wider political context" (1948, 13). In light of the existing reports from this century, Evans-Pritchard maintained that the reth's function was best described as "sacerdotal rather than governmental," and immediately went on to pen the justly famous line: "The king of the Shilluk reigns but does not govern" (1948, 16).

Rather than viewing a particular king as the political center of the system, Evans-Pritchard insisted that the office, rather than the holder, functioned as the mystical center of the Shilluk nation. The polity itself realized its coherence in the "structural dichotomy" (1948, 21) between the northern and southern halves of Shillukland. According to Evans-Pritchard, this balance of opposed forces consistently produced rival claimants to the throne, which undermined political centralization.

Those conversant with the writings of Evans-Pritchard (see in particular 1940) will of course recognize the familiar fission and fusion, and unity through opposition of parts, model of society generated in his study of the acephalous Nuer. However, in this instance, the schema is applied to a social system replete with political offices. Without denying the applicability of the argument to a wide range of political and social processes, it is nonetheless possible to suggest that this idealized balance of forces was an intrinsic aspect of Evans-Pritchard's political philosophy and view of social life in general. Yet there is also a particular strain here with regard to the general inclination of Evans-Pritchard to de-emphasize the significance of political leaders in his interpretation of Nilotic ethnography (Arens 1983). In the Shilluk instance (Arens 1979), Evans-Pritchard's interpretation, while not devoid of generous insight, does not always fit well with other ethnographic or historical facts (Wall 1976; Yunger 1985).

At the more immediate level, and without deviating radically from Evans-Pritchard's model, it is also possible to suggest that the political function of the reth should not be seen in an "either\or" perspective. Within a restricted area, and depending on historical circumstances and the personal political qualities of a reth, his word was indeed law (Arens 1979).

Considering the sacred nature of this dual office, this proposition does not contradict the notion of this position as a central and unifying symbol of the Shilluk people. Everywhere the institution was viewed in this august light, but as Evans-Pritchard suggested, it was the position, rather than the incumbent that refracted the divine light. In sum, the belief in the divinity of the kingship was universal among the Shilluk, while both the political legitimacy and actual authority of any given incumbent was restricted by particular circumstances. As suggested, this interpretation is in general agreement with previous arguments, including those of Evans-Pritchard, except with regard to his insistence on eradicating the idea that the reth had actual political power by converting him into a one-dimensional sacerdotal figure playing out his role in a cultural arena of mystical values. This tendency to de-secularize office holders should be borne in mind in a consideration of the political system of the Anuak, which also fell under Evans-Pritchard's ethnographic scope.

The Anuak

At the time of Evans-Pritchard's investigations in 1935, an estimated thirty thousand to forty thousand Anuak were living in a riverine and marshy environment along the Sudan-Ethiopian border. As with the Shilluk, with whom they share related traditions recalling their former unity and then subsequent separation, the Anuak subsist primarily on agriculture in a series of compact and relatively self-sufficient villages often isolated from each other by local ecological conditions and seasonal rainfall. In the northwest the less populated savannah land floods during the rainy season sometimes forcing village relocation and reducing interaction among them for long periods. In the southeast, higher elevations and woodland allow for both greater population density and intervillage communication. This ecological diversity is mirrored by a variation in political organization and processes.

The western zone has been characterized by Evans-Pritchard (1977) and subsequently confirmed in greater detail by Lienhardt (1957, 1958) as one in which the dominant form of political organization involves village headmen who neither recognized nor owed any higher formal governmental allegiance. The eastern half of the country, however, was associated with both village headmanship and a dispersed noble clan that produced candidates for the Anuak throne. It was in this area, and for the specific purpose of investigating Anuak kingship, that Evans-Pritchard spent most of his time described as..."a brief ethnological survey" (1977, 4). It is also worth noting that, as with the Nuer research, he was asked to undertake the project by the Anglo-Egyptian administration, which in Evans-Pritchard's words "...had encountered some difficulties in its dealings with the Anuak nobility" (1977, 5). He suggested, therefore, that the results be considered an instance of "applied anthropology... so that the government can organize its administration in light of them" (1977, 5-6).

As usual, Evans-Pritchard considered prevailing environmental circumstances and economic arrangements with an eye toward an eventual understanding of the political system in question. He noted that its agricultural base and productivity allowed each Anuak community to exist as a self-sufficient unit lacking the need for intervillage economic cooperation. As a consequence, any political amalgamation was temporary, in contrast to the more typical "balanced opposition" among the communities associated with descent groups. As a result, fighting and feuding were frequent among the Anuak villages (1977, 25-26).

Historically, this form of political organization allowed the Anuak to be pushed into the more inhospitable marsh and riverine environment by expanding neighboring groups. The Anuak were able to bring a halt to this decline in the late nineteenth century with the introduction of firearms from Ethiopia into the eastern part of the country, associated with the nobility and kingship.

In commenting on the Anuak politics in more synchronic fashion, Evans-Pritchard referred to the arrangement as "very peculiar," since in effect there were two "distinct political systems" (1977, 38). The first, in the western half of the country, was characterized by headmanship; the other, to the east by a more complex mixture of village headmenship and nobility competing over a circulating kingship. Evans-Pritchard warns that little research has been done on this "dual system," and notes that in more recent times headmen have fallen under the control of nobility (1977, 38). Thus, although he draws attention to both political structure and processes, Evans-Pritchard eventually comes down on the side of a dichotomized arrangement rather than a single, competitive system viewed over time.

Evans-Pritchard argued that the historical association of the Anuak with the Shilluk, as well as the use of such terms as "king," "sultan," "royal house," and "royal emblems" by others, ". . . obscured the real nature of their political organization" (1977, 51). Evans-Pritchard noted that, although there may be a single term (*nyiha*) for the large group he translates as "nobles," there exists no one term for "kingship." Thus, "there is no single king" (1977, 52) as opposed to the existence of a large number of nobles who dispute for possession of emblems of mythological and historical prestige. For Evans-Pritchard then, there was no objection to speaking of an Anuak "king" as long as it was understood that this status involved only belonging to the noble clan and being the current holder of certain emblems.

For Evans-Pritchard, the manner in which these emblems circulated "constituted" (1977, 86) both the office and the historical stages of Anuak kingship. In the first phase, the emblems normally remained under the control of a king until his death, when they were peacefully passed on to a son. In the subsequent era, assassinations characterized the movement of the emblems in a restricted area of eastern Anuakland. In the third phase, sometime in the nineteenth century, the emblems began to circulate more rapidly and peacefully as holders turned them over to rival claimants.

The late nineteenth or early twentieth century, which saw the first appearance of firearms in the area, ushered in another and more distinct political stage of Anuak kingship. Three nobles of two different lineages became so powerful during this period as to be able to maintain their control over the emblems, though they eventually passed them on peacefully to relatives.

The final two stages involved the establishment of effective external government control in 1921, when one incumbent had firm control over both the office and a wide area of eastern Anuakland. As such, he was able to pass on the office to his son. Henceforth, colonial officials appointed or confirmed Anuak kings in some accordance with Anuak customs and an eye toward a cooperative attitude on the part of the recipient. This description of the stages of Anuak kingship is taken primarily from Evans-Pritchard (1977, 86-99).

Having considered the relevant data, two primary concerns remain: (1) an evaluation of these two societies with reference to the meaning and significance of the dual nature of divine kingship, and

(2) a reconsideration of the manner in which Evans-Pritchard marshalled and interpreted the material. The latter is called for since, despite obvious political differences between these culturally related peoples, there emerges an underlying structural similarity in Evans-Pritchard's style of presentation, which continues to affect how kingship is viewed today.

With regard to the office of kingship, the Shilluk reflect a classic instance of a "divine kingship." The officeholder not only claims direct descent from the deity but is also spoken of as its living representative. Other elements associated with divine kingship are present at least in ideological form. These elements include the previously mentioned officeholder's and rivals' concern for the potentiality of both revolt and assassination. Thus king-killing, which figures so prominently in the literature (Young 1966) on this institution is an ideal for the Shilluk if not a verified practice. Finally, there are the extensive and integrated ceremonies attending to the death of one king and installation of his successor, which draw attention to their immortality by a variety of cultural fictions and forms denying the actual demise of any particular reth (see Arens 1984).

The Anuak, on the other hand, cannot claim such a commanding significance for their kingship. There is a claim to descent from mythical figures, but no hint of divinity attached to these past or more recent figures; no prescribed rituals of societal well-being; and little ceremony in recognition of their investiture or death. Equally significant, Anuak kings had little if any political power in comparison to their Shilluk counterparts.

Evans-Pritchard was aware of these variations in political arrangements and in trying to account for them he drew attention to ecology, economics, population density, geographical location, and historical peculiarities that separated these two societies. Yet, in addressing his greater concern for these two institutions of kingship, Evans-Pritchard adopted a position which in effect denied the power of the office in either political system. Yet this interpretation cannot be substantiated by the reported facts, particularly for the Shilluk and possibly not for Anuak kingship as it developed in the twentieth century.

Evans-Pritchard's consistent mode of interpretation for the political arrangements of the Shilluk and Anuak, and even the quite different Nuer with specific regard to their prophets, can be linked up with a number of different considerations. As suggested previously (Arens 1983), without denying the value of the models he offered, Evans-Pritchard was intent on denying the political significance of indigenous leaders who were the object of both manipulation and pressure by the Anglo-Egyptian administration in their pacification projects. This policy included removal from office, arrest, imprisonment, exile, and in some instances execution for resistance to the imposition of colonial rule or the failure to cooperate with its agents or policies. It is difficult to imagine from his published remarks on this charged atmosphere (Anon. 1972; Evans-Pritchard 1937, 1938) that Evans-Pritchard could have countenanced such a policy. His response to the situation involved contradicting the assumption that such figures had significant authority.

In this revisionary process, Evans-Pritchard made a similar contribution to our understanding of kingship by shifting attention away from political arrangements to a cultural perspective. Writing with Fortes he argued:

> An African ruler is not to his people merely a person who can confer his will upon them. He is the axis of these political relations, the symbol of their unity and exclusiveness, and the embodiment of their essential

values. He is more than a secular ruler.... His credentials
are mystical and are derived from antiquity (1940, 16).

The text goes on to suggest that, in effect, these "sacred persons" are themselves like the other items, symbols of unity (1940, 17).

Clearly prescient of his remarks on the Shilluk, Evans-Pritchard wrote that: "Among the Anuak,... there is a kingship but no central government" (1977, 136). Recognizing that "this good example of the ritual character of African kingship" had no ritual functions to perform, he suggested that the position itself was "the ritual object" (1977, 137-138). Thus, kingship becomes a cultural artifact, a symbolic representation of shared values and sentiments, rather than viewed as the arena of political relationships.

Evans-Pritchard also remained faithful to this approach in his estimation of the history of these two "realms" of kingship. He viewed their expansion and acceptance as a matter of ever more encompassing political values rather than actual influence. For the Shilluk at the time of analysis, this entailed the recognition of the prestige of the kingship throughout the land as the king "reigned." For the Anuak, he argued for the recognition of a "field of kingship" (1977, 104) that grew without any concomitant recognition of authority. On the one side, headmen continued to struggle to maintain effective political control over their villages, while on the other, rival claimants to the throne continued to compete for the royal emblems from their maternal strongholds rather than accept their control by the present holder.

By implication, this argument suggested that the structural field of kingship values might permeate a society prior to the spread of political arrangements, creating in the process the groundwork for potential centralization of authority. In effect, this orientation implies that legitimacy, in this instance in the form of royal values, precedes the spread of political power through coercion or imposition. This was indeed the case for the Anuak, as headmen, in their capacity as maternal relatives of nobles, invited such figures to reside in their villages and share political authority. The headmen then supported the nobles' claims to the royal emblems in order to garner the prestige this would entail for the community. Viewed from this perspective, kingship becomes a "civilizing process" as its associations confer prestige to a community and its residents.

This perspective not only makes sense in the two instances under consideration here; it was subsequently adopted by others in their studies of the spread of the centralization of authority in Africa (Southall 1956; Fairley 1978) in opposition to the then more attractive conquest theory of state formation. Without denying the potential validity of this perspective, and because of a variety of philosophical, personal, and theoretical inclinations, Evans-Pritchard drew our attention to a different model of political systems. As much of the recent literature in both history and social anthropology (Cannadine and Price 1987) suggests, this cultural interpretation of kingship now dominates our understanding of this institution. The emphasis on the cultural aspects of kingship alone, "the theater of power" as Cannadine and Price (1987, 1) so eloquently put it, tends to ignore the actual power of kings, including those imbued with divinity. Admittedly the cultural residue of kingship is often all we are left with as rituals are now sometimes performed "...merely as entertainment to please the people" (Gilbert 1987, 298) or as the divine king becomes a helpless "fetish" for his people (Friedman 1985, 249). Maybe this is the justifiable fate of kings in response to their quest for, or in the exercise of power. Yet in our attempt to understand this institution we should not permit the notion of the theater of power to prevent a recognition of the exercise of power.

Note

1. Limited field research among the Shilluk was conducted from February to May, 1978, during a period that turned out to be a lull in the ongoing civil war between the Northern and the Southern Sudan. This research was made possible by the Social Science Research Council and the Institute for Asian and African Studies, University of Khartoum.

168

References

Anon. [E.E.Evans-Pritchard]
1972.   The anthropologist as colonialist. *Times literary supplement.* (May 12):54.

Arens,W.
1979   The divine kingship of the Shilluk. *Ethnos* 44:167-181.
1983   A note on Evans-Pritchard and the prophets. *Anthropos* 78:1-16.
1984   The demise of kings and the meaning of kingship. *Anthropos* 79:355-367.

Bruce,J.
1905   *Travels to discover the source of the Nile.* New York: Horizon.

Cannadine,D., and S.Price, eds.
1987   *Rituals of royalty.* Cambridge: Cambridge University Press.

Evans-Pritchard,E.E.
1937   *Anthropology and administration.* Oxford: Oxford Summer School on Colonial Administration.
1938   *Some administrative problems in the southern Sudan.* Oxford: Oxford Summer School on Colonial Administration.
1940   *The Nuer.* Oxford: The Clarendon Press.
1947   Further observations on the political system of the Anuak. *Sudan notes and records* 28:62-97.
1948   *The divine kingship of the Shilluk of the Nilotic Sudan.* Cambridge: Cambridge University Press.
1977 (1940) *The political system of the Anuak.* New York: AMS Press.

Fairley,N.
1978   *Mianda ya Ben'Ekie.* Ph.D. dissertation. State University of New York, Stony Brook.

Fortes,M., and E.E.Evans-Pritchard, eds.
1940   *African political systems.* London: Oxford University Press.

Frazer,J.
1963   *The golden bough*. London: Macmillan and Co., Ltd.

Friedman,K.E.
1985   Sad stories of the death of kings. *Ethnos* 50:248-272.

Gilbert,M.
1987   The person of the king. In *Rituals of royalty*, edited
            by D.Cannadine and S.Price. Cambridge: Cambridge
            University Press.

Lienhardt,G.
1954   The Shilluk of the Upper Nile." In *African worlds*,
            edited by D.Forde. London: Oxford University Press.
1955   Nilotic kings and their mothers' kin. *Africa* 25:29-42.
1957   Anuak village headmen, part 1. *Africa* 27:341-355.
1958   Anuak village headmen, part 2. *Africa* 28:23-36.

Seligman,C.G., and B.Z.Seligman
1932   *Pagan tribes of the Nilotic Sudan*. London:
            Routledge and Kegan Paul.

Southall,A.W.
1956   *Alur society*. Cambridge: W. Heffer and Sons.

Wall,L.L.
1976   Anuak village politics, ecology, and the origins of the
            state. *Ethnology* 15:151-162.

Young,M.
1966   The divine kingship of the Jukun. *Africa* 36:135-153.

Yunger,K.
1985.   Nyikang, the warrior priest. Ph.D. dissertation. State
            University of New York, Stony Brook.

The Sudan in Reverse: Northern Separatists And Southern Integrationists

Ali A. Mazrui

Albert Schweitzer Professor in the Humanities
State University of New York at Binghamton, United States

The Sudan is still in the throes of upheaval and deprivation. It is not clear which is more elusive, national cohesion or national development. What is clear is that political allegiances have not been stagnant. At least from that point of view, the country is undergoing profound change.

There was a time when it was taken for granted that Northern Sudanese were basically national integrationists (committed to one Sudan) while Southerners were latent separatists, many of them even potential secessionists from the boundaries of the Sudan as created by British imperial rule. In reality this formulation has always been too simplistic. But in the 1990s the distribution of separatist sentiment, on one side, and integrationist commitment, on the other, is bound to become much more complicated. The majority of Sudanese may still be committed to their country's national integrity, but the distribution of separatism versus integrationism no longer correlates neatly between South and North.

For one thing, there seems to have been a greater commitment to a single Sudan in the South in the second civil war (since 1983) than there was in the first civil war (1955-1972). *Civil wars can be*

The argument of this essay is based on Mazrui's oral presentation to a special session of the Steering Committee of the National Dialogue of Problems of Peace in Sudan, held on Monday, October 16, 1989, at Friendship Hall, Khartoum, Sudan.

distinguished as primary or secondary. Primary civil wars seek to redraw the *boundaries* of the political community. Secessionism precipitates a primary civil war. A secondary civil war is a disagreement about the *goals* of the political community rather than its boundaries.

The **American** civil war of the 1860s involved secession. It sought to redraw the boundaries of the political community. It was therefore primary. The **Spanish** civil war of the 1930s was essentially a disagreement about the ideological goals of the political community. It was therefore secondary. The **Nigerian** civil war was primary-- targeted at boundaries. The Angolan civil war is probably secondary-- a disagreement about goals.

It is in the same sense that the second civil war in Sudan is secondary, a fundamental disagreement about directions and goals for one Sudan. On the other hand, the first civil war from 1955 to 1972 was decidedly primary, seeking to redraw the map.

Given that distinction, this second war in the Sudan has been at a higher level of national integration than the first, in spite of the fact that the second war has cost more lives and caused more devastation than the first.

Typology of Southern integrationists

There are different kinds of integrationists in the South. First, there are radical integrationists who believe that the Sudan as a whole is a more appropriate theater of social transformation than the South on its own. Although the evidence is ambiguous, John Garang, leader of the Sudan People's Liberation Movement (SPLM) may well be one such radical integrationist.

He has sometimes articulated the view that Sudan is potentially a stronger theater for revolution and democracy than the rural South on its own. He has sometimes defined the goals of the Sudan People's Liberation Army (SPLA) in terms of "liberating" the whole of the Sudan from a "reactionary oligarchy."

Second to the radical integrationists there are ethnic integrationists in the South. These are the smaller groups in Southern Sudan who feel safer in a bigger Sudan than in the South on its own.

There are similarities elsewhere in Africa's experience. Biafra did not consist only of the Igbo. The smaller communities like the Ibibio preferred to remain part of the bigger Nigeria than to be in a Biafra under Igbo control.

The Dinka may be the Igbo of the Southern Sudan. There are Southern Sudanese who are afraid of what they perceive as "Dinka domination." The regional minorities are the equivalent of the Ibibio.

The third category of Southern integrationists (after the radical and ethnic categories) are the professional integrationists. These are those who believe that there are greater professional opportunities in the bigger Sudan than in the South on its own. As the South has got better educated in the modern sense, this category of believers in one Sudan has expanded.

Professional integrationists include military as well as civilian subcategories. An integrated Sudanese army is perceived as potentially more fulfilling for a career soldier than the army of an independent Southern entity. A majority of the national army may already consist of Southerners, though not a majority of their officers. Southern journalists, broadcasters, engineers, professors, and school teachers may also prefer the wider professional market of an integrated Sudan over the smaller one of their region.

Fourth, there are the Arabophilic integrationists. Perhaps a small majority of Southern Sudanese have a love-hate relationship toward Arab culture, sometimes more hate than love.

But there are some Southern Sudanese who have crossed the line from Arabophobia (hostility toward the Arabs) to Arabophilia (fascination with the Arabs). Some of the Arabophiles have intellectually invested in the Arabic language and aspects of Arab culture. They may not be quite as infatuated with Arab civilization as Francophone Africans are with France, but the phenomenon of Arabophilia in Southern Sudan, though weaker than Francophilia in Senegal, is nevertheless real. The Arabic language is, after all, spreading fast as a lingua franca in Southern Sudan.

The fifth category of Southern integrationists is the category of genuine Sudan-wide nationalists and Sudan-wide patriots. These people may come from the Southern region and may indeed have a lot of complaints about their country (who does not?), but this category of Southerners may be genuinely loyal to the concept of a single Sudan beyond the calculations of ideological radicalism, or ethnic anxieties in the South, or professional prospects in the wider market, or a love-hate relationship with the Arabic language and Arab culture.

The sixth category of Southern integrationists are Southern Muslims, who have strangely been marginalized by both the North and the South. The majority of Southerners are still followers of traditional African religions. Christianity and Islam command allegiance from about forty percent of the Southern population. The Islamic fraction of the total population of the South is estimated at seventeen percent. The Christian population may be about twenty-three percent.

Typology of Northern separatists

Many of these reasons for integration may also apply to northern believers in a single Sudan. Northerners may also perceive themselves as, in any case, the majority in the nation as a whole, and therefore spared some of the anxieties of cultural minorities. The greater degree of Islamization and Arabization has also tended to help the cause of national integration.

But on the eve of the 1990s, what is more distinctive about the North is the emergence of a clear school of Northern separatism. It is still a small minority, but it seems to have become more articulate.

Again we find there are different categories of actual or potential Northern separatists. First, simply the war-weary, those who feel that if the price of maintaining a single Sudan is a civil war every ten years, the North had better cut its losses and go its separate way.

Such sentiments have been heard in a comparable context in England with reference to Northern Ireland. There is a sizeable popular opinion among people in England who would rather see Britain pull out of Northern Ireland--"and let the Irish fight it out among themselves."

In Sudan the second category of Northern separatists are economic pragmatists. Most of these currently complain about the £11 million (Sudanese pounds) spent each day on the war in the South. But some of these economic pragmatists believe that the South would remain an economic drain and would destabilize the North even if actual military hostilities ended. Instability would continue to carry a price tag for the North.

The third category of Northern separatists (cultural separatists) believes that it is not just the Southern culture that is endangered by the union between north and south; the northern culture itself is held hostage by the demand of saving the union.

Some of these Northern separatists believe that "abandoning Islam" is too high a price to pay for national integration. Of course Northerners are not really being called upon to stop being Muslims.

The debate is about whether the September laws (described by some as the *Sharia* itself) should remain the legal code of the Sudan. But the Northern cultural separatists believe that the September laws are a test case. Is the religion of the North being held hostage?

Fourth, there may be a category of Northerners who are racial separatists. In reality, of all the countries of the world, racism makes least sense in Sudan. The Arabs of Sudan are among the most racially mixed in the Arab world, and probably the most ethnically mixed ruling elite in Africa. The very name *Sudan* is derived from blackness.

But there may be a minority whose Pan-Arabism has taken racial overtones--some who may even object to any further racial intermingling with the blackest of blacks.

On the other hand, there is a fifth category of Northern separatists who are moral self-determinationists, who believe that most Southerners would prefer their own country and ought to be allowed to break away.

A few writers and intellectuals in Northern Sudan have taken that position almost since 1955, though it has not always been prudent to morally support Southern separatism too openly.

The proportion of Northerners who are separatists is still significantly smaller than the proportion of Southerners who are so. But there has been some shift in balance.

Toward the future

The fact that the distribution of separatism and integrationism is now criss-crossing between North and South can itself be integrative. National integration does not necessarily mean the evolution of a universal national consensus. It can merely mean that the differences in principle do not coincide with differences in ethnicity or race.

For example, in Nigeria the relationship between Christianity and Islam would have been far less divisive had the religious differences not coincided with ethnic differences. Almost all Hausa are Muslims; almost all Igbo are Christian. The Yoruba are split fifty-fifty.

In his political reforms, President Ibrahim Babangida has been trying to encourage ideological secular parties instead of ethnic, regional, or sectarian political groupings. Babangida's hope has been that the new Nigerian political parties would be truly based on secular ideology--cutting across the old divisive frontiers of ethnicity, regionalism, and religion.

I realize that important sections of opinion in the Sudan are profoundly distrustful on what they regard as "ideology." General Joseph Lagu's open letter to Colonel John Garang warns Garang about the dangers of promoting "ideology" in Sudan.

And yet one way of reducing the politics of regionalism and sectarianism in Sudan is to increase the politics of criss-crossing secular ideology. Southern liberals would need to ally with Northern liberals, in competition with, say, Northern socialists in alliance with Southern socialists.

Another criss-crossing allegiance is class allegiance. I understand that solidarity within Sudanese trade unions (across ethnic and religious divides) has been quite impressive.

There has been evidence that Sudan is ahead of most of the rest of Africa in the development of both secular ideologies like Marxism and class-consciousness. After all, it was not by accident that Sudan until 1971 had the largest indigenous communist movement in Africa. The movement briefly captured power from Jaafar Numeiry in 1971.

It took an external factor--Libya's capture of the supreme Sudanese communist leader on a plane from London to Khartoum via Tripoli-- to crush the communist coup.

Even if present-day Sudan survives, it will nevertheless be a long time before the North-South divide ceases to be painful and often disruptive. But elements of hope exist in this tormented society. Among those optimistic rays are the social forces which, against all odds, are producing Southern integrationists on one side and Northern separatists on the other. New forms of coalitions and new patterns of alignment are in the making. It is hoped that they will be more integrative and potentially more humane.

Dialectical Marxism and the Segmentary State

Stephen L. Mikesell
University of Kathmandu
Nepal

In the theory of the "segmentary state," Aidan Southall (1956) identified empirically the characteristic that Marx had ascribed to states generally, that the state is a society divided against itself, vertically in terms of class divisions, and horizontally by the limitations of both the divisions within the dominant class and of the state machinery to implement that class's control. In his early work, Southall presented the "segmentary" state as an alternative to the theory of a "unitary" state, criticizing the assumption that the latter was universally applicable, but nevertheless accepting its validity in describing the modern capitalist state. In succeeding years, however, Southall (n.d., 1984, 1988) explicitly closed his position with Marx methodologically.

Yet, he continued to see the problem of the state in terms of segmentary versus unitary. Although he showed that a unitary state theory was not universally applicable, he was unable to bring the unitary state theory under criticism as itself being an ideological construct in its entirety. This was the revolutionary implication of the theory of the segmentary state from the start. By turning to Marx's theory, Southall all but took the next step. However, he was thwarted by the "mode of production theory," brought to anthropology from Althusser, Balabar, and Establet who, misrepresenting Marx, destroyed the essential dialectical content of Marx's materialist method.

Exhuming Marx and dialectical materialism

A careful rereading of Marx and Engels (1983, 30-31) shows that they conceived of the production of life as appearing as a double relationship encompassing three simultaneously existing "aspects or... moments." Marx (1970) in a later work, presents the same position in a greatly truncated version. This later work has been used as the basis of the development of the Althusserian school, but its ambiguity and inconciseness led to the misinterpretation of essential features of dialectical materialism. Unfortunately, both early Marxist anthropology and cultural materialism repeated these mistakes. First, the relationship in which people produce two fundamental aspects or moments of their existence appear (but do not exist in reality) as a natural relation, a point that Marx and Engels (1983, 27-30) made in a discussion of Feuerbach. The first aspect is production of the means to satisfy the primary needs of life (which "involves before everything else eating and drinking, a habitation, clothing and many other things") or "material life itself," which confronts humans as the fundamental premise or condition of history. The second aspect is production of new needs that lead from the satisfaction of the first ones.

Second, production appears as a social relationship, consisting of "the co-operation of several individuals, no matter under what conditions, in what manner and to what end." This relationship consists of the third aspect of production, the production and reproduction of social life.

> Humans who daily remake their own life, begin to make
> other humans, to propagate their kind: the relation
> between man and woman, parents and children, the
> family. The family, which to begin with is the only social
> relationship, becomes later, when increased needs create
> new social relations and the increased population new
> needs, a subordinate one...and must then be treated and

analysed according to the existing empirical data, not according to the "concept of the family",...[Marx and Engels 1983, 31].

Marx and Engels (1983, 31) used the term "mode of production or industrial stage" to refer to the first relationship, and "mode of co-operation or social stage" to refer to the second, both of which occur historically in particular combinations. They specifically point out that not only the mode of production, but "the mode of co-operation is itself a 'productive force'" as well.

For Marx, the productive forces were the combination of historically created relations in things and people, not only by which individuals produce and reproduce themselves and their society, but which they confront in shaping their lives. The productive forces determine the nature of society, as "a materialist connection of humans with one another" (1983, 32). This materialist connection "is determined by their needs and their mode of production which is as old as men themselves." In other words the premises of history (needs) and the first two aspects of production (mode of production), the production of the means for the satisfaction of the premises and simultaneous production of new needs or premises, are determinate. It follows from the determinative nature of production that "this connection is ever taking on new forms" and that this history "thus presents a history independently of the...political or religious..." (i.e., the consciousness).

According to Marx and Engels (1983, 33), consciousness is itself a social product, which extends through increased productivity, needs, and population (which arise from the three respective aspects of production). The division of labor also develops on the basis of these developments, first spontaneously or naturally, according to natural predisposition, then "truly" for the first time with the appearance of the division of mental and physical labor. Marx and Engels associate the latter with the rise of the city. But both Southall, with the segmentary state, and Marx (1972), in his notebooks on Morgan (1877), show that not only did this division occur prior to the cities, but that it arose out of a division of labor based on gender and age. The division of labor (activity), simultaneously takes form as unequal distribution (product of activity), or the power of disposing the labor power of others (i.e., property).

Marx and Engels write that the contradiction of the interest of the separate individual or individual family versus that of the communal interest of all the individuals arises from the division of labor. The communal interest takes concrete form in the mutual interdependence among those whom labor is divided. It takes independent form in both the state, divorced from the real interests of the individual and community, and the illusiory communal life. "As long as a cleavage exists between the particular and the common interest...man's own deed becomes an alien power opposed to him, which enslaves...instead of being controlled by him" (Marx and Engels 1983, 35). If contradictions arise within the state and the consciousness, it is because these themselves extend from a contradiction between the whole collection of forces, which seem to be developing independently of human will and confronting humans as a huge alien power, and the particular existing productive relations as a dialectical source of change and transformation.

For Marx and Engels, the productive forces are represented in the full extent of human intercourse and contact. They are not limited by a particular mode of production; they are the combination of all the various modes and relations of production that are in intercourse and contact. This intercourse and contact, even if it is between groups of vastly different modes of production (in Marx and

Engels' sense), represents the full extent of "co-operation between individuals as it is determined by the division of labor" (Marx and Engels 1983, 36). It is these "multiplied productive forces" (ibid.) that people confront as the alien power, and which, in contradiction with their own particular modes and relations of production, are continually giving rise to a new society.

The reburial of Marx: Alhusser's antidialectic

When Engels buried him, Marx's deeds lived on after he died; with Althusser, they were buried with his bones. As diagrammed in the table, the Althusserian Marxists not only totally switched around Marx's theory, they changed the contents of its elements beyond all but the most superficial resemblance.

First, the Althusserian paradigm switches the term "productive forces" with Marx and Engels' term "mode of production," imposing a much shallower meaning onto the former, while unjustifiably expanding the latter. From the Althusserian perspective, productive forces refer only to the "material and intellectual means...to work upon nature and to extract from it their [referring to members of a society] means of existence" (Godelier 1978, 763). Thus they refer only to physical and mental instruments. For Marx and Engels, mode of production refers to two aspects of production, the production of means and of secondary needs.

Thus from the start, the Althusserian perspective shifted the emphasis from production, with its implication of creation and becoming, to instruments, removing the dialectical basis of Marx and Engels' entire argument. Worse, productive force as social power, based in and encompassing production, constantly changing and therefore historical, has been reduced to force defined merely as physical and mental force, static, requiring human productive activity

Marx and Engels	Althusserian Marxism
Premise: Humans must live to make history: life implies certain needs and production to satisfy these necessarily follows (contingency is identified in production itself). *	**Premise:** Structures of human life which takes historical existence within separate "social formations," leaving the contingency of how one social formation begins and another ends.
(No corresponding category)	*Infrastructures*
Production: Three simultaneous aspects or moments of production	**Structures:** Three instances or levels of social reality or substance
(Humanized nature means a nature that has entered into social relations and thus is not separate from production or history.)	1. <u>Ecological and geographical conditions</u>
1. <u>Mode of production/industrial stage</u> 1st aspect: production of the material means * 2d aspect: production of new needs *	2. <u>Productive forces</u> Material or intellectual means in order to work on nature
2. <u>Relations of production/social stage</u> 3d aspect: people create their social existence or reproduce themselves as social beings	3. <u>Relations of production</u> Relations that assume either or all of: a) determining the social form of access b) allocating a labor force c) determining the social form of redistribution
Productive forces: arise from production and exchange	Mode of production: particular combination of productive forces of relations of production
Consciousness, division of labor/distribution, contradiction/property, classes, the state (the content of society that arises from production	*Superstructure:* ideas, religion, political, legal, etc.

*Determine the "material connection of men".

rather than encompassing it, therefore devoid of history rather than created by it. The full significance of this is discussed below.

Second, "social relations of production" is the same term and occupies the same corresponding position in the Athusserian theory as it did in that of Marx and Engels. However, it ignores Marx and Engels' definition of relations of production in terms of production and reproduction of human social existence. Rather it has to do with "determining the social form of access to resources and control of the means of production, allocation of labor, and determination of social form of distribution" (Godelier 1978, 763). For Marx and Engels, these are attributes of distribution, which are given by the division of labor. The social division of labor is itself derived historically from production, both material and social. To define the social relations of production in terms of division of labor is to shift the focus from production to its social product. The former implies dialectical process, requiring historical analysis to apprehend it, the latter implies structural relationships, which may be reduced to structural analyses devoid of history.

Third, while forces of production had been placed in the position of mode of production without the content of the latter, mode of production itself was switched to the position of Marx and Engels' forces of production. It thus encompassed forces of production and social relations of production. But since, as pointed out, both categories lacked the dialectical content of Marx and Engels' categories, the mode of production merely consisted of a structural correspondence between two static categories.

Fourth, Althusserian reduction of productive forces into mere instruments totally removes the contradiction of the existing social relations with productive forces arising as an alien power. Whether they are tools or knowledge, instruments are not in themselves a force, but require intervention of living, human labor power to move them. This may exert force, but only in a mechanical or physiological sense and thereby in a manner totally different from the meaning given by Marx and Engels. For Marx and Engels, productive forces, as created by the combination of production of means and new premises on the one hand, and relations of production on the other, can become a power that contradicts the relations in which the individuals or individual families find themselves. Because they arise from production that was defined as itself in constant flux, these social forces are themselves in a constant flux of becoming. As such, they are defined and understood by the history of their development, not by a particular configuration.

As shown above, the Althusserian "mode of production," is not an equivalent of "forces of production," because not only were the categories rearranged, they were robbed of their content. Indeed, because the terms were all switched around, they ceased to have organic connection with their content, and they became bundles of formal categories used to identify and define static structures of relations within different modes of production. The problem was reduced to one of fitting different historical situations into these bundles of formal categories.

Since the forces of production had been reduced into a static, sterile category on an entirely different level of abstraction from that of Marx, the contradiction between it and relations of production lost its significance. The only contradiction that could be found was located as arising between population categories or groups of people defined by different Althusserian modes of production (usually merely a different name for the stale categories of society, tribe, nation state, and so forth, depending upon the problem). If there was intercourse, then the problem was how to explain this intercourse, since these societies/states/ tribes of different "modes of production" were already defined by their different structures of production and therefore exclusive of each other. So the Althusserians set out to look for "articulation" of modes of production. Of course, since mode of production was created out of a failure to understand Marx, the whole project was a contrived one.

Althusserian Marxism was an antidialectical and counterrevolutionary regression from Marx. Raya Dunayevskaya attributes it to the identification of many European Marxist intellectuals with Stalinist "state capitalism," as she called it. However, it has played just as well into the hands of transnational corporate capital and corporate bureaucracy, with which these intellectuals may just as well have identified. It has detoured Marxists from developing a revolutionary theory of the world, in which all people, although engaged in a variety of modes and relations of production, are involved in a global division of labor and are in confrontation with the same productive forces. While individuals may find themselves in particular relations with their own particular circumstances, the character of these relations, whether in Africa, India, Eastern Europe, or the Anthropology Departments in the United States and Western Europe is now determined by these same global productive forces, according to their historical circumstances.

Beyond mode of production

Southall's works are a record of a struggle with such categories and pretensions, allowing many of us to move ahead to address entirely new problems. In his unpublished magnum opus, *The City in Time and Space*, Southall (n.d.) eschewed the modes of production and progressed in terms of the development of productive forces represented by the rise, expansion, and finally global merging of urban civilization. Thus it was a regression for Southall (1984, 1988) to return to the theory of modes of production, which forced him to retrack the ground covered by Marx and Engels in the *German Ideology*, with which he was familiar. In the later work, therefore, he identifies the basic problems in the Althusserian mode of production theory, but, apparently unaware that the whole theory is a total perversion of Marx and Engels, he revises rather than discards it.

> The formulation of a theory of modes of production tends, through the limitations of words, to concentrate the suggestion of change between modes rather than within them, in a way which fails to conform with the flow of events in history. Even according to the theory, change is always present in the potential contradiction between the forces and relations of production, and in the development of both, which eventually leads to increasing contradiction.
> Historical periods which are represented in the theory as transitions from one mode of production to another have to be seen as periods of the most rapid and significant change and are commonly referred to as revolutions. But even Marxist historians treat the transition from feudalism to capitalism as taking place over a very long period of several centuries and there is little reason to suppose that other transitions would have been any more rapid. In recognition of this, revolution is sometimes treated as though it were a conceptual rather than a historical fact (Southall 1988).

We have seen that blame for the problems raised by Southall arise not from Marx's theory, but from the Althusserian school's misrepresentation of Marx. When mode of production and productive forces are set in their correct relationship and attributed the content originally given them by Marx, whether changes occur between or within modes of production ceases to be a problem. Marxist theory becomes dialectical once again and history, rather than diverging from it, becomes its tool. The contradiction of forces and relations of production, rather than being subordinated within a mode of production defined in terms of structures between static elements, again makes mode of production defined by the dynamic of production its basis. And thus the contradiction itself becomes a dynamic, dialectical one, constantly in flux. Since the contradiction arises from productive activity (including that of undialectical theorists) and not structures, the goal of analysis becomes not one of identifying how structures articulate, but of creating a new consciousness that causes individuals to transform their old activity into revolutionary practice to create new conditions that serve rather than thwart their social interests. Southall's second paragraph merely follows from this.

Marx himself always analyzed capitalism in terms of the total span of human history, and in the last years of his life, like Southall, he was looking for the origins of the divisions of labor, property, class, and the state within the clan itself (Marx 1972). Although he identified particular historically arisen modes of production in the different stages of history, he never called these stages "modes of production," and he always rooted them in real history, defined them in terms of historical not formal categories, and described them in terms of a dialectical sense of "becoming," not static, structures (Marx 1973, 1983). Only the Asiatic form of property was not derived from an actual historical stage of development, although it was based on contemporary understandings of real societies (1983). In his ethnological notebooks, Marx (1972) had turned away from all these categories and was progressing in the manner suggested by Southall.

At the end of his article, Southall (1988) concludes that the segmentary state is not limited to a "kinship mode of production" (in an Althusserian sense), but is cross-contextually applicable to different stages in the transition between the kinship mode of production and the Asiatic mode of production. In the latter, the extent of the state is equated with the extent of the mode of production; this is logical, given that within the Althusserian framework all contradictions between the forces of production and relations of production are reduced into the mode of production. But when the productive forces are placed into their proper position over and against the present relations of production, with the mode of production subordinated to both the forces and the relations of production, then the relations, consciousness, and so forth of the particular nation state exist in contradiction to the productive forces that transcend particular states as well. Since these encompass the extent of human production and intercourse as a power alien to them, it is unlikely that any particular nation state encompassed them, and thus it is questionable that any nation state has been unitary.

Although Southall argued that China exemplified the unitary state, its productive forces must be seen as including "barbarians" beyond its borders. The Great Wall and the invasions it was meant to stop underscore this; centuries or even millennia of trade with Arabia and Europe similarly preceded and contributed to the growth of the global productive forces that greatly reshaped China within the last couple of centuries.

Generally, as Southall (n.d.) showed, the development of the productive forces consisting in capitalism started when the first cities in Mesopotamia, Africa, East Asia, and America arose to confront the Neolithic segmentary states that gave birth to them as a great new power. The subsequent commerce, conquest, migrations, and so forth represented a quickening of this process, until finally, as a product of commerce global in extent, and thus also the product of a global human effort, production itself became subordinated to commerce in the formation of the most powerful combination of productive forces:

industrial capitalism. But, because it arose from cooperation in the old restricted division of labor, it also is the most alienating and oppressive one.

The productive forces of industrial capitalism, growing out of the combined production and cooperation of all nations, stand in opposition to the relations of people in every nation state as never before. The division of labor and thus the classes determined by it are global. Thus the dominant class interest and its independent form, the state, are global. In the collection of particular nation states, however, it remains segmented, although these nation states themselves are far more integrated in terms of production, intercourse, consciousness, and administration than many if not all segmentary states in the past.

Thus, finally, the segmentary character of the state extends from the the character of human production, especially in that it takes form as an independent power in the productive forces. Taken as a generic type, applicable cross-contextually, in opposition to the "unitary" state, the segmentary state is meaningless. The theory of the unitary state, like the Brahmanic conception of the state in Rajput or Cola India, is a cultural construction used to serve the interests dominating society. It should be returned to the political science departments, only entering anthropology (along with the political science department itself) as an object of study, not a basis of theory.

Following Southall (1988), I argue that the segmentary state is a developmental or genetic type of state that occurs as a logical stage in the development of the state. However, having proposed that segmentation arises from production as a character of the state generally, I would prefer to limit Southall's term to states that take the categories of gender and age as their basis. Long before Marx's (1972) own work on the subject became generally available, Southall

(1956) discovered not only that class and the state exist within societies that had previously been described as stateless, but that the first and most important, truly historical division of labor, between intellectual (ritual clans) and manual labor (commoner clans), which Marx had attributed to the rise of the city, preceded the city and provided its basis. The significant difference between the segmentary state and other states is not in its form, but in the division of labor, contradictions, form of property, and particular class interests that make its basis. Whereas the segmentary state represented interests based on kinship, particularly of ritual over other clans, subsequent states represented the sacred intelligentsia, landed property, capital, and secular bureaucratic intelligentsia classes. Nevertheless, in the history of its development and dissolution, the segmentary state stands as the historical premise of all subsequent states, while in its segmentation it provides the essence of the state.

References

Engels,F.
1983   The origin of the family, private property and the state in light of the researches of Lewis H.Morgan. In *Selected Works*, by Ka.Marx and F.Engels, 5th printing, 191-334. Moscow: Progress Publishers.

Godelier,M.
1978   Infrastructures, societies, and history. *Current anthropology* 19(4):763-771.

Marx, K.
1970   *A contribution to the critique of political economy*, edited by M.Dobb. New York: International Publishers.
1972   *The ethnological notebooks of Karl Marx*, edited by K.Krader. Assen: Van Gorcum and Company, N.V.
1973   Forms which precede capitalist production. In *Introduction to the critique of political economy* (Grundrisse), translated by M.Nicolaus, 471-514. New York: Vintage Books.

Marx,K., and F.Engels
1983   Feuerbach. Opposition of the materialistic and idealistic outlook (chap. 1 of the *German Ideology*). In *Selected works*, vol. 1, 5th printing, by K.Marx and F.Engels, 16-80. Moscow: Progress Publishers.

Morgan,H.L.
1877   *Ancient society or researches in the lines of human progress from savagery through barbarism to civilization.* New York: Henry Holt.

Southall,A.W.
n.d.   The city in time and space. Unpublished manuscript.
1956   *Alur society.* Cambridge: W. Heffer and Sons.
1984   The significance of Marx's view of urban evolution for a theory of cities. Paper for the workshop,"Meanings of the City," at Wingspread Conference Center, Racine, Wisconsin, October 25-27.
1988   The segmentary state in Africa and Asia. *Comparative studies in society and history* 30(1):52-82.

Economic Parameters of an Archaic Polity:
Nanun, Northern Ghana

Peter Skalnik, Professor
University of Cape Town, South Africa

Nanun is an indigenous polity of the Voltaic type, which presently forms the Nanumba District in northeastern Ghana. Its traditional council is incorporated into the imported modern state structure of Ghana and the economy of Nanun is also integrated in many ways into the modern Ghanaian economy. The latter is to a considerable degree a state economy because the state is a major employer, entrepreneur, and distributor of wealth. The state collects taxes, owns and finances the infrastructure and development projects, and it has the monopoly of the state currency, the Cedi. The state of Ghana imposes law and order, is responsible for defense, and represents the population in the world arena. It is also a major foreign trade agent. It is widely believed that up to forty percent of the working population of Ghana is officially employed by the state and even though their salaries and wages do not constitute a decent living, the money thus earned is a kind of guarantee of economic security.

Interesting questions arise when one considers the functions fulfilled by a polity such as Nanun in precolonial times. Is a comparison possible with the modern Ghanaian economy or with economic systems of other modern states? Was there anything like a state economy in Nanun? Did the chiefs, for example, employ and exploit their subjects for the sake of chieftancy or *naam*? Serious answers to these questions require, first, clarification of what is meant by "Nanun polity." On the one hand, it can be argued that all people who recognized the superiority or sovereignty of the *Bimbilla Naa*, or paramount chief of Nanun, made up Nanun as a polity. However, if we look at economic activities, there are problems in deciding whether or not activities such as animal husbandry or gardening are part of a "state" economy. Leaving aside the question of whether Nanun was a state at all, which I have answered in the negative (Skalnik 1983, 1987), it is necessary to look more closely at each economic activity in order to decide how it relates to the polity. In one sense, of course, any economic activity in Nanun took place under the general umbrella of Nanun as a polity that was expected to keep order and defend its population so that the population enjoyed the security flowing out of its allegiance and loyalty to the local chief and the paramount.

If we look more closely, however, at the links between the subjects and the representatives of Nanun, such as chiefs and other dignitaries, we might be disappointed. In Nanun, each household, including that of the chiefs, cared for its own subsistence. Every male in Nanun, the Bimbilla Naa included, was a farmer. There was never a regular tax system, but once a year, on the occasion of the Damba festival, farmers *could*, if they so desired and were in a position to do so, give samples of their harvest to the chief as tokens of their loyalty. But those who did not were not in any way disadvantaged.

Nevertheless, there were a few economic duties of the population toward the chiefs: annual hoeing of the chiefly fields and supplying of a hind leg from each first animal killed at ritual funerals. There were also extraordinary duties: skins from lions and leopards killed by the hunters had to be given to the Bimbilla Naa. The chiefly house originating from the first immigrant leader, Nmantambu, is the lion's house (*Gbuxmayili*). Elephant tusks had also to be delivered to the Bimbilla Naa, and hind legs of buffaloes, antelopes, or hippos had to be presented by the hunter to the local chief. Fish was treated in a similar manner, and riverine chiefs were entitled to samples from each catch.

The abuse of these rules could have unpleasant repercussions. When Nakpaa Naa Abudulai sold a tusk from an elephant killed on Nakpaa territory and bought a horse with the proceeds, the then Bimbilla Naa, Salifu, took the horse from him as punishment. However, when Naa Abudulai became the Bimbilla Naa, he revenged his humiliation by not promoting to naam any male children of Naa Salifu. Perhaps in this sense we could speak of the political economy of Nanun. To this day the competition for naam is central to the polity, and the economic factors that may influence it are also essential. Any candidacy for naam must be accompanied by gifts to the person who decides (i.e., most often the Bimbilla Naa). Also, arbitration and other judicial activities bring the chiefs some revenue in the form of payments for adjudication or arbitration. Still, it must be reiterated, most ordinary economic activities could not be used in the affairs of the polity; this was only possible in indirect ways.

A good example were activities on whose success the whole destiny of the polity was believed to depend. *Naakuli* or the chief's ritual funeral had to be organized by the *gbonlana* or regent, the eldest son of the deceased. The regent could "blackmail" his subjects by demanding big amounts for food under the pretense of having to care for funeral guests. So gbonlana Mahama Dasana delayed naakuli for his father Naa Dasana Abudulai for more than half a year in 1982-1983 by demanding "100 cows, 100 bags of maize and 100 guinea-fowls." This was an obvious pretext for prolonging the "rule" of the Gbuxmayili chiefly house and for wreaking a promise from the electors of the new Bimbilla Naa that he (gbonlana) would be promoted by the new paramount to the naam of Nakpaa, a "gate" town, giving him strategic advantage in a future competition for the naam of Bimbilla. Ironically, he, in turn, was subjected to "blackmail" by the people from the sacred villages of Dalaanyili, Ponaayili, and Binda, who are solely entitled to carry out secret rituals making the deceased Bimbilla Naa fully recognized and introduced into the rank of ancestors (Skalnik 1988). These ritual specialists also demanded from the regent quite massive sums of money and food before they were prepared to start with the funerary rituals.

Another clearly economic aspect of naam is the fact that when a village chief became a Bimbilla Naa, he almost instantly married a large number of wives. Had he had several wives before, as chief of a "gate" town, he would then be in charge of several dozen wives. This of course leads to the expansion of the chiefly household into an unprecedented size. However, the labor force thus gained was mitigated by the number of juvenile dependents. There were considerable expenses involved in clothing the wives and children as well as obligations toward visitors who had to be offered cola nuts at the very least if they came to greet the chief. The Bimbilla Naa was expected to be a good and generous host.

Even though I have serious doubts about the existence of any specific chiefly wealth that could be used for antagonistic relations between the chiefs and other inhabitants of Nanun, I must admit that I was not able to establish the exact size of the main wealth in Nanun, namely cattle. The Bimbilla Naa Dasana, under whose rule the first part of my research was done (1959-1981), was known to have cattle in several places in Nanun, allegedly in order to avoid decimation through illness. But this dispersion also served the purpose of keeping secret the extent of his cattle wealth. Only after his death, when relatives complained that the regent (i.e., his eldest son) had sold and consumed many cattle, comprising virtually all the

Gbuxmayili wealth, was it obvious that paramount chiefs can be rich in cattle. The Dakpam Naa, the present Bimbilla Naa Abarika, reported in 1981 the loss of more than two hundred head of cattle in the hostilities between the Nanuma and the Konkomba. However, as cattle are a form of family wealth, it is doubtful whether we can connect them with the polity in any way. It is true that cattle ownership confers prestige to the Bimbilla Naa and other chiefs, as does horse ownership. However, because of the secrecy surrounding cattle ownership, which is common in Nanun among all sectors of the population, the utility of cattle wealth in politics is limited. The chief would rather be expected to offer a bull to visitors who came for ceremonies like funerals or annual festivals or all night praise singing, common under the Bimbilla Naa Natogmah (1945-1957).

At this point, it is also worth mentioning house slavery. The chiefs held slaves or captives in larger numbers than did the ordinary people. This can be explained by the fact that they were superordinates of the warriors who usually were responsible for catching slaves in adjacent "acephalous" territories. There was also debt slavery. I could not secure any facts concerning permanent use of domestic slaves in polity service except as pages and eunuchs of the chiefs. There were no "state" farms on which slaves would work for the chiefs like they did in Songhay. Chiefs' farms were tilled only once a year by the young men supplied by the heads of compounds. During the rest of the agricultural activities, the chiefs' own wives, sons, sons-in-law, and daughters-in-law did the bulk of the work on the farms. Certainly village chiefs, but even the Bimbilla Naa, himself, did farm work like weeding and sowing. I witnessed on a number of occasions that the Bimbilla Naa or the regent went to inspect their farms in order to check for themselves how the yams or maize were growing. They showed keen interest in their herds as well.

In conclusion, I would argue that economic resources were used for political purposes in Nanun but not for the accumulation of wealth as an end in itself. Redistribution of wealth to supporters was expected from the chiefs. There was no institutionalized "state" economy in Nanun. Only a very Eurocentrist analysis would reveal purely economic aspects of politics in Nanun. Thus in Nanun one cannot really speak of "early state economics," as there was hardly any discernible public economic domain. The continuation of the polity required no particular economic activity or institution. However, there were several areas of an economic nature, which within the framework of the general embeddedness of politics, economics, and ideology, played important roles in the competition for chieftancy. There was no ownership of land, and cattle were mainly owned by groups of relatives. The chiefs did not run any specific economic undertaking in the name of the polity and really had no chance to exploit economically their subjects. Each wife had her own economic sphere of interest and the sheer number of wives diminished the possibility of their exploitation by the chief. Contemporary chiefs in Nanun show keen interest in the government allowance, which though small, is enough to indicate that their own "traditional" economy is not a major source of wealth. The political and religious emphasis in Nanun, as in many other African polities, made economic concerns relatively insignificant. Economics were an individual and family concern.

References

Skalnik,P.

1983   Questioning in the concept of the state in indigenous Africa. *Social dynamics* 9(2):11-28.

1987   On the inadequacy of the concept of the "traditional state." (Illustrated with ethnographic material from Nanun, Ghana.) *Journal of legal pluralism* 25-26:11-28.

1988   Power symbolism and political culture in Nanun, northern Ghana. Paper prepared for the 12th International Congress of Anthropological and Ethnological Sciences in Zagreb, Yugoslavia, 24-31 July 1988.

Robbers and Aristocrats: Power, Potency, and Leadership Among the Punan Bah of Borneo

Ida Nicolaisen, Associate Professor
Institute of Cultural Sociology
Copenhagen University, Denmark

Every now and then the rumor of *penyamun* spreads like wildfire among the ethnic groups of Borneo and upsets the daily life of the longhouse communities and the picturesque Malay *kampong*. Families return from their swiddens to find safety behind the solid walls of the communal houses and/or the comforting nearness of neighbors and kin. Women venture but in the immediate vicinity of the settlement to scout for vegetables and shrimp, men postpone hunting and fishing activities. After a few days' food supplies get low, the atmosphere becomes correspondingly tense. Shrill voices of mothers, who order their boys to stop playing at the riverbank and stay on the longhouse veranda, pierce the ears and get at nerves. The longhouse echoes with admonitions not to stray into the rain forest, and stories about penyamun spice the conversations. No one usually knows from where the rumor stems, and after a week or two, concern about penyamun fades away, only to turn up again after some time.

This widespread phenomenon has so far hardly caught the attention of social scientists working with Bornean societies. An exception is a paper by Anna Lowenhaupt Tsing (1985). Information

---

The essay is based on close to three years of fieldwork among the Punan Bah carried out in 1973, 1974-1975, 1980-1981, 1983-1984, and 1985-1986. The research was supported by grants from the Danish Social Science Foundation.

about penyamun crop up in newspapers from time to time. In the Sarawak Gazette, that wonderful chronicle of events big and small, first published by Rajah Charles Brooke in 1870, we learn here and there about penyamun. In the July issue of 1874, we read

> "PENYAMUNS. Excitement has been caused in the Kampongs by the appearance of "Penyamuns" or robbers; they are described as men with long hair, dressed in black clothes. Although we believe this report to be without foundation, yet penyamuns do appear every year in Sarawak, and in fact in all large Malay towns. They are not really robbers, as they rarely appropriate property, and although armed, they seldom commit an assault. Their only object seems to be to cause alarm, which they soon thoroughly succeed in doing (Malays are proverbially cowards in the dark), one night startling one part of the Kampong, the following appearing in a quite different quarter. They almost invariably escape without being captured; and we think they sally out in quest of adventure simply to gratify their love of excitement.

The understanding of the editor of the *Sarawak Gazette* at the time was clearly that penyamun were robbers, if they existed at all, that is. The same point of view is held today by Westerners and Chinese familiar with the area, as far as my investigations went. Like the late editor, they explain penyamun as persons driven by sheer economic lucre if they do not discard the phenomena as being altogether unfounded. Among the many ethnic groups of the interior, penyamun is a reality, the cultural significance of which still needs investigation. We shall turn to one of these, the Punan Bah, among whom the notion of penyamun can be fully understood only as an expression of key premises of their cultural construction of reality, more specifically as this relates to concepts of power, wealth, and leadership. The Punan Bah tell of penyamun that

(1) They are hairy, awesome men, strangers on the outlook for people, in particular children, whom they want to catch and kill.

(2) They are sent on their missions by people of power, generally described as *tuan*, a Malay word with which the Punan Bah denote British and other Westerners. In this context it may refer as well to others of genuine power in their country, Malaysia.

(3) They kill by tearing out the heart of their victims.

(4) The purpose of the killing is to present a sacrifice of blood to the guardian spirits of the tuan or people of power.

(5) Such sacrifices are prerequisite to the successful outcome of major projects and undertakings by those who have sent the penyamun, endeavors that present themselves to the Punan Bah as visual manifestations or proofs of the extraordinary capabilities and powers of these tuan.

Rumors about penyamun flourish among the Punan Bah when news about major construction work reaches their society. During my stays among them, the rumors were associated with a renewed exploration for coal at Nanga Merit, below the Punan Bah settlements at the Rejang, to the setting up of an oil rig off the coast of Miri, and to dynamite explosions at the rocks of the Pelagus and Bakus rapids in preparation of the building of the proposed hydroelectric plants there.

The thought of facing a violent death by penyamun is frightening to the Punan Bah, the more so as the consequence in their understanding is that the victim shall not be reborn; rather, his or her soul will be doomed to an existence in eternal misery and unhappiness.

We shall take the notion of the penyamun as a point of departure for the ensuing exploration of cultural concepts of power and leadership, a topic to which Aidan Southall (1989) has devoted himself. In a fairly recent paper entitled "Religion and Political Economy in State and Stateless Societies," he advocates the idea that sequence of power, which he characterizes as benign, malevolent, righteous, and oppressive, corresponds to changes in political economy and religion associated with it, as well as changes in size and scale, in specialization and technology. We shall not pursue Southall's comparative line of investigation but explore how cultural premises of power, wealth, and leadership among the Punan Bah condition their understanding of changing socioeconomic and political conditions and shape their political behavior as citizens of the modern nation state, Malaysia.

The Punan Bah is a minor ethnic group of about fifteen hundred persons living in seven longhouse settlements in the fourth and seventh Divisions of the State of Sarawak. They subsist on swidden agriculture, fishing, hunting, and gathering. Cash-income is procured by selling game, fish, ironwood, and jungle produce; by tapping rubber; and working as wage laborers for timber companies. Punan Bah society is stratified. It consists of a small but highly influential aristocracy *lajar*, and a larger category of commoners, panyin. Slaves (*lipien*) were possessed by the aristocrats in former days, enabling these to live in relative leisure. Masters and slaves formed common households, addressed one another with kin terms, as parents and children, respectively, and enjoyed different rights and obligations. Slaves could achieve great responsibility, represent the aristocrats at ritual and political occasions, and they were respected, sometimes feared, by their masters.

The Punan Bah perceive of the hierarchical order of their society as divinely ordained, as stated in their myths, and to be respected lest the wrath of the divine ancestors shall befall the presumptuous. The aristocracy traces its descent directly back to Bua, the Creator. It is believed to be semidivine, *pabeta otu*, and should be venerated accordingly. Aristocrats are known as the great people, *linou ajo*, the aristocratic ruler as the great one of the longhouse, *ajo lovo*, or as the father of many people (i.e., commoners, *oman linou owad*). There is only one aristocratic household in each longhouse, and formally its head holds the social, political, economic, and also the religious leadership. Today only three out of the seven longhouses are ruled by aristocrats. Aristocratic leadership is nevertheless not only preferred, it is the only form of leadership that the commoners truly recognize, that is, if carried out in accordance with the norms of exchange and responsibility that ideally define relations between aristocrats and their subjects.

The hierarchical social organization is idealized by the Punan Bah. Societies without a hereditary aristocracy (e.g., the Iban) are said to be without tradition or custom, *adet*, a characterization that, among the highly status-concerned Punan Bah, carries the connotation of ultimately lacking culture and prominence, of being nothing. Commoners look up to and respect the aristocracy, and as we shall see, fear their divine powers.

The relationship between the aristocratic ruler and the commoners is described by both parties as one of mutual dependence and respect. The aristocrat receives corvée labor by the commoners, or what is considered its equivalent in kind. Commoners are obliged, moreover, to provide housing and means of transportation for the aristocratic family. On them rests the economic burden of paying bridewealth when a male aristocratic ruler marries, of providing labor, food, cash, and valuables at his or her burial, as well as at certain other ritual and social occasions, if so required. The aristocratic leader offers leadership and management. The commoners expect him to take upon himself not only political and religious duties, but also economic decisions such as the overall planning of swidden agricultural activities and related rituals, and other communal endeavors. The aristocrat should solve social conflicts and problems in consultation with elder members of the longhouse community. He is expected to take care that the needy are provided for in return for the labor and services rendered by the commoners. He must serve their interests in order to pay back their loyalty. He should be theirs in all matters, as he and his family is fed (*makkan*) by the commoners.

Reality is often far from this ideal, however. Aristocrats are selfish and increasingly so, the commoners complained to me. They eat people, *koman linou* (i.e., claim labor and other services from the commoners), yet do not fulfill their obligations toward these commoners in return, nor do they handle the communal interests vis-a-vis the state to the satisfaction of their subjects. Not that selfish aristocrats are a new phenomenon. The problem is that the commoners have no means to curb poor and unjust rule, nor do they dare openly to defy the aristocratic leaders. For commoners cannot disobey aristocrats without risking not only their personal retaliation but also, and that is the core of the issue, the divine wrath of the ancestors. This conception of reality is of consequence to the participation of the commoners in political life and modern development in Malaysia. To understand why this is so, we shall look closer at the Punan Bah notion of power. We shall first cast a glance, however, at the historical events that have influenced political leadership among these people.

Up to the beginning of the twentieth century (i.e., before the rule of the Brooke Raj had a thorough impact on the lives of the ethnic groups of central Borneo), aristocratic power was culturally justified by descent as it is today. In practice, however, it relied as well on the personal qualifications of the aristocrat: his generosity, personal bravery, success in dangerous head-hunting expeditions, his ability to organize communal activities, his knowledge of traditional customs and rituals, his decisions being just, and social conflicts kept at a minimum within his longhouse. His personal appearance and behavior were also significant. If he was a gifted leader, his community prospered and commoners would flock around him. His power both over his own community and vis-a-vis other longhouses and ethnic groups could be measured more or less by the number of commoners who stayed with him. If he was selfish and stingy, on the other hand, did not "respect his children," as the Punan Bah say, then the situation became different. Open opposition was and is out of the question in this society, where the cultural reality is such that aristocrats are considered semidivine and believed to be backed by powerful spirits. The only strategy open to dissatisfied subjects was to make themselves unavailable. By keeping out of reach, staying on their farms and in the forest over prolonged periods of time, they sent a strong message to the aristocrat. If his behavior did not change and conditions were judged intolerable, then the commoners would move. We know of cases where this happened, and the aristocrat was left utterly disgraced with but a few relatives. There are stories of aristocrats who fled the community upon such a humiliation. The commoners established new and independent longhouse communities around a commoner of standing. In the long run, he might be proven an aristocrat himself through personal achievement, the manipulation of genealogies, and dreams that revealed that he was supported by aristocratic guardian spirits, a sign that he was of proper aristocratic descent. There is ample evidence that Punan Bah society, despite an overall conception of society as hierarchically founded and ruled by a hereditary aristocracy, has operated as well by principles much more akin to a Big Man system. This is not in concordance with the established wisdom of the sociopolitical systems of the ethnic groups in Sarawak, which have been described as either egalitarian (e.g., the Iban and the nomadic Penan) or hierarchical with hereditary aristocracies (e.g., the Melanau, Kenyah, Kayan, and Kajang group), to which the Punan Bah belong.

The Brooke Raj unknowingly put an end to this flexible political structure. The Brookes governed, as the British did later and as does the current Malay-dominated government, through a system of native leaders. At the lowest level are the headmen, *tuai rumah*, who are held responsible by the administration for carrying out government regulations and for the collection of taxes. We cannot elaborate on the changes in Punan Bah society brought about by the state. It suffices to stress that the loyalty of the aristocracy toward the commoners was diverted and its dependency on these gradually weakened. A most significant factor was a regulation that forbade commoners to leave their longhouses to settle elsewhere, without the permission of the tuai rumah. The purpose of the regulation was purportedly to curb the spreading of swidden agriculture to protect the rain forest, but it upset the power balance between aristocrats and commoners by preventing the latter from fleeing poor leaders. Thus the way was paved for a petrification of the political system and corruption of the aristocracy, and cases of aristocrats who appropriated the property of their subjects are unfortunately not unheard of. During the 1980s, the gulf between aristocrats and commoners widened along with conflicts of interest in respect to the extensive logging of the rain forest in Punan Bah territory. Yet commoners rarely oppose the aristocrats openly. They are afraid, *buud*, as they say. They react as previously by evasion and passivity. Nor do they respect the leadership of those commoners, who in some instances have been appointed tuai rumah by the government. These hold no true power, they are unable to rule, it is said. To find an explanation of these phenomena, we must now look closer at the Punan Bah conception of power.

A key premise of Punan Bah understanding of power and its uneven distribution in the world is related to the concept of *etun*. Etun is perceived as an immanent and inseparable part of everything alive, a force of condensed potency. Etun is the essence that animates all beings, visible and invisible. Etun lets the eagle fly, the deer run, the fruit trees grow. The etun of spirits lend these the ability to undergo metamorphosis and change bodily form, to become visible or invisible, exert incredible strength, and move unimpeded by time and space. The more condensed the etun, the more potent its holder, a notion the Punan Bah express in metaphors of confined form. Modern technology sustains Punan Bah beliefs in such an innate extraordinary force. The satellites, telephones, and construction of wonders like the dam at Batang Ai confirm the existence of such potency, as does video. In Chinese Kung Fu films and Western science fiction they witness how persons fly through the air, possess supernatural strength, and transform themselves into various bodies and shapes. It may be pointed out to them by a visitor that this is fiction, but such a concept holds little meaning to most of them. They interpret such experiences in accordance with their concepts of potency and hierarchy.

Etun does not exist as a general, free-floating force. Ultimately it is localized, though of different strength or intensity in various categories of beings and among individuals within these. This uneven allocation lies at the foundation of the hierarchical power structure of both the society and the wider cosmological order. The way in which etun is assigned represents a divine scheme, a given not disputed. Those of potent etun hold higher rank and greater power, and defer respect accordingly. To fight beings of more potent etun than one's own is at best in vain, but more likely to bounce back on the improvident with fatal consequences. Aristocrats are thus distinct from and above commoners because they hold etun of greater potency, in much the same way as the *mana* of Polynesian chiefs sets these apart from and makes them superior to people of lower rank.

The Punan Bah conception of etun shapes their explanations of personal achievement, the accomplishment of wealth and influence, and changes in political leadership. Though localized at any one point, etun is conceived as ultimately unbound by time and space. The etun of human beings, for example, is transmitted from one generation to the next in the course of rebirth. The etun of spirits is of such potency that it can be bestowed upon other spirits or human beings. The Punan Bah believe that man is unable to stay alive and accomplish anything unless assisted by guardian spirits. Individual success in life depends on the etun, bestowed upon him or her by such spirits. The spirits hold different potency, however, and only aristocratic ones are believed to be truly powerful. They are the ones who assist and guard men and women of high rank, while commoners are aided by spirits of a more humble status. Odds do thus differ for aristocrats and commoners, and a commoner does not hold the innate potency nor can he muster the support of spirits that can make him or her successfully beat an aristocrat, it is believed.

Power then relies on etun, and only those aided by powerful guardian spirits succeed in this world. A major problem is, consequently, how to secure the benevolence of these invisible beings. Like man, spirits are unable to read the mind. What counts in dealing with them, as with fellow human beings, is behavior and presentations. Punan Bah understanding of the stuff of which relations with those of power are made comply in essence with the principle of reciprocity, the moral obligation to reciprocate a freely given gift, as formulated by Marcel Mauss in his essay on the gift (Mauss,M. 1923-24). The Punan Bah offer respect, labor, and food to those of power, be it at rituals for the spirits or in terms of political loyalty toward and material support of the aristocrats. In return they expect to be protected, assisted, and given material aid, as we have heard. The obligation of the aristocratic leaders to reciprocate is a moral plight backed by supernatural sanctions, it is believed. Commoners explain the prevalent childlessness among their aristocrats (e.g., a punishment by the ancestors). These refuse to let themselves become reborn by the aristocrats in protest of aristocratic neglect of their liabilities toward the commoners.

The decisive gift to spirits is one of blood. It is on this that spirits thrive. Having very little blood themselves, they rely on blood sacrifices, preferably human, to sustain their strength. Blood sacrifices have to be carried out regularly or the powers of the spirits dwindle, as does their ability to aid human beings. It is through an extrapolation of this conception that the Punan Bah explain the extraordinary achievements of the Europeans and the Malay politicians. As they themselves, it is believed, these people rely on potent spirits to be successful. They, too, must present their powerful guardian spirits with sacrifices before they start any major endeavor. No wonder there are penyamun around.

Conclusion

Over the last one hundred years, the period in which we can follow the Punan Bah fairly closely, their society has been transformed in many ways. Leadership is traditionally vested in the hands of an aristocracy believed to descend directly from divine ancestors, on whose powers the society claims itself utterly dependent. Commoners who became head of longhouse communities had to prove themselves to be aristocrats by manipulation of genealogies and by establishing relations with the divine aristocratic spirits (i.e., through successful head-hunting and dreams, an option not open to them today. The relation between temporal and spiritual power has been little differentiated in this society then; power was moreover symbolized as good, facts well in accordance with Southall's thesis about the symbolic representation of power in pre-state societies. State intervention and the modern way of life that literally bulldozes its way right into the heart of Punan Bah territory has changed relations between aristocrats and commoners. Yet for the Punan Bah to accept a modern secular political system is a question of giving up basic cultural premises and values. So rumors of penyamun still flourish. While these may neither be robbers nor on the outlook for human hearts, as believed by the Punan Bah, those by whom they were sent may well prove men of less than noble hearts.

References

Mauss,M.
1923-1924   *Essai sur la Don. L'année sociologique.*

Nicolaisen,I.
1986   Pride and progress: Kajang response to economic change.   *Sarawak Museum Journal* 36(57).

Southall,A.W.
1989   Religion and political economy in state and stateless societies.   In possession of author.

Tsing, A.L.
1985   Government headhunters and cosmic cuisine: Meratus stories of the state and local politics.   Presented at the American Anthropological Association meeting held 4-8 December 1985 in Washington,D.C.

The Quest for the Agent of Liberation: Mongo Beti's Fiction on Tyranny, Neocolonialism, and Liberation

Josef Gugler, Professor
University of Connecticut, United States
University of Bayreuth, Federal Republic of Germany

Established as the foremost author of anticolonial fiction in the 1950s, Mongo Beti resumed his literary oeuvre after a sixteen-year hiatus in the 1970s. The five novels to appear between 1974 and 1984 have a common theme: they denounce the postcolonial regime in an African country that is easily identified as Cameroon, his native country. Lament about the failures of independence and denunciation of the African elites now in power are common themes in African literature. Indeed they were heard as early as 1960 from so powerful a voice as Wole Soyinka, whose play *A Dance of the Forests* (1963) was written specifically for the independence celebrations of Nigeria. Mongo Beti's writing, however, is distinct in that he characterizes the postcolonial regime as a tyranny installed and maintained in power by the departing colonial power. A few other authors have described and analyzed tyrannical regimes in Africa, but Mongo Beti broke new ground in analyzing the postcolonial dispensation as a neocolonial system. (For an account of Wole Soyinka's plays exposing tyrants and pondering the lust for power and Nuruddin Farah's trilogy, "Variations on the Theme of an African Dictatorship," see Gugler 1988). While individuals are held responsible for the betrayal of the

An earlier version of this paper was presented at the African Literature Association Conference at Cornell University, Ithaca, New York, April 1987. I wish to thank Reinhard Sander for helpful comments.

hopes of the new nation, they are shown to act out the rules of political and economic arrangements inimical to the masses. Central to these arrangements is that the departing colonial power installed a puppet regime that continues to do the bidding of the French government. Mongo Beti's analysis is thus quite distinct from that of Ngugi wa Thiong'o who, in *Devil on the Cross*, also adopts a new colonial perspective, but focuses on the role of multinational corporations in Kenya. (For a comparison of the neocolonial paradigms of Mongo Beti and Ngugi wa Thiong'o, respectively, see Gugler (1986)).

Mongo Beti's description of tyranny and analysis of neocolonialism *à la francaise* shall not detain us here. Rather our interest focuses on the solutions the author offers to subvert the system he so forcefully denounces. Indeed, each of the five novels concludes on decisive action by protagonists revolted by tyranny. However, the action taken varies from one novel to the next, a fact all the more remarkable as two of the novels are presented as sequels. Here, then, we have an author exploring a great variety of responses to oppression under a neocolonial regime.

Perpétue et l'habitude du malheur (Beti 1974) is the story of an inquest. Essola, imprisoned for his involvement in a radical nationalist movement, learns of the death of his younger sister Perpétue. He renounces the movement, is released, and sets out to reconstruct Perpétue's life from her school days, to her marriage, to her death. Imprisoned just before independence, he finds, six years later, that his country's independence has been betrayed. The French have installed a puppet regime, a regime that furthers French economic interests in the ex-colony and represses all forms of opposition. Essola learns that Perpétue was forced to abandon school and to marry against her will by their mother intent on a large dowry.

She had been ill-treated by her husband, the local party tyrant. In her third pregnancy she had lacked medical care, had given up the will to live, and had died after a vain appeal to their brother for help. The tragedy of the betrayal of the independence of Cameroon is paralleled by the tragedy of the sufferings and death of Perpétue. All are guilty in these tragedies, not least Essola whose single-minded commitment to the revolutionary cause deprived his sister of his protection. (For a sensitive discussion of the tragic character that distinguishes this novel from Beti's other works, see Mouralis (1984, 495-517)).

Essola deliberately sets out to avenge the sufferings and death of his younger sister. He cruelly kills his brother, and through the death of her favorite son, hurts their mother. When she curses him as a parricide, he responds:

> Comme toi, mère dénaturée. En vendant Perpétue à son bourreau, tu l'as bien livrée au supplice, toi. Et quand Perpétue a été au plus mal, tu ne l'as pas ignoré, tu ne pouvais pas l'ignorer, puisque ton Martin avait été témoin de son agonie. Veux-tu que je te dise les dernières paroles de Perpétue? les voice - elles étaient adresses à ton Martin: "Martin, tu es mon frere; emmène-moi auprès de notre mère. Ne me laisse pas assassiner par mon mari, ce monstre." Et sais-tu ce que ton Martin a repondu à sa soeur? "Je ne mettrai pas le doigt entre l'écorce et l'arbre." Oui, je suis un parricide, mais un parricide comme toi. (*Perpétue*, 294)

Perpétue then presents us with the classic tragedy of family retribution for family injustice. But Essola expressly establishes the relationship between such family injustice and an unjust society, taking the elimination of Ruben Um Nyobe, the radical leader in the struggle for independence, as the decisive event marking Cameroonian society as a society of the unjust:

> Tu n'es que ma mère. Ruben était, lui, un homme juste. Quelle vénération ses assassins ont-ils eue pour Ruben? Quand un peuple accepte le lâche assassinat de son seul

juste, quelle vénération desormais les mères attendront-
elles de leurs fils, les pères de leurs filles, les maîtres de
leurs valets, les chefs de leurs subordonnés? Vous avez
tué Ruben ou bien vous vous êtes accommodés de son
meurtre pour continuer à vendre vos filles, sans pour
autant avoir à répondre des souffrances infligées à ces
esclaves par la cruauté de leurs maris. Vous avez
assassiné Ruben ou bien vous vous êtes accommodés de
ce crime pour que vos fils préférés, rendus irresponsables
par votre excessive indulgence, continuent à festoyer
impunément avec la rançon de leurs soeurs, à se repaître
en quelque sorte du sang de ces malheureuses, comme
des cannibales. Vous avez souhaité la mort de Ruben
pour bannir la Justice et évite qu'elle porte le fer dans
l'épaisse routine de vos moeurs sauvages. Quelle
importance désormais si l'on extermine dix, cent ou mille
d'entre nous. Maudits, oui, nous le sommes tous depuis
ce 13 september 1958 où le seul Juste de Sodomeet
Gomorrhe est tombé au coin d'un obscur fourré sous les
balles de vils mercenaires (*Perpétue*, 294-295).

Mongo Beti purports to show how oppression permeates
throughout society even into the most intimate family relationships.
(Nuruddin Farah (1981), in a similar manner, relates family tyranny
to political tyranny in his trilogy on tyranny in Somalia; the
oppression of women is central to the middle volume, *Sardines*, as
it is to *Perpétue*). It doesn't matter how many are eliminated among
us: we are all guilty, the only just has fallen. The Christian mea
culpa surprises from Mongo Beti, or from his militant revolutionary
protagonist for that matter. And in fact Essola perceives the injustice
and dispenses justice. The difficulty with the solution proposed in
Perpétue, then, does not lie at this religio-philosophical level, but
arises from the severe constraints on such retributive justice effected
at the family level. Essola is prepared to go to prison but escapes
persecution under rather fortuitous circumstances. If many perceive
injustice, how many are prepared to administer justice on their own
and bear the consequences? And, furthermore, how will the

elimination of injustice in interpersonal relationships translate into chasing neocolonialism and its puppets from Cameroon?

Remember Ruben, the first volume in the Ruben sequence, was published like *Perpétue* in 1974. But while *Perpétue* calls for individual awareness and action to establish justice in interpersonal relationships, the solutions proposed in the Ruben sequence revolve around collective action to free Cameroon from neocolonialism and its puppets. Having told how the French violently repressed the labor movement, manipulated the elections, prohibited the opposition party in 1955, and installed a puppet government that was to be handed independence in 1960, *Remember Ruben* explores the urban insurrection strategy. An underground movement establishes itself in Kola-Kola, the largest African township of the nation's capital and major port, Fort Nègre as Mongo Beti calls it (i.e., Douala). Tracts are distributed, and contributions are collected. Politicized youngsters audaciously confront the police. They gain control of the streets, burn down the two police stations, and force the police to abandon the township. The parallels to the urban insurrectionary tactics that led to the overthrow of the Somoza regime in Nicaragua in 1970 and that have become prominent in the resistance to the racist regime in South Africa since 1984 are striking. For the argument that, in contemporary revolutions, the urban confrontation is determinant, see Gugler ([1982] 1989). When a large police contingent attempts to secretly invest the township at night, it is put to flight. But such victories are ephemeral. Kola-Kola cannot confront the combined might of the Cameroonian state and the French government that stands behind it. "*Kola-Kola est telle une patrouille qui s'est aventurée trop loin du gros de la troupe, et dont la position a été revelée a l'ennemi*" (*Remember Ruben*, 305).

The urban resistance movement is exposed and vulnerable, the future lies, according to the Ruben sequence, with the rural guerilla. Throughout *Remember Ruben* there are repeated references to the rural guerilla war, led by Ruben Um Nyobe, that indeed confronted first the colonial regime, then its neocolonial successor in Cameroon for over a decade. The sequel, *La Ruine presque cocasse d'un polichinelle* (*Remember Ruben 2*), appeared in book form in 1979. It is the story of the liberation of Ekoumdoum, a small, quite isolated town, far from Fort-Nègre, the liberation from the chief, imposed by the French, who tyrannizes his subjects, just as did the country's president imposed by the French.

On the very day of independence, as guerillas attack the crowd at the presidential palace, the police headquarters, and the airport, three Rubenists set out to liberate Ekoumdoum. Their long trek is arduous, a Cameroonian version of the Long March. Its high point comes when they arrive in a village being terrorized by four policemen, and they lead the young men in getting rid of the police. After a long series of exploits and misadventures, the three protagonists eventually liberate Ekoumdoum from the corrupt chief imposed by the colonial administration, his tyrannical son, and a scheming missionary. The women of the town play a decisive role in the victorious struggle against physical and ideological oppression. This emphasis on the revolutionary potential of women, the most oppressed, is reminiscent of Ousmane Sembene's *Les Bouts de bois de Dieu.*

In contrast to the somber tone that characterizes both the tragedy of *Perpétue* and the epic drama of Remember Ruben, humor erupts time and again in *La Ruine*: the liberation movement is on the march, claiming its first victory, however small. At the same time,

La Ruine pursues reflections on guerrilla tactics already begun in the closing days of *Remember Ruben*: How to raise the consciousness of the masses? How to direct the anger of the masses? How to confront the enemy? What revolutionary justice in victory? *La Ruine* eventually opts for an integrative stance that forgoes retribution.

The liberation of Ekoumdoum is a small and precarious victory. The Rubenist leader advocates prudence, but the elimination of the chief is bound to come to the attention of the authorities. If prudence can channel their reactions, it is difficult to see how such a liberation can spread through the countryside without provoking a crushing response from the overwhelming repressive apparatus at the service of the state.

The Ruben sequence takes the long view. *Remember Ruben* ends with the guerilla leader's assessment:

> Surtout pas de précipitation, les gars. Prenez tout votre temps, faites soigneusement les chose, ne vous souciez pas des délais, le temps ne compte pas pour nous. L'Afrique est dans les chaînes pour ainsi dire depuis l'éternité, nous la libérons toujours assez tôt. Notre combat sera long, trés long. Tout ce que vous voyez en ce moment dans Kola-Kola et dans toute la Colonie n'est qu'un prélude puéril. D'ici quelques années, quelques mois peut-etre, et même aprés la prochaine destruction de Kola-Kola au cours de laquelle pourtant seront immolés des milliers et des milliers des nôtres, y compris des femmes et des engants, il se trouvera des gens pour sourire au souvenir de ces préliminaires brouillons; ainsi fait-on en songeant aux jeux innocents de l'enfance (*Remember Ruben*, 312-313).

And the narrator concludes his story in *La Ruine*:

> C'est ainsi que cela a commencé, mais nous autres nous ne l'avons su que plus tard, beaucoup plus tard. Car, en dépit des apparence, c'est ici que commence véritablement cette histoire, drame aux mille

retournements, visage de femme ruisselant tantôt de
larmes commela cascade melodieuse, tantot de rires de
rires comme un ciel ensoleillé, écho retentissantun jour
de salves, un autre de chants, destin de notre peuple
voué aux déclins répétés, mais se réveillant tourjours, se
redressant quand même chaque fois. . . . (*La Ruine*,
313).

*Les Deux méres de Guillaume Ismaël Dzewatama, future
camionneur* appeared in book form in 1983. It provides a detailed
account of the mechanisms employed to co-opt those trained abroad
to serve, on their return, the neocolonial regime characterized by
corruption and repression. If the memory of Ruben Um Nyobe, the
leader of the radical opposition to the colonial regime, situated the
three earlier novels in Cameroon, there is no longer such a direct
reference. But the account certainly fits this particular country, even
to the point that one commentator recognized a real life figure in the
character of an execrable French advisor to the president (Bjornson
1987, 17).

Guillaume Ismaël's father, former head of the militant student
organization in France, is the prime example of the radical critic co-
opted to the point of signing the death sentences for political
opponents of the regime.   Eventually, however, he becomes
disaffected and joins a group of intellectuals and young officers in a
coup attempt. Singularly inept, it fails. In any case, as a historian
points out: "*on ne peut faire une révolution simplement par
ésprit de vengeance*" (*Les Deux méres*, 197).

La Revance de Guillaume Ismaël Dzewatama, sequel to
Les Deux méres, and the last novel of Mongo Beti published to date,
appeared in book form in 1984. After the arrest of her husband, the
French stepmother of Guillaume visits his home village and initiates
an effort to bring basic amenities to it. Deprived of any access to her

husband, sexually assaulted in secret service offices by French officials, she agrees to return to France to mobilize public opinion there. On a farewell visit to her husband's village she discovers that the old men have been co-opted by the regime and that the cause of her imprisoned husband is supported only by the women led by his mother.

This last volume, then, focuses on the task of mobilizing public opinion in France, a task that has been accomplished to support those opposing regimes behind the iron curtain, others oppressed by Latin American dictatorships, but that reveals itself uniquely difficult when it comes to francophone Africa. The French government that cooperates with African tyrannies--more, that has installed them and maintains them in power--spies on their opponents in France, subverts their meetings, infiltrates humanitarian organizations such as Amnesty International, and persecutes the most prominent opponents (here we hear faint echoes of the very serious difficulties Mongo Beti himself has experienced in France): Guillaume who had come with his stepmother to France is forced to return to Cameroon.

Remember Ruben is preceded by what starts out as the customary disclaimer to turn into a sarcastic commentary:

> Toute ressemblance avec des événements passés, des personnage réels ou des contrées connues, est totalement illusoire et, en quelque sorte, doit être considérée comme regrettable (*Remember Ruben*, 6).

At the end of *Les deux méres*, the author explores the possibility of presenting the entire story as just an unfortunate nightmare, but decides otherwise:

> Le lecteur qui aime les histoires heureuses serait rassuré; le militant qui réclame la vérité sans fard se prendrait tout à coup a rêver, oubliant quelques instants son gout de la littérature engagée. Mais l'auteur a préféré, comme à l'accoutumée, dédaigner les sentiers riants,

mais sémés de remords, de la réussite ainsi que les plaisirs frélates de la démagogie littéraire. Il assure donc que ce recit n'est nullement un mauvais songe, que c'est bien réellement ainsi que tout cela est arrivé (*Les Deux méres*, 200).

For the ending of *La Revanche*, however, Mongo Beti chooses the opposite strategy. Guillaume has returned to Cameroon and become a soccer star. His skills and those of other players in the rebellious African township of the capital are needed to assure that Cameroon will again win the African championship. They make their collaboration conditional on the release of all political prisoners. And the reader is forewarned:

Et voici le tournant de cette chronique jusqu'ici bien modeste, trés banale. Voici l'instant où elle bascule dans l'inimaginable, le fabuleux (*La Revanche*, 224).

La Revanche, then, has a happy ending, Guillaume Ismaël has taken his revenge, his father and the other political prisoners have been released, his stepmother has returned to Cameroon. The political leverage of soccer players is explored in *Perpétue* as well, but in a less optimistic fashion. After a series of defeats at the Pan-African Games, a soccer star who may have induced the team to undiscipline and irresponsibility is accused of opposing the regime and belonging to the underground movement, tortured, and executed in his home village. The glimpse we are given of the workings of the neocolonial regime leaves us in no doubt, however, that if this is the end of the story, it is not the end of the regime. The tyrant acted on the advice of the French ambassador. Refusing the demands of the soccer players and losing the championship quite possibly would have led to public disturbances. To repress the popular reaction would have entailed casualties likely to be reported in the French press now that public opinion in the metropole has been sensitized by the efforts of

Guillaume's stepmother and a Cameroonian opponent in France. But the meeting ended with the French ambassador assuring a French official of increased funding for the secret services--in Cameroon.

Both the *Remember Ruben* and the *Guillaume Ismaël* sequel end in upbeat fashion. But the liberation of Ekoumdoum is precarious, and it is difficult to see how its experience could be expanded throughout the countryside under the noses of a powerful and alert regime. And the revenge of Guillaume belongs in the realm of the happy ending. And, indeed, how could it be otherwise, given the longevity of tyrannical regimes virtually always assured of support from foreign powers? Mobutu has been solidly installed in Zaïre for over two decades. Siad Barre has run Somalia as his personal chief for nearly as long, finding ready United States of America sponsorship once his Soviet supporters had deserted him. How could Mongo Beti offer us a realistic solution to the problems of neocolonialism and tyranny when the successor regimes often turn out little different from their predecessors? As has indeed been the case in Cameroon after the change in leadership in 1983.

Mongo Beti has no more a ready solution to the common African predicaments than anybody else. There is no blueprint for the revolution he judges necessary. Rather, all possible options have to be pursued in the struggle for liberation. Indeed, a ready-made solution would solve little. A systematic problem requires a systematic solution that must arise out of a transformation of consciousness. It has to be transformed to perceive injustice and to react to oppression in both interpersonal relationships and the political system. To transform consciousness is precisely the task Mongo Beti is working at: in his widely acclaimed fiction, but also in the political essay; *Main basse sur le Cameroun: autopsie d'une décolonisation* was sufficiently powerful for the French government to resort to illegal measures to repress it (for a succinct account of the affair, see Mouralis (1981, 73)), and the literary political journal *Peuples noirs-, Peuples africains* he established in 1976 and has edited since. Mongo Beti, while making his living as a *professeur de lycée*, while harassed by the French authorities, has undertaken these enormous efforts to transform consciousness in Africa and also in France, whose public opinion, according to his analysis, affects the state of affairs in the neocolonies. And indeed, the pen of a writer as distinguished as Mongo Beti, unlike Don Quichote's lance, changes the world because it changes the way we look at the world.

References

Beti,M. (A.Biyidi)

1972   *Main basse sur le Cameroun: autopsie d'une décolonisation.* Paris: François Maspero. *Petite collection Maspero,* 2d rev. ed. Paris: François Maspero, 1977.

1974   *Perpétue et l'habitude du malheur.* Paris: Editions Buchet/Chastel.

1974   *Remember Ruben.* Paris: Union Générale d'Editions.

1978   *Perpetua and the habit of unhappiness,* translated by J.Reed and C.Wake (African Writers Series 181). London: Heinemann.

1979   *Remember Ruben,* translated by G.Moore. London; Nairobi: Heinemann (African Writers Series 214). Ibadian: New Horn Press, 1980; Washington,D.C.: Three Continents Press, 1980.

1979   *La Ruine presque cocasse d'un polichinelle (Remember Ruben 2).* Paris: Editions des Peuples Noirs. (Serialized in *Peuples noirs - Peuples africains* between 1978 and 1979).

1982   Quotations from reissue of *Remember Ruben.* Paris: Editions L'Harmattan (Collection encre noires).

1983   *Les Deux méres de Guillaume Ismaël Dzewatama, futur camionneur.* Paris: Editions Buchet/Chastel.(Serialized in *Peuples noirs - Peuples africains* in the 1980s).

1984   *La Revanche de Guillaume Ismaël Dzewatama.* Paris: Editions Buchet/Chastel. (Serialized in *Peuples noir - Peuples africains* in the 1980s).

1985   *Lament for an Africain Pol (La Ruine presque cocasse d'un polichinelle (Remember Ruben 2)),* translated by Richard Bjornson. Washington,D.C.: Three Continents Press.

Bjornson,R.

1987   The concept of neocolonialism in the late works of Mongo Beti. Script.

Farah,N.

1981   *Sardines: A novel.* London: Allison & Busby.

Gugler,J.

[1982]1989   The urban character of contemporary revolutions.

226

Studies in comparative international development 17(2), 60-73. Reprinted revised in *The urbanization of the Third World*, edited by J.Gugler, 388-412. Oxford; New York: Oxford University Press.

1986   Not Yet Uhuru: Ngugi wa Thiong'o and Mongo Beti. Paper presented at the African Literature Association Conference, Michigan State University, East Lansing, April.

1988   African literary comment on dictators: Wole Soyinka's plays and Nuruddin Farah's novels. *The journal of modern African studies* 26:171-177.

Mouralis,B.

1981   *L'Oeuvre de Mongo Beti*, comprendre. Issy les Moulineaux: Les classiques africains.

1984   *Littérature et développement: essai sur le statut, la fonction et la représentation de la littérature négro-africaine d'expression française.* Paris: Silex.

Sembéne,O.

1960   *Les bouts de bois de dieu: Banty mam yall.* Paris: Le Livre Contemporain.

1970   *God's bits of wood (Les bouts de bois de dieu)*, translated by F.Price. London: Heinemann (African Writers Series 63), and New York: Doubleday.

Soyinka,W.

1963   *A dance of the forests.* Oxford: Oxford University Press.

Dissent in the Empire: Serfs, Peasants, And Lords in the Upper Black Forest

Hermine G. De Soto, Assistant Scientist
University of Wisconsin-Madison, United States

In 1725, when the abbot of the monastery of St. Blasien ordered the peasant village masters to sign their village units over to the monastic Upper Jurisdiction Right, one master called for resistance and refused to sign. At that moment a rebellious situation arose in the Upper Black Forest. Was the resistance of the one master also a moment of historical consciousness?

The questions of why, when, and how peasants resist, protest, or rebel, and whether such practices can be considered political factors in social change, have been given diverse degrees of attention by various scholars. Shanin (1966), Wolf (1969), Blok (1972), and Hobsbawm (1979), for example, generally seem to agree that peasants' protests and rebellions do not entail demands for structural changes; instead, they only call for reforms in social justice. However, according to Tanabe, while peasants' demands might encompass "retrospective aspects," "...peasants often pursue old values which were outwardly 'reactionary' but were to be converted into a tactical weapon by, and in course of, the protest movements themselves" (1984, 88). A point of apparent agreement among these authors is that such movements implicitly suggest a period of time in which social tensions and existential uncertainties have increased due to structural changes; for example, particular relations of production may be in a period of transformation. Another important point in this analysis is whether peasants' protests and rebellion are "political" or "prepolitical" actions.

For Hobsbawm, social banditry, as "a phenomenon of social protest and rebellion" is a prepolitical action limited to the social structure of a specific locality (1974, 14). This social protest, writes Hobsbawm, is based on an "ambiguous position" because the protesters lack an ideological platform, or stated differently, they lack a class consciousness "for itself." In contrast to Hobsbawm, Blok argues that banditry is a phenomenon consisting of "various links that tie the peasant community to the larger society" (1972, 496). He emphasizes that when conceptualizing social banditry in a wider societal context, the "ambiguous position" might be explained "as an element of class conflict" (1972, 495). This position opens up a new dimension in the analysis of peasant uprisings, to include the whole structure of society, not just local concerns.

How peasants contest hegemonic elites, and what forms of ideological practices they might create, calls for a reexamination of the classical theorem of the formation of consciousness from a "class-in-itself" to a "class-for-itself."

To limit ourselves to these classical concepts of class consciousness *an sich* or *für sich*, does not allow us to recognize, as Kulluk (1985) maintains, the resulting changing power relations "among and within classes, status groups and the state," in the process of "tactical mobility."

If we continue to search for the existence of a "true" class consciousness, and then conclude on the basis of this "found" *Klassenbewusstsein* whether or not people are politically engaged, we might not only miss the fact that the contradictory social forces leading to the formation of political practices are a continuous movement in history, but we will also miss the fact that peasant and community struggles entail a call for a social transformation that often includes outcries for abolition of diverse forms of "extra-class" oppressions such as racism and patriarchy. For instance, E. P. Thompson suggests that peasants' ideological practices in a preindustrial state develop a class consciousness through the "cultural content of social life." Tanabe, elaborating on this point, writes,

> the class consciousness of peasants can be formed historically only through their ideological practices which are directed, consciously or unconsciously, towards a conflict of interests and values between classes based on existing primordial loyalties in a society. This historical and sociological process is structurally linked to ideological practices carried out within the cultural context, where battles are taking place over ritual symbols, value systems and ideas (1984, 85).

He links this formulation to Gramsci's concept of counterhegemony, stressing that the ideological practice in peasant rebellions entails political, economic, cultural, and moral elements that are critically and creatively reinterpreted during such movements (1984, 88, 103).

While Thompson and Tanabe point to the formation of ideological practices within class societies, we need also to address the problem of differentiation within classes, since on the practice level this factor of differentiation often determines how potential alliances and counteralliances are formed and re-formed in political movements.

Wolf (1962) points to such fluid practices when he writes

> If we now follow out the hypothesis that it is middle peasants and poor but "free" peasants, not constrained by any power domain, which constitute the pivotal groupings, then it follows that any factor which serves to increase the latitude granted by that *tactical mobility* (my emphasis) reinforces their revolutionary potential (1962, 292-293).

Wolf's hypothesis seems to point toward class factions that are being formed in peasant uprisings, and toward social strata within a class which organize and mobilize themselves into political forces. These factions and strata may contest either for the reconstruction of a dominant hegemony, or the creation of a counterhegemony.

Continuing in this debate, Stoler recently emphasized the interrelationship of structural, and human forces, which we have to understand in the social reality of the "making of the revolution." For Stoler, "we must appreciate the local relations under which people labor as much as the political context in which they fight" (1988, 227). We may add here that dual forms of "tactical" reorganizations are occurring on the level of dominating classes and the level of subaltern classes. This duality has been stressed by Kulluk (1985), who writes that a dominant strata will contest for the reproduction of its oppressive forces, which will simultaneously serve the interests of dominant classes (or social strata) for creating solidarity "for the sake of their extra class interests, such as control over women's sexuality/fertility or the psychological rewards of being the Master Race" (Kulluk 1985, 221). It is this dual aspect--the contradictory relationship between the dominant and nondominant classes--which becomes a vital force in the political organization in community struggles.

Peasants use everyday forms of life culture (Silverman 1979, 64), such as religion, regional dialects, history, and customary village gatherings, for forming an ideological practice culminating in a rebellion in which they combine cultural, moral, political, and economic elements in relationship and in response to domination. I argue that a peasant culture carries the potential for development of either a nonautonomous or an autonomous consciousness. In the first process, a peasant culture can feed the ideology of the hegemonic classes; in the latter development, peasants can form and participate in counterhegemonic movements. In such political actions peasants do not feed the ideology of the ruling classes; instead, they challenge hegemonic powers. An abbreviated case study of a continuous peasant struggle in the Upper Black Forest illustrates the above proposition.

Structural conditions of the classes

The geographical region of the Black Forest was and still is an agro-ecological marginal location. It is currently in the Federal Republic of Germany. During the Salpeter movement of 1725, this region was part of the Austrian Empire and formed a state similar to what Michael Adas calls a "contest state."

> Central to this form of political organization is rule by a king or emperor who claims a monopoly of power and authority in a given society but whose effective control is in reality severely restricted by rival power centers among the elite.... There was a constant struggle between the ruler and his nobility, between factions of the elite at various levels, and between supravillage elite groups and village notables and peasants for the control of labor and the agricultural production which formed the basis of these predominantly agrarian states (Adas 1981, 218).

The essential relationships among the Hapsburgian rule, the monastery, and the peasants of the Upper Black Forest consisted of the feudal principle of binding the peasants to the land, which was the major force of production. As direct producers, the peasants owned their means of production needed for reproducing themselves, and rent extraction was enforced through a noneconomic compulsion, which was embedded in and institutionalized through a jurisdictional power, a power expressed in the Upper Black Forest, in the ownership of High and Low Jurisdiction Rights. The High Right over the Upper Black Forest was owned by the Austrian ruler, while the Low Right was held by the monastery. The owner of the High Right had the power to control the jurisdiction of the law-enforcing system, which included taxation and high crimes, while the Low Right held by the monastery settled local disputes such as petty quarrels, thefts, verbal insults, or fights that caused minor damages or injuries.

Between the local domination and the central power was the so-called Amt or Office. The Office, represented by the forest magistrate, or state officer, was seated in the *Ackerbürgerstadt* of Waldshut, where a first appeal would be made. The next stage of appeal would be made in the town of Freiburg, the third stage in the Upper Austrian city of Innsbruck, and the final stage of appeal would be made in the imperial metropolis of Vienna. The Office on the one hand was the enforcing and controlling organ of the central and territorial state power; on the other hand, it supported the local secular lords in case of failure of the local legal domination.

Both Rights could be sold, lent, or pledged by the owners, and either power could in theory or practice own both Rights. Owning both Rights translated concretely into increased power to enhance financial gains, hence the hegemonic elites often contested for these Rights. In 1655 Emperor Joseph I was short of money to pay his debts from the Spanish War of Succession. This caused him to pledge his ownership of the High Jurisdiction Right to the abbot of St. Blasien, who anxiously had awaited such an opportunity (Haselier 1973, 43-45).

Although the cloister owned both Rights then, the emperor remained the territorial sovereign. However, St. Blasien, with its enhanced legal power, began to level the status of the peasants in the units in order to extract additional serfdom labor. Until then there were peasants with hereditary land tenure subjected to the territorial ruler, and there were those who were under serfdom and subjugated to the monastic ban-and-command right. Whereas the former peasants had to pay rent in kind and in money, the latter peasants had to pay rent and additionally had to perform feudal services as subjects of the manor.

The changing ownership of the High Right from the Hapsburgian emperor to the local monastery meant not only a change of status for the peasants, it also meant the loss of the Hapsburgian long-time guarantee of village government. The Upper Black Forest consisted of eight units. Each unit comprised ten to eighteen villages, and each unit had a main village and a main parish. Each unit had a unitmaster who was annually elected on St. Georgi day (April 23) by married men under open sky settings. The eight masters formed a *collegium* called the *Achtmann* or Eightmen. The Eightmen, with their predecessors of the previous year, elected a *Redmann* or Speaker as the representative of the Eightmen (Haselier 1973, 30).

This village government formed the basis for identity and solidarity among the peasants, and it was important as a political and economical force with a code of order governed by the peasants. The elected representatives of the peasants participated in rent bargaining with the local state officials, mediated external rent demands to comply with the productive realities of the village, and collected the rent together with the state officials. Furthermore, they advised the forest magistrate in legal disputes. When ending their annual services, the departing masters and the newly elected ones had to call a meeting in which the vacating masters reported the annual accounts to the new masters. Then each departing master was obliged to give the same account to villages in his unit (Haselier 1973, 30-34).

Bringing all peasants of the Upper Black Forest under the leveling monastic jurisdiction meant that all peasants could be called upon for serfdom labor, and that their local peasant organization would lose its relatively autonomous rights guaranteeing participation in the secular and nonsecular power relations. In 1705 those representatives of the peasants who rejected the monastic policies traveled to Vienna to try to influence the emperor to redeem the pledge of the Upper Jurisdiction Right, but they failed. After that failure, the mistrust and anger about the cloister's *de jure* embodiment culminated in 1725 in the tense situation in which the abbot called upon the masters to sign their units over to the monastic Upper Jurisdiction Right and one master called for resistance and refused to sign. With Hans Salpeter's resistant act, he became the peasants' "Robin Hood."

Salpeter's resistance

This village master was known in the locality as Hans Salpeter. He was not a full-time peasant, but, primarily, a collector of saltpeter (potassium nitrate), which was collected from either rock salt or, more common at the time, from stables and manure piles where nitrogen developed in the decomposition process. His collection routes took him across village boundaries, so Salpeter's social relationships extended not only to the immediate vicinity but to the entire southern region of the forest.

Salpeter's biographical sketch seems at variance with Hobsbawm's type of bandit or rebel, who emerges usually from the ranks of young, unmarried, and unemployed men lacking in skill and education (Hobsbawm 1974, 151-153). Salpeter's piety and pilgrimages as a married man, combined with his intelligence and wisdom, earned him wide respect among the peasants. During the seventy years of his life he had taught himself to read and write, which was unusual among the rural people of that time. Furthermore, the peasants of his village had elected him as their village master (Lehner 1977, 31-41). Salpeter exemplified an organic intellectual whose consciousness was based not only on literacy but also on what Tanabe, and E. P. Thompson, called "the cultural content of social life" (Turton and Tanabe 1984, 85).

After his refusal to sign the contract, Salpeter traveled to the villages of the units and gave public speeches. Salpeter's power of speech was based on the native dialects, in which he attacked the renegade village masters and the monastic contract. He told the peasants that the monastery had no right to call the villagers for serfdom duties since the peasant rights of village self-government were based on nonserfdom status and had been guaranteed 300 years ago in a letter signed by a Hapsburgian duke. As he recalled the contents of this letter in his speeches, Salpeter used religious, symbolic, and moral elements familiar to the peasants from their everyday life. He told them, "God creates humans in His own image. He created mankind and redeemed everyone through His martyr. His love was indistinguishable for the poor and the rich. It is incomprehensible to my senses that someone should be the property of someone else" (Lehner 1977, 16).

Salpeter transformed an already experienced struggle. By verbally attacking the local elites, he engaged in an ideological practice which he expressed and explained to the peasants in a familiar cultural discourse. This in turn helped the peasants to become convinced about their resistance. In other words, Salpeter was instrumental in supporting the peasants to express their autonomous consciousness, a consciousness that developed into a counterhegemonic movement in which economic, moral, and common cultural elements were geared toward larger social goals ready to confront the power relationships of the contest state (De Soto and Valdez 1986, 9-12). Salpeter's actions as the peasants' "Robin Hood" cannot be explained, as Hobsbawn (1974, 15) has suggested, as "prepolitical." Rather, Salpeter's ideological practice--when conceptualized in the larger context and in relation to the power aspirations of the prevailing feudal class--prodded the peasants to react politically against the mistreatment.

Convinced by Salpeter's action and speeches, the peasants, infuriated about previous oppressive modes by the local state and monastic nobility, gave full support to the resistance. In the meantime, Salpeter traveled to Vienna to consult with the monarch about the peasants' grievances.

Arriving in the city, the monarchical staff refused him admittance, and he was forced to return home. Upon his return to the district's capital, at the end of 1725, he was asked to participate in a meeting arranged by the forest's magistrate; however, upon his arrival he was arrested as a rebel.

As soon as news of this arrest reached the peasants, they counterattacked not only by questioning the renegade peasant leaders (i.e., the village masters) but also by removing them from office and calling for new elections. In spite of the feudalistic power strategy of Salpeter's arrest, the peasants proceeded with an election that resulted in a victory for the Salpeter followers. Hans Salpeter was again elected, in absentia, but he never returned to his village; he died one year later in jail (Lehner 1977; Haselier 1973; Müller-Ettikon 1979).

The continuation without "Robin Hood"

It was planned in the spring of 1727 that the new abbot would visit the units and call for the performance of a public ritual during which the peasants would be asked to swear the symbolic oath of homage. The peasants refused to appear, insisting that they could only swear the oath of homage to the emperor. The historical and sociological process of the resistance was structurally linked here to "the ideological practices carried out within the cultural context, where battles were taking place over ritual symbols. . ." (Turton and Tanabe 1984, 85). They also found unacceptable the terminology of the oath, which granted ownership over body and will to the abbot. When the state forest magistrate ordered the peasants to swear the oath, the peasant struggle widened to include the renegade masters, the monastic, and the state local lords (Haselier 1973, 46-48).

All parties hoped for a favorable intervention from Vienna, but when Vienna interceded, it sent a royal commission supported by 1,000 state soldiers, forcing the insufficiently armed peasants to pay the feudal oath of homage. The imperial staff, fearful of a counterattack by the peasants in response to the use of force, called for a legal investigation in which both the peasants and St. Blasien could state their grievances.

The peasants, employing a Swiss lawyer, worked out a list of complaints against the monastery, taking advantage of the legal discourse to express their rejections, refusals, and petitions. Some of their complaints were refusal of ownership rights, denial of swearing an oath, contesting increases in rent, and taking as serfs the children of nonserf women. Additionally, the peasants protested paying a marriage rent when a serf married a nonserf. They rejected a tenfold increase of general rent, and the increase in the number of chickens they must donate annually to the carnival. They refused paying rent for moving to other units, and they contested paying higher taxes for using village roads. They also fought against the prohibition of dividing their plots, and they fought the rent for marriage, and paying a salary for excess visits of the monastic rent collector. The peasants refused to pay increased interest rates for monastic loans given to the parishes, and they opposed the despotic manners employed during compulsory sales and the exchanging of serfs with other regions. They petitioned to keep their elections, and they pleaded for more humane conditions during feudal services. Finally, they rejected the use of all categories expressing ownership of their bodies (Haselier 1973, 48-49); Müller-Ettikon 1979, 16-212).

When the monastery reviewed the grievances, it first achieved, through an appeal to Vienna, a dismissal of the Swiss lawyer. Then the cloister's legal staff presented its list of counterdemands. Peasant elections would be approved only when the cloister chose the masters and upcoming elections would be postponed for six years. The forest magistrate would have the right to keep the most loyal masters in service longer than a year. The bargaining power for setting rent payments would be shifted from the masters to the magistrate. All songs of protest and other verbal insults would be punished with a half year of forced labor. A police force of 50 to 100 men would be created for the magistrate, and the right of appeal of judgment through peasants' rights would be nullified. The magistrates would be released from the oath of granting the peasants their customary rights. The loyal speaker and loyal masters, together with state officials, would record all behavior of unmarried male peasants so that oppositional behavior could be ascertained early.

In order to instill obedience to the abbot, the monastery advised that the emperor should elevate the abbot's title to "Upper Austrian Imperial Secret Adviser." They commanded further that the magistrate work with an informant familiar with the indigenous peasant culture. St. Blasien required that the mayor's and the magistrate's offices should be united lest some burghers might conspire with the peasants. Finally, the villages were forbidden to take in transient Lumpencountrymen because their unpredictable behavior might turn in favor of the peasants.

The royal court, after investigating and reviewing the legal sets of policies, generally concurred with the monastic policies. Vienna's only refusal was to promote the abbot to an Austrian Imperial Adviser, in anticipation of keeping his power aspirations localized.

Following the legal procedures, all nine leading rebels were punished. The sentences included eternal banishment combined with forced labor in Hungary; lashing and a five-year banishment with forced labor in Belgrade and eternal expulsion from the Black Forest; three years of forced labor in the Black Forest with renouncement of all rights for election participation; and five sentences of forced labor in the region. In the end, those villagers proven to have shown varying degrees of support for the movement had to pay differing amounts of all the legal expenses (Haselier 1973, 43-45); Müller-Ettikon 1979, 95-194).

Conclusion

I have argued that the Salpeter rebel was an organic intellectual who was instrumental in forming a movement directed against the producers of hegemony of the contest state.

For Salpeter the marginal location of the Upper Black Forest vitally assisted his assuming leadership of a resistance movement (because the major political power was located externally, in Vienna). Additionally, the relatively autonomous organizational structure of the village-based units was an important basis for the fast growing peasant solidarity. Salpeter, as a well-known and accepted village leader, was culturally sensitized and thus able to consolidate the cultural consciousness of the peasants at the critical moment of transfers of ownership rights among the elites.

In his ideological practice, he used familiar cultural and symbolic elements such as language, religion, regional history, and morals in order to transform an already experienced struggle of the peasants. In Gramsci's terms, Salpeter helped to alter the "common sense culture" or popular knowledge into an autonomous consciousness. This in turn gave rise to the counterhegemonic rebellion in which the peasants resynthesized the previous mistreatments and anger into a political consciousness, which found its final expression in a legal discourse. In this counteraction, the peasants not only refused increasing economic demands; they also rejected political, moral, and symbolic oppressions prior to and during their resistance.

With that they confronted the sacred and the secular elites who in turn ordered severe countermeasures against the peasants. These new orders were unacceptable for the Salpeter followers. In 1730, 1743-1744, and in 1750 they formed new counterhegemonies.

These struggles continue even today, within current global capitalistic relationships rather than the feudalistic. Twelve years ago--in 1977--two Salpeterists wrote the following:

> We want to continue our tradition of resistance because today there are many reasons for it. We have to protest against the senseless destruction of the forest through the construction of reservoirs. We protest against bureaucratically introduced settlement policies which will destroy our dialect and the old village names. We protest against the bureaucratic reform introduced from Stuttgart planning a systematic abolishment of peasant agriculture. We protest against the opening up of the Upper Rhine for industrial boat traffic--and the industrialization of the Upper Rhine valley, and we also protest against the existing nuclear reactors in our region. Our successful resistance against the construction of a nuclear reactor in Whyl was important because it showed that we can do something . . . !
> (Lehner 1977, 122-123).

References

Adas,M.
1981   From avoidance to confrontation: Peasant protest in Precolonial and Colonial Southeast Asia *CSSH* (2): 217-247.

Blok,A.
1972   The peasant and the brigand: Social banditry Reconsidered. In *Comparative studies in society and history* 14" 404-505.

De Soto,H., and N.Valdez
1973   Lukács, culture, and social transformation. Presented at the international symposium, "The Other Lukács." University of Wisconsin-Madison, March 7-8.

Haselier,G.
1973   *Geschichte des Hotzenwaldes.* Lahr: Verlag Moritz Schauenburg.

Hobsbawm,E.
1974   Social banditry. In *Rural protest: Peasant movements and social change*, edited by H. Landsberger, 142-157.
1959   *Social bandits and primitive rebels.* Glencoe, Illinois: The Free Press

Kulluk,F.E.
1985   The uneven and contradictory development of the revolutionary process in late capitalism: An exploratory case study of workplace and community struggles in Western Europe, 1960-1975. Master's thesis. Madison: University of Wisconsin-Madison.

Lehner,T.
1977   *Die Salpeterer.* Berlin: Verlag Klaus Wagenbach.

Müller-Ettikon,E.
1979   *Die Salpeterer.* Freiburg: Verlag Karl Schillinger.

Shanin,T.
1966   Peasantry as a political factor. *Sociological review* 14(1):5-27.

242

Silverman,S.
1979   The peasant concept in anthropology. In *Journal of peasant studies* 7:46-69.

Stoler,A.L.
1988   Working the revolution: Plantation laborers and the people's militia in North Sumatra. In *The journal of Asian studies* 47(2) (May): 227-247.

Sütterlin,B.
1968   *Geschichte Badens I.* Karlsruhe: Verlag G.Braun.

Turton,A., and S.Tanabe
1984   *History and peasant consciousness in Southeast Asia.* Senri Ethnological Studies No. 3. Osaka: National Museum of Ethnology.

Wolf,E.
1969   *Peasant wars of the twentieth century.* New York: Harper and Row.

IV. SYMBOLIC MANIFESTATIONS: KINSHIP, IDEOLOGY, AND TEXTUALITY

The Organization of Social and Cultural Diversity: An Historical Inquiry

Sandra T. Barnes, Professor
University of Pennsylvania, United States

Throughout his career and in varying ways Aidan Southall grappled with the problem of representing sociocultural diversity in a single society. In confronting this issue he was consistently at the forefront of his discipline. Where others took refuge in a structuralist perspective that placed emphasis on integration and homogeneity, Southall strived to capture the fluidity and complexity of societal systems without, as he put it in his classic study of the Alur peoples,

Research for this article was conducted in Nigeria and in European archives in 1983, 1984, and 1986-1987 as a Research Associate of the Institute of African Studies, University of Ibadan. It was supported at various points by a Fulbright Research Fellowship, a grant from the American Philosophical Society, and a Basic Research Grant from the National Endowment for the Humanities, all of which is deeply appreciated.

without resorting to a "confusion of detail" (1956, 7). This sensitivity to the analytic challenges posed by ethnic heterogeneity continued in his many studies of African urbanism (e.g., 1957, 1961, 1973). More recently (1989), this theme reappeared in his penetrating analysis of the multiplicities of symbols and cultural practices among the Alur as well as their Nilotic neighbors. Yet during this time, early assumptions concerning the homogeneity of African societies persisted in analytic models despite a mounting body of evidence that suggests cultural heterogeneity may have been more the rule than the exception. Cohen points to the same problem, and suggests that early students of African culture were unaware of the heterogeneity of most precolonial populations (1985, 209).

Mobility is one of the most persistent themes in sub-Saharan Africa's social and demographic history (Cohen 1985, 214). If oral traditions share a common element, it is the migration story relating where people came from and who their alien ancestors were. Aside from the standard subsistence reasons for movement--fishing, gathering, pastoralism, or shifting horticulture--mobility also manifested itself as travel, itineracy, and migration for permanent, temporary or even cyclical periods. Men, women, and children, and individuals and groups, traveled to new places and opened new frontiers for a host of reasons, not the least of which were trade and commercial opportunities, marriage, warfare, or religious pursuits.

Political and social boundaries were relatively porous in spite of hostilities, or they were overlapping, shifting, or ambiguously drawn (Asiwaju and Law 1985, 425-427); indeed their definition was less geographical than social. Migration across these boundaries in response to shifts in ecological, climatic, or other environmental forces was common. So, too, was migration in response to political, military, and social conflict, or even opportunism. Peel's careful account of the Yoruba kingdom of Ilesha opens with a lengthy examination of the diverse and geographically widespread origins of each descent group (1983, 19-26; see also Agiri and Barnes 1987, 21-25). As indicated, Southall presents oral histories that tell of the diverse alien origins of both the politically centralized Alur peoples and their acephalous Lugbara neighbors, the very people he expected to lay stress on their homogeneous ancestry. In explaining the Nilotic context, Southall managed to capture one of the most pervasive and dynamic aspects of sub-Saharan life, for at the deepest levels of their identity, he wrote, "however distinctive they feel themselves to be, [people] conceive of themselves as derived from a fusion of other peoples coming from other places in opposite directions" (Southall 1989, 188-189). Furthermore, people were not the only bodies that moved.

In West Africa, armies were institutions on the move. The desire for expanded trade opportunities, wealth (both material and human), territory, and political or ideological reform led to extensive warfare and raiding. The famed conquest states of coastal West Africa (Ashanti, Benin, Dahomey, and Oyo) were known for operations that extended through large expanses of territory and, in fact, ultimately brought some of them into military contact with one another. Lest it be thought that only large polities fielded armies, it should be said that military operations, raids, and other hostile maneuvers were common to polities of nearly all sizes and descriptions.

Military campaigns were often organized as step-by-step operations that left chains of camps in their wake (Smith 1989, 100). Expeditions lasted for weeks, months, or even years, but even then control of new holdings could require long-term supervision. Conquerors sometimes annexed their new holdings, colonized them, gave them to the conquering general (as a way of keeping potential rivals away from the ruling centers), or simply turned them into allies. The outcome was that military operations served to deposit and disperse personnel across large stretches of culturally alien territory for varying periods of time, sometimes permanently.

Armies were accretive systems, as well as distributive ones. Most armies recruited as the occasion demanded, since standing armies or even professional warriors such as those of the Kingdom of Oyo, were limited to the largest states. For a more extensive discussion of military recruitment patterns in West Africa, see Smith (1989, 42-48). Both Ashanti and Benin, for example, expected their tributaries and allies to contribute personnel to their military expeditions (Bradbury 1973, 53-54; Smith 1989, 48). By far the largest sources of personnel were captives and slaves who often provided the backbone of a military unit. Mercenaries sold their services to foreign powers. Hostages, exiles, clients, and other dependent people were expected to participate in military operations of their hosts. Armies also grew as they moved. Staging posts, camps, and occupied villages provided manpower, provisioners, guides, and various types of experts such as the Iso canoemen who guided land-based forces when they engaged in campaigns along the coastal lagoons and waterways (Smith 1970, 530). In many ways a dwindling military unit could recruit and rejuvenate its forces from a variety of sources.

The point is that many, if not most, West African military organizations depended on the incorporation into their ranks of individuals of diverse origins in order to function and reproduce themselves (Awe 1973, 68; Smith 1989, 57). Recruitment was not an in-group or ascriptively determined process that operated according to status- or kin-defined rules. Although in most communities free-born males and most slaves were expected to serve in time of need, anyone could be incorporated into a military unit where the idiom governing relationships among members was according to leader-subordinate norms.

The military was an institution for upward mobility. Indeed, in order to replace casualties in the field, reward valor and success in battle, and engender loyalty and stability within the organization, military leaders needed to advance talented soldiers through the ranks. How high in the ranks a lowly soldier could rise varied from one polity to another (Smith 1989, 53). Among the city-states along the Bight of Benin during the period of roughly 1760 to 1860, the military was an institution within which individuals could achieve high posts and later, in peacetime, convert them into positions in the system of civic authority.

The military was described as an "in-up-out system" in which an individual entered the military as a subordinate, rose up through the ranks, and moved out and into the community as a leader (Prince Tajudeen O. Olusi, personal communication, 1986). The route to the top was open to the slave who emerged with rights to act as a freeborn member of the society and the alien who emerged with rights to function as a citizen. The military served as an incorporative, status-conferring institution, whose actions regarding the status and rights of individuals could be recognized and perpetuated by the wider society (Nadel 1942, 98-99; Howard and Skinner 1984, 8). The rationale for this achievement-oriented system, aside from recognizing and rewarding good talent, had an even more pragmatic base. Rulers could not risk alienating powerful warriors, so there were established ways of rewarding and co-opting them into the established authority structure. The conventional rewards were a land grant where the successful warrior established himself and his soldier-following, a chiefly title, and the right to sit on the royal council of chiefs.

The reward in this in-up-out system was tantamount to conferring citizenship rights on someone who, in many instances, had previously been unable to achieve or exercise such rights. The result, of course, was to create people who were capable of operating in two societies: the society of origin and the society into which he or she had been adopted.

The more significant consequence of the in-up-out system was that through the military, the wider society gained bicultural actors who, by virtue of a transformation in their status and positioning in the community, could as title-holders influence political decisions and cultural practices. An important example was Oshodi Tapa, a Nupe-speaking war captain, who lived in Lagos between c. 1816 and 1868. The following biographical sketch is based on interviews in 1986 with his descendants, principally Lawyer M. Ola Oshodi.

> Enslaved as a child, Oshodi Tapa served in the *oba*'s palace as overseer of the women's quarters and, later, as his trading agent. [Oshodi Tapa's given name was Landuji (Folami 1982, 126). Oshodi is a title, derived from Benin, where it also was conferred on the guardian of the royal women's quarters (Bradbury Papers, Birmingham University Library, BR Series, BR 332). Tapa is the Yoruba term for Nupe.] It was customary for owners to give a share of the profit to their agents which then allowed them to augment their own purses. Tapa used his earnings to purchase his own slaves.
>
> Tapa also established a Nupe ritual cult, called *Gunnu*, which drew a large number of people to its ceremonies. It was customary for people to carry their deities or cults when they moved to new places. Warriors also took their protective charms and war medicines on military excursions. It was impossible for slaves to take the actual artifacts of a cult to new places, but they frequently reconstructed rituals and practices of their homelands.
>
> Tapa's owner, the *oba*, died and in the ensuing succession dispute Tapa backed the losing candidate and was forced into exile with him. [In succession matters,

slaves made their loyalties known. Technically, they were
to be inherited by the next ruler who, because he was not
usually one of the deceased ruler's direct heirs, might
instead have been a member of a rival royal faction.]
The dispute devolved into civil war and Tapa became a
war chief with his slaves and *Gunnu* cult followers
serving as warriors.

Eventually Tapa's master was invited to return to
Lagos. So impressed was the reigning king with Tapa's
military expertise and his large following that he gave
him a chiefly title and a large parcel of land on which
Tapa established himself as head of his own chieftaincy
"house" and following, consisting of some 200 family
heads, their wives, children, clients, slaves, and others.
Tapa laid out the settlement as a war camp and erected
a chiefly palace in its center; a short distance away was
a *Gunnu* shrine and ritual lodge. The settlement,
palace, and shrine currently occupy a large area
consisting of 21 compounds in the center of Lagos Island.

In one generation, Tapa went from slave to chief, from alien to
citizen, and from the bottom of the status hierarchy to the top.
Clearly it was safer for the ruler to co-opt a warrior's influence than
to vie with it; safer to share power than monopolize it; safer to
designate a powerful person as a legitimate actor in the established
authority system the ruler controlled than allow him to be a free
agent.

The Oshodi Tapas of Lagos and similar communities left the
military with a different status than when they entered. Furthermore,
by virtue of their bicultural orientations, they came out with an
expanded share of cultural capital with which to make their way as
well as the status to make use of that capital, that is, to influence the
cultural configuration of their new societies.

In most instances people who succeeded in making their way
through the in-up-out system in old Lagos also established a ritual
cult. Tapa used his knowledge of Nupe mystical traditions to attract
a ritual following and to instill in that group and his warrior followers

a sense of solidarity and distinctiveness. As a Lagos chief he could then bring their interests to bear on matters taken up in the public arena. By the same token, his influence had added significance due to the large, organized group behind him.

The descendants of Oshodi Tapa and his original followers continue to stage an annual Gunnu ceremony in Lagos which, in fact, has been incorporated into the public ceremonial calendar. Moreover, they continue to claim and use their dual participation in the Gunnu ritual lodge and the wider society, as well as their dual identities as Nupe and as Lagosians, as cultural capital in competing for a dominant place and the public resources that are embedded in the Lagos civic hierarchy. Which identity is used, of course, depends on a host of factors including the context and one's positioning in it.

Oshodi Tapa's biography is a paradigmatic one. The histories of many of Lagos' chiefly houses and descent groups involve alien origins, entry into Lagos or citizenship via the military, and the use of alien culture in drawing together a ritually solidified following. What is more important here is that then (and now) groups of people shared knowledge that was unevenly distributed. Furthermore, that restricted knowledge was embedded in an institutionalized context where routine ritual practices kept it alive and culturally distinctive. Yet these same people shared, not completely but more generally, with a wider group: civic knowledge, practices, and representations that were more evenly distributed as part of the public ritual domain. In Lagos, Gunnu represented one kind of sharing/nonsharing pattern.

One of the arguments for the homogeneity of precolonial, preliterate African culture comes from Goody, who, in comparing the characteristics of oral and literate societies, maintains it is difficult for cultural knowledge to accumulate and thus support a complexly organized social order in the absence of written texts. In an argument more subtle than can be recapitulated here, Goody suggests that for a society to be heterogeneous, it must contain competing systems of knowledge that are sustained through the kind of skeptical scrutiny that, in turn, is derived from written evidence that can be accumulated, compared, and consulted over time (1987, 69-77).

Taking a slightly different approach, Horton argues that homogeneity in a community's culture is a logical by-product of social practice. His view is that in small-scale societies members must engage in face-to-face debate in order to reach the consensus-producing decisions by which their sociocultural order is maintained and this produces a singular cultural order (1982, 254-255).

Both positions assume that social practices take place and knowledge is shared on a full community level. Thus, social interactions underpin and produce a homogeneous, integrated, clear set of rules, meanings, and ideologies that constitute a shared core culture. Additions, subtractions, syncreticisms, and transformations occur within the core, but it is treated as hegemonic. The direction of cultural influence flows outward from a dominant center to the rest of the community through the discourse involved in face-to-face relationships or civic performances, or through discourse that is undifferentiated because the oral texts themselves cannot be differentiated. Neither position allows for the embedding of separate knowledge in separate groups or for social practices that involve subsets of a society. Nor do they take account of the widespread use of knowledge as a scarce resource in African societies and the competition for power among groups that scarcity produces (Murphy 1980). In short, neither position takes into consideration the intrinsic unevenness in the distribution of cultural knowledge that exists in any community or the consequences of that unevenness.

The institution of kinship also has played a significant role in reinforcing notions of cultural homogeneity. Studies that take kinship to be the dominant institution of social organization take as given the fact that the kin group is the basic unit for incorporating aliens into a society. Briefly, the position is that kin groups are the basic social units of most African societies; social status is based on membership in a kin-defined group; and rights and obligations in society derive from that status. Entry into a new society is at the bottom of an ascriptively defined kin-based social hierarchy, and upward mobility, which is indeed possible, takes place within the idiom of kinship. Until they have negotiated the kin hierarchy, newcomers are viewed as marginal and thus deprived of the rights of citizenship and consequently of the ability to perform as fully legitimate actors in public bodies (Kopytoff and Miers 1977, 14-27).

The point is that in a kin-centered analysis the status of outsiders and rights and obligations accruing from that status are interpreted as being dependent on processes occurring within a single field of relationships. By the same token, social assimilation is seen as kin-mediated and by extension cultural assimilation is interpreted as part of the same process. Hence the process of achieving entitlements in a new community is one of being assimilated into a kin group and thereby into the core culture.

The problem with this well-known scenario is that it overlooks other social institutions and cultural practices--such as the military or ritual groups--that organize diversity. Furthermore it conflates the processes of social and cultural incorporation. Inasmuch as social incorporation in a kin-based society is dependent on an individual's being subject to the ascriptive principles of a kinship group, it is taken as given that cultural incorporation also is ascriptive in the sense that the individual either is born or assimilated into the society's existing culture via that group. The cultural influence of members who have alien origins are *ipso facto* denied.

Here, then, lies the reasoning behind the hegemony of the culture core. In the process of social and cultural incorporation, conflated as it is, the cultural knowledge that the outsider brings to an adopted community is lost. The assumption is similar to that of religious conversion in that, in a strict interpretation, the convert's change to the new ideology is complete.

In contradistinction to these views, Wallace has long held that, from a cognitive point of view, diversity is intrinsic--indeed, necessary--to all societies. Complete uniformity is dysfunctional in that survival depends on the pooling of specialized orientations and knowledge rather than the mastery of all knowledge by all members. In his view, analytic priority should be on how a society organizes difference rather than on how it achieves integration (1970, 109-110). Fredrik Barth moves a step further. For him "Culture is *distributive* in a population." At the most basic level, cultural knowledge and practices are distributed according to gender, age, occupation, or experience; they are "shared by some but not by others" (1989, 134). If we add to Barth's demographic categories the incomplete distributions in knowledge that result from the incorporation of outsiders (or from the outside experiences of a society's members), complexity takes on added dimensions. At this point then, our ability to understand sociocultural dynamics depends, to some extent, on understanding and explaining *patterns of nonsharing* and the way incompleteness plays itself out in terms of conflict, competition, and resistance to authority, as much as it depends on examining the forms through which sharing takes place (1989, 134).

In the case of the Nupe presented earlier, knowledge of custom and practice was used as a basis for organizing difference. Such

254

knowledge kept a group of people together as a distinct unit in a small society enabling it to compete for public resources. Certain secret aspects of its ritual and language were not shared beyond the group, and this served to symbolize and maintain the group's separateness. On the other hand, certain aspects of Gunnu ceremonies were publicly performed and shared at the civic level as a way of symbolizing the group's having attained a legitimate place in the wider community. The public performance of Gunnu signaled that Nupe was both a separate cultural presence in Lagos and that it also was part of the full community. Gunnu was simultaneously specific and general. It could be taken and used in either direction.

This essay began by describing the significant amounts of movement that have taken place in sub-Saharan Africa. The ramifications of mobility are apparent in every aspect of life, from the mystical to the pragmatic. To focus on practices such as ritual, and institutions such as the military, that articulate with mobility by incorporating and organizing diversity helps direct attention to two-way exchanges of cultural knowledge. This focus provides insight into ways that bicultural or multicultural identities come into being and are then borne by single individuals. It reveals the ways in which people come to perceive a multiplicity of choices, and ways of being in the world, which in turn yield a multiplicity of strategies for achieving their various ends. To have cultural diversity is to have contexts where cultural negotiation and interaction occur. Military or ritual groupings are two kinds of context in which people can trade on their bicultural capital that, in competitive relationships, can be transformed into power: power that exists at various levels and flows in multiple directions.

References

Agiri,B.A., and Sa.T.Barnes
1987   Lagos before 1603. In *History of the peoples of Lagos state*, edited by B.A.Agiri, A.I.Adefuye, and J.O.Osuntokun, 18-32. Lagos: Literamed Ltd.,

Asiwaju,A.I., and R.Law
1985   From the Volta to the Niger, c. 1600-1800. In *History of West Africa*, vol. 1. 3d ed., edited by J.F.A.Ajayi and M.Crowder, 412-464. New York: Longman.

Awe,B.
1973   Militarism and economic development in nineteenth century Yoruba country: The Ibadan example. *Journal of African History* 14(1):65-67.

Barth,F.
1989   The analysis of culture in complex societies. *Ethos* 54(3-4):120-42.

Bradbury,R.E.
1973   *Benin studies*. London: Oxford University Press for International African Institute.

Cohen,D.W.
1985   Doing social history from *Pim*'s doorway. In *Reliving the past*, edited by O.Zunz, 191-235. Chapel Hill: University of North Carolina Press.

Folami,T.
1982   *A history of Lagos, Nigeria*. Smithtown, N.Y.: Exposition Press.

Goody,J.
1987   *The interface between the written and the oral*, Cambridge: Cambridge University Press.

Horton,R.
1982   Tradition and modernity revisited. In *Rationality and relativism*, edited by M.Hollis and S.Lukes, 201-260. Oxford: Basil Blackwell.

256

Howard,A.M., and D.E.Skinner
1984   Network building and political power in northwestern
              Sierra Leone, 1800-65. *Africa* 54(2):2-28.

Kopytoff,I., and S.Meiers, eds.
1977   African "slavery" as an institution of marginality. In
              Slavery in Africa, 3-81. Madison: University of
              Wisconsin Press.

Murphy,W.
1980   Secret knowledge as property and power in Kpelle
              society: Elders versus youth. *Africa* 50:193-207.

Nadel,S.F.
1942   *A black Byzantium*. London: Oxford University Press
              for International Institute of African Languages and
              Cultures.

Peel,J.D.Y.
1983   *Ijeshas and Nigerians: The incorporation of a
              Yoruba kingdom, 1890s-1970s*. Cambridge:
              Cambridge University Press.

Smith,R.S.
1970   The canoe in West African history. *Journal of African
              history* 11(4):515-533.
1989   *Warfare and diplomacy in precolonial West
              Africa*, 2d ed. Madison: University of Wisconsin Press.

Southall,A.W.
1956   *Alur society*. Cambridge: W.Heffer and Sons.
1961   *Social change in modern Africa* (ed.). London:
              Oxford University Press for International African
              Institute.
1973   *Urban anthropology*, edited by A.W.Southall. London:
              Oxford University Press.
1989   Power, sanctity, and symbolism in the political economy
              of the Nilotes. In *Creativity of power: Cosmology
              and action in African societies*, edited by W.Arens
              and I.Karp, 183-222. Washington: Smithsonian
              Institution Press.

Southall,A.W., and P.C.W.Gutkind
1957   *Townsmen in the making: Kampala and its suburbs*. Kampala: East African Institute of Social Research.

Wallace,A.F.C.
1970   *Culture and personality*, 2d ed. New York: Random House.

The Sakalava: A Case for Religious
Continuity in Madagascar

Thomas K. Park, Assistant Professor
University of Arizona, Tucson, United States

Madagascar's Sakalava kingdom of Menabe traced some of its royal ancestors to the sixteenth century, formed its essential institutions by middle seventeenth century and then flourished and expanded on the west coast until partially succumbing to Merina expansion in the nineteenth century. It ended its political history with French colonial efforts at the end of the century (Lombard 1988, 55). The key to Sakalava royal legitimation was a ritual of possession (*tromba/bilu*) and a cult of royal relics (*dady*) linking Sakalava society to God and the spirit world (Lombard 1986, 152). Trance played a crucial role in Sakalava religion as did cults of relics as means for linking individuals or communities to the ancestors and the spirit world.

The significance of these religious elements to the Sakalava expansion and domination of the west coast of Madagascar for two centuries has long attracted scholarly attention (e.g., particularly since Rusillon 1912), but two main scholarly interpretations have been put forward. The first (Kent 1968, 1970) suggests that the Sakalava dynasty adopted these religious elements by 1650, from late sixteenth century immigrants to the west coast of Madagascar (specifically to the town of Sahadia) from the Mozambique coast. Kent claims that this religious legitimation was crucial to Sakalava expansion and dominance of other societies because for other societies this religious apparatus was both new and persuasive in legitimating Sakalava claims to royal dominance.

The second interpretation (Lombard 1986, 1988) suggests that the religious elements were adopted in the same time frame (first half of the seventeenth century) but from societies on the southeast coast of Madagascar who had brought some of the religious elements to the north coast of Madagascar in the thirteenth century. Originally Muslims, the immigrants split into several groups and one, migrating down the east coast, gradually lost its Islamic religion while keeping elements of Islamic divination and founded the kingdom of Antemoro on the southeast coast in the fourteenth century (Lombard 1988, 11).

This kingdom split into four polities in the sixteenth century, which gradually assimilated other groups. The resulting political and religious institutions combined elements from both the immigrant traditions and the indigenous traditions. Lombard, in distinction to Kent, stresses that the Sakalava adoption of religious elements from groups on the southeast coast did not mean that Sakalava expansion involved a religious rupture for the conquered peoples; rather, the Sakalava institutions "revealed" or brought out religious elements that were already present in Madagascar (Lombard 1986, 145, 1988, 15).

This brief paper provides support for Lombard's thesis in the form of a middle seventeenth century account of religious ritual on the southeast coast of Madagascar that seems to have been completely overlooked by scholars of Madagascar's history. The account is by Urbain Souchu de Rennefort, published 1688, but describing a visit in 1667 to Fort Dauphin and parts north. Though the book is extremely rare and its title, *Histoires des Indes Orientales*, does not mention Madagascar, I am still puzzled why no scholars concerned with Malagasy ritual mention it (e.g., Deschamps 1959, Estrade 1977, Faublée 1954, Kent 1968, 1970, Lombard 1988, Ottino 1965, Raseta-Ravelomanantsoa 1968, Rason 1968, Rusillon 1912, Vig 1973). The work is cited in the major compendium of early works on Madagascar

(Grandidier 1903-1920) and a study discussing early works mentioning the exploits of Le Vacher dit La Case (Gautier and Froidevaux 1907) cites it repeatedly for its accounts of La Case's exploits.

The paper begins with a discussion of the Sakalava conceptions of the linkages between the spirit world and the world of people based on Lombard (1988). It then briefly expands the discussion to variations found among the Bara, Betsimisaraka, and Vezo, which facilitate elucidation of elements of the 1667 southeast coast account. A number of different points will be made but at least the following are worth mentioning in advance: (a) there are common religious expressions of a dichotomy between royal-dominant-dominating spirits and spirits in league with non-elite people and their appropriate symbols, (b) women's chorus or singing plays a significant role, (c) possession is the immediate connection to the ancestors and the spirit world, (d) cults of relics/talismans (*oly, ody, sampy, dady*) play an important role in facilitating possession or contact with the spirits and (e) skilled /knowledgeable individuals (*ombiasy*) have special access to spiritual power.

The two interpretations

Kent's (1970, 196) history of the Sakalava hypothesizes that the Maroseraña dynasty formed in Mahafaly in c.1550 and had adopted the dady and the tromba from a proto-Sakalava group by 1650. The dady is described by Mariano, a Jesuit who visited the west coast between 1613 and 1630, as "ugly wooden images, ornamented with beads and other jewelry" in which precious relics are placed (1970, 182). The presence of the tromba in Sahadia, Kent deduces from statements that people believed the dead could aid the living and an account of people assuming the role of *Afo* (meaning fire and later symbol for king) and inciting people to do things. Kent notes that commoners and nobles alike engage in these practices. Kent claims these institutions were crucial in building the Sakalava empire established by the Maroseraña (1970, 162-163). The evidence for this uniqueness is mostly negative: thus Kent adduces Mariano's account of the afo and dady institutions among the Sukulambes of Sahadia (1970, 182) and refers to oral tradition that traces the royal institution of dady to the death of Andriandahifotsy or the reign of Andriamisara, dating to about 1670 (1970, 197). This limited evidence is implicitly complemented by the large lack of counterevidence.

Lombard reconstructs the Sakalava Menabe kingdom primarily from oral traditions, complemented by travelers' accounts, and like Delivré (1974) for Merina traditions, finds the royal traditions quite reliable (Lombard 1988, 24 ff.). The earliest archaeological dates for Madagascar are from about A.D. 900 (Verin 1986, Wright 1986). This and the close relation between all Madagascar's languages and certain Indonesian language families suggests that Madagascar was settled by migrants from Indonesia sometime in the A.D. first millennium. There is quite persuasive evidence for some immigrations by African and Arab Muslim groups subsequent to A.D. 900, but it is likely that few demographically significant immigrations occurred from the fourteenth to the eighteenth centuries other than to some Muslim towns on the northwest coast (the nineteenth and twentieth centuries saw significant immigration of Europeans to Madagascar). This last point is one of Lombard's reasons for viewing Sakalava expansion as an indigenous movement, benefitting from earlier Afro-Arab immigrations by reinterpreting religious elements by this time generally present in Madagascar. Development of this ritual complex in Sakalava times, in Lombard's view, did not imply a radical imposition of new religion on conquered peoples (Lombard 1988, 15).

Lombard places the introduction of new ritual practices of Muslim origin (centered around **sikily** or divination techniques) from the thirteenth to fifteenth centuries. Lombard (1988, 17, 77-82) suggests that the immigrants brought pastoralism, religious specialists (*ombiasy*), and religious knowledge (*hasina*) and divination (*sikily*) to combine with the west coast recession agriculture, kingship, and more general Malagasy genealogical ritual (cults of relics). Sakalava oral tradition glosses the pre-Sakalava religious practices as Vazimba (the term for a putative autochthonous group) and attributes to them ancestral cults involving offerings of honey, bananas, and tortoises under the guidance of ritual specialists (also called ombiasy) (1988, 17). As the Sakalava royal tradition develops in the seventeenth century, ombiasy are incorporated as exclusive masters of improved ritual systems and are involved in transforming indigenous ideas into royal ritual to the point that they make major political decisions for the developing Sakalava dynasty (1988, 20-21).

Sakalava conceptions of religion and health may be summarized from oral tradition as follows (from Lombard 1986, 1988, 104-134). Sickness is due to an intervention from the spirit world. Unsolicited possession (trance) is also an intervention from the spirit world while human induced possession is the primary means of making contact with the spirit world. Sickness can be classified along a scale from minor to fatal and along this same vector the appropriate treatment runs from food and plant medicines through use of trance via talismans (oly, ody, sampy, dady) to the use of prayer or trance and the intervention of an ombiasy. The world of spirits includes two levels (*jiny* and *raza*) and several groups of spirits. The top level spirits, the jiny, include four levels of spirit ancestors of the first inhabitants of the earth two of which groups are capable of direct intervention in human affairs. The raza level inclues the *koko* (*a* group of spirit ancestors of oldest local inhabitants viewed as half (amen and half spirit living in the forests and capable of intervening in human affairs by way of talismans), the seventy-seven errant spirits that cause sickness and carry out orders of the higher spirits, the dady (royal ancestor spirits, also the term for their relics/talismans), the *razabe* (noble ancestor spirits), and the raza (ancestor spirits of historically important lineages).

Basic access to the spirit world is via trance; different kinds of trance exist, depending on which aspect of the spirit world is being linked to whom in the world of humans and what (who) the intermediary linkages are. To simplify, trance linkages between the raza level and humans are called *bilo*, between the dady and humans are called both bilo and tromba, between the jiny level and people are called tromba, and between the koko and people (via talismans) are called tromba. In the southern Sakalava areas tromba and bilo serve to link various social factions in dialogue with the spirits. In the northern Sakalava areas, bilo is replaced by the term *jama* which specifically designates possessions organized by the nobility as opposed to possessions organized by dominated groups (tromba). Lombard (1988, 125) suggests that within the Sakalava system this opposition appears as one between ritual organized symbolically in terms of dynastic ideology (by the nobility) and ritual organized in terms of Sakalava territory (for those who for reasons of political prudence cannot claim to trace genealogies back to pre-Sakalava times). In areas less central to the rise of the Sakalava dynasty, the various elements seem to be used more explicitly to emphasize the dichotomy between dominant and dominated.

Ethnographic range for associated ritual elements

Among the Bara, in south central Madagascar, men can call on powers associated with *auli*, charms involving sikily. Similarly, the women can invoke life charms. Among these are *fuli velu*, life threads; *ranu velu*, water of life; and *tani velu*--earth of life, a white clay (Faublée 1954, 9-11).

Associated with specific sacred places and generally dispersed in nature there are *helu*, or spirits, that can haunt or possess people. There are two basic sorts of *helu*: *helu mena--helu mena panjaka*: red helu--red king helu and *helu meti*: dark or black helu. The former are bad, dangerous, don't cure people, and do throw stones, while the latter, also called *fanahi mitili*, flying spirits, are favorable to people (Faublée 1954, 34-35).

Though both men and women can be possessed, the helu are associated with women: (1) *tani*, a terrestrial goddess and the general parent of the helu, is the enemy of patriarchal gods; (2) women pray and offer directly to helu without needing an intermediary other than the possessed person; and (3) unpossessed men pray to ancestors and gods through the intermediary of the *pitata* (a male ritual expert). This distinction is even more marked in that women sing in chorus for all life rites, avoid sikily and avoid complex magical charms, while men perform circumcision, funerals, and sikily. In general, the helu impose prohibitions and observances on the possessed and can be called on by the person linked to them for inspiration, aid, or to cure someone else's illness (Faublée 1954, 37).

The similarities between helu possession and the bilu are many, but some differences should be pointed out first. Bilu is a rite, the person possessed, and the state of the possessed. Some of its crucial characteristics are (1) it can be provoked or spontaneous: in the former case an ill person who hasn't been cured by the prayers of the *nitata* or by the men's auli may be taken into hand by women of the patient's family or neighborhood who sing in chorus to the rhythm of a tambourine until the patient becomes *bilu*, dances, and is possessed; (2) every bilu chooses a companion, washes in water containing silver, and wears some dark glass beads on left hand; (3) the bilu assists at circumcisions but avoids funerals and anything red; and (4) the bilu gives orders that are obeyed. The bilu is followed by a crowd of youth and musicians. Wherever she goes she dances to the accompaniment of a chorus of women. The role of bilu only lasts for a few days to several weeks but there is apparently rarely a Bara village without a bilu (Faublée 1954, 40).

These two forms of possession emphasize an opposition to royal authority structures. The predominance of women in both forms of possession are crucial. Faublée points out that both bilu and helu must avoid death, gold, and red: three very clear symbols of Sakalava ancestral political power (1954, 59). A point that is missed at one's peril is that in some forms of both bilu and helu possession, the name *Resurati* is given to the possessed person, and it is said that the bilu is a prince and that the princes are the parents of the helu (Faublée 1954, 42,46). This means that, while both oppose themselves to the recognized royal ancestral authority, both may have recourse to alternative noble traditions.

Faublée divides the tromba of the Vezo, in southwest Madagascar, into two types: *raza* and *sandratsi*. A raza extended up to a week or more for illnesses, dreams, or dangers (1954, 71). The Vezo say the *vurumbu* (spirits) possess people and ask them to build an *anjumba* (a house for the spirits). An *anjumba* (also *andrumba*) is a miniature house that is raised by spirits, is separated from residential houses when these are plural, has a door facing west, is painted white, and contains bottles of rum, bowls, glasses, incense, *tani futi*--white clay and glass beads on cotton threads called *fuli velu*. The anjumba is called the house of birds (Faublée 1954, 65,67).

The raza type involves anointing with tani futi, a chorus of women, incense, libations, and supplications (Faublée 1954, 70). The sandratsi type usually involves the possessed speaking in foreign languages, dancing, and anointing with water. It stops at sunset and then continues until late at night (Faublée 1954, 81, 86). The Vezo identify the sandratsi with the bilu and oppose the spirits of life to complex magical charms and gold as do the Bara. Faublée points out that anjumba are particularly numerous among endogamous fishing groups of the Vezo, which do not practice circumcision, while exogamy, cattle raising, and patriarchal rites go together in other Vezo groups (Faublée 1954, 99). Thus Faublée's analysis supports a claim that the tromba/bilu/helu have little to do with supporting the ancestral political apparatus.

Koechlin has in minute detail analyzed the *tzumba* (tromba) among the Vezo. He contrasts two types of tzumba. The Vezo have two altars: the first holding calabashes of honey alcohol, pieces of bamboo, ceremonial necklaces, honey, water, and incense. Each of four altar supports is marked with white clay and "life charcoal." In front is the second, lower altar containing, for the modern seance: rum (*tuoko mena*--red alcohol), wine, soda water, brea, mirrors and flasks, carafes, glass bottles, etc. (1970, 186). The style of the "modern" seance contrasts with that of the old: the old uses Vezo gestures and the Vezo dialect, the modern seance uses European gestures: fists, insolent attitudes (including direct eye-to-eye staring), index fingers directed at the assistant,and the words are either

French, English, Norwegian, Merina, or Arabic. Koechlin writes: "*il s'agit, dans les diatribes des possedés, d'imitations admirablement fidèles des gueulantes des colons . . . des capitaines sur leur navire ou, encore, des admonestations des hauts fonctionaires.*" He notes down that the possessed in the modern tzomba wears white with a red belt and harness rather than pure white, presumably in imitation of colonial military uniforms. He concludes that the roles played by the possessed seem to be interpretations of coercive powers, in the traditional seance of very ancient powers--those of kings, in the modern seance those of Merina, Arabs, and Europeans (1975, 187).

Althabe studied a group of Betsimisaraka, on the east side of Madagascar, who had been forced, following a revolt in 1947, to engage in tobacco production under unreasonable conditions and had as a result ritually isolated themselves from the administration in both its French and Merina manifestations. The tromba appeared in 1960 and began increasingly to compete with and dominate traditional ancestral ceremonies (1969, 95). Althabe (1969, 100) distinguishes three types of spirits: (1) kings, queens, and generals of the pre-colonial period--usually Sakalava or Merina; (2) ethnic: Marin, Sakalava, or Comorien tromba; and (3) mythological: Vorambe (the great bird) Ampelamena--the red women, etc.

Among the Betsimisaraka the tromba has the following major aspects: (1) indirect communication through the possessed person's assistant, (2) reenactment of master servant relationships complete with European garments and language, (3) exclusively European paraphernalia (Althabe 1969, 96-98). The tromba takes place in the hills near the rice tavy: in direct opposition to the traditional ancestral ceremonies which also take place there in that, except for the tromba, no European clothes are ever worn when in the hills.

Althabe suggests that the participants and the possessed regain their psychological autonomy on various levels: vis-à-vis their peers and vis-à-vis their administrative coercers. This involves a reorganizing of relationships and a reevaluation of old traditions. Thus the tromba challenged the role of diviners (*Mpisikidi*) and strengthened the position of astrology (*sorobe*) on which the tromba depended for predicting the date and importance of possession ceremonies (Althabe 1969, 112).

Souchu de Rennefort's account

Souchu de Rennefort describes (1688) a ritual, observed in the 1660s on the southeast coast of Madagascar, that seems to combine aspects of the Vezo anjumba and the Sakalava dady. Recall (1) The Vezo call the anjumba (andrumba) the house of birds, (2) the omnipresent chorus of women, (3) that the anjumba itself resembles the dady in being a carefully built container for various sacred objects, and (4) the numerous references to flying spirits (helu, fanahi mitili, vurumbe). Souchu de Rennefort (1688, 188) writes as follows:

> Ils adorent une manière de Grillon qu'ils nourrissent au fond d'un grand panier bien travaillé, oú ils mettent ce qu'ils ont de plus précieux, and appellent tout cela leur Oly. Ils dansent autour avec emportement, s'excitent comme des furieux: and animans leur imagination, ils croyent que cet Oly leur inspire de faire ce qu'ils executent.
>
> Un françois curieux, s'informant d'un des ces sçavans, surquoy il fondoit l'adoration d'un si vil animal que celuy qu'ils nourrissoient dans leur Oly: Il luy répondit fort gravement, que dans le sujet il respectoit le principe, & qu'il falloit determiner un sujet pour fixer l'esprit.

The savant (referred to later as an ombiasse) thus explains that the sort of cricket in the large, well-worked basket is merely an object for localizing a spirit and it is this spirit that inspires them. The basket is clearly referred to as the Oly as well as the cricket and the precious objects included in the basket. The similarities with the Vezo anjumba are undeniable and, given the ethnographic variety described for groups from the east coast to the west coast, it would be difficult to argue that Rennefort's "Oly" is unrelated to Mariano's "dady." Yet, it is equally significant that there are major differences.

Discussion

It is clear that this all too brief description is that of a ritual at once too removed in form as well as in space for the odds to be high that it came from Sahadia and was modified drastically all in less than fifty years. Yet if it did not, either we have an improbable coincidence or we entertain some doubts at least about the Sahadia origin of two key Sakalava characteristics. It is likely that Lombard is correct in surmising that such ritual elements were already fairly widespread in Madagascar by 1600.

The prevalence of an antiauthoritarian or antidomination theme in the ethnographic cases fits well Lombard's suggestion that the development of these ritual elements in the Sakalava tradition was an adaptation of indigenous elements and not the introduction of a completely new religious system. It would be far more puzzling if all the noncentral-Sakalava ethnic groups had used what was hitherto a unique Sakalava tradition for antiauthoritarian purposes. It makes more sense to view the ritual trance and talisman traditions as a broader Malagasy one that the Sakalava and the dominated ethnic groups each adapted to their own purposes.

References

Althabe,G.
1969   *Oppression et liberation dans l'imaginaire.* Paris,
            Maspero.

Delivré,A.
1974   *L'Histoire des Rois d'Imerina - Interprétation
            d'une tradition orale.* Paris: Klinsiek.

Deschamps,H., and S.Vianès
1959   *Les Malgaches du Sud-Est.* Paris: Presses
            Universitaires de France.

Estrade,J.-M.
1977   *Le tromba, un culte de possession à Madagascar.*
            Paris: Editions anthropos.

Faublée,J.
1954   *Les espirits de la vie à Madagascar.* Paris: Presse
            Universitaires.

Gautier,E.-F., and H.Froidevaux
1907   *Un manuscrit arabico-malgache sur les compagnes
            de La Case dans l'Imoro de 1659 á 1663.* Paris:
            Notices et extraits des manuscrits de la
            Bibliotéque Nationale et autres bibliothèques, vol.
            39.*

Grandidier,A., and G.
1903-1920   *Collection des ouvrages anciens concernant
            Madagascar,* (C.O.A.C.M.) Paris, Union Colonial.

Kent,R.
1970   *Early kingdoms in Madagascar 1500-1700.* New
            York: Holt-Rhinehart.
1968   Madagascar and Africa: II- The Sakalava Maroseraña,
            dady and tromba before 1700. *Journal of African
            History* 9(4):517-546.

Koechlin,B.
1975   *Les Vezo du sud-ouest Madagascar.* Paris: Mouton.

Kottak,C.P., J.-A.Rakotoarisoa, A.W.Southall, and P.Vérin
1986   *Madagascar: society and history.* Durham, North
          Carolina: Carolina Academic Press.

Lombard,J.
1988   *Le Royaume Sakalava du Menabe Essai d'analyse
          d'un système politique à Madagascar 17è - 20è.*
          Paris: *Editions de l'ORSTOM collection travaux et
          documents* 214.
1986   *Le temps et l'espace dans l'idéologie politique de
          la Royauté Sakalava-menabe.* In *Madagascar
          society and history*, by Aidan Southall et al., 143-156.

Ottino,P.
1963   *Les economies paysannes du bas Mangoky.* Paris:
          Editions Berger-Levrault.
1965   La tromba-Madagascar. *L'homme revue francaise
          d'anthropologie.* Paris (January-March):84-93.

Rennefort,U.S.de
1688   *Histoire des Indes orientales.* Leide: Marchand
          Libraire.

Raseta-Ravelomanantsoa,A.
1968   *Le tromba et la vie traditionnelle betsimisaraka.
          Civilisation Malgache* 1:167-179. Tananarive.

Rason,R.
1968   *Le tromba chez les Sakalava.* Civilisation Malgache
          2. Tananarive.

Rusillon,H.
1912   *Un culte dynastique avec evocation des morts chez
          les Sakalavas de Madagascar le tromba.* Paris,
          Alphonse Picard.

Vérin,P.
1986   Origines malgaches: histoire culturelle et archéologie de
          Madagascar, mise au point et commentaire. In
          Madagascar society and history, edited by Kottak et
          al., 45-52. Durham, North Carolina: Carolina Academic
          Press.

Vig,L.
1973   *Les conceptions religieuses des anciens Malgaches*,
            translated from German by Bruno Hübsch. Tananarive:
            Impr. Catholique.

Wright,H.T.
1986   Early communities on the island of Maore and the coasts
            of Madagascar. In *Madagascar: society and history*,
            by Kottak, et al., 53-87.

Chipimpi, Vulgar Clans, and Lala-Lamba Ethnohistory

Brian Siegel, Associate Professor
Furman University, Greenville, South Carolina
United States

Common to the matrilineal peoples of eastern central Africa is their clan system, and the reciprocal joking, or "funeral friendship," relations that exist between clans with figuratively complementary names (Cunnison 1959, 62-71; Richards 1937; Stefaniszyn 1950). This paper, however, focuses on the southeastern Shaba Pedicle, and the anomalous, one-sided joking between the Vulva and (pubic) Hair clans of the Lala and Lamba chiefs. It suggests that this joking, like the claim that these clans share a common mythical ancestor, is best explained in terms of nineteenth century Lala and Lamba history, and of their competing claims to the Pedicle's easternmost end. This region of Bukanda lies between the Aushi to the north (in Bwaushi), the Lala and Swaka to the east and south (in Ilala and Maswaka), and the Lamba (of Ilamba) to the west. The main distinction between these closely related and adjacent peoples, with their similar customs and languages, is in the histories and traditions of their chiefs.

The bizarre relationship between the chiefly Vulva and Hair clans is not widely known. I only heard of it during my fieldwork in Ilamba. The Lala, like the Lamba, straddle both the Zairois and Zambian sides of the Shaba Pedicle, and the literature on this region in both French and English, is fragmentary and marked by an ahistorical and uncritical acceptance of oral traditions. The Lala are

Presented at the Spring 1991 SERAS meetings, College of Charleston, Charleston, South Carolina, 13 April 1991.

probably best known in relation to Mwana Lesa's Watchtower movement of the 1920s (Verbeek 1977, 1983). Norman Long's *Social Change and the Individual* (Manchester, 1968) is the only modern ethnography on the Lala, yet this study of the enterprising Jehovah's Witnesses has little to say about their history or clans. Fortunately, Léon Verbeek's *Filiation et usurpation* (1987) has sorted through the oral and colonial histories, and has paved the way for comparative ethnohistories of the peoples on both sides of the Shaba Pedicle.

The matrilineal peoples of eastern central Africa share a number of common culture traits (Richards 1939, 16-17, 1950, 221-236). Among these is an assortment of some thirty to forty exogamous clans, each bearing the name of a plant, animal, or some other feature of the natural or cultural world. This clan system is common to the matrilineal peoples found between the southern end of Lake Tanganyika and the Luangwa River in the east, and west to the Lualaba and Lunga Rivers. The peoples involved are, in alphabetical order, the Ambo (or Kambonsenga), Aushi, Bemba, Bena Chishinga, Bena Kabende, Bena Mukulo, Bena Ngumbo, Bisa, Kaonde, Lala, Lamba, Lima, Luano, Kazembe's Lunda, southern Lungu, Sanga, Seba, Senga, Swaka, Tabwa, and Unga (Cunnison 1959, 62n; Grévisse 1956, (32) 77-80, (35) 95-97, (38) 120; Richards 1939, 16-17, 1950, 221-222; Slaski 1950, 86; Whiteley 1950, 5). I do not claim that these are all distinct peoples; some, like the Lala and Ambo, the Bisa and Senga, the Lamba and Seba, and the Sanga and Kaonde, are clearly cognate groups. Nor do I claim that this list is exhaustive. The marital histories I collected suggest that the Lenje and Soli should also be included, and Smith and Dale (1920, vol. 1, 287-298, 308-313) describe very similar clans and joking relations among the Ila.

The same or similar clan names are so widely distributed across the region that they probably predate its current ethnic labels, and the supposed migration of these peoples' ancestors from the western, Luba or Lunda land of "Kola." The claims to Luba origins are most frequently found in Zambia, while those to Lunda origins, as one might expect, are common to the Shaba Pedicle (Verbeek 1987, 164-166, 326-328). Thus the Zambian Lamba claim Luba, while those in Shaba, Lunda origins. Such claims seem to be self-serving assertions of these chiefdoms' antique legitimacy. None of the current ethnonyms are primordial, yet the "Muiza" (Bisa) informants Lacerda encountered during his 1798 journey to Kazembe clearly refer to the hostile "Uemba" and "Mussucuma" (Bemba and Sukuma/Nyamwezi), and to the peaceful "Aramba" (Lamba) and "Ambo" (Burton 1873, 99). Regardless of ethnic identities, people with the same clan name (or referent) are theoretically related. And since every person is considered a "child" of both his mother's and father's matriclans, and a "grandchild" of his mother's father's and father's father's matriclans, a traveling stranger can claim hospitality from a wide network of clan relatives.

But the same clan system also establishes reciprocal partnerships between those whose clan referents stand in a relation of symbolic complementarity or interdependence. While church congregations have not completely eliminated the role such "funeral friends" once played in burying each other's dead, the reciprocal baiting between joking-clan partners remains a vital part of everyday life, and one which establishes warm, kinlike relations between relative strangers (Boswell 1969; Epstein 1981, 194-198). Using the language of chiefly master-servant relations, the Iron clansfolk, for example, berate the Grass clan as their "slaves," arguing that iron (knives and hoes) kill grass. The Grass clan, in turn, assert their superiority on the grounds that grass (thatch) saves iron from being eaten by the rain.

Joking-clan partners abuse one another in ritualized enmity. The very names for these partners--*balwani* or *baali* (Lala), *balongo* (Lamba), or *banungwe* (Ambo, Aushi, Bemba, and Sanga)-- are those for "enemies." Their reciprocal banter entails a licensed disregard for the code of good manners (*mucinshi*). Thus, while these peoples ordinarily "use a variety of euphemisms when discussing sex relations, and are in particular careful of referring to sex matters when members of different age groups are present" (Richards 1940, 17), joking-clan partners employ *amatuka*, or vulgar sexual insults, to engage in "mutual cursing of the grossest kind" (Stefaniszyn 1950, 291). Lambo (1946, 325) says, "These insults [amatuka] are frequent; they generally call into question the virtue of one's relatives and allude to the private parts of one's maternal ancestry. The Lala possess a very rich vocabulary in this domain." Doke (1931, 77n) offers the following "typical examples" of Lamba amatuka: "Little [but connoting "big"] penis of your mother!" [incest] "Little anus of your mother!" "Your little penis!" and "Your little testicle!". As provocations to a fight, such amatuka are punishable offenses against customary law (Doke 1931, 67, 77, 213; Grévisse 1956, (39) 126; Stefaniszyn 1964b, 101). Smith and Dale (1920, vol. 1, 374-378) say that the Ila must not only avoid references to private parts and natural functions when in mixed company, but should also "avoid the use of words and expressions of the same or similar sound" (1920, vol. 1, 377). Their compulsive and privileged license serves as "a highly efficient ice-breaker" at any social gathering (Cunnison 1959, 70).

Of all these peoples, however, the peoples along the southeastern Shaba Pedicle actually have clans with vulgar (amatuka) names. I discovered this during the course of my fieldwork when I tried making sense of my informants' common claim that the *Bena*

Mishishi (Hair clan) chiefs of the Lamba and Seba (Lamba offshoots) are somehow related to the *Bena Nyendwa* chiefs of the Lima, Swaka, Lala, and Ambo (Lala offshoots). Doke (1931, 195) called the latter the "Needle" clan, for he, like Stefaniszyn (1964b, 5), was evidently told that they were named for the *nyenda*, a wooden mat-making needle. I saw no symbolic complementarity between these Hair and "Needle" clan names. And getting no help from my surprised and amused, but evasive, friends, I decided to try eliciting Doke's "Needle" clan translation while interviewing a gregarious Lamba age-mate at his father's old, established village, just inside a Lima chiefdom.

Fishing for phallic symbols, I steered him to the topic of clan names and, in spite of his evasion, that of the Lima chiefs. My indirection failed, for he claimed ignorance of the Lima's chiefly clan and, then, of what their name meant! So, as his sisters tittered and his father guffawed, I reduced him to an embarrassed silence by asking just what kind of animal the *nyendwa* (vulva) was.

As matters of good manners (mucinshi) and shame (*nsoni*), one should never raise sexual issues with one's parents or members of their generation, or with siblings of the opposite sex, so my questions were doubly indecent. The same sexual etiquette is expressed in the social distance between adjacent generations, and the social solidarity of alternate ones. (See Watson 1954, 16-23; also Epstein 1981, 200-204; Richards 1940, 15-17, 25; Stefaniszyn 1964b, 11-12, 87-88).

He suggested that we retire to a neighborhood Chibuku tavern, and, on our way, told me about vulvas and the shame (nsoni) my amatuka had caused him. Doke, by the way, got it straight as well, for the sexual entries in his Lamba *Vocabulary* (1963) are marked with an "M" for amatuka, or "vulgar terms."

But the Vulva clan is not the only vulgar clan along the Shaba Pedicle. Here one also finds the *Bena Bi* or Anus, *Bena Mwanso* or Penis, and *Bena Mubinda* or Breechcloth clans. Mwanso properly denotes the male genitals. A Lala told me it was the same as *ubwaume*, the Bemba term for "virility," "male organs," and, more commonly, "penis." One of Verbeek's (1982, 182) informants, an elderly Lala female, pointed to a billy goat and described it as "that thing dangling down" (*kilye ikikolebela mu*). Thus, while Lambo (1946, 248) translates the Bena Mwanso as the "Testicles" clan, most call it the Penis clan (Boswell 1969, 281n; Mitchell and Barnes 1950, 50; Munday 1961, xvi; Stefaniszyn 1964b, 5).

The mubinda (or mobinda) of the Bena Mubinda (Breechcloth clan) is draped over the buttocks, tied around the waist, and is then drawn up between the legs and through the tie in front. While Stefaniszyn (1964a, 16; 1964b, 1) calls it a "loincloth," Lambo (1946, 248) and Verbeek (1987, 355) call it a "cache-sexe." In this respect, it may be a euphemism for the *bukushi*, a small cloth strip suspended front and rear from a woman's beaded waist string (Stefaniszyn 1964a, 16; White Fathers 1954, 46). In the idiom of joking-clan relations with the Anus and Musamba Tree (source of barkcloth) clans, it conceals the vulva (Stefaniszyn 1950, 301).

Smith and Dale (1920, vol. 1, 313), in a list of foreign clans among the Ila, include the "Vulva" (Nyendwa) clan from the "Batema and Walenje," and the "Anus" (*Chibanda*) and "Vagina" (*Ntoto*) clans from the "Balamba (Badima)," west of the Lukanga Swamp. While I doubt that the Anus is a Lima ("Badima") clan, chibanda is not "anus" (Ila *inyo*, Lamba *inyenu*), but a common term for "evil spirit" or "devil." And since ntoto is the Ila term for "vaginal orifice" (vol. 1, 233), their "Vagina" clan is the same as the Vulva clan.

The Swaka and Lima are not included with the Lala and Ambo here because, while their chiefs are Bena Nyendwa, I have no evidence that they have the Anus, Penis, or Breechcloth clans. Munday (1940, 447, 1950, 25-26, 40-41, 1961, 24-28) claims that both the Swaka and Lima chiefs derive from the Swaka's Mwewa lineage who, after the Lala conquest, changed from the *Bena Ng'ona* (one of the many Mushroom clans) to the Vulva clan. If true, this may explain the apparent absence of these other vulgar clans among the Swaka and Lima. Having never encountered any reference to the Anus, Penis, or Breechcloth clans in the Lima marital histories I collected, I place no credence in Moffat Thomson's claim (in Brelsford 1965, 50) that the Lima are a Lala offshoot.

These are even more narrowly localized, for they are as specific to the Lala and their Ambo offshoots as the Hair clan is to the Lamba and their Seba offshoots (Stefaniszyn 1964, 1; Verbeek 1987, 326). Thus, of 299 marital histories I collected from the Lamba and Lima areas in Ndola Rural District, fifteen of the seventeen Hair clan spouses came from Lamba chiefs' areas, and ten of the thirteen Vulva clan spouses came from Lima or Lala chiefs' areas. The remaining five spouses--from nearby Lima, Lamba, or Swahili chiefs' areas--were presumably of Lamba or Lima ancestry (Mitchell and Barnes 1950, 50). The Anus clan was never mentioned, but one Lala each had a Penis and Breechcloth father.

It is futile to ask the origins of these vulgar clans, for all are either attributed to Lesa (God) and Kola, or to the ancestors who broke some prohibition at a funeral, and were then named for the thing responsible for their impropriety (Doke 1931, 182, 193-197). Lambo (1946, 247-248) records just these sorts of just-so stories for the origins of the Anus and Breechcloth clans. According to the less "indecent and scatological" accounts, the Anus clan were cast out of the Vulva clan for breaking the taboo against burying their own clansman (also Munday 1940, 441, 1961, 13). And the Breechcloth clan were outcast from the Blue Monkey clan because their women, while serving beer at a funeral feast, wiped their fingers on their genitals. The Penis clan's origins must be equally indecent, for it is attributed to their members' former prolificacy (also Stephenson 1937, 131).

Such stories are not to be taken literally, for they merely reflect the ribald joking-relations that exist between the Vulva and each of its other mutual and intimately related "sister-clans." To bury a chief with his full crop of pubic hair would be doubly scandalous. First, when female initiation rites (*cisungu*) were still practiced, the instruction in wifely duties included that of plucking (later, shaving) the husband's pubic hair and giving it to him for safe burial (Doke 1931, 169; Grévisse 1956, (32), 122; Marchal 1933-34, 125; Stefaniszyn 1964b, 92). The Bemba probably did this, too, for the White Fathers' *Dictionary* (411) includes the phrase "to shave or depilate pubic hair" (ukusesa maso). Second, given the elaborate (and grisly) care given chiefs by their funeral attendants, it is difficult to see how such pubic hair could have escaped notice. (See Edme 1944, 87-93; Doke 1931, 186-190; Lambo 1946, 283-285; Marchal 1933-34, 103; and Stefaniszyn 1964b, 52-60). This origin fable, like the "pubic hair" label, is a vulgar insult against the Hair clan).

Just as the Sorghum and Finger Millet clans share sisterhood (*bwanankashi*) because their referents are both grains, the Vulva, Anus, and Breechcloth clans are considered such because breechcloths cover vulvas and anuses. The breechcloth is treated as a woman's garment, so the Breechcloth and Penis clans' opposition, like that of the Vulva and Penis clans, is based upon sexual complementarity and "physical dependence." And though the Anus clan says "only wizards do it," the joking between it and the Vulva and Penis clans is based upon the anus being a poor (and proscribed) substitute for the vulva (Stefaniszyn 1950, 299-304).

The one exception to these just-so stories appears to be the origin of the Vulva clan, which is only described by Munday (1940, 440-441, 1950, 3-4, 1961, 7). It seems that two chiefs, Chisenga Mushili and her brother, Malama, left Kola in search of their land. Upon reaching the Itumba Hills, west of Serenje, in the heart of Ilala (Verbeek 1987, 249), they met a woman fetching water. They refused a drink from her gourd, so she urinated into her water pot, and the chiefs bent down and sucked it up. Thus "all changed to the name Nyendwa because they drank water which had come from the loins [*lubunda*, crotch] of a woman" (Munday 1940, 440-441). This bizarre vulgarity does make some sense, for the drinking of a clanswoman's urine, symbolizing clan solidarity, figures in both the cleansing of burial parties and the ritual curse-removal between estranged clan members (Munday 1961, 7; Stefaniszyn 1964b, 3, 126).

Others claim that the Bena Mishishi, the Hair clan of the Lamba (and Seba) chiefs, is the "Pubic Hair" clan, and a member of the Vulva clan's set of vulgar sister-clans. Since the Bena Mishishi are named for the hair of the human head (mishishi), its members deny that their name is a euphemism or synonym for pubic hair (*amaso*) (Doke 1931, 194; Stefaniszyn 1964b, 92). Yet this is such an open secret that studies of the Swaka, Lala, and Ambo invariably refer to them as the "Pubic Hair" clan. "Chirupula" Stephenson, who served in Ilamba and Ilala, and was the polygynous husband of a Lala Vulva clanswoman, suggests that the Hair clan had a vulgar origin (Stephenson 1937, 131). What is more damning, Verbeek (1987, 29) cites three Lamba sources for the tale that the Hair clan were outcast from the Vulva clan after burying a chief with his pubic hair intact.

The Vulva's "sister-clans" are mentioned by Boswell (1969, 281n), Munday (1961, xv-xvi, 19), and Stefaniszyn (1964b, 5-6). Among the Ambo, these also include the *Bena Nyangu* (Bean clan), and beans symbolize pubic hair and the clitoris in the neighboring Nsenga's cisungu rites (Stefaniszyn 1964b, 6; Munday 1961, viii). *Kankomba* (Scraper), the praisename of the Lala chiefs, supposedly derives from a version of the Chipimpi myth in which a Vulva clan ancestor scrapes clean the relish pot of beans (nyangu) while his cross-cousin (Kabunda) of the Hair clan works in the clay pit (Munday 1940, 436-438, 1950, 6-7, 1961, 9-10). This again suggests that such vulgar clans are specific to the Lala.

The Anus is a special sister-clan. Since it originated from the Vulva clan, the two do not intermarry (also Lambo 1946, 247; Munday 1940, 441, 453). Boswell (1969, 281n) reports the existence of an Anus clan chief among the Lala.

These supposed links between the Vulva and (pubic) Hair clans are all the more interesting in light of Munday's Western Lala-Maswaka oral traditions, which claim that these clans share a common ancestor in Chipimpi, the first chief of Lamba legend (Munday 1940, 1950, 1961).

The origin of the Lamba's chiefly Hair clan is found in the far more elaborate myth of Chief Chipimpi. It explicitly explains how he lost his people, his head, and his chiefdom to the Hair clan. (The most accessible version of the Chipimpi myth is in Doke's Lamba ethnography (1931, 31-35). Increasingly more satisfactory versions are those in Doke (1922), Marchal (1936), and Verbeek (1982, 22-120). The myth is discussed in Siegel (1985) and Verbeek (1987, 9-26)).
The Lamba conventionally assign the Hair clan's origin and praisename, *Mwansekanda*, to that episode in which Chipimpi sent a nephew and his son, Kabunda, into a pit (*ikanda*) to extract

plastering clay. Once done, the nephew accepted and killed a goat. But Kabunda, goaded by his mother, refused to leave the pit until given a person, whom he killed, and in whose blood he bathed. This son and future chief thereby declared Chipimpi's people to be the Goat clan, and himself to be one of the Hair clan. Since the term *mwansa* denotes an animal's "mane," this clan's praisename might best be translated as "Mane of the Pit" Mwansa does have alternative meanings. It was once a popular personal name, and Verbeek (1987, 14-16) prefers to render it as such. It also appears in an exploit of Kalulu, or Little Hare, the folklore hero in "Mwansa the aimer who aimed at five people with the arrow at his navel" (Doke 1927, 400). This is probably a reference to the epithet *mwansa kabinga*, a cruel, savage, and proud fellow (Lambo 1946, 342; White Fathers 1954, 510). This, too, is consistent with Kabunda's patricidal exploits.

While the myth alone does not support the conventional Lamba belief that Kabunda either seized his victim by the hair, or washed his hair with the victim's blood (Verbeek 1987, 14-16), the Hair clan's identity is consistent with at least two other episodes in the myth. In the first, Chipimpi's newly found wife, Kashanga (Kabunda's mother), introduced his people to fire and, from a plaited hollow in her hair, the seeds of all cultigens. Later, after the episode in the pit, the Goat and Hair clans quarreled and, before separating, divided Kashanga's seeds. But while the Goat clan got those she had secretly roasted, Kabunda and his sister were given the fertile ones. These, again, were concealed in a hollow of plaited hair. So throughout this myth, the mwansa portion of the Hair clan's praisename seems firmly rooted in the hair of the human head.

Now most of the Zairois (i.e., Shaban Pedicle) Lala know of Chipimpi, but deny any links through him to the Lamba chiefs (Verbeek 1987, 247-248). Such claims are specific to the Mushili lineage of Lala chiefs, the family of Vulva clan chiefs who conquered the Lamba of the Bukanda region (Verbeek 1987, 254-260) and, under Chief Bwashi, the Swaka of Maswaka. The same lineage continues to rule the Western (Mkushi District) Lala and Ambo (Petauke District) chiefdoms in Zambia. The Eastern (Serenje District) Lala chiefs, however, appear to represent a different lineage (Brelsford 1965, 49-52); Lambo 1946, 235; Munday 1940, 443-452; Stefaniszyn 1964a, 5-9, and 1964b, xx-xxii). Munday's Western Lala-Maswaka version of the Chipimpi myth is clearly linked to the Mushili lineage, for a number of his unnamed informants told him "they had heard their story from one Nkufye, who was storyteller to Chief Bwashi" (Munday 1961, xiv).

It is the Mushili lineage that claim Chipimpi as the ancestor of the Lala, Lamba, and Aushi chiefs. They do so either by having him travel through Bwaushi, or by investing him with additional wives from the clans of the Lala and Aushi chiefs (Verbeek 1987, 232-47). Thus, in Munday's Western Lala-Maswaka traditions, Chisenga Mushili (mentioned previously), an original founder of the Vulva clan, is one of Chipimpi's wives; her daughter crosses the Luapula to marry an Aushi chief of the Wild Pig clan; and her daughter's son abandons his uncle's western lands in Bukanda, west of the Munyengashi River (Munday 1940, 436-442, 1950, 3-24, 1961, 8-18).

Such myths do not constitute a plausible historical record. Yet it is interesting to note that Verbeek's Lala informants were unable to trace any clear connection between Chipimpi and the Lala and Aushi, had no knowledge of Chisenga Mushili and five other characters in Munday's genealogy, and were unfamiliar with many of the Chipimpi myth's central episodes, characters, and clans. They explicitly said it is a Lamba story. By contrast, none of the Lamba versions of this myth mention the Lala nor their Vulva clan. There is, then, no particular reason to believe the Mushilis' claims of a common ancestry (Verbeek 1987, 239, 248-249). Nor is there any reason to believe that the Lamba's Hair clan belongs with the Lala's set of vulgar sister-clans. Given their limited distribution, it is far more likely that the Vulva and its vulgar sister-clans are specific to and originated among the Lala.

There are a number of more or less plausible reasons for the association between the Hair and Vulva clans. First, the mishishi (head hair) of the Bena Mishishi is certainly a euphemism for pubic hair (Doke 1931, 194); Stefaniszyn 1964b, 92), and the scandalous fable of how this clan was outcast from the Vulva clan plays upon this semantic ambiguity. In effect, this unlikely story degrades the Hair clan: first, by suggesting that they derive from an earlier, more legitimate chiefly clan; and second, by reducing them to the status of the Vulva's other vulgar sister-clans.

That the Lamba might entertain such vulgar notions about their chiefs is aptly demonstrated in two remarkable versions of the Chipimpi myth recorded by Verbeek (1982, 38-41, 54-59). It seems that Lesa (God) separately sent Kashanga and Chipimpi, or their parents, out of Kola to find their land. The woman left with her firesticks and seeds. The man was given their genitals in two bundles, but, offended by its smell, tossed Kashanga's bundle by the way. No sooner did they meet when, like joking-clan partners, they began arguing over who was whose chief. Their bantering continued long after Kashanga retrieved her bundle and they put on their genitals. Chipimpi got a huge erection, but Kashanga refused him and berated him for his penis which, waking or sleeping, continuously (and contemptuously) spat "salvia" at her. Kashanga relented after accepting an axe in tribute, but she warned Chipimpi that he would never be her master, and would always have to beg and pay to sleep with her.

The antagonism between the mythical couple in this episode not only reflects the matrilineal war between the sexes, and the subsequent triumph of the Hair over the Goat clan, but is just the sort of banter one might expect from an encounter between the Lala's vulgar sister-clans.

In addition to their sexual sense of humor, the Lamba also have a healthy disregard for unbearably proud chiefs, and share the common Central African tales of the villagers who burned their tyrannical chief to death in a pit of boiling water, and of the foolish chief who tried to catch the moon with a bamboo Tower of Babel (Doke 1927, 15, 277-279). Commoners, as their chief's "slaves," should show their respect with tribute, gifts, and decorous speech. But the chief must also respect and be generous to his "children" lest they abandon him to be chief over all the trees (Doke 1927, 429, 476, 489-490, 509). Thus Lamba commoners presumably perpetuate the association between head and pubic hair to subvert the Hair clan's royal pretensions. This is what Lamba commoners mean when, in confidence, they claim that the Hair and Vulva clans are related.

Yet the most compelling reason for this association between head and pubic hair and the Hair and Vulva clans is to be found in the Lamba-Lala encounters of the nineteenth century, when the Vulva clan chiefs expanded their territory in all directions and, in the west, conquered the Lamba peoples of Bukanda (Verbeek 1987, 249-252, 311), the easternmost end of the Pedicle which, the Lala say, is so rich in honey, mushrooms, and wild fruits that its residents need never fear famine (Lamba 1946, 233). It is no accident that the Lamba and Lala chiefdoms in Bukanda contain a generous mix of both Lala and Lamba residents (Boone 1961, 96-103; Lambo 1943, 26-27), for in the middle 1800s the Vulva clan chiefs extended their control to the west of the Munyengashi River, the present ethnic boundary. It was only around 1900 that the Belgians established the Munyengashi boundary, and they did so after a Lala chief went to war (Lambo's (1946, 236) "revolt") on the disloyal Lamba villages that refused to help fill his food and rubber levies (Verbeek 1987, 229, 252-258, 264-267).

Yet this association between the Hair and Vulva clans is much more than yet another example of a joking-relationship between peoples who formerly warred upon each other (Mitchell 1956, 35-42). For it seems that the Mushili lineage of the Lala's Vulva clan chiefs, the one that claims common mythical ties to the Lamba and Aushi chiefs, appropriated the Chipimpi myth to mask their late nineteenth century misfortunes, and to preserve the memory of their former rule. For the Mushili lineage in Shaba fell from power in the early 1900s when, following Chief Mushili's death, the Belgians awarded his chiefdom to their appointed go-between from a different Vulva lineage (Verbeek 1987, 240-244, 256-258, 263).

The territory of Chief Mushili's Vulva clan lineage was usurped by the same Chief Namopala who, with neighboring Chief Mufumbi, was deposed and died in prison for hosting Tomo Nyirenda (Mwana Lesa), the Watchtower prophet, and for concealing his murder of at least forty-eight "witches" during his 1925 tour of Katanga. Like Lala chief Shaiwila, just below the border, neither Namopala nor Mufumbi were wholly legitimate chiefs, and a number of these "witches" are known to have opposed their rule (Verbeek 1977, 89-94; 1987, 258-263; Verbeek 1983, 37-108). The Mushili lineage, as stated earlier, did stay in power among the Western Lala and Ambo chiefdoms in Zambia's Mkushi and Petauke Districts.

The other misfortunes center upon the chiefdom of Mushili's mother, Ngosa Mupeta, on the western (i.e., Lamba side of the Munyengashi. Her nickname, Nabayeke (Mother of the Yeke), refers to the Yeke occupation of the early 1870s, when the Lala chiefs in

Bukanda submitted to the Yeke. Ngosa Mupeta then married a Yeke of the Goat clan. Then, during the Aushi invasion of the late 1880s, her youngest daughter, Musonda Kaseba, was taken hostage and disappeared across the Luapula. Though Ngosa Mupeta's second husband, Mumbilima the elephant hunter, shared the usual occupational reputation for witchcraft, they are supposed to have lived in brother and sisterly harmony, for both came from chiefly clans. Mumbilima, who succeeded her on her death, was a Lamba from the Hair clan, and her chiefdom, now that of Chief Kumbwa, has remained in control of the Lamba's Hair clan ever since (Lambo 1943, 27-28; Verbeek 1987, 12, 49-50, 254-256, 274-276).

It is the history of Ngosa Mupeta's chiefdom that best explains the tie between the Lala's Hair clan and the Lamba and Aushi chiefs. For, as in Munday's Western Lala-Maswaka version of the Chipimpi myth, her daughter, Musonda Kaseba of the Vulva clan, did cross the Luapula as an Aushi hostage to live among the chiefs of the Wild Pig clan. Presumably it is this same Musonda who appears with Ngosa Mupeta in a Western Lala list of ancestresses as "Nampongela [literally, "I have lost myself"], alias Musonda, who appears to have been of the least significance," and whose "offspring [kin] ... are [were among] the Lala chiefs in Congo territory" (Moffat Thomson, in Brelsford 1965, 49-50). And just as in the Western Lala's Chipimpi myth, the Mushili lineage really did lose its rule in Bukanda after Ngosa Mupeta's chiefdom passed from the control of her Goat clan husband to that of the Hair clan chiefs.

There is no evidence to indicate that the Lamba's Hair clan began or belongs with the Lala's Vulva and its vulgar sister-clans. Yet its name is ambiguous, and Lamba commoners enjoy and perpetuate its scandalous implications. While the symbolic opposition of joking-clan partnerships goes a long way in explaining this association between the chiefly Hair and Vulva clans, it probably derives from the nineteenth century rivalry between the Bukanda Lamba and Lala chiefs, and, as symbolized in the myth of Chief Chipimpi, from the consequent redemption of Ngosa Mupeta's chiefdom by her Hair clan successors. There is power in myth and symbols, but it is particularly satisfying to show how such constructs reflect equally real historical struggles for legitimacy and power.

References

Boone,O.
1961   *Carte ethnique du Congo: Quart sud-est. Annales, sciences humaines* 37. Tervuren: Musée Royale de l'Afrique Centrale.

Boswell,D.M.
1969   Personal crises and the mobilization of the social network. In *Social networks in urban situations*, edited by J.C.Mitchell, 245-296. Manchester: Manchester University Press.

Brelsford,W.V.
1965   *The tribes of Zambia*, 2d ed. Lusaka: Government Printer.

Burton,R.F.
1873   *The lands of Cazembe: Lacerda's journey to Cazembe in 1798*, translated and annotated by R.F.Burton. London: Royal Geographic Society.

Cunnison,I.
1959   *The Luapula peoples of Northern Rhodesia.* Manchester: Manchester University Press.

Doke,C.M.
1922   A specimen of the folk-lore of the Lamba people of Northern Rhodesia. *Bantu studies* 1:30-37.
1927   *Lamba folk-lore.* New York: G.E.Stechert.
1931   *The Lambas of Northern Rhodesia.* London: G.G.Harrop.
1963   *English-Lamba vocabulary*, 2d rev.ed. Johannesburg: Witwatersrand University Press.

Edme,P. [E.Bourgeois]
1944   *Nkoya Kalambwa: scènes de la vie noire.* Elizabethville: Editions Congolaises.

Epstein,A.L.
1981   *Urbanization and kinship.* London; New York: Academic Press.

Grévisse,F.
1956-58   *Notes ethnographiques relatives à quelques populations autochtones du Haut-Katanga industriel. Bulletin du centre d'etudes des problèmes sociaux indigènes*: 32-41.

Lambo,L.
1943   *Organisation judiciaire et procedure du tribunal coutumier de Kumbwa. Bulletin des juridictions indigènes et du droit coutumier congolais* 11(2):26-30.

1946   *Etude sur les Balala. Bulletin des juridictions indigènes et du droit coutumiers congolais* 14(8): 231-256; (9): 273-300; (10): 313-346.

Long,N.
1968   *Social change and the individual.* Manchester: The University Press.

Marchal,R.
1933-34   *Moers et croyance des Balamba. Bulletin des juridictions indigènes et du droit coutumier congolais* 1(4):62-66, (5):82-86, (6):103-106; (7):124-127, (8):153-155.

1936   *Origine des Balamba. Artes Africaines* 3(4):14-28.

Mitchell,J.C.
1956   *The Kalela dance.* Rhodes-Livingstone Paper No. 27. Manchester: Manchester University Press.

Mitchell,J.C., and J.A.Barnes
1950   The Lamba village: Report of a social survey. African Studies Communication No. 24. University of Cape Town.

Munday,J.T.
1940   Some traditions of the Nyendwa clan of Northern Rhodesia. *Bantu studies* 14:435-454.

1950   *Inyendwa (W. Lala-Maswaka traditions)*, 3d ed. Cilala: Lovedale Press.

1961   *Kankomba.* Central Bantu historical texts I, Part I, Rhodes-Livingstone Communication No. 22. Lusaka: Rhodes-Livingstone Institute.

Richards, A.I.
1937   Reciprocal clan relationships among the Bemba. *Man* 37:188-193.
1939   *Land, labour and diet in Northern Rhodesia.* London: Oxford University Press.
1940   *Bemba marriage and present economic conditions.* Rhodes-Livingstone Paper No.4. Manchester: Manchester University Press.
1950   Some types of family structure amongst the Central Bantu. In *African systems of kinship and marriage,* edited by A.R.Radcliffe-Brown and D.Forde. London: Oxford University Press.

Siegel,B.
1985   The binary mind and the immortal head: A structural analysis of the myth of Chief Chipimpi. *Furman studies* 31 (December):36-55.

Slaski,J.
1950   *Peoples of the lower Luapula valley.* Ethnographic Survey of Africa, East Central Africa, Part II. London: International African Institute.

Smith,E.W., and A.M.Dale
1920   *The Ila-speaking people of Northern Rhodesia,* 2 vols. London: Macmillan.

Stefaniszyn,B.
1950   Funeral friendship in Central Africa. *Africa* 20:290-306.
1964a   *The material culture of the Ambo of Northern Rhodesia.* Rhodes-Livingstone Museum Occasional Paper No. 16. Manchester; Manchester University Press.
1964b   *Social and ritual life of the Ambo of Northern Rhodesia.* London: Oxford University Press.

Stephenson,J.E.
1937   *Chirupula's tale.* London: Geoffrey Bles.

Verbeek,L.
1977   *Kitawala et détecteurs de sorciers dans la Botte de Sakania (1925-1975). Enquêtes et documents d'histoire africaine* 2:86-107.

1982   *Mythe et culte de Kipimpi (Rep. du Zaire).* Series 2, vol. 80. Bandundu: CEEBA Publications.

1983   *Mouvements religieux dan la region de Sakania (1925-1931). Enquêtes et documents d'histoire africaine* 5.

1987   *Filiation et usurpation: Histoire socio-politique de la région entre Luapula et Copperbelt. Annales, sciences humaines* 123. Tervuren: Musée Royal de l'Afrique Centrale.

Watson,W.
1954   The Kaonde village. *Rhodes-Livingstone journal* 15: 1-30.

White Fathers
1954   *The White Fathers' Bemba-English dictionary,* rev.ed. Cape Town: Longmans, Green.

Whiteley,W.
1954   *Bemba and related peoples of Northern Rhodesia.* Ethnographic Survey of Africa, East Central Africa, Part II. London: International African Institute.

The Nuer Prophet: Personification of Dialogue

David Parkin, Professor
University of London
United Kingdom

I have had opportunity already to draw attention to two main areas in which Aidan Southall has made pioneering contributions (Parkin, 1978, xii, 1990, 189-193). The first refers to his extraordinary knowledge of Nilotic cultures and languages. At the present time, when the depth of modern anthropologists' understanding of the languages and cultures of the peoples they study is often questioned, the exceptional quality of Southall's cannot be overemphasized. Anyone who has been with him among Nilotic-speakers in East Africa will have marveled at a degree of empathy and sociolinguistic facility that is all too rare nowadays and may not have been that common during the years when he did his most intensive fieldwork. The second major contribution is to the reshaping of East African ethnography and of anthropological thinking generally. It may not often be recognized that it was Southall who, with his paper published in 1970, entitled *The Illusion of the Tribe*, ushered in the period still with us during which a whole series of Africanist concepts, including those of lineage, segmentation, linguistic and cultural isomorphy, statehood, and ethnic boundedness, have been radically revised or rejected. Indeed, this frame of questioning went back to his first major monograph, *Alur Society*, published in 1956, in which he copiously established the theory of the segmentary state, an idea now so widespread in one form or another that its original inspiration is often unacknowledged or forgotten, a common enough occurrence but one worth noting in the present context.

The third main area to which Southall has contributed, but on which I have not yet commented, is that of Marxism in anthropology. It is typical of Southall's scholarly approach that, unlike many of the earlier fellow travelers, he did not abandon this line of enquiry when the initial euphoria evaporated. His work continues to be underlain by it, though perhaps more directly with the Marxist critique on materialist infrastructures than with, so to speak, the second related Marxist critique, namely the extent to and manner in which religion and ideology shape or mystify human consciousness.

Partly in the spirit of the latter, I offer a reanalysis of the relation between priest and prophet among the Nilotic-speaking Nuer, suggesting that they represent a kind of dialectic between the overarching constraints of society, as expressed in agnation via the priest, and individual ambition and inventiveness, expressed nonagnatically via the prophet. It is obvious that such contrasts can be as much the product of the ethnographer's and analyst's imagination as that of the Nuer themselves. Nevertheless, the many later exegeses on Evans-Pritchard's work in particular, together with our knowledge of adjacent Nilotic cultures, suggest that, though not sharply demarcated, such broad distinctions may well approximate what was once a Nuer reality.

Let me then begin with the concept of the Nuer prophet by briefly summarizing some of the main views. Both Johnson (1979) and Southall (1976) criticize the analytical and artificial concreteness of the groups distinguished as Nuer/Nath and Dinka/Jieng. For Johnson, this exaggerated separation of Nuer from Dinka arose as a result of the Nuer Settlement of 1929-1930, but was not customary. For Southall, the concreteness of this distinction results from a semantic confusion of folk terms for "person" and what outsiders have translated as separate tribes. In fact, Naath came to denote peoples who were attackers, while Jieng referred to those who were attacked. But taken together, the two verbal concepts constituted a dynamic model of shifting sociocultural boundaries operating under ecological directives and constraints.

Southall's view of Naath and Jieng dynamic complementarity can be compared, analytically, with that of Beidelman (1971) of the priest and the prophet, the relationship between whom is also not sharply demarcated but rather represents different combinations of traditional authority and charismatic power. Southall supports this interpretation of priest and prophet as alternating characteristics of what may in fact be the same person, and as paradigmatic of other aspects of Nuer life and thought.

Johnson's emphasis is less on a kind of shifting politico-ritual complementarity expressed in the role of priest and prophet. Rather, in confining himself to the prophet, he suggests that the ritual or religious mediatory role was fundamental, and that the political and militant aspects of his behavior were exaggerated by the circumstances of the Nuer Settlement.

All three views depart from that of Evans-Pritchard. The four views can be expressed briefly as follows:

1. Johnson
   Priestly Prophet > warring prophet (i.e., the mediatory role of the prophet is customary).

2. Southall
   Priest = Prophet (i.e., they involve essentially the same cluster of role characteristics).

3. Evans-Pritchard
   (a) Priest : Prophet :: addressing God : addressed by God
   (b) Yet Priest → (can become) Prophet

   ←————————————— charismatic power
4. Biedelman

Priest   Prophet :: other   aspects   of   Nuer
                        life/thought
traditional ══════════⟶
authority

Rather than judging these as being either wrong or right, let me take them to be different perspectives on the place of the prophet in Nuer definitions of the person.

By comparison, I suggest that the way the Nuer see the relationship between what we call priest and prophet may be a metaphorical way of talking about the main channels and limitations on personal destiny and achievement among men, otherwise identified as *buth* (agnation) and *mar* (kinship).

Because dialogue of this kind goes beyond such static equations as A : B :: C : D, and must involve evaluative relations of inclusion, exclusion, entailment, presupposition, implication, and so forth, my own view can be put as:

5.   Parkin
     Priest ⊂ Prophet :: buth ⊂ mar   (i.e., the concept of priest is entailed in that of prophet in much the same way as agnation (buth) is entailed by, or included within, kinship (mar)

Moreover, I would suggest that it is a characteristic of both the prophet and of kinship, that they each express inconsistent and sometimes contradictory elements:

Priest ⊂ Prophet :: buth ⊂ mar
         ↓   ↓
   contradictions   contradictions

In other words, the concept of prophet and the concept of mar (kinship) are saying similar things: that they include within them the ideas of the priest and of agnation, respectively, but that they confuse them, even to the point of threatening their distinctiveness. Thus, just as an overemphasis on cognatic kinship can dissolve the power of agnation, so a privileging of the status of prophet can supersede that of priest. This built-in debate, so to speak, on human and kinship agency gets to the heart of Nuer ideas of personhood. It is a debate in which it is difficult to disentangle the contributions of the ethnographer and of the Nuer themselves. Or, to put this another way, how much the ethnographer has unwittingly imposed his distinctions and how much he has been influenced by Nuer ideas on the subject.

Let me start briefly with Evans-Pritchard. *Nuer Religion* (1956) carries furthest his exhortation that we should study not just relations but relations between relations. The difference between priest and prophet is presented analytically as based on a series of opposed characteristics: traditional versus modern; set versus indeterminate functions; inherited versus charismatic functions; official versus personalized status; noncultic versus cultic features; and speaking to God versus being spoken to by God, this latter being " . . . the most outstanding conceptual difference" (Evans-Pritchard 1956, 304). The outstanding significance of this latter feature is of central importance to my argument.

There are a number of terms for priest and prophet, and for other functionaries (Howell 1954, 211-217). It is therefore unsurprising that Evans-Pritchard should say that the Nuer themselves see priests and prophets as merely different rather than opposed, which was a view erroneously taken by government, and that they recognize that their activities may overlap, such that both priests and prophets may mediate disputes and make sacrifices, and that some priests led war raids like prophets.

No doubt there is situational variation in the use of the terms for priest and prophet that would give us more idea as to how much their characteristics are regarded as opposed or overlapping. The two main terms for prophet do suggest some special characteristics. *Gwan kwoth* consists of two words that are of central semantic significance. The first, gwan, means father, owner, or respected, and apparently denotes lineal authority; and the second word, kwoth, means immanent Spirit and refers to a divinity that transcends lineal restrictions. The use of these two key words together to mean prophet suggests, then, an archetypal joining together of lineal authority and nonlineal divinity. My impression is that the personal struggles of the prophet reflect this and tell us something of how ordinary Nuer also have to cope with contradictory demands of lineage and nonlineage ties.

The second term for prophet, *guk*, actually means both a bag and also two species of bird (Stigand 1923; Huffman 1933). The etymological idea is that Spirit enters the prophet as if he were a bag, suggesting a sexual parallel and the prophet as a spouse of Spirit or God. With regard to the second term, the prophet is also a bird, which, as we know from elsewhere in Nuer ethnography, is a child of God (*gaat kwoth*). As both spouse and child of God, the prophet here confuses lineal affiliations, which should be kept distinct.

None of the main terms for priest, however, *kuaar muon*, *kuaar twac*, *gwan twac*, and so forth, connote ambivalence or contradiction. A priest belongs to the realm of earth rather than of sky or Spirit, and he carries out tasks that are consistent with earthly matters, including the fertility of the soil, and of people and livestock, and of maintaining life-saving peace during feuds.

The impression I have is that, while a person may be a priest and no more, a prophet includes but goes beyond this role. That is to say, the concept of prophet encompasses that of the priest but is also associated with such additional features as voluntary possession by

Kwoth/Deng (Spirit), a wide geographical scale of activities, the occasional inclusion of women as prophetesses, a revelational as well as sacrificial role, and speech that is believed to compound the prophet's with that of his/her spirit.

It is because these are differences of scale and degree that Nuer might refer to the same person by any of the different terms. The classification of what we translate as priest and prophet is clearly polythetic, to use Needham's concept (1975), with Nuer sometimes referring to a particular clustering of features as constituting gwan kwoth or *guth*, which we then please to translate as prophet.

For example, were the priests ("leopard-skin chiefs" *sic*) who had "considerable [persuasive] powers in bringing together disputants in the Zeraf Valley tribes" (Howell 1954, 28), (my bracketed inclusion), regarded by Nuer as conforming more to the characteristics of prophets than priests? Lel, whom Evans-Pritchard calls "a leopard-skin priest and also a prophet" (1956, 11) was summoned at a distance to officiate at a sacrifice. Was this because he was, in that situation, associated with geographical distance and dispersion rather than locality and lineal restriction, these being features that supplement those of the local priest? If so, we can say that identifying someone as a prophet does not negate his priestlike attributes, but may entail and include them. The prophet is a kind of metonymic transformation of the priest.

Even the most important contrast made by Evans-Pritchard, namely that between the priest who speaks to God and the prophet through whom God speaks to man, may be reformulated as a relationship of serial inclusion. Evans-Pritchard says that "spirits of the below" (*kuth piny*) are opposed in Nuer thought to "sky or air spirits" (*kuth nhial*) (Evans-Pritchard 1956, 63). This is part of an "implicit metaphor, which runs through Nuer religion, of light and dark, associated with sky and earth... (Howells, 97). Prophets are possessed by sky-spirits or by Spirit (i.e., the sky-god kwoth or *deng*) in its immanent aspect (Evans-Pritchard 1940, 172, 185). We might even say that as immanent Spirit inspires prophets, so prophets aspire to immanence through their wanderings in the wilderness. It is through air-spirits that God instructs prophets in battle (Evans-Pritchard 1956, 45). God creates prophets just as prophets create hymns and are otherwise innovative (1956, 47, 50). In their immanence, the air spirits assume no specific form and "are easily thought of, once people are familiar with their names, quite independently of the person in whom they manifest themselves" (1956, 63). They expand beyond the restrictions of conventional form.

Contrast this with the spirits of the below, which manifest themselves only in earthly creatures and things that are known by reference to these specific forms alone (1956, 63). Though priests are not especially associated with such earth-spirits, they are themselves characterized by their mild mystical association with the earth. They represent man's identification with the earth as distinct from God's identification with the sky (1956, 291-292). Priests, spirits of the below, and mankind are thus each associated with the earth. But the prophet, while sharing the greed and ambitions of all men including priests, themselves, transcends them through association with God, who at least is thought of as benign (1956, 51).

The immanence of Spirit, the higher status enjoyed by air spirits over earth spirits, and their association with the prophet and his wider field of activities is given material representation. Thus, a Nuer killed by lightning is said to have been taken by God as a kinsman or friend, and a small, pyramidal mud shrine should be built for him. He becomes a *colwic*, and may later need to be appeased with another slightly more elaborate mud-shrine to take the place of the first (1956, 59-60). But the pyramid built by a prophet is the biggest and most elaborate of all. That built by Ngundeng in honor of Deng and for Ngundeng's personal glory was fifty to sixty feet high and made of ashes, earth, and local debris, with large elephant tusks placed round the base and on top (Evans-Pritchard 1940, 186, 1956, 48). This morphological progression from small earth mound to large pyramid reaching up to the sky parallels in a way the pursuit of God in the sky by these prophets who may, themselves, have begun "at the bottom" as earth priests. The point is that, just as the pyramid of many substances is not simply opposed to the earth mound but rather encompasses it as the final stage of a morpho-ritual progression, so the prophet encompasses the priest as the final position that living men can reach in their attempt to be near God. The association of a pyramid with the highest mystical potency is nicely illustrated by the story of the barren woman of Garjok who lacked sons and who made a pilgrimage to Dengkur's mound in the Lau country, placing ivory tusks, beads, and sacrificial cattle there. They were, it seems, duly made pregnant (Stigand 1918). We may note here how lineal perpetuity through women was made possible by their crossing boundaries: from men to prophet pyramid; and from Garjok to Lau country. The prophet then here transcends lineal divisions, yet makes their continuation possible.

> The relationship can therefore be expressed not as one
> of opposition, such that priest : prophet, but rather as
> priest ⊂ prophet.

Encompassing so much, it is not surprising to find the prophet personifying contradictory elements. He is closest to God. Contact with God is dangerous. Therefore, contact with the prophet can also be dangerous, though to a lesser extent. He embodies the double aspect of spirit, which aids and sustains and yet can also harm and destroy (Evans-Pritchard 1956, 195-196). A concrete illustration of this may lie in the suggestion by Beidelman that prophets might especially appeal to Nuer dissatisfied with the status quo. These would include young men lacking livestock needed for marriage payments, probably junior sons or men whose fathers were poor. Such men might respond to the prophet's admonition to go and raid other lineages or areas for cattle (Beidelman 1971, 397). His exploitation of the frustrations of economically deprived young men in need of wives would contrast strikingly with the prophet's mediatory role practiced elsewhere for elders to whom the prophet preaches peace. In offering peace to the elders, the influential, and the materially comfortable, he preserves the lines of genealogical and generational differentiation, yet urges the young and poor to flout these same sources of authority.

Earth priests may sometimes have instigated cattle-raids (Beidelman 1971, 382), but they are more locally confined than prophets, and might have to conform more to the wishes of the senior than junior generation, while remaining neutral with respect to their disputes. They may well covet the apparent freedom of the prophet to transcend such limitations, but there is a price to pay. Prophets are prepared to risk intense possession by kwoth, while other Nuer avoid it or control their intake (Beidelman 1971, 389-391). If priests will not take the risk, they remain priests. The source of the prophet's contradictory attributes is the kwoth that fills him.

Perhaps here is a sense in which the mediatory *kuaar mon* who remains somberly unpossessed by Spirit, best represents lineal and generational consistency, the supreme expression of which is the segmentary lineage structure. The gwan kwoth may represent the transcendence or blurring of lines of generation and descent.

Some observations by Southall may be relevant here (1976, 473, 484). He suggests four things. First, that Dinka (Jieng) spearmasters are basically similar to Nuer (Nath) leopard-skin priests, except that the Dinka spearmasters are politically and ritually central, while Nuer priests are peripheral. Second, that Dinka spearmasters are therefore more like Nuer prophets in leading large-scale fighting against strangers and the British. Third, that Dinka spearmasters and Nuer prophets are most found in areas lacking a unitary agnatic structure, and in fact compensate for this lack. And fourth, that the peripheral Nuer leopard-skin priests are, by contrast, found in areas with a unitary agnatic structure, the political foci in which were the "bulls" (*tut*). That is to say, where the pyramidal segmentary system operates as a unitary agnatic framework, "bulls" are politically dominant, and ritual roles are dispersed among different incumbents, of which the leopard-skin priest is one. Where, by contrast, the agnatic framework is not unitary, then priests appear to have a greater chance of becoming ritually and politically central prophets. Prophets represent the absence and, by implication, the negation of the unitary agnatic structure.

If we gloss this unitary agnatic structure as the strongest expression of the concept of buth, then its opposite is that of mar, kinship and affinity. So, as kuaar muon is to gwan kwoth, so buth is to mar.

However, just as kuaar muon is encompassed by, rather than simply opposed to, gwan kwoth, so is buth encompassed by mar (i.e., buth $\subset$ mar). That is to say, buth, agnation, is one of the components of mar, the others being uterine and affinal ties and patrikin of up to only three generations. In a quantitative sense, then, mar is buth but much more besides. It is not simply the negation of buth. There are differences in the equation of these two pairs of concepts. As

Beidelman argues (1971), the authority associated with priests may be sought by prophets. But in actual cases, the career path seems to be largely one way: priests seeking to add charisma to their authority and becoming prophets (Beidelman 1971, 400). The relationship between buth and mar is the other way round. Buth is the concept quantitatively encompassed by mar, but is the one which ambitious men most wish to build up in order to become "bulls." Beidelman portrays mar as a resource of mainly nonagnatic ties which enterprising men can, through skillful manipulation, convert into the strong, corporate lineage relations called buth, and can themselves become renowned "bulls" (Beidelman 1966, 456). In other words, buth is contained in mar, from which it must be extracted in order to flourish.

We may note here the problem of legitimization faced by the prophet who seeks public recognition of his fatidical (prophetically gifted) status, one aspect of which might well be to institute his prophetic power as heritable in his own agnatic line like the status of priest (Beidelman 1971, 399-401). It is as if here the prophet tries to extract from his own dispersed affiliations, which we might call a personal mar, an agnatic line that will become clarified as buth, a fatidical corporate lineage. Since prophetic powers are in some ways based on confounding rather than clarifying lineage loyalties (Beidelman 1971, 399-401), this attempt to acquire the lineal respectability of a priest may well be at the price of losing charisma.

Thus far, we can see that the static equation,

1.   priest (kuaar muon) : prophet (gwan kwoth)
      :: corporate lineages (buth) : kinship (mar)

may be expressed more dynamically as

2.   priest $\subset$ prophet : agnation $\subset$ prophet

"Relations between relations" continues to be the object of study. But, expressed as relations between relations of entailment, they give us a clearer picture of how actual practicalities and preferences are generated.

The generative power lies in the fact that each relationship of entailment is unbalanced. Kinship contains agnation, and prophetic contains priestly status, with the result that in neither relationship are the components of equal value. Agnation is valued more than kinship by "bulls," even though contained by kinship, while prophetic is valued more than priestly status, even though acquiring it may mean forsaking the value normally placed on agnatic perpetuity.

The generative power comes from the source of contradictions: prophetic status and kinship, respectively. Prophets, it will be remembered, support young men and urge them to flout the authority of elders, and so, in this and in other ways, cause lineage boundaries and sentiments to be transgressed. Yet a prophet himself may want to establish a lineage in his own name (her own name, also?) and, on occasion, may require the support of corporate lineages on raids and in war. Moreover, in his occasional role as peacemaker, he needs the cooperation of lineage elders and aristocrats, whose position he thereby implicitly supports. Since there is no permanent reconciliation of these contradictory forces, prophets move to and from between fatidical and priestly attributes.

In a similar manner, mar contains contradictions. It is kinship and affinity, and is therefore the web of all possible relations out of which agnatic lines are built. But mar is also divisive. For, through the exchange of women in marriage, it includes the ties that divide lineages. In other words, mar contains the materials out of which corporate lineages are made but also contains the forces that may weaken or destroy them. Women come into lineages and, as co-wives and mothers, produce the competing groups of sons that will eventually divide the lineage. The term mar appears related both to the Nilotic variants of *maro/miro*, meaning to love "platonically" or, alternatively, to lust, and also to the term for mother (*man*), the one who divides agnates, as distinct from the term for agnation, buth, meaning to share (Beidelman 1966, 457). Beidelman (ibid.) suggests a range of other ways in which offence against mothers may be particularly harmful to the offender and, we may assume, to his own lineage, especially if he is afflicted by *nueer* (Howell 1954, 209). Perhaps, also, the fact that between a quarter and a third of the bridewealth cattle received for a sister goes to a man's maternal kin (Howell 1954, 97-110) reinforces the ambivalent nature of his ties with them.

In a similar manner, a man's affines may be his son's maternal kin. A man may struggle with the demanding affines from whom he took his wife and try to prolong the delivery of cattle, but to his son by this wife, these same affines are, at least until his sister's marriage, benevolent kin. Father and son may therefore be divided in their perceptions and judgments of the same group of people. In being able to refer to affines as well as kin (Evans-Pritchard 1951, 6,12), mar as a concept leaves unresolved this conflict of sentiments and loyalties between agnates.

In comprising various kinship terms of address, the concept of mar is even able to convert genealogical fathers and sons into members of the same generation, or alternatively, distant into clan kin (Evans-Pritchard 1951, 175).

The concept of mar does, then, seem to denote dispersed relationships, yet also allows for their common abridgement in specific situations. As I mentioned before, as well as containing a threat to agnatic continuity, it is the stuff out of which agnation grows.

Evans-Pritchard has argued that the Western Nuer prophets "personified the structural principle of opposition in its widest expression, the unity and homogeneity of Nuer against foreigners" (1940, 189). One can also argue that, in demonstrating and, through Spirit, embodying the strengths and weaknesses of dispersed, cross-lineal relationships, the prophet also personifies mar. In a similar way, the priest in his role of lineal patrolman, personifies buth.

Is it too much to claim that when Nuer discuss the merits and faults of *kuaar muon*/kuaar twac/gwan twac and *gwan kwoth*/*guk*/*cok kwoth*, and the transformation of one into another, and when they speak of relationships as alternating in character between buth and mar, they are talking, paradigmatically, and perhaps wistfully, of the same thing: of a structured as against personally inventive existence?

For K. Gough, agnatic structuring would be the privilege of being aristocrats (*dil*), while personal inventiveness would be that used by individuals and small "stranger" lineages to attach themselves through kinship (mar) to the dominant lineages characterized as buth (Gough 1971, 98-99).

We see now why the outstanding conceptual difference between priest and prophet is in their speech relationship with God. Priests speak to God seeking to reaffirm the lineal structure. God sometimes answers back, not always directly to them however, but to the prophets, suggesting ways round the structure. It is reassuring that God here seems less on the side of the angels and more on that of the artists, for it is an intelligent God who breaks the rules. God is not therefore Nuer society, but rather Nuer person recognizing itself.

References

Beidelman,T.O.
1966   The ox and Nuer sacrifice. *Man* 1:453-467.
1971   Nuer priests and prophets: charisma, authority and
            power among the Nuer. In *The translation of
            culture*, edited by T.O.Beidelman, 375-415. London:
            Tavistock Pulbications Limited.

Evans-Pritchard,E.E.
1940   *The Nuer*. Oxford: Clarendon Press.
1951   *Kinship and marriage among the Nuer*. Oxford:
            Clarendon Press.
1956   *Nuer religion*. Oxford: Clarendon Press.

Gough,K.
1971   Nuer kinship: a reexamination. In *The transition of
            culture: Essays to E.E.Evans-Pritchard*, edited by
            T.O.Beidelman. London: Tavistock Publications.

Howell,P.
1954   *A manual of Nuer law*. London: Oxford University
            Press for International African Institute.

Huffman,R.
1933   *Nuer-English dictionary*. Berlin: D.Reimer.

Johnson,D.
1979   Colonial policy and prophets: The "Nuer Settlement."
            Journal of the Anthropological Society of Oxford
            10:1-20.

Needham,R.
1975   Polythetic classification: convergence and consequence.
            Man 10:347-369.

Parkin,D.J.
1978   The cultural definition of political response: Lineal
            destiny among the Luo. London; New York: Academic
            Press.
1990   Eastern Africa: The view from the office and the voice
            from the field. In *Localizing strategies: Regional
            traditions of ethnographic writing*, edited by

310

R.Fardon. Edinburgh: Scottish Academic Press; Washington: Smithsonian Institution Press.

Southall,A.W.
1956   *Alur society.* Cambridge: W.Heffer and Sons.
1970   The illusion of tribe. *Journal of African and Asian studies* 5:28-50.
1976   Nuer and Dinka are people: Ecology, ethnicity and logical possibility. *Man* 11:463-491.

Stigand,C.H.
1918   Warrior classes of the Nuers. *Sudan notes and records* 1:116-118.
1923   *Nuer-English vocabulary.* Cambridge: Cambridge University Press.

Tsimihety Exogamy and Conquest

Peter J. Wilson, Professor
University of Otago, Dunedin
New Zealand

Aidan Southall has made the most succinct and coherent attempt to weave together the divergent strands of Malagasy culture into a single unified model (1986). The unity ramifies from the concept of "cumulative kinship" and the variations, it is suggested, rest upon such contrasting emphases as those between rice growing and cattle keeping, environmental differences between lowland coast and upland plateau, and on the degree of richness of the economic infrastructure. Two features of Malagasy unity are endogamous marriage and cognatic kinship, bound up with the need to maintain continuity with ancestors and to ensure exclusive access to tombs. One of the exceptions cited by Southall is the Sakalava who "have lost one of the fundamental features of the kinship system present everywhere," namely, cognatic emphasis and endogamy, because commoners have developed a cult of dead kings rather than an ancestor cult. They do not need to maintain exclusive lines to tombs and property, but there is a hint of endogamy among the kings. Well, Tsimihety, neighbors of the Sakalava, but also of the Betsimisaraka (to the east) and Sihanaka (to the south) have no cult of dead kings, do not recognize political hierarchy but they do insist very strongly on a rule of exogamy, members of the same *foko* not being allowed to marry, though the degree of forbidden kinship varies from a minimum of three generations to not being related at all. Why should this be? There have been, in the past, close contacts between some Tsimihety and some Sakalava, but if the connection between exogamy and a royal cult is the crucial one, then there is no way Tsimihety would have borrowed the idea of exogamy from the Sakalava. For if there is one thing insisted on even more emphatically by Tsimihety, it is that they admit no ranks to their society, least of all such sacred rulers like the Sakalava *mpanjakas* or the Merina kings. Tsimihety do not recognize a hierarchy of their own and only grudgingly admit agents of modern state bureaucracy. The split in Sakalava society between commoner and royalty in which commoners are said to be "more" unilineal and royalty to be more "cognatic," a split that still preserves the essential kinship characteristics Southall proposes for Madagascar, does not apply to Tsimihety. Tsimihety have patrilineally slanted ancestral associations (foko), which are strictly exogamous. At the same time, they attach importance to cognatic kinship.

I would like to link Tsimihety exogamy and the devolution of chieftainship not only to each other but also to a subject that has been central to Aidan Southall's interests, the state. Madagascar provides anthropologists and historians with one of the few examples where detailed information is available on the formation of indigenous, non-Western states. Much is known of the expansion of Sakalava groups and even more is known about the origin and growth of the centralized Merina state. It is not at all surprising that historians and anthropologists have been fascinated by the ritual and secular constitution of Merina state power and by the details of administration, supply, command, and military campaigning. But Merina expansion in the last years of the eighteenth and the first decades of the nineteenth centuries has another side. History all too often is history of the winners. The other side, of course, is the history of the effect of Merina state formation on the people who were forcibly incorporated to be ruled and administered. Among such people were those who are now called Tsimihety. The area in which they lived was at the limit of Merina reach, but oral and written history indicate quite clearly that much of this region was occupied increasingly in the nineteenth century by immigrants from the east coast (i.e., Betsimisaraka). These were people caught under the heel of the Merina state who chose to flee rather than stand and fight or cooperate as part of the state. When Merina influence extended into the region of Androna, where these migrants settled, the problem caught up with them again and required further solution.

What anthropologists often treat as structural constants engrained in a culture, such as a rule of exogamy and chieftainship, can be pried loose by utilization for other than social functions. In the present example, I suggest that gradually Tsimihety came to deploy exogamy and named exogamous associations and to deny hierarchy for political purposes of resistance against outside domination, first by the Merina, then by the French, and finally by the centralized Republican government. These were not the only tactics employed for such purposes and to some extent isolating these features from their political context is misleading, but necessary given the confines of this paper.

Tsimihety individuals identify themselves as belonging to a named foko, as a result of which they observe certain *fady* (taboos), are entitled to use a particular ear mark to identify cattle, are obliged to follow a rule of specified exogamy, may enjoy a joking relationship with another association (*lohateny*), claim status of *zafintany* over a bounded territory and the right to be buried in tombs located in the *tanindrazana* (territory) occupied by other ancestral members of the foko. I was able to record eighty-eight foko names within the region of Androna, the "heartland" of Tsimihety in the northeastern interior of Madagascar, around the town of Mandritsara. Tsimiheti villages, which are small, averaging about forty inhabitants, contain a core consisting of people of the same foko. This core is most commonly male, but not exclusively so. These small villages tend to be clustered within the ancestral territory and their claim to live on and work the land is unequivocal and unconditional. However, spouses, both male and female who are not of this proprietary status (i.e., zafintany), live in these villages and any Tsimihety, after going through the formality of asking permission, may live in and work the tanindrazana (ancestral land) of another foko. Since the pastures and rice lands vary in fertility and availability from year to year, people often live where they may only enjoy the formal, secondary status of *vahiny* (guest).

Although village houses are nowadays built of relatively solid mud and dung plastered over a wattle or raphia palm framework, they are not considered either permanent or valuable enough to restrain people from continually moving. In the dry season, families move around from one village to another to resettle for one, two, or more years. Distance is no object, nor are the reasons for moving always economic. Strained relations with others in a village may best be resolved by exit; a simple desire for a new view was often cited to me as a reason for moving; advice from the ombiasa to move as a means to avoid bad luck, or to counter illness were often cited reasons. One other circumstance resulting in moving, which I was often witness to, as well as it being explained to me, was to avoid the notice of the authorities if, for some reason, there was a threat of too close a contact. It is worth examining this reason historically.

Official records and oral accounts from the past suggest that Tsimihety mobility was as, if not more, pronounced than at present (i.e., middle 1960s). Villages were really no more than hamlets in most instances with an average of four to five houses in 1911, and two or three in 1927. From the time of occupation, French officials in their reports bemoaned the difficulty of collecting taxes in either cash or kind from Tsimihety because, so often, villages were found to be deserted. Enforcing corvée was at times and in some places extremely difficult. Censuses were nearly impossible because of the constant changing of residence (though this did not prevent population figures being issued, and not surprisingly, these were full of contradictions).

The Androna region is still, today, sparsely populated (about 5.53 per square kilometer is the estimate given by Molet (1959, 83), a generous estimate in my opinion). It was almost certainly even emptier during the time of the Merina occupation and at the time of French occupation in 1896. There is plenty of room to move and a reasonable disposition of natural resources to allow for subsistence. Such conditions one may regard as fundamental to any sort of physical freedom. It was surely this emptiness of Androna which attracted east coast Betsimisaraka migrants fleeing from Merina oppression in the first place. And it is the tradition of mobility within Androna that continues, both for the intrinsic attractions of an idealistic freedom and for the affordance it provides for political freedom, in a context in which for one hundred sixty-five years Tsimihety have been surrounded by aspirants to dominance.

Androna today, however, is not as empty as many parts of it were in the late 1700s. It is mapped out according to boundaries known to and recognized only by Tsimihety themselves and quite invisible on the official cartographical maps of the Service Geographique. The principle of such a mapping is the principle of foko. Everyone is affiliated through his or her father to a foko, which gives the individual a right to expect a place in a tomb, place to live, and access to rice fields and pastures. For the most part, most Tsimihety do not wander aimlessly and settle in some anonymous spot.

They actively seek out, first, kin of the same foko whom they can join as zafintany or landlords, where that foko has first rights in several areas, depending on whether or not foko ancestors were the first to clear the land and institute a tomb (*fasana*). In this way a settler secures rights to the use of pastures and rice lands, to the protection of his own ancestors, which can be exercised directly, and he/she lives in the presence of his future, the tomb, and its ancestors.

Foko associations lack any formal segmental, hierarchical organization. They are not nests of lineages within clans like African structures, and there are no political offices with decision making powers or jural authority. A foko is split up and dispersed over the landscape, and any members who happen to be living together at a particular time make up an effective "cell." Whoever is the senior male of the senior generation is *mpijoro* and offers prayers and sacrifices on behalf of the others and the village as a whole. In some instances I came across, the mpijoro was a woman. In secular affairs the assembly of adults (*rayamandreny*) is presided over by the *soja* (who is usually mpijoro), but this "headman" has no authority of his own separate from the rayamandreny. When members of a foko assemble together from far and wide, on the occasion of a funeral, for example, seniority determines office, and those who reside where the tomb is located have the status of guardian (*mpiambinjana*) and take on the duties of hosts. But otherwise foko association contributes little to political and social solidarity and control. Tsimihety, notoriously as far as other Malagasy and outsiders are concerned, are individualistic. The household is, perhaps, the most effective social grouping.

There is evidence that Tsimihety have lacked a politically constituted cohesion and organization from about the last decades of the nineteenth century. Further evidence suggests that political devolution occurred gradually and more as a result of circumstance than planning, from the beginning of the nineteenth century. Tsimihety seem to possess only a sketchy oral history, but one event known to all is the marriage of Ramarohosigny, the Antivohilava mpanjaka with Renimanana, the Sakalava princess. Together they stopped the expansion of the Sakalava Zafinmena across the Sofia River. For many of the people I spoke to, this union of Vohilava, the indigenous inhabitants of Androna, with Sakalava was the beginning of Tsimihety. The story clearly indicates a well-established chieftainship. Grandidier argued that the dynasty was not a strong one and controlled only a small area of Androna. The rest of the region was lived in by independent groups loosely linked together and ruled by local chiefs--a pattern similar to that of the Betsimisaraka. In 1824, Radama I, the Merina ruler, invaded Androna where he met little resistance. Radama appointed his own men as *komandy* or military overseers, and among other things, they had to collect a tax. Within a few years after Radama's arrival, numerous localized rebellions broke out, and were suppressed, it seems with unnecessary force. So humiliating were these constant defeats that, apparently, there was a rash of suicides of Tsimihety chiefs, who were replaced by Merina komandy (Grandidier 1958, 128, n.1). In other words, the relatively weak political hierarchy of Tsimihety was decapitated and seems never to have been replaced. What is more, there is no evidence from either history, or from my observation, that Tsimihety have ever wished to restore a hierarchical social and political way of life. The last mention of a Tsimihety chief or *sojabe* is of one Bosy who sided with the French against the Merina, but who was then dropped.

In a short paper, I cannot go into the details of the reasons as to why Tsimihety, unlike the Sakalava for example, chose to let political hierarchy go. Not just let it go, but develop a fiercely egalitarian ethos with which to defy any imposition of hierarchy, either their own or one imposed from the outside. Without chiefs or some sort of official recognized by the people to be administered as having legitimate, ritually sanctioned authority, an external regime has great difficulty getting its wishes fulfilled and commands obeyed. In effect, it has to confront the entire population as individuals, since that population is not represented under an egalitarian system by select individuals. Foreign officials, though they may summon superior force, have power but they do not enjoy authority. They cannot call upon the sense of duty, allegiance, and loyalty that an autochthonous official commands. As to the command of power through force, this can, to a large extent, be countered either by overt resistance or by covert evasion and noncompliance. Evasion, avoidance, stalling, and noncompliance are Tsimihety tactics and have been at least ever since the French colonialists sought to administer Androna. Reports are full of frustrated comments about the noncooperativeness of Tsimihety, of their failure to keep promises, of their vanishing from the scene whenever officials went to see for themselves. I might add here that I, too, as a *vazaha* or outsider was subject to the same "treatment."

So much of Tsimihety organization of life has to be considered with this backdrop of resistance against outside domination and cannot be explained simply by reference to some sort of eternal and universal Malagasy culture. Only a full study can demonstrate this, but allowing for the fact that in a short paper one must leap over many other factors, the question that remains is, Where does exogamy fit in?

Whereas Malagasy endogamy is viewed as a means to reinforce the unity and solidarity of the group as a tomb and property-owning entity, Tsimihety exogamy can be understood as a mechanism by means of which the political weakness and isolation of foko is compensated for socially. Tsimihety tombs, unlike those of most other Malagasy people, are not monuments to wealth, labor, and investment requiring exclusive access and ownership. And, except in a few instances, land is not a scarce commodity exerting subtle pressures for stability. Emphasizing exclusiveness is not, then, a requirement for Tsimihety foko. If anything, countering the inherent independence of foko is desirable. And the reason is that the need for avenues of escape and evasion, the attendant requirements of cooperation and trust, and the opening up of as wide a degree of choice as possible among Tsimihety--all these as functions of the political situation--makes advantageous the idea of establishing as many nonpolitical links as possible. When Tsimihety look for wives or husbands, one contacts one's own kin living elsewhere, one's affines, and one's friends. The searchers often go far afield geographically, though they keep within close social bounds. One ideal, apart from the ideals of securing a properly qualified spouse, is to establish links with people in a part of Androna where no links exist at present. It is almost as desirable to reinforce links with people to whom one is already connected by marriage because doing so would provide a possible option available to members of the foko for a place to go and maybe hide, and live. Exogamous marriages or unions expand the network of cognatic and affinal kinship, the obligations, sentiments, and duties of which are nearly as strong as those of patrilineal kinship. An expansion of such kinship helps to create a criss-crossing network of ties and obligations among people that, in turn, creates the invisible paths along which they pursue their seminomadic lives. This network is also part of the infrastructure of Tsimihety political cohesion and political evasion, the two principal means by which Tsimihety organize their resistance to outside powers in the absence of traditional leaders and a coordinating political structure.

References

Grandidier,A., and G.Grandidier.
1958   *Histoire de Madagascar*, vol. 4. *Ethnographie de Madagascar*, vol. 1. Paris: L'Imprimerie Nationale.

Molet,L.
1959   *L'Expansion Tsimihety*.   Mémoires de l'Institute Scientifique de Madagascar, series C, vol. 5.

Southall,A.W.
1986   Common themes in Malagasy culture. In *Madagascar: Society and History*, edited by C.Kottak, J-A.Rakotoarisoa, A.Southall, and P.Vérin. Durham, North Carolina: Carolina Academic Press.

Morality and Ethical Values According To the Iteso of Kenya

Ivan Karp, Curator of African Ethnology
Smithsonian Institution
Washington, D.C.
United States

The concepts I examine are not the product of individual thinkers reflecting on life, but are instead the terms used by almost all Iteso in making sense of their experience of self, society, and nature. In this sense I am not examining what H. Odera-Oruka calls "sagacity," the product of systematic reflection by individuals. Instead I am describing what Oruka-Odera (1983) terms "cultural philosophy."

For Odera-Oruka, cultural philosophy is the systematic set of beliefs characteristic of a society at a point in time and capable of explicit expression. Sages are usually conversant in cultural philosophy but often transcend it in their reflections. Hence their attitude is more critical of popular opinion than is found in the discourse Odera-Oruka characterizes as cultural philosophy. One of his primary examples of cultural philosophy is the work, *Conversations with Ogotemmeli*, in which a blind elder was assigned the task of describing the world view of the Dogon of Mali to the French anthropologist, Marcel Griaule (1965).

This paper is based on research conducted among the Iteso for short periods between 1986 and 1988. I was assisted by Mr.Steven Omuse of Amukura. Mr.Omuse collaborated with me in all aspects of this work, and I have greatly benefited from his own extensive research and knowledge of Iteso culture. I also wish to thank Dr.D.Masolo and Dr.Corinne Kratz for their generous comments on an earlier draft.

Actually *Conversations with Ogotemmeli* is a problematic text, since it is unclear how much is conventionally known and how much is the product of systematic elaboration by ritual specialists. There is little evidence for Griaule's implicit claim that the material in the book is the world view of all the Dogon people. Still there is obviously much there that Dogon apply in practices such as ritual. I would argue that *Conversations* is actually a synthetic work, the sagacity of Ogotemmeli, and the speculative thinking of the anthropologist Griaule. This presents no problem in and of itself, but Griaule makes rather grander claims to have uncovered an authentically **Dogon** world. This work demonstrates the sorts of difficulties that arise in attempting to describe cultural philosophies.

Odera-Oruka, unlike Griaule, actually constructs criteria for distinguishing between cultural philosophies and sagacity. For him the difference between the two emanates from the truth claims made by the two forms of discourse. Cultural philosophy is based on a *mythos*, an absolute set of values and ideas not subject to question. A sage who is an expert on that mythos and expounds it, such as Ogotemmeli, does not qualify as a producer of "philosophic sagacity." To do so the sage has to have the capacity to reflect on the claims inherent in a cultural philosophy, perhaps even to rebel against it. The sage produces a second-order thought that reflects on the first order of cultural philosophy.

Odera-Oruka's formula has the merit of separating the products of the critical and reflective capacities of people from their everyday activities. I find the idea of different truth claims valuable but do not find so useful the notion that the truth claims of cultural philosophy are based on a mythos. The very idea of a mythos implies that attitudes to knowledge in cultural philosophies are defined by notions of what is eternal and sacred. Thus cultural philosophies are defined as a form of religious thought. The problem with reducing cultural philosophies to religion is that much of the everyday categories of a people, such as moral and ethical concepts, may not be religious in motivation. Certainly ideas about wisdom, education, or even such culturally based skills as principles of mathematical calculation are omitted from consideration on an a priori basis.

What I want to argue is that the idea of a cultural philosophy is most useful when thought of as having two dimensions. The first I will call the "idioms of everyday life," in which people use concepts to interpret their experience, formulate future actions, and make judgments about themselves, other people, actions, and events. Idioms of everyday life are neither terribly systematic nor necessarily formulated in explicit terms either by ordinary people or specialists. They emerge in practice and are more directly related to conduct than the second aspect of cultural philosophies, which I call "consciously elaborated world views."

All societies possess idioms of everyday life and often have more than one set. An example of one such set are scientific theories as they are applied in laboratory settings. Recent work in the history and philosophy of science has shown that even the most innovative researchers are not conscious of the fundamental principles of basic science and are unable to articulate the underlying framework out of which their discoveries arise. There is an extensive literature on the relationship between "ordinary science," in which work relies on taken-for-granted assumptions and "revolutionary science," in which scientific theories are subject to explicit critical evaluation (Kuhn 1962). Appiah provides the best account of the literature on the parallels between scientific thinking and "traditional" African systems of thought (1987). Idioms of everyday life are not restricted to language but can be manifested in such spheres of conduct as ritual.

This was recognized by Austin when he included ritual actions in his account of how speech acts perform deeds (1962).

The second dimension of cultural philosophies is more the product of theoretical and contemplative activities of specialists, such as diviners, prophets, and other ritual practitioners. It is far more systematic and capable of being formulated in precise, propositional form. World views are related to idioms of everyday life through a process of exposition and elaboration. One example from East Africa is Roy Willis' examination of ideas about the causes of illness among the Fipa people of Tanzania (1972). Willis found that Fipa diviners had a theory of illness that related sickness to "paths" of social relations. Using this theory, diviners were able to discriminate among different Fipa medical conditions and social relations in a manner more complicated and complex than the ordinary Fipa who consulted diviners and healers. Still the elements of the thought of ordinary people could be found in the theories of Fipa medical practitioners.

This pattern is not uniquely African, but characteristic of many modes of thought in Africa and elsewhere. It is a commonplace of studies of American medical practice, for example, that in the United States, doctors' prescriptions and remedies are often not followed by patients because the physician has failed to explain the remedy in terms that will allow patients to monitor their own illness. What has not been investigated, however, is the relationship between idioms of everyday life and the systematic elaboration of them in world views. This may even involve historical studies that examine how and whether there are divergences between the two. The existing literature only hints at what we might discover. For example, in his classic studies of world religion, Max Weber distinguishes between two forms of religiosity, that of the masses and the more developed religiosity of the masses. He sees them as developing different standards of ethical conduct and moral ideals over time (1956). Weber describes a situation in which different segments of the same society may embrace moral values that not only differ but are in complex and changing relationships.

I describe the two dimensions of cultural philosophies--idioms of everyday life and systematically elaborated world views--at some length for four reasons:

(1) In studies of modes of thought in African societies, there has been far too great a tendency to fail to distinguish whose belief system is being described (specialist or laity) or even how the expressions of one segment of society relate to the expressions and actions of another.

(2) Under conditions of rapid change, idioms of everyday life and world views can often move in different directions. I would think that it is a critical research problem to assess the range of concepts and practices found at one time and place.

(3) Idioms of everyday life emerge in action and are not so capable of being collected by interviewing selected knowledgeable persons. The best way to make accounts of these idioms is to collect instances in which they are used, such as cases of misfortune, and then to ask people to explain their usage after the fact. This is so because the implicit beliefs used in the production of action become explicit primarily in situations of conflict or where two competing beliefs call each other into question.

(4) Finally, idioms of everyday life are directly related to morality and ethics. They are the language of moral judgments, the terms through which people evaluate the actions of others. If we are to describe moral values as they are used on a daily basis then we have to begin with the idioms of everyday life.

Iteso idioms of everyday life

I turn now to examine some Iteso idioms of everyday life and consider how they imply underlying ideas about moral standards. The Iteso are a Nilotic speaking people living across the Kenya-Uganda border in Busia District, Kenya, and Bukedi District, Uganda. They are related to the Iteso of Teso district, Uganda, but in some ways their language is closer to other members of the "Teso speaking cluster" of peoples, such as the Turkana in Kenya. There is considerable intermarriage between Iteso and the surrounding Baluyia-speaking peoples, especially the Babukusu and Bakhayo. An important project on cultural exchange would be to assess the degree to which intermarriage and social intercourse have facilitated the exchange of custom and belief. An overview of Iteso culture and social change is given in Karp (1978). Articles that describe the Iteso beliefs, ritual, and symbolic structures include Karp 1979, 1980, 1986, 1987, and 1989.

One way in which cultural differences have been maintained between Iteso and Baluyia has been through the general refusal of the Iteso to adopt the custom of circumcision. This has some implications for their ideas about the moral qualities of the person, discussed below.

I wish to discuss some concepts relating to moral judgments among the Iteso, and then to assess what these judgments imply for moral judgment.

The first such set of concepts relate to Iteso ideas about the person. Concepts of personhood are the most significant in my opinion because they enable an observer to examine whether a set of ideas can be termed moral concepts or not. This is an issue that has been raised by the philosopher Kwasi Wiredu (1983). Wiredu argues, rightly I think, that a concept can properly be termed "moral" only if it is neither customary (simply used because of tradition) nor religious (reinforced by mystical sanctions). For Wiredu morality must imply a "sense of virtue" such that actions are deemed to be moral in and for themselves rather than for some other reason. Yet Wiredu is too rigid in the way he draws his distinctions, since virtually any concept can be customary, religious, and moral at one and the same time. Moreover his idea of religion seems to me to be tainted by protestant fundamentalism. Even for Christianity it can be argued that many actions are viewed as good in and of themselves and not advocated because of divine retribution.

Still the person in Western philosophy and religious belief tends to be the isolated individual whose actions are judged in relationship primarily to himself or herself. Persons are good because they desire to do good or their actions show them to be good. Whether that good is defined in terms of social interaction is not determined by the Western "sense of virtue." Protecting the environment can be a virtuous act regardless of whether other people gain or lose by such actions. Not so for the Iteso. The good entailed by protecting the environment cannot be defined without reference to the effects of such an act on other people.

The Iteso have a rather different and far more collective sense of personhood. As a result, they believe that a good person directs his actions toward other persons because that is the very definition of what is good. One does not "do unto others as you would have them do unto you." Instead one does unto others because doing so defines proper moral behavior.

Let me explain this in terms of Iteso concepts. A person is composed of two faculties, the head (akou) and the heart (etau). The head is the seat of accumulated knowledge and skill (acoa), and the heart is the source of emotions and energy. Persons are only capable of exercising their full capacities when they possess adult physical strength and health (*agogong*).

The capacities of the head alter as the person grows. Ideally the adult person acquires skill and knowledge over time and acts in a "cool" fashion, guided by his or her head. The heart can also be hot or cold, and changes according to the person's feelings. These feelings, however, do not significantly alter as the person grows older. When a person is bad tempered and subject to jealous moods, for example, that person will feel the same way throughout his or her life. How these feelings are expressed can change over time. The reason for this is that the head has the task of managing the heart. In most people the capacity for managing emotional dispositions grows with age, as their head becomes "cooler." Some people, however, have such strong tendencies to act in certain ways that their heart overcomes their head. In some situations, anyone can be overcome by their emotions, but some people are simply unable to manage themselves, either because they have a weak head or a bad heart. The extreme cases of uncontrolled behavior such as drunkenness, madness, and possession by spirits of the dead are instructive. In these cases the head is overcome by an external agent, allowing the heart to act without guidance. Spirits of the dead are thought of as rather childlike, motivated by greed for meat and beer, revenge, and other such desires. More than one informant described them as "etau kijokis," all heart.

Young men are notoriously "hot" because their head is unable to control the "hot" emotions of the heart such as anger. (The Iteso phrase for anger is *Emwan' etau keng*, "His heart is hot." Elders have "cool" heads. These Iteso accounts of the personal characteristics of young and old have a superficial resemblance to conventional English idioms. But in English we speak of a man as "hot-headed," not "hot hearted." The difference is that for the Iteso the heart is hot and not the head. The capacities represented by the image of the head, sound judgment, and skill at controlling the person, are simply insufficiently developed in young men. They cannot control their hot hearts. Older men, however, are able, by virtue of knowledge and skill, to strike an appropriate balance. Iteso say of persons who control themselves that *Isomae akou*, "the head works." How the head works is to achieve the balance that enables them to interact skillfully and morally with others. Women are not as often judged in this manner as they are believed to have innately weak heads. I have not questioned women about whether they share this sentiment. The care with which they guard other women in settings in which the head can be made weak, such as beer drinking, indicates that they do.

When adults achieve the ideal balance between heart and head, they are described as "happy" (*elakara*). The happy man is someone who is controlled in his actions but open and sharing with other persons. A major ideal of Iteso sociability is the sharing of food (Karp 1978, 1980). Obviously this has functional significance for a society subject to seasonal and yearly fluctuations in food supply. Still the Iteso go further than simply appreciating sharing. For them sharing is the sign of happiness. The happy man eats out of doors, frequently brews beer for his neighbors, and is willing to cooperate in working parties and share his resources. Another way of describing a person who is happy and a good person is *epaparone*, roughly "self possessed." This is someone who takes such care of himself or herself that he or she strives to help others.

Persons lacking these qualities are described as "selfish," (*ationus*) or "proud", (*epoq*). These are two of the worst insults among the Iteso. The proud and selfish man is very much one who lives alone, does not cooperate in neighborhood labor and beer parties,and eats hidden in the rear of his hut, rather than outside where anyone who passes by can share his meal. To Iteso it is obvious that the man who eats alone also fears poisoning. This is not simply a casual observation. As many Iteso themselves note, the person who is concerned with witchcraft and poisoning is often the person who has much to fear from his fellow man. This recalls the anthropologist Godfrey Lienhardt's observation about the Dinka concept of witchcraft. "One can only accuse another of being a witch if one knows in one's heart how a witch feels" (1951).

The fear of witchcraft and poisoning is not uncommon among the Iteso. The beer party is the setting for poisoning to occur and everyone knows of instances where this has happened. Hence the return from open sociability is countered by its risks. The risks associated with interaction indicate why I think that Iteso ideas about the person display their "sense of virtue." I have never heard Iteso say that they are happy for the material possessions they have acquired. They express their happiness at positive interactions, seeing a person after a long time, receiving a gift, giving to someone else. This happiness is itself the product of the balance between heart and head, between knowing and feeling. The result is that virtue can only be manifested through actions with others and never by oneself. Even when the return is great, personal risks are involved.

A proud man cannot be virtuous, almost by definition. He does not exhibit actions toward others that are associated with virtue. No precise equivalent to the English sense of "virtue" exists in the Iteso language. A virtuous man is *ejokana*, "good." Ejokana is derived from the root, *jok*, referring originally to the happy nature spirits associated with divinity, called *ajokin*. This meaning has been corrupted through missionary influence, where *ajokin* have come to refer to the devil and evil. Among the Iteso, virtue manifests itself in social interaction. It is located not in the isolated individual but in the person's interactions with others. It is based on, but not defined by, the achievement of personal balance. Iteso moral judgments are judgments of interactions, which themselves are a product of the capacities of the person. The Iteso, however, reverse the movement from individual capacity to social interaction in their specific judgments. They do not judge the capacities of persons but rather their actions. Then they infer individual capacities and intentions from interactions.

A person is not evil for being mad, but a mad person is evil if he does harm to others. These judgments themselves have a hierarchy. Of all the forms of harm that one person can do to another, the worst is called *akicud*. For an action to be defined as akicud, it must have two defining characteristics, done secretly with homicidal intent. Poisoning and other forms of sorcery are all described as akicud.

I can only briefly indicate a significant difference between the Iteso and the neighboring Bagisu, closely related to the Baluyia speaking peoples and living next to the Iteso in Uganda. Like the Iteso the Bagisu have an idiom of personhood that distinguishes between the capacities of the head and heart. One major difference, however, lies in attitudes toward emotional capacities. The Bagisu believe that circumcision is associated with the production of an emotional state called *lirima*, which is the capacity both for adult action and violence. This is an attribute of all circumcised men (Heald 1982). For the Iteso the closest thing to lirima is a "hot" heart, an individual difference rather than the attribute of a whole class. Furthermore, if the Iteso judge this emotion to be more than transient in a person, they define him as a morally bad person. For the Bagisu (and possibly the Babukusu), lirima is a necessary emotional condition for the assumption of adult status. Only an excess of lirima makes a person morally bad. This contrast demonstrates differences between ideas about both the capacities of the person and the effects a person can have through his actions. An account of the effects that different capacities can have, of personal agency, is the second most important aspect of moral concepts among the Iteso.

A full account of Iteso ideas about agency, the effects persons bring about, would lead me into a discussion of Iteso ideas about evil, manifested in their concept of the witch. In what space I have left I can only begin this task. I will take an Iteso concept related to their idea of creation and show both that it is morally neutral in principle and that moral judgments are manifested not in what people do but in the purposes to which their actions are put. My argument is that morality is not innate in actions but are derived from the assessments made of the motives for actions.

The Iteso concept of *akisub* is translated in dictionaries as equivalent to the verb "to create." It is used in a number of ways that may guide us to its core meaning. The first translators of the New Testament translated the name of God, as *Nakasuban*, "the creator." But this term is equally applied to a potter fashioning her pot out of clay. In fact, any act that gives shape or form to matter is described by the verb akisub. This suggests that creativity is not the divine act implied by Christian ontology, creation out of nothing, but always action that fashions an already existing material world.

The moral content given to the verb akisub derives from its contrasting uses. Akisub is used to describe acts that are both good and evil. *Isuben*, acts of akisub, are usually translated as "blessings," but really mean actions that create a relationship between two entities. Thus the individual who calls out to the high god in a moment of crisis is said to be doing an isuben. Also rites directed at the *Ipara*, spirits of the dead, are referred to as *Isuben ipara*.

These rites are always done to remove a misfortune caused by a spirit by creating a new relationship with it. What is created is a new connection, a path or relationship that is fashioned through the actions of men.

Akisub can also refer to actions that are harmful. These range from the relatively harmless act of *anunuk* (tying up), by which a wife renders her husband impotent, through to homicidal acts of witchcraft that involve using a person's bodily waste to kill. What these actions all share with isuben is that they create a relationship between two separate entities. What makes these actions morally good or bad is what the relationship intends. In the case of isuben ipara the intention is to heal; in the case of some instances of akisub the intention is to kill. If the intention is to kill by means of creating a mystical relationship, then the act is defined as *akicud*, sorcery. Iteso are absolutely clear that what makes an attempt to harm by secret means such as poisoning or sorcery akicud is its secret, homicidal intention, as I stated previously.

Intentionality thus is a fundamental element in Iteso moral judgments. For them an action is morally neutral until colored by the intention to do good or to harm. Although they have no separate word for "evil" that is distinct from "bad," *erono*, the notion of akicud illustrates that the most evil action for them is made evil by its homicidal intention.

Intentionality must be coupled with action, and action must lead to a relationship. These three elements are all necessary for a moral judgment to be made. But intentionality is the basis for such judgments. This returns us once again to the sense of virtue manifested in Iteso ideas about the good person. The evil person is the good person inverted. Both types of persons create relationships. For the good person, relationships are motivated by a sense of virtue, the pleasure derived from doing good with others. For an evil person, relationships are motivated by the absence of a sense of virtue. The envy and hatred of the witch are the motives for the relationship the person fashions. One acts for the good of self and others; the other acts only for himself. This observation finally brings us back to the other theme I found in Iteso notions of sociability. Ideas about good and evil elevate the ideal of the person acting with others over the image of the person acting alone and against others. Goodness and evil are not innate in the individual but a product of intention and practice. Hence questions of good and evil are profoundly social and not individual.

This final remark leads me to make two concluding observations about Iteso moral concepts. The first is that for the Iteso the domain of the moral is not defined by essences, but by actions. A person is not good because of some innate quality, but by virtue of how he or she acts to other persons. In this sense they are rather existentialist in their definition of the moral. The second observation is that Immanuel Kant might have approved of their moral concepts. For the Iteso the good consists of doing good in and for itself. This is the definition of the happy man. Their moral imperative is categorical, absolute, and unqualified. It most definitely is not what Kant termed "hypothetical," based on technical skills, or done for prudent reasons. The hypothetical element enters into the skilled attainment of balance between heart and head that is the achievement of adults. This is a necessary but not sufficient condition for Iteso moral acts.

References

Appiah,K.
1987   Old gods, new worlds: Some recent work in the
              philosophy of African traditional religion. In
              Contemporary philosophy, vol. 5, *African
              philosophy*, edited by G.Floistad. Dordrecht: Martinus
              Niehoff.

Austin,J.L.
1962   *How to do things with words.* Oxford: Oxford
              University Press.

Griaule,M.
1965   *Conversations with Ogotemmeli: An introduction
              to African religious ideas.* London: Oxford
              University Press.

Heald,S.
1982   The making of men. *Africa* 52(1).

Karp,I.
1978. L   *Fields of change among the Iteso of Kenya.*
              London: Routledge and Kegan Paul.
1979   With P.P.Karp, Living with the spirits of the dead. In
              African therapeutic systems, edited by
              Z.A.Ademuwagun, et al. Waltham, Massachusetts:
              Crossroads Press.
1980   Beer drinking and social experience in an African
              society. In *Explorations in African systems of
              thought*, edited by I.Karp and C.Bird. Bloomington:
              Indiana University Press.
1986   African systems of thought. In *Africa*, 2d ed., edited by
              P.O'Meara and P.Martin. Bloomington: Indiana
              University Press.
1987   Laughter at marriage: Subversion in performance. In
              The transformation of African marriage, edited by
              D.Parkin and D.Nyamweya. Manchester: Manchester
              University Press.
1989   Power and Capacity in Rituals of Possession. In *The
              creativity of power: Cosmology and action in
              African societies*, edited by W.Arens and I.Karp.
              Washington: Smithsonian Institution Press.

Kuhn,T.
1962   *The structure of scientific revolutions.* Chicago:
            University of Chicago Press.

Lienhardt,G.
1951   Some notions of witchcraft among the Dinka. *Africa*
            21(4).

Odera-Oruka,H.
1983   Sagacity in African philosophy. *International
            philosophical quarterly* 23(4):383-393.

Weber,M.
1956   The social psychology of world religions. In *From Max
            Weber.* Glencoe: The Free Press.

Willis,R.
1972   Pollution and paradigms. *Man* 7:369-378.

Wiredu,K.
1983   Philosophy in Africa: Trends and perspectives.   In
            Philosophy and culture, edited by H.Odera-Oruka and
            D.Masolo. Proceedings of 2d Afro-Asian Philosophy
            Conference, October-November 1981, Nairobi. Nairobi,
            Kenya: Bookwise Limited.

Slim Textuality, Linguistic Anthropology, And Speaking

Lukas D. Tsitsipis, Professor
Aristotle University of Thessaloniki, Greece

In honoring a scholar whose work has been focused on the materiality of social structure in the context of urban anthropology, I consider it suitable to discuss some problems concerning the materiality of speech in the context of linguistic anthropology. This article is primarily theoretically conceived although certain specific problems pertaining to the author's particular research interests will be ultimately addressed. In fact, it is the specificity of the problems that has generated in a dialectic manner the theoretical considerations.

The issue of **slim textuality**, which I initiated in another paper, is taken up and discussed here in more detail and in the wider theoretical framework that I consider appropriate.

Theoretical discussion

Vološinov (1973) in his *Marxism and the Philosophy of Language* has criticized Saussurean structuralism for introducing an *abstract objectivism* into the study of language reifying thus human language. Bakhtin (1981, 1984) has shown primarily for the novel but by extension for human speech, that the only level at which linguistic study is interesting is not that of structure abstracted from human communication but also, and even more so, the level of the word as a positive term, the meaning of which is built on the borderline between interacting individuals. The word is full of resonances of other, previous speakers' nuances when used by a member of the society. The Bakhtinian philosophy of language has come over the last years as a tour-de-force in linguistic anthropology, and many scholars have suggested that we profit from the opportunities that the perspective offers for the anthropology of language and sociolinguistics. Hill (1986) sees these opportunities emerging out of Bakhtin's **translinguistics**, which allows for the study of centrifugal forces of speech, and Cazden (1989) compares the Bakhtinian concepts with the ones developed by Hymes in his ethnography of speaking and the study of communicative competence. Cazden's article is to the point, and although not exhaustive, touches explicitly on some of the most crucial areas of convergence between the two. Hill also points in the beginning of her article to the need for a transcendence of the deconstructionist project which denies the **materiality** of speech, and takes Bakhtin's conception of language as a good ground for the refiguration of the anthropology of language. Hanks (1987) introduces a combined methodology where the Bakhtinian study of discourse genres meets the theory of practice as developed by Bourdieu (1977).

Before I introduce my conception of linguistic anthropology in a materialistic frame of reference, I should bring up some further similarities in the traditions of Bakhtin-Vološinov and the Hymesian ethnography of speaking. These similarities might reiterate the obvious but help us sharpen the focus of later discussion. Following this, some critical comments about deconstruction will be presented. Both Bakhtin and Hymes understand language as a social phenomenon par excellence and start from variation rather than take the abstract code as the point of departure. Hymes (1974) has systematically explored the second elementary function, that of the stylistic or socioexpressive side of language, bringing concern with it to the center from the periphery of linguistic investigation. Vološinof

(1973, 103) talks about the social evaluative accents of language use that complement the theme and meaning of words. Bakhtin takes the double-voiced word to be the point where dialogism expresses itself in the most explicit way (see both his 1981 and 1984 treatments).

In the Anglo-American philosophical tradition, the **Speech Act** theory has made the significant switch from the referential-propositional axis of language to language as action. However, this tradition, in spite of its important impact on linguistic and sociolinguistic thinking, has not taken the decisive step to incorporate its theoretical premises in a socially constituted understanding of language. Critical examinations of the horizons and limitations of this trend of linguistic philosophy have shed light on some of its deficiencies (Rosaldo 1982). Furthermore, broad universalist schemes such as Grice's maxims and implicature along with speech act theory have come under criticism for their lack of sensitivity to the broader social context (Hymes 1986). Indeed, speech acts are mostly framed in an individual-speaker perspective. The very intentionality of the speaking subject has been criticized in domains such as ritual speech (DuBois 1987). This and other approaches bring to the fore some of the Western ethnocentric philosophical biases of speech act theory and its cogeners. (I refer here to the major philosophical treatments of Austin and Searle.)

There is no doubt that notions advanced by Austin and Searle, such as felicity conditions and illocutionary force, are extremely useful for detection of the sociolinguistic conventions of a community's situational and other constraints on speaking. Nevertheless, the theory becomes an unfinished business when it focuses on a rational-individual actor. To paraphrase Vološinov, the speech act is inherently dialogical and therefore is located on the border between two interacting beings. Therefrom emerges its social essence, and its materiality and social contextuality. Furthermore, if we carefully consult Searle's major treatise on the conditions governing the acts, we discover room for the conventional but not for the emergent (Searle 1969, 57-61). This point merits a rather more detailed discussion. Literary critics, political philosophers, and cultural theorists alike take into serious consideration the emergent property of discourse (Williams 1977). Traditional speech act theory can tell us something about the conventional status of an act. Its arguments are in the line of sociolinguistics: that act is to be taken as such and such generally under these conditions. But this is the maximum that we get from the theory. On the contrary, ethnographers of speaking and performance take the emergent qualities of discourse seriously as parts of communication that enter decisively into the structural conditions of relations, evaluation, and the constitutive role of speaking (Bauman 1977, 1986).

More will be said about emergence, conventionality, and collusion later in my discussion of slim textuality. This more specific discussion may bring to bear on my conception of linguistic anthropology, that is, close to the refiguration proposed by Hill (1986) along the Bakhtinian lines, and along the major teachings of the ethnographic focus on speech. Also, the subjective aspect that Caton (1987, 251) takes to be quite significant for the ethnography of speaking will be touched upon.

A few words about deconstruction are now in line. One of the most crucial aspects of a distance between deconstruction and a speaking perspective has been recently put down for consideration by Robin Lakoff (1989, 975), who argues that working in the specifics of language and taking steps, example by example, you lay the whole field wide open for examination, which turns out to be more democratic. Deconstruction operates obviously on an opposite dimension where authority comes philosophically first. There is no room in deconstruction for the emergence for instance of narrative, its acquisition, and functions in the communicative economy of a community (Hymes 1982 for a brief comment on deconstruction). Although it is not part of my specialty and usual competence to try to hit hard rock in matters concerning the detailed aspects of deconstruction, the appearance of some of its teachings in modern academia should not go unnoticed and uncommented. I would hardly resist the temptation to cite a few phrases from Eagleton, which come to me as a word of warning against uncritical adoptions of doctrine. Says Eagleton (1984, 97-99),

> Deconstruction had its root in France--in a society whose ruling ideologies drew freely upon a metaphysical rationalism incarnate in the rigidly hierarchical, authoritarian nature of its academic institutions. In this context, the Derridean project of dismantling binary oppositions and subverting the transcendental signifier had a radical potential relevance which did not always survive when deconstruction was exported. The creed, in short, did not travel well: transplanted to the liberal empiricist rather than rationalistic cultures of Britain and North America, its complicity with liberal humanism tended to bulk as large as its antagonism to it

and

> It would perhaps be more accurate to argue that the Anglophone varieties of deconstruction rejoin the liberalism of the ruling critical ideology at the very moment that they challenge its humanism--that such deconstruction is, in short, a liberalism without a subject, and as such, among other things, an appropriate ideological form for late capitalist society (98-99).

For an anthropology of language, such comments cannot be treated without some interest and appreciation given our concern with speaking as **praxis** in a sociocultural milieu. What seems to me to be the significant point made by Eagleton is his insistence on both incongruities between intellectual currents and their new host-academias and emergence of new varieties nurtured in the foreign line of thinking but reflecting a more universal function than that of the ruling critical ideology of late capitalism.

Now the above presented transplanting of deconstruction from its original motherland hardly resembles the other transplanting, that of the Bakhtinian philosophy of language. Here analytical and methodological concepts and techniques point to a matching of ideas and congruity. Hymes reports that he was "scooped" by the Bakhtin-Vološinov ideas (Cazden 1989, 117). Both traditions pursue the study of language by crossing through the rigidly built disciplinary borders. Hymes crosses the boundary heading in the direction of the artistic-literary properties of oral narrative (see also Bauman 1986) from a concern with ways of speaking of the communities, whereas Bakhtin does not seem to be so clear in the direction he takes. One could claim, with a fair amount of certainty, that the direction is from the silent register of the novel to the broader aspects of speaking but not actually in a chronological sense, but rather, in a philosophical one. Different works seem to me to have the one or the other focus more strongly emphasized, problems of authorship notwithstanding.

By stating that Bakhtin does not appear to be so clear in the line he takes, I do not intend to criticize his intellectual struggle. On the contrary, globality, multidirectionality, and unfinalizability have been some of the major features of his thought and writings. I, therefore, address the average reader for whom Bakhtin is primarily a literary scholar when I claim that he starts from the novel. For the complex lines of influences from neo-Kantianism to Marxism to modern theoretical physics on Bakhtin's thought, see Holquist (1990). For a discussion of disputed texts, see Clark and Holquist (1984).

Nevertheless, differences between the Vitebsk school of philosophical critical tradition and the Western anthropologically based sociolinguistics should not be underestimated. The serious and careful ethnographic detail obviously lacks in the Bakhtinian tradition due primarily to its literary focus. For those of us who wish to use the scientifically promising and politically emancipatory Bakhtinian perspective, these differences pose problems that call for a critical view of the model adopted. I have encountered such difficulties when I discussed the issue of **authoritative discourse** in a previous work, and will come back to that in my discussion of slim texts in the specific part of my article.

It seems worthwhile to elaborate further the point just raised, since more than once in the history of science, model-building, and application, the transfer of ideas and principles from the one field to the other has caused headaches and procrustean frames. If we take as an example the distinction that Bakhtin makes between the monological status of poetry and the polyphony of the novel, at least the mature stage of the genre (1981, 278), we soon find out that discourse written to be read does not match the requirements of an orally performed genre (see Mannheim (1987, 285) who makes exactly this point for the folksong). There are, of course, some theoretical consequences of this observation at least in what concerns the two theoretical directions under scrutiny here. The task of linguistic anthropology is by and large to study the cultural patterning of speech in its ethnography of speaking version and the other domains of interest that we usually associate with discourse analysis, sociolinguistics, and pragmatics. Literary critical study focuses on the socioesthetic value of what is called differently by different schools the literary product, its process of production being included. If the literary work is to enjoy a relative autonomy as an ideological form, it has to be selective in regard to the types of natural discourse that chooses to refract through its medium (see Bakhtin 1986, 61-62 for a discussion of primary and secondary genres, and Hymes 1974, 443 for minimal and complex genres). What is left for us to do is to take seriously the Bakhtinian observation in the above cited work that the transformation of a primary genre to a literary, secondary one is not a mechanical process but one incorporating qualitative shifts.

Slim texts: A close examination

In the remainder of this article I will discuss what I have elsewhere called slim texts (Tsitsipis 1991). Since in my earlier treatment the whole issue of slim textuality was embedded in a wider context, my analysis of the specific phenomenon has not been as exhaustive as it could have been. I take slim texts to be a good empirical locus for the critical view of the various positions and notions that appear in the previous theoretical part. In fact, my main motive for opening up here the issue of slim texts has been a comment of a reviewer of the article just cited that the concept needed further specification and definition, since it seems to be a rather new concept. Although I attempted to do so to a certain extent in the earlier paper, there is reasonably good cause to pursue the problem in more detail and more systematically here.

I defined slim texts as **set discourse material which can be quoted in order to comment on some element of the cultural backdrop or of the immediate situational context, differing thus from routine ways of performing some linguistic action directly** (Tsitsipis 1991). Thus, whereas these texts have a property of length or internal density as a crucial feature, it is in functional and social terms that their meaning and significance become complete. The term is used by Sherzer (1987), who briefly compares the slim textuality of a greeting formula with a myth narration that displays a more complex structure. Sherzer does not define slim text and I consider it crucial to try to circumscribe certain characteristics of this category of texts so that we can recognize them in other contexts. I first differentiate them from formulas and from narratives of some complexity. In narratives, reframings occur in various forms such as footing shifts or complex manipulations of points of view, and so forth. In distinguishing between them and slim texts, therefore, we face fewer problems than those showing up in a distinction between slim texts and formulas. For this second distinction, I have adopted a frame put forward by Sperber and Wilson in their study of irony (1981). These scholars understand an ironic statement as being a mention rather than a use of a proposition. This means that the statement refers not to the situation described but to the proposition itself. Slim texts, and particularly those I am about to discuss, are closer to this metalingual function than formulas, strictly speaking. In the case of the formula, one performs a speech act directly; one does something by uttering it. Slim texts do not behave in the same way. Several points are to be made in connection with the notion discussed here. First, the rigid institutional framework presupposed by Searle (1969) in his classical treatment of speech acts does not seem to hold for slim texts. Thus, if we take, as a case in point, his conditions for a happy illocutionary act, we find out that the nonobviousness condition, for instance, is almost irrelevant. The condition states that for the act to be successfully carried out, it should not be obvious to the participants that the speaker would carry it out anyway (Searle 1969, 57-62, for an analysis of the prototypical act of **promising**). It is not my goal here to discuss further developments in speech act theory, and of course, the various categories of illocutionary acts differ from one another in complex ways. I only want to stress the point that a rigid institutional frame does not allow for the emergent properties of slim texts, that is, how they are embedded in the ongoing discourse once produced. Whether it is obvious or not that the speaker who utters a slim text would produce it is not what counts here. It can go without saying that texts are surrounded by certain cultural norms that function as blueprints or abstract frames helping participants in their interpretive activity.

Second, in light of our first observation, one is led to look into the total discourse situation for clues as to the status of slim texts. Both the cultural background and the immediate backdrop are relevant here. Restricting our analysis to the individual-intentional actor, as much of recent speech act theory would do, leaves things quite unexplained. Slim texts profit more from a use of the Bakhtin/Vološinov approach, which considers meaning as not inherent in the monological word but as generated in the context of interaction and as inhabiting the area shared by participants in conversation, that is, as being collaboratively constructed (Duranti 1986, 239-247).

Third, in order to make more explicit some of the dimensions of slim texts, I propose to look into their framing potential. In the cited work (Tsitsipis 1991), I suggest that slim texts, due to their brevity, are easily framed and reframed in various directions. One essential feature, particularly of the texts examined here, is their embeddedness in slightly ironic or joking frames. The texts achieve their goal by being **oblique** (Mannheim 1987). As the examples will show, if these texts are taken literally, they violate basic norms as to who is entitled to perform a speech act. If they are framed, emergent appropriateness through coparticipants' collusion centers them as nondeviant discourse. In this way, therefore,

> text...is centered insofar as it is grounded in a locally
> defined social context, which functions as the source of

> information an author [here read also speaker] and
> reader [here read also hearer and audience] draw on to
> flesh out the interpretation of the textual artifact....
> (Hanks 1989, 106).

This point leads us to the definition of slim texts as commenting rather than directly performing an act. Fourth, I introduced (Tsitsipis 1991) the notion of emergent nondeviance or appropriateness.

Slim texts of the type to be examined here are initially deviant discourse chunks that are embedded in the communicative situation as appropriate texts through the complicity of the other participants in the event. If this complicity or collusion were not an important factor and if the texts should be uttered unframed, they would offer grounds for serious contradictions as to who is entitled to conduct appropriately a speech act, as our examples will suggest. I distinguish this initial deviance transformed to nondeviance from **conventional** inappropriateness as attested in the ethnographic record. In this latter case, certain complex norms governing speech and attitudes allow for what we may call the competence of incompetence (Albert 1972; Irvine 1973; Hinds 1981). In the cases of slim texts that I have examined in context, no prior conventionality shows up allowing the reading of their uttering as legitimately inappropriate. It is in the interaction mainstream that they emerge as nondeviant. In light of this last observation, to be further elaborated later, it makes sense to claim, as I did before, that we cannot apply conditions of the current **speech act** theory to this case. The tests' relevance and ultimate acceptability relies on participants' complicity informed by their implicit evaluation of their language, and appropriate conduct in its use. It is therefore the cultural background that is in a dialectical play with the immediate backdrop.

The role of collusion in properly interpreting what is going on in discourse has been recognized by researchers working in various areas of speech and its cultural shaping. Thus, Irvine (1982, 257) in her discussion of mediumship and possession in connection with various types of religious speech says,

> the emergence of an interpretation will also depend on contexts of situation; it will depend on the observers' knowledge of participants' past histories; and it will depend on the motives and interests of the various observers who interpret what is going on. In other words interpretation is a creative process, incorporating a historical trajectory, and involving active collusion among participants.

Irvine's observations hold true for a wide variety of situations warranting our adoption of the Bakhtinian philosophy of interaction that centers meaning in the interspeaker territory.

Let me now give concrete substance to my analysis by examining specific texts from the community in which I have worked. The slim texts of my corpus come from low-proficiency speakers of a dying variety of Albanian as spoken in Greece. On linguistic and sociolinguistic grounds, members of the Greek-Albanian (the language is locally known as Arvanítika) communities can be divided into fluent and terminal speakers (see Tsitsipis 1983 for details on the distinction). Terminal speakers show a diminished competence in the contracting language. Their situation resembles Dorian's East Sutherland Gaelic semispeakers (1981). Terminal Arvanítika speakers, whose strong code is the Greek language, frequently produce texts which, through slight irony, mockery, and joking intonation, reproduce in an imitative frame fluent Arvanítika speech. I first reported on this behavior in Tsitsipis (1989) but without the present analytical framework. Gal (1989), in her discussion of the contracting Hungarian in German-Hungarian bilingualism in Austria, points to the need for linguistic anthropology to reject a simplistically minded understanding of the communicative situations of speakers of

350

a contracting language. She views these speakers as facing pressures from both the wider society and the local networks, and therefore, as having to communicate with both successfully. Arvanítika terminal speakers, in spite of their heavy reliance on the wider urban context, still need to be communicatively adequate, even to a small extent, within their local communities. In the face of contradictory pressures, speakers of this category have to be creative and able to embed their speech in the immediate backdrop of the various speech events. As a consequence, their texts must be or become appropriate in the ongoing conversations. I will suggest that slim textuality as embedded in participants' complicity helps this nondeviance surface in the proper manner. I will then compare these texts with similar ones from other research.

Arvanítika terminal speakers participate frequently in natural conversations with fluent speakers but differ from them most of the time in the ways they choose to make their contribution. A long narrative session cannot be sustained by terminal speakers qua speakers due to their losses in the control of Arvanítika language. In these bilingual communities, fluent speakers build on both Greek and Albanian languages for the intracommunity interaction. Terminal speakers' severely diminished competence in the contracting language is a more complicated problem than one would think from a rather superficial contact with the communities. Texts uttered by these speakers are generally oblique by making continuous reference to the language, older people's ways of speaking, and so forth. What therefore strikes the observer is the use of the language as a citation object rather than as a use tool. Since terminal Arvanítika utterances refer obliquely to the community's speech, they form a framed behavior. I suggest that such framing transforms texts to acceptable speech that unframed would be unacceptable. Thus, one hears frequently expressions such as *haróve gljúhë në?* (did you forget the language?), *e di Arvaníte?* (do you know Arvanítika?), *fljet Arvaníte?* (do you speak Arvanítika?), u-shkurtúa ménda (mind is being lost), *ashtú ist pram* (that's the situation), and so forth. I have analyzed such texts in Tsitsipis (n.d.) and discussed the complex process of their surfacing.

I want to pursue here some of the theoretical consequences of these cases. If slim texts of the kinds shown by the examples were to be taken as unframed chunks of speech, they would perform an illocutionary act, and specifically an act of control. Such an act would not be acceptable in view of the fact that speakers of a low proficiency level cannot properly exercise control with regard to the linguistic abilities of the wider community or of the fluent speakers. There are two factors that accommodate the nondeviance of these initially deviant texts: First, their framing through slightly ironic and teasing intonation and the complicity shown by other discourse participants. Fluent speakers present in such natural interactions ratify terminal speakers by providing answers to their "control" acts or by shifting the interactional focus, as for instance, when they remind those present that young people know how to speak Arvanítika when they are adequately exposed to grandparental speech. Slim texts, therefore, do not perform an act but exhibit the properties of metalinguistic and metacritical commentaries. Younger and terminal speakers' point of view is fused thus with the traditional point of view of the communities. As Sperber and Wilson (1981) suggest, **ironic** statements do not make direct reference to the situation propositionally described but refer obliquely to the proposition itself. Terminal Arvanítika texts should be interpreted in the same spirit. They refer to the portions of speech of the community through imitative slight irony brought about through the proper intonation.

And this imitative, teasing, or slightly ironic tone of voice must be negotiated as such because outright irony would jeopardize the status of the texts rather than incorporating them in the interaction. It is, thus, a joking and ambiguous critical activity that provides grounds for the texts' appropriateness, and not aggressive irony.

In the theoretical discussion of this article, I elaborated on the significance of the Bakhtinian philosophy of language. It is in the context of slim texts, among other discourses, that the element of praxis is best foregrounded in interaction. Terminal speakers' utterances show features of the Bakhtinian double-voiced or polyphonic discourse. They incorporate the traditional voice of the community and through framing introduce the younger speakers' own point of view. The texts can be interpreted as instances of the **internally persuasive discourse** (Bakhtin 1981, 348; Tsitsipis n.d.), which merges a critical view and an acceptance. Such a discourse is internalized but also critically exposed. This discourse grasps very characteristically the contradictions faced by speakers with a marginal position in the communities of their upbringing. Traditional community utterances become the target of scorn and criticism and a second layer of meaning is thus built into the slim text.

Before I examine further examples, I want to notice that the understanding of complicity (or collusion) as an important dimension of culture seems to become prominent in many cultural studies oriented toward practice. Abrahams (1986, 223-237) analyzes this significant factor. This scholar observes that "through stylized voice modification...community members not only cross-refer to each other, but draw upon the voices of tradition..." (Abrahams 1986, 229). Abrahams, providing a coherent description of **pragmatic ethnography**, understands complicity as pointing to the activity of practical involvement in the various cultural events, scenes, and acts.

Such a complicity allows for rule-altering and licit activities, and the furnishing of signals that conventionally cue them. This perspective, based on principles of dialogism in the Bakhtinian sense, allows us to make sense out of our Arvanítika slim texts.

Not all speech genres and kinds of context, though, allow for a complicity to transform rule-altering to appropriate discourse. In long narratives offered by fluent speakers, terminal-speaker conduct can become detrimental to the performed status of the narrative. I have elsewhere elaborated on that with a focus on how terminal speakers' inappropriate interjections destroy the performance of narratives (Tsitsipis 1988). Of course, here we are talking about terminal speakers as audience and not as speakers. Terminal speakers cannot control the structural features that long narratives require in order to be appropriately rendered as successful performances. Slim texts on the contrary are not in any confrontation with the community norms if they become genuine slim texts, that is, commentaries rather than illocutionary acts. Abrahams (1986, 230) grasps the difference between more formal and everyday interactions when he observes that

> There are many other dimensions of expression that may alter between everyday interactions and more formal or performed occasions. In attempting to get at where storytelling enters into the interpretive apparatus of culture perhaps the most important of these variables are those of stylization and intensity. In the more formal kinds of storytelling, the level of intensity rises: the encounter now is more than an interaction, more like an event.

This explains a great deal of the license around slim texts versus long narratives.

For a narrative to successfully occur, it has to be performed and hence to appear as an event, that is, to be marked as interaction outside the spontaneously enacted everyday talk. It is here that the linguistic-stylistic resources that the two languages provide cannot be adequately controlled by terminal speakers (Tsitsipis 1988). Let us therefore examine an example of slim textuality in which terminal speakers merge the various voices.

The following text is an attempt by a terminal speaker from the community of Spáta, in southern Greece, to tell a joke of the anecdote type. Anecdotes are small genres characterized by turns at talk, and therefore, reported speech is a crucial feature of their structure (Bauman 1986). The comments that are volunteered by the terminal speaker before he engages in the telling of the anecdote are significant for the framing of his attitude and speech. He is a twenty-one-year-old graduate of a technical college and, despite his strong ties with the urban center of Athens, he retains a close contact with the local networks of the community. He is actually a resident in the community. The session involves both a testing of his competence in Arvanítika and various sequences of natural conversation. In the course of the interaction he offers the following comments, here given in their English translation:

> If we run into a person who is also of Arvanítika origin, let us say in Athens, "we use routines such as si véte (how is it going?) in order to suggest that we are Arvanítes, and then we switch to Greek. Or, once in a while we want to **imitate the old folks** and say a joke or two.

The idea of imitation is brought up by the speaker himself, and indeed it is this imitative-joking activity that is to be found at the center of these speakers' slim text production. There are various subtle ways from the most to the least explicit that terminal speakers merge their voice and point of view with the traditional voice of the communities. It is definitely part of their conscious knowledge that the Arvanítika language is for them a citation and not a use code. Recognition of this surfaces in many ways. The speaker of our example says at another juncture of our conversation, "There are even words and expressions that **do not enter in a conversation** [he means naturally]; you utter them if you want just like that, **out of the blue** like, for instance, the expression **Kugóva** (I took Holy Communion)."

The above statement alludes to more than just a recognition of the diminished lexical competence of terminal speakers. It brings to bear on the reduced contexts for full-fledged narrative discourse and other kinds of natural use of the language. In fact, the reduction of complex grammatical structures like subordination in the repertoire of terminal speakers is in a dialectic relation with the restriction of argumentative and narrative discourse in the contracting language for these speakers (Dressler 1988; Tsitsipis 1984).

In light of the above information, we can now turn to an examination of the anecdote. It is as follows and is given with interlinear translation (In the transcribed parts of Arvanítika discourse, phonetic symbols have been avoided for simplicity. Graphemic clusters such as kj, hj, ch, and so forth, are used to indicate palatalization. The symbol ë stands for the schwa which is produced irregularly and inconsistently by terminal speakers.):

(1)   Kápjos, ihje fkjáksi i jinéka tu kulurákja
        somebody, his wife made cookies

(2)   ipírhe mja paraksíjisi me ti jinéka tu
        he had an argument with his wife

(3)   Do t'has koc? jo, do véte per gjum
        Do you want to eat Kóstas? No, I'll go to bed

(4)   píje kjimíthikje, katá tis dhío-tris ton ékove pína to vrádhi
        he went to sleep, at about two or three o'clock after
        midnight he got hungry

(5)   sikóthikje, tahje váli sto fúrno, kj'árhjise kj'étroje
He got up--the cookies were in the oven--and started
eating

(6)   pái i jinéka tu: *koc, tíje re? Koc?*
his wife shows up: "Kósta, is it you?"

(7)   aftós ékane to skjilí ke aftí:
this one pretended to be a dog, and she:

(8)   nji kjen ist bérdha në furn
a dog is in the oven

The above text is offered mainly in Greek. In Albanian are line
(3), the italicized part of line (6), and line (8). Actually, the quoted
words of the story's protagonists are given in Albanian. The
significant point is that the anecdote does not culminate with its
punchline, which is supposedly line (8). The following comment is
added directly after the main body of the joke, which I give here in
English translation: "They tell jokes in such a way and in very specific
contexts that jokes in Arvanítika make you laugh."

We are dealing here not with the performance of a small genre
directly but with the creation of an oblique context for the reference
of the genre to other older and authentic performers. The anecdote
is cited and not told. No accountability for the successful telling is to
be expected. The terminal speaker is not held accountable for a
performance. His comment disclaims this responsibility.

In spite of the fact that in this anecdote the speaker manages
to provide a good balance between the Greek- and the Albanian-
language parts by rendering in Arvanítika the reported speech of the
protagonists for dramatization, his intonation is that of a colorless
citing of information, and not of a climactic narration leading to a
punchline (for a difference in the handling of quote speech, see
Tsitsipis n.d.), where reported speech and diegetic part are not

properly rendered by the terminal speaker). Furthermore, the fact that the anecdote is not part of the speaker's active repertoire becomes obvious in the manner in which he initiates his move; as line (1) suggests the expression, "**somebody, his wife made cookies,**" is syntactically messed up. One of the most significant deviations, however, from the proper performance of the genre is the noninclusion of a specific scene-setting in the plot; **someone, somebody, somewhere** are not generally selected by fluent speakers to dramatize or authenticate the story.

As suggested previously, there is a continuum of explicitness that terminal speakers fuse their voice with that of the traditional community. Comparing the text above with the "control questions" and authoritative sounding statements cited previously as well as with other anecdote renderings (Tsitsipis n.d.), we notice that here the speaker exploits the opportunity to refer it to traditional narrators explicitly. Thus, the subversive attitude so characteristic of slim texts as effected through slight irony and joking intonation does not take hold as strongly here as elsewhere. Nevertheless, the comment with which the speaker culminates the anecdote is not completely free from a slightly ironic or skeptical tone becoming thus a locus of double-voiced discourse of the internally persuasive type.

As discussed in some detail earlier, for slim texts to be fully incorporated in the ongoing discourse, complicity between participants is required. This complicity is a very powerful factor in giving the endorsement of appropriateness to initially improper discourse materials. The emergent appropriateness starts out, no doubt, from the framing of the texts by the terminal speakers themselves. It is being completed with the culturally appropriate rejoinders by the fluent speakers. Thus, discourse centering is effected. Throughout the conversation of which the terminal-speaker interjection was cited, older speakers become complicitous in various ways. The terminal speaker's grandmother, present during a long part of the discussion, shows supportive attitude by commenting:

E léi kamjá *chë bën jajá, si véte?* dhen da miláne; emís tus miláme eliniká

"E he uses a couple of expressions 'how are you doing grandma, how things are?,' [young people] don't speak it [Arvanítika]; we speak to them in Greek."

The text of the fluent speaker reveals a complicity. A lot of attitude and speech habit recapitulation is effected through it. The old woman utters her words in Greek except for the italicized part in which she cites expressions of the type usually uttered by terminal speakers. Such a complicity is not always shown in the same way by fluent speakers. Here the woman takes responsibility for the contracted competence of younger community members by stating that these people are not adequately exposed to Arvanítika talk. In other cases, the point made is different. Fluent speakers frequently point emphatically to the situation in which terminal speakers know how to use the language, since they are exposed to grandparental conversations. It is, therefore, obvious that the deviance of terminal-speaker slim texts emerges as nondeviance through a collusive enterprise.

In the theoretical part of my discussion, I pointed to the need for a critical application of Bakhtin's discourse theory in view of the variation of speech use and function in the communities studied by ethnographers. I want to elaborate in what follows on the relation between slim textuality and authoritative discourse. The significance of this subject stems from an apparent contradiction between the tests' polyphonic status and their target, that is, the traditional community speech patterns. Bakhtin (1981, 342, 348) contrasts authoritative to internally persuasive discourse. The former cannot be questioned, and thus, it cannot become the object of refraction through another discourse; it is only transmitted as such since it has been acknowledged in the past. The latter allows for a dialogue because it starts out and continues as a resistance to and questioning and exposure of another word. I found that terminal-speaker slim texts fall comfortably within this last category. Such a categorization of slim texts is not contradicted by another classification also of Bakhtin's, that of the partial coincidence between external and internal discourse. Terminal speakers in their "control" comments and questions as well as in their pretentious "tellings" of anecdotes become the addressers or animators of texts that should be addressed to them under "normal" circumstances. But the problem lies elsewhere, that is, how should we take the ways of speaking of the traditional and continuous communities themselves? Is there any component of authority in the traditional speech patterns? If there is, then how are we to explain the framed slim texts? According to Bakhtin, such a discourse is not the object of dialogical engagement of the type I claim here for terminal speakers. In order to answer these questions, we have to provide some picture of the sociolinguistic shift in the communities.

Socioeconomic restructurings in the communities have caused a gradual subjugation of the symbolic power of the Albanian variety spoken locally under the hegemonic ideology of the state. Speakers' self-deprecation was already obvious in the past decades (Tsitsipis 1983; Hamp 1978). A gradual shrinkage in the functional load of Arvanítika has gone hand-in-hand with the reduction of complex grammatical-syntactic structures for the terminal-speaker group. However, the language retains some of its power for fluent speakers by indexing through the use in domestic discourse of interpersonal relations and solidarity (see Woolard 1989 for a discussion of language death as a social process). In Arvanítika, the functional shift has been the opposite of what Hill (1983, 269) recognizes as the **Latinate** type of change where the most elevated styles are more viable than domestic discourse. Here everyday discourse is more viable, and higher stylistic levels along with genres addressed to children, abundant in the past (Meyer 1896) are swept away. Even the use of Arvanítika in the Orthodox Mass, as evidenced by bilingual New Testament texts, occurred by concession (Hamp, personal communication), which suggests among other things that Arvanítika, which has been and still is a traditionally oral culture, faced literacy as the medium of the formal aspects of religious practice only under the orbit of the state. In fact early enough in the last century, a bifurcation was taking place gradually between the most prominent Arvanítika-speaking community leaders and the rest of the community. The expression *érdh Búbuli* "Búbuli is here (has come)" recapitulates the experience of the church's congregation and the priest who were notified to switch over to Greek in the mass because Búbuli showed up and Arvanítika should be quit. Such information suggested, on the one hand, that Arvanítika monolingualism was still the norm and only through this code the Holy Word could become intelligible, and on the other, that any use of the language for high purposes such as the religious practice was already on shaky grounds.

Terminal speakers of the present-day communities face a rather reduced authority of the Arvanítika language. Nevertheless, a traditional authority is not completely absent from Arvanítika discourse. Because of its limited functional load locally and the partial dependence of terminal speakers on the Arvanítika language resources, the traditional voice is not fully stripped of authority. This of course explains the limits on how far terminal speakers can go in addressing the community linguistic habits in mockery and slight irony. Through a close scrutiny, therefore, it appears that the contradiction between the requirements of authoritative discourse and the double-voiced slim texts dissolves. If we accept that, although no utterance is to be accepted without authority (Du Bois 1986, 322), authority or control over an utterance admits of degrees and gradations (Du Bois 1986, 227-228), then internally persuasive discourse is suitable to characterize slim texts. I would rather judge Bakhtin's distinction between authoritative and internally persuasive discourse as too rigid if we intend to make use of it in the context of ethnographic and sociolinguistic cases.

The analysis advanced so far is also consistent with recent tendencies to take language shift studies out of the metaphorical frame of the pastoral ideal according to which scholars are searching for the pristine and pure forms of a language or culture (Gal 1989). The analysis is further consistent with Vološinov's position against a reifying perspective in linguistics. In fact, it is interesting that dying, foreign, or dead languages have been taken by Vološinov as being at the root of inspiration for the reification of linguistic theories. Says Vološinov,

> The dead language the linguist studies is, of course, an alien language. Therefore the system of linguistic categories is least of all a product of cognitive reflection on the part of the linguistic consciousness of a speaker of that language....Inevitably, the philologist-linguist's passive understanding is projected onto the very monument he is studying from the language point of view, as if that monument were in fact calculated for just that kind of understanding, as if it had, in fact, been written for the philologist (1973, 73).

Viewing things from the perspective of community dynamics and contradictions, I hope that I have established the sociological as well as the textual and communicative status of slim texts.

It still remains, however, to examine the phenomenon under discussion in the context of the notion of **tradition** corroborating thus further the interpretation offered so far. The linguistic habits and speech patterns that constitute the targets of terminal slim texts are part of a local tradition, as is obvious from earlier discussion. They are invested with some degree of traditional value for fluent speakers. This conception of traditional value comes close to what Williams (1977, 116) calls a weaker notion of tradition, that is, "...points of retreat for groups in the society which have been left stranded by some particular hegemonic development." On the other hand, as already shown, the symbolic power of Arvanítika has come under the hegemony of the then emerging nation-state and it is this hegemonical process that is best exemplified in the self-deprecation that Arvanítika people show. In fact, fluent speakers incorporate in their everyday domestic narrative discourse explicit or oblique references to their internalizaton of the process (Tsitsipis 1988). Thus, through a combination of the effects of hegemony and those of the residual, weaker points of retreat, ambiguous attitudes toward the language have grown (Tsitsipis 1983). This further justifies our claim in the present analysis for a nonabsolute authority surrounding Arvanítika, which opens the potential for discourse by terminal speakers that questions these traditional values.

Williams (1977, 115-117) provides an innovative understanding of tradition that grasps those features and processes that a static historicized notion cannot. Between a selective tradition in the service of hegemony and the weaker sense, Williams holds that the hegemonic is always the most active. The weight is leaning toward the questioning of traditional Arvanítika discourse, and its being blocked from developing features of authoritative discourse that, per Bakhtin, cannot be questioned or fused with another discourse.

In the theoretical part of my discussion, I alluded to the subjective aspect of the problem, and the moment is ripe now to elaborate on that. Although the macroprocesses of language shift and attitude development are not in any simple sense the conscious product of actors in the speech community, undoubtedly speakers have a knowledge of how they should manipulate their resources. Caton (1987, 251) observes that the ethnography of speaking must explore fully the subjectivity implicated in the notions of speaking and the appropriateness conditions as held by actors. Arvanítika speakers, in their production of slim texts and in the complicity shown by all those present in an interaction, provide a good example of subjectively or, more accurately, intersubjectively held notions of speech appropriateness. Furthermore, if slim texts offer an oblique critical commentary of types of traditional discourse, they become the expression of intersubjectively built attitudes subversive of the absolute authority of traditional patterns of speaking. Speaking interaction itself is therefore the locus of linguistic and social change. How this questioning of authority becomes possible is revealed in our discussion of tradition in the preceding paragraphs. It is thus rewarding to embed speaking in the recent and promising line of anthropological research with an emphasis on **praxis** (Ortner 1984).

At this point of my research, I have not fully developed all these dimensions of **slim textuality** that would permit an adequate comparison of various cases that appear in the ethnographic record. Nevertheless, certain similarities suggest themselves. Basso (1979, 41), in a detailed account of Western Apache joking performances, discusses the building of portraits of "The Whiteman," that is, staged imitational frames that serve as cultural commentaries. These portraits are successfully effected through the appropriate use of speech resources on the basis of some guiding principles. The slices of unjoking activity serve as the models, or **primary texts**, on which the **secondary texts** of joking performances are built.

The relation between primary and secondary texts holds also for the Arvanítika situation the sociolinguistic and cultural differences between the two cases notwithstanding. Basso (1979, 44) notes that the major strategy that jokers use to achieve their effects is **epitomization**, which is guided by two basic principles: **contrast** and **distortion**. The underlying principle informing these two, and perhaps other cases of the ethnographic record in which slim texts serve the ideological purposes of speakers, is the appropriation of others' voices, which become freshly refocused carrying within themselves a different, and frequently opposite, ideological point of view.

Conclusion

Since focus on discourse and natural interaction brings to bear on the notion of praxis, I considered it profitable to discuss the concept of slim text in the broader context of linguistic anthropology exploiting the dialectic between data and theoretical constructs. Although no specific reference has been made throughout my text to particular works by Southall, I would claim that there is a congruity between what I am saying here and his fundamental contributions to both urban and Marxist anthropology. To put it in a more specific manner, both social anthropology and its linguistic aspect tend nowadays to develop less localized models in which broader networks replace the hard community boundaries and structure looks to praxis or a fuller understanding of processes of change. Furthermore, ideology that figures prominent in current treatments of social issues by anthropologists and linguists takes a very concrete and material substance if viewed through the light that interaction sheds on it.

References

Abrahams,R.D.
1986   Complicity and imitation in story-telling: A pragmatic folklorist's perspective. *Cultural anthropology* 1:223-237.

Albert,E.M.
1972   Culture patterning of speech behavior in Burundi. In *Directions in sociolinguistics: The ethnography of communication*, edited by J.J.Gumperz and D.Hymes, 72-105. New York: Holt, Rinehart and Winston.

Bakhtin,M.M.
1981   Discourse in the novel. In *The dialogic imagination: Four essays by M.M.Bakhtin*, edited by M.Holquist, 259-422. Austin, Texas: University of Texas Press.
1984   *Problems of Dostoevsky's poetics.* Minneapolis: University of Minnesota Press.
1986   *Speech genres and other late essays.* Austin, Texas: University of Texas Press.

Basso,K.H.
1979   *Portraits of "The Whiteman": Linguistic play and cultural symbols among the Western Apache*, with a foreword by D.Hymes. London; New York: Cambridge University Press.

Bauman,R.
1977   *Verbal art as performance.* Rowley, Massachusetts: Newbury House.
1986   *Story, performance, and event: Contextual studies of oral narrative.* London: Cambridge University Press.

Bourdieu,P.
1977   *Outline of a theory of practice.* Cambridge: Cambridge University Press.

Caton,S.C.
1987   Contributions of Roman Jakobson. *Annual review of anthropology* 16:223-260.

Cazden,C.B.
1989   Contributions of the Bakhtin circle to "communicative competence." *Applied linguistics* 10:116-127.

Clark,K., and M.Holquist
1984   *Mikhail Bakhtin.* Cambridge, Massachusetts: The Belknap Press of Harvard University Press.

Dorian,N.C.
1981   *Language death: The life cycle of a Scottish Gaelic dialect.* Philadelphia: University of Pennsylvania Press.

Dressler,W.U.
1988   Language death. In *Linguistics: The Cambridge survey. IV Language: The socio-cultural context,* edited by F.J.Newmeyer, 184-192. Cambridge: Cambridge University Press.

Du Bois,J.W.
1986   Self-evidence and ritual speech. In *Evidentiality: The linguistic coding of epistemology,* edited by W.Chafe and J.Nichols, 313-336. Norwood: Ablex.
1987   Meaning without intention: Lessons from divination. *Papers in Pragmatics* 1:80-122.

Duranti,A.
1986   The audience as co-author: An introduction. *Text* 6:239-247.

Eagleton,T.
1984   *The function of criticism: From the spectator to post-structuralism.* London: Verso.

Gal,S.
1989   Lexical innovation and loss: The use and value of restricted Hungarian. In *Investigating obsolescence: Studies in language contraction and death,* edited by N.C.Dorian,313-331. Cambridge: Cambridge University Press.

Hamp,E.P.
1978   Problems of multilingualism in small linguistic communities. In *International dimensions of*

bilingual education, edited by J.E.Alatis, 155-164. Georgetown Round Table on Languages and Linguistics. Washington,D.C.: Georgetown University Press.

Hanks,W.F.
1987   Discourse genres in a theory of practice. *American ethnologist* 14:668-692.
1989   Text and textuality. *Annual review of anthropology* 18:95-127.

Hill,J.H.
1983   Language death in Uto-Aztecan. *International journal of American linguistics* 3:258-276.
1986   The refiguration of the anthropology of language. (Review article.) *Cultural anthropology* 1:89-102.

Hinds,J.
1981   The interpretation of ungrammatical utterances. In *A festschrift for native speaker*, edited by F.Coulmas,221-235.   Paris; New York; The Hague: Mouton.

Holquist,M.
1990   *Dialogism: Bakhtin and his world*. London; New York: Routledge.

Hymes,D.
1974   Ways of speaking.   In *Explorations in the ethnography of speaking*, edited by R.Bauman and J.Sherzer, 433-451. Cambridge: Cambridge University Press.
1982   Narrative form as a "grammar" of experience: Native Americans and a glimpse of English. *Journal of education* 2:121-142.
1986   Discourse: Scope without depth. *International journal of the sociology of language* 57:49-89.

Irvine,J.T.
1973   Caste and communication in a Wolof village. Ph.D. dissertation. University of Pennsylvania.
1982   The creation of identity in spirit, mediumship, and possession. In *Semantic anthropology*, edited by D.Parkin, 241-260. London: Academic Press.

368

Lakoff,R.
1989   The way we were; or; The real actual truth about generative semantics: A memoir. *Journal of pragmatics* 13:939-988.

Mannheim,B.
1987   Couplets and oblique contexts: The social organization of a folksong. **Text** 7:265-288.

Meyer,G.
1896   *Albanesische studien V: Beiträge zur kentniss der in Griehenland gesprochenen Albanesischen mundarten.* Vienna: Wiener Akademie Sitzungsberichte.

Ortner,S.B.
1984   Theory in anthropology since the sixties. *Comparative studies in society and history* 26:126-166.

Rosaldo,M.
1982   The things we do with words: Ilongot speech acts and speech act theory in philosophy. *Language in society* 11:203-237.

Searle,J.R.
1969   *Speech acts: An essay in the philosophy of language.* Cambridge: Cambridge University Press.

Sherzer,J.
1987   A discourse-centered approach to language and culture. *American anthropologist* 89:295-309.

Sperber,D., and D.Wilson
1981   Irony and the use-mention distinction. In *Radical pragmatics*, edited by P.Cole, 295-318. New York: Academic Press.

Tsitsipis,L.D.
n.d.   Terminal-fluent speaker interaction and the contextualization of deviant speech. *Journal of Pragmatics* 15. (Forthcoming.)
1983   Language shift among the Albanian speakers of Greece. *Anthropological linguistics* 25:288-308.
1984   Functional restriction and grammatical reduction in

Albanian language in Greece. *Zeitschrift für Balkanologie* 20:122-131.

1988   Language shift and narrative performance: On the structure and function of Arvanítika narratives. *Language in society* 17:61-86.

1989   Skewed performance and full performance in language obsolescence: The case of an Albanian variety. In *Investigating obsolescence: Studies in language contraction and death*, edited by N.C.Dorian, 117-137. Cambridge: Cambridge University Press.

Vološinov,V.N.

1973   *Marxism and the philosophy of language*, translated by Ladislav Matejka and I.R.Titunik. Cambridge, Massachusetts: Harvard University Press.

Williams,R.

1977   *Marxism and literature.* Oxford; New York: Oxford University Press.

Woolard,K.A.

1989   Language convergence and language death as social processes. In *Investigating obsolescence: Studies in language contraction and death*, edited by N.C.Dorian, 355-367. Cambridge: Cambridge University Press.

V. CULTURAL PRACTICE, EPISTEMOLOGY, AND REFLEXIVITY

The Past and the Present in the Future

Concepcion del Castillo, Development Anthropologist
Food and Agriculture Organization of the United Nations
Rome, Italy

In his work, Aidan Southall has shown a deep interest and concern, both theoretical and practical, about the study of social change. Concepts and assumptions about social change are used in the design and implementation of foreign donor-assisted development projects in Third World countries, and I argue against the notion that the theoretical and applied facets of anthropology are separable.

Professional involvement in this type of development work presents moral, philosophical, and theoretical dilemmas for anthropologists. Because of our training, we have an unspoken "populist commitment to the people," in the phrase of A.F. Robertson (1984, 295), and often the notion of donor-assisted development is perceived with skepticism if not hostility. We are more comfortable in the role of showing people as they are rather than speculating on what they can be. "Although the business of anthropology is to look at the empirical reality of what might be termed alternative cultures, it does not speculate about what might be" (Belshaw 1976). This stems from our preoccupation with objectivity, values, and judgments, but most of all with a distaste for political involvement.

It is naive, as many have indicated, to assume that theory and practice are value free, and that in conventional fieldwork we are not involved with these problems. We all face them to a lesser or greater degree, and for those who choose to work as applied anthropologists, these problems are central. I would argue that one of the messages of Southall's work is that we are in a better position to meet these challenges, and to contribute to the theoretical debate about social change, if we examine the concepts and premises behind the framework of action that surrounds development work.

From the personal perspective of an applied anthropologist, this framework combines two different kinds of premises: (1) conceptual or theoretical, which refer to systems of ideas about how social change occurs; and (2) instrumental or practical, which refer to how the process of social change can be analyzed and interventions created. These two premises are held by development organizations and by states and their agents, though the premises are different for each and may conflict in the design of programs, policies, and specific interventions.

The premises on which anthropologists or other social scientists base their models of society are a third set of assumptions, but they are not dealt with here. I will list some key premises and discuss their implications for applied anthropological work.

Premises of the development agencies

Conceptual level

- Change can be predicted and directed, and can occur through external intervention;

- Induced social change should reduce social and economic inequalities and promote general welfare;

- Development results in a new kind of political culture that legitimizes broad political participation;

- Development and social change should promote participatory institutions that will increase the self-awareness of the people and improve their capacity to identify and solve their own problems, thus reducing their reliance on government resources and ensuring sustainable development.

Instrumental level

- Empirical research can point out the causes of poverty and underdevelopment;

- Interventions can be designed to specifically address and modify these causes;

- Country-specific cultural factors (thought and action systems) must be considered and evaluated in the design of projects;

- A priori Western assumptions concerning reactions to development interventions in specific (non-Western) contexts are not valid;

- Institutions to encourage grass-roots participation in the process of development can be designed on the basis of empirical analysis.

Premises of the state agents/agencies

Conceptual level

- The state works for the welfare of the people and popular will is expressed in the actions of officials;

• State officials know the empirical realities of the country and what changes (in the form of interventions) are required;

• State officials are best placed to decide on interventions, and popular participation is not necessary.

Instrumental level

• Effective action is generated through plans;

• Macrolevel information is sufficient for the design of effective plans;

• Centralization of organizational functions is the best way to implement action, and delegation of power diminishes efficiency.

These two sets of premises do not operate independently, and their interaction and the manner in which they are eventually translated into action are not frequently examined, which results in deficient projects and in changes within the recipient system that are unintended and/or deleterious. In what follows I outline ways in which this interaction is significant for both theory and practice.

What we mean by the study of social change is not some grandiose and abstract process but the observation and explanation of *specific* differences, replacements, or changes in material conditions, power relations, or ideologies, that affect a particular socioeconomic system through time. The dimensions of power relations and ideologies are essential to the understanding of the process but these are usually not highlighted in development models.

Methodologically, a proper investigation or analysis requires us to formulate models of *real systems* and these should (1) make all the facts visible and intelligible, (2) explain the conditions under which elements in the system are transformed, (3) describe the magnitude of changes and their effects on other elements in the system, and (4) predict how the system will react if one or more of its elements are submitted to modifications.

By definition, these systems are dynamic and diachronic, and these features are the most critical ones for models of social change. The baseline identification of components and empirical information concerning their relative value are usually met through empirical research and observation. On the other hand, the model's requirements about conditions of transformation, the description of magnitudes of change, and of predictability, cannot be fulfilled unless we include the elements of ideology, and their uses in specific contexts. It is the dialectical interplay and contradictions between ideology and the power relations in specific environments that drive the systems under observation.

The importance of ideology and local power relations in the process of development and social change are not outrightly recognized by most development agencies. The relatively steady increase in the use of social scientists, other than economists, in development work over the last ten years, however, reflects a gradual shift (not quite a change) in paradigms of development. Thinking is increasingly oriented toward the definition of a paradigm that goes beyond the examination of material conditions, and focuses on concrete cultural processes and their ramifications. This is a positive step, but one that has not been pushed far enough. This change in perspective reflects altered concepts about "traditional" societies and their dynamics, as well as on what factors can promote certain kinds of social change, and the change in perspective begins to focus on heterogeneity, stratification, and the social organization of production, as well as on linkages between communities and statewide systems. However, the analysis of the power relations in local-level systems and their linkages, which are the structuring principles of class order that uphold and enforce the system of resource distribution, have not been stressed and have been only peripherally incorporated into the models. A recent illustration of this reluctance to examine intrinsic causal factors of poverty and underdevelopment is the World Bank's report where it distinguishes between poverty and inequality:

> poverty is concerned with the standard of living in a part of society--the poor--inequality refers to living standards across the whole society. At maximum inequality, one person has everything and, clearly, poverty is high. But minimum inequality...is possible with zero poverty as well as with maximum poverty (1990, 26).

They do not stress the correlation of these two factors. We are not dealing squarely with the factors that lead to the cycles of impoverishment and indebtedness. The danger of this omission is that it risks reproducing the social and economic inequalities development, which interventions are seeking to eliminate.

In particular, the premise that development implies a certain kind of political culture, outlook, and ideology, which legitimizes and facilitates political participation, has become the *sine qua non* of development programs. The thinking is that the participatory process will result in increased self-awareness and an increased capacity of local people to identify and solve their own problems. This process would enable the people to plan and implement their own long-term sustainable development programs, which are less reliant on government interventions and foreign assistance. The topic of participation and its outcome, specifically how it affects economic change and political systems is complex and lengthy. Here we would only suggest that the causal chain is not as simple as some would have it and should be subject to careful scrutiny. Few practitioners with an egalitarian bent would dispute the ultimate welfare goals behind this notion, but very practical problems are associated with it. The problem is that here the goals of the development agencies are set for a head-on collision with the premises of the state and its agents. While international donor agencies may be sincere about their wish to address the issues of poverty and underdevelopment, the implementation of interventions must be accommodated within the development strategies of specific countries. It is at this level that the ideological and political system articulates with the premises of external development agencies, and with those people whom the projects are designed to aid, and the nature of this articulation critically affects the results of development.

By ideology we mean a system of signs and social consciousness, founded on the historic economic and social relations that exist in a society, which reflects the total life situation of a social group, and which serves as the mental grid through which that situation is experienced by the group. For an interesting discussion of these concepts, from which I have derived this definition, see Sumner (1979). Ideologies, in addition, serve as the crucial support for the state, which transforms them into a form of discourse designed to ensure its own maintenance and secure its own interests. It is through ideology that the state or selected portions of a population assert their political and moral legitimacy and acceptability presenting themselves as natural, legitimate, and unchallengeable, and whereby alternative or oppositional cultures (or discourses) are co-opted, downgraded, or silenced. These concepts paraphrase the views presented by Taylor and Turton (1988, 177).

Development thinking and local ideologies are often largely incompatible paradigms, and yet neither international donors nor individual states wish to withdraw from the development game. To the contrary, the trend is toward institutionalization of dependency on foreign assistance. The incompatibility of these paradigms leads to practical problems with implementation in the form of obstacles that were not foreseen at the time of project preparation. No state wants to foster significant structural changes by instituting programs if they will undermine the existing status quo. On the contrary, the state and its agents seek to protect their own interests.

Given this framework, there is a conversion of a project's cycle of activities into terms the state's agents can cope with (i.e., subverting the process, playing for individual gains against long-term change). Bureaucrats or other agents of the state controlling the resources of development projects become the patrons of certain groups, typically the local elites. The state agents become the legitimate monopolizers of an almost supernatural source of funds, and through the provision of needed and welcomed services, they mobilize support from their clients, further entrenching themselves and legitimizing even more pervasive control. Any material improvements constitute potentially larger surpluses, which perpetuate rather than change the existing system.

Some would argue that small quantitative changes in material conditions eventually change the superstructure, that quantitative increments lead to qualitative change. Even if this is true, the direction of that qualitative change may not be the one sought.

Until recently, the assumptions underlying development project design and implementation focused the study of social change on those elements that stressed a system's maintenance and stability. We are now entering into a phase that includes the examination of forces that can alter conditions and potentially produce systemic long-term change. But if there has been an increased awareness on the part of development agencies of the need to examine local systems of thought and action, anthropologists are still placed in a position of conducting relatively conventional ethnographic descriptions. This occurs in part because, as stated initially, a reluctance and distaste is associated with political involvement among anthropologists. Nevertheless, applied anthropologists **can** make a more significant contribution by transcending the boundaries of conventional description and superficial analysis by focusing on the interaction between the state and the groups on whose behalf projects are being designed. This means consideration of what interests are involved, who stands to win and to lose, and what specific conditions led to the evolution of the current system. Unless the dimension of ideology and its manifestations and contradictions represented by the unequal distribution of power and competition for resources (both ideologic and material) within communities, and between communities and the state, is placed at the center of the investigations and incorporated into models of social change, the models will remain incomplete and of limited usefulness.

The formulation of models that incorporate these dimensions is not a new idea, certainly not to academic anthropologists, and these are concepts that we have all seen reflected and debated in Southall's writing for over thirty years. But a lag persists in thought between academics and applied anthropologists, and for many ideological and practical reasons the methodological and theoretical change in the investigation of social change this essay describes is only now beginning to take place. While formulating such models is not the exclusive domain of anthropologists, it is certainly an area where we have the theoretical and methodological tools to make a contribution. This is one way in which we can put our training and expertise to work toward the formulation of alternative futures and the reduction of inequalities between the West and the Third World.

380

References

Belshaw,C.
1976   *The sorcerer's apprentice: An anthropology of public policy*, cited in *People and the state: An anthropology of planned development*, by A.F.Robertson, xiv. Cambridge: Cambridge University Press.

Robertson,A.F.
1984   *People and the state: An anthropology of planned development*. Cambridge: Cambridge University Press.

Sumner,C.
1979   *Reading ideologies: An investigation into the Marxist theory of ideology and law.* London: Academic Press.

Taylor,J.G., and A.Turton, eds.
1988   *Sociology of "Developing Societies": Southeast Asia.* London: Monthly Review Press.

World Bank
1990   *World development report.*

Culture and Contradiction in the Practice
Of Development Anthropology in Africa

Michael Brown, Project Director
PVO-NGO/NRMS Project
Washington, D.C., United States

Anthropologists, and gifted ones at that, are sometimes forced to assume humility in the face of incomplete data not fitting neatly into comfortable analytical categories. Southall (1970, 41) candidly notes that for uncentralized or stateless Nilotic societies, where rank is defined and expressed largely in terms of ritual, one must often defer to the primacy of cultural choice and confess ignorance when attempting to explain why societies with similar degrees of political specialization may develop different degrees of ritualization. Or in a case of assumption driving a crucial aspect of analysis relating to the evolution of two of the most studied and discussed ethnic groups in both the ethnographic and development literatures (Evans-Pritchard 1940; Howell 1954; Sahlins 1960; Lienhardt 1961; Newcomer 1972; Gough 1971; Southall 1976; Kelly 1985), demographic factors may in fact, when all brilliant argumentation is said and done, have impelled population expansion of proto-Naath (Nuer) leading to their sociocultural divergence from proto-Jieng (Dinka) (Southall 1976, 474).

Persuasive theories have been and no doubt will continue to be proffered as to why Nuer and Dinka diverged from a common stock into distinguishable ethnic groups. Yet *the driving force* behind the choices, in no small part cultural, of individual Nuer to effectively organize to expand their collective territory through raiding at the expense of Dinka, and of Dinka, to not develop an effective large-scale organization of defense against Nuer raiding (Lienhardt 1958), will remain speculative. For after all, the crucial demographic and socioeconomic data from the most pertinent years of Nuer/Dinka coevolution (the 1500-1800 period) remains "too far removed from the ethnographic present to be susceptible to detailed explication" (Kelly 1985, 22).

It could be argued that even data generated during the 1800-1880 period, from which much of Kelly's argument for the precedence of a sociocultural and socioeconomic explanation for Nuer and Dinka divergence versus a demographic argument (Southall 1976), is highly conjectural and of only rough orders of magnitude of precision. This is probable bearing in mind Evans-Pritchard's blunt assessment (1940, 12) on Nuer informant reliability generally: "Nuer are expert at sabotaging an inquiry and until one has resided with them for some weeks they steadfastly stultify all efforts to elicit the simplest facts and to elucidate the most innocent practices."

The necessity to argue for logical possibility in retrospective analysis or interpretation of sociocultural phenomena is characteristic of the most interesting sociocultural anthropology. This necessity is itself a function of sociocultural anthropologists' customary reliance on partial and disparate data sets. That different analysts may come to different, even contradictory conclusions over interpretation of cultural phenomena is hardly surprising given the often tenuous nature of the data and the incredibly complex nature of the processes involved.

The reliance on partial and disparate data sets is a hallmark of applied anthropology as well, and of development anthropology in particular. It is rare that development projects provide the luxury to permit the fullest gathering of data for the most optimal of planning. In cases where data gathering is prioritized, the political will to utilize the information engendered may not always be forthcoming. Admittedly however, there is no perfect correlation between maximal data and effective development execution in projects where excellent data exists (i.e., the Jonglei Canal Project in Sudan, or the Juba Valley Analytical studies Project, Somalia).

Somewhat analogously, it is precisely at the difficult-to-predict (or explain) level of cultural choice that much of the practitioner specialization of development anthropology operates: the prediction of what and how people will choose in particular sociocultural contexts; the solicitation of views of what interventions (if any) in a given situation will be most appropriate to improve the quality of peoples' lives; the mobilization of grass-roots participation in implementing projects of purported benefit to groups within communities, or to communities as wholes.

In this paper I discuss how development anthropologists confront and work through ambiguity and potential contradiction vis à vis different aspects of culture and cultural choice. Discussion of the assumptions and the limits of objectivity in development anthropology is broached. Finally, examples of how development anthropologists work with and through contradiction are provided based on ambiguous, culturally complex/contradictory experiences I have been involved with in Somalia and Mali.

Development anthropologists' assumptions

If such a thing as a "program" for development anthropology can be identified, it is, I believe, rooted in a number of premises about others and the world they live in. A nonexhaustive list of premises includes the following:

(1) The developing world is peopled with sociocultural units of various types: ethnic groups, hybrid socioeconomic categories, gender

groups, religious confessions (tribes in the restricted sense!)--which in dealings with "outside change agents" require "sympathetic" advocates, of which anthropologists qualify better than most.

(2) Others are "knowable," or components of socioeconomic and cultural life can be apprehended, to permit design of projects promoting optimal social change.

(3) Planners work on the basis of "objective" knowledge (even if development experience has proven the contrary true time and again (Horowitz 1988).

(4) Anthropologists, despite frequently working for purveyors of international capital, donor agencies, firms, and private voluntary agencies which often implement projects for them, believe that their work is directed to the poorest of the poor, and is thus counter hegemonic.

Objective grounds for anthropological knowledge

In recent years, the epistemological foundation upon which anthropology as a science of man has been called into question, and interest in the **grounds of objective anthropological knowledge** has been pronounced (Clifford 1983; Clifford and Marcus 1986; Marcus and Fischer 1986). The focus has been on cultural knowledge as depicted in texts (i.e., Is that which anthropologists have interpreted and rendered through participant observation, empirically credible, or rather a creative interpretation of a given anthropologist's mind?).

The political motives of anthropologists have also been questioned (Asad 1975; Hymes 1970). Issues concerning anthropologists' power through control of information and "knowledge," and the witting or unwitting perpetuation of facile explanations for the sake of maintaining unequal structural relations of power and dependency of first world over third world cultures (now "northern" over "southern"), have all been raised. Clifford, in what could serve as partial apology, notes for ethnography that

> even the best ethnographic texts--serious true fictions--are systems, or economies, of truth. Power and history work through them, in ways their authors cannot fully control.... Ethnographic work has indeed been enmeshed in a world of enduring and changing power inequalities, and continues to be implicated. It enacts power relations. But its function within these relations is complex, often ambivalent, potentially counter-hegemonic (1986, 9).

Limits of objectivity in development anthropology

The plight of development anthropologists is analogous to the plight of cultural anthropologists. Both are responsible for deciding how complex social realities are best depicted using smatterings of information, the cohesiveness of which requires supposition, massaging of embedded assumption, and leaps of faith in presentation of the reality interpreted. Both deal with, and construct, "economies of truth."

Any pretense that development anthropologists, any more than cultural anthropologists, can and do in any way act as independent, value-free, wholly objective analysts is admittedly incorrect. Development anthropologists are inevitably implicated in what Giddens, regarding another context, calls the "dialectic of control" (1983). All personal often progressive political agendas aside, anthropologists formally represent particular class interests of development agencies, usually informed by capitalistic paradigms of socioeconomic development.

A multiplicity of eager interest groups/constituencies exist, furthermore to shape the pace, content, and outcome of development anthropologists' work, be it on the order of research/analysis or development intervention. An inexhaustive list of such groups include donors, employers, host country ministries, governmental administrative structures, political parties, nongovernmental organizations (NGOs), ethnic group leaders, cooperatives or rural associations which may crosscut ethnic lines, and finally, the people, or "beneficiaries." Clearly within this context, development anthropologists' abilities to objectively analyze, recommend, and implement will be constrained by the conflicting class-determined ends striven for by the varied constituencies.

To avoid being a co-opted pawn (i.e., someone who prepares innocuous intellectual prattle that is easily buried within project documents and subsequently ignored) and to catalyze equitable development in the face of conflicting often contradictory constituent demands, requires creativity and dexterity by anthropologists committed to participating in a development process that is riddled with ambiguity and potential contradiction.

Development anthropology works with contradictions

Following are two themes from my experience in development projects in Africa that illustrate the kinds of ambiguous and culturally contradictory situations development anthropologists may confront.

(1) In order to reach target beneficiaries in northern Mali, **how flexible** do you have to be with elites?

(2) What is the **appropriate social organization** for Western-inspired range management in Somalia?

Mali. Effectively reaching target beneficiaries with agricultural and natural resources management activities in the Sahel requires inducing both capital-rich elites and marginalized agropastoralists to participate in a process. This must be done without allowing elites to co-opt the process. Saying this however is easier than accomplishing it in practice, and implies contradiction and ambiguity from the outset.

As background, my position in agricultural and natural resources management activities in Mali has involved promoting cooperative development through farmer participation in planning and management, rural credit, and motorized irrigated technology transfer in northern Mali (1986-87) (Activities Paysannes Project, Africare, funded by USAID/Mali), and broad-based technical and institutional capacity building activities within natural resources management (1989-90) PVO-NGO/NRMS Project, The Experiment in International Living, CARE, and World Wildlife Fund, funded by USAID/Washington). This has been predominantly among Bouremboro Songhay, and to a lesser extent Tamashek, and Peulh· agropastoralists in the first instance, and through the NGO sector countrywide in the latter.

In the northern Malian example, social organization and behavior is still largely operative along the basis of noble/captive lines of social stratification embedded in chiefdoms (Brown 1986). Based on a reading of the ethnographic and historic literature (de Sardan 1982; de Sardan 1984; Baier 1980) it could be argued contradictory, presumptuous, and paternalistic for an anthropologist to promulgate abstract participatory democratic principles derived from the political philosophy of "northern" countries onto Sahelian societies. There is scant precedent in the history of northern Sahelian societies for a tradition of democratic pluralism. Much presumably "cutting edge development," similar to that which I have worked on and continue to work on, is attempting nonetheless to promote such broad-based participation.

A major challenge for development anthropologists in the Sahel today is to determine how to integrate production and resources management planning needs and strategies of the poorest segments of Sahelian society with those of elite, capital-rich agropastoralists. The transfer of technologies in the highly drought-prone Sahelian environment must be promoted in a way that does not increasingly stratify wealth differences and access to productive resources between those owning the most productive (and potentially damaging) technology from those that do not.

Just *saying* that participation is needed and that participatory process is being promoted *does not*, in the context of stratified Bouremboro Songhay society, mean that participation will actually be achieved. To promote participation in the project I coordinated, areas of common interest between capital-rich elites and the capital-poor majority had to be identified. This involved linking cooperatives' continued access to seasonal credit for purchase of inputs for motor pump irrigation together with obtaining irrigation infrastructure improvements to the process of equitable cooperative farmer participation. Both elite and poorer agriculturalists within a cooperative would benefit only as the cooperative as a whole made its repayments for outstanding credit.

In those cooperatives where repayment rates were high, productivity across individual farm units, while variable, met minimal consumption needs. Farmers knew that production variability did not relate to inegalitarian access to either project resources or land or water distribution within the cooperative. Where repayment was most problematic, in the cooperatives managed by the strongest chiefs (particularly the *chef de canton* of the Bouremboro), inequalities in water and quality land distribution were important.

Here ironically, contact between project staff and farmers was most easily facilitated, at least on the surface. In cooperatives where chiefs were weakest, understanding of "project culture" and/or maintaining appropriate irrigation systems' management was most constraining. Empirically speaking, in the chef de canton's own cooperative, farmer participation in project activities was correlated to low productivity; while cooperative labor for the construction of irrigation infrastructure was successfully obtained since political leadership was strongest, individual repayment rates toward the cooperative's incurred credit liability was weakest, as input distribution within the cooperative was inegalitarian and intra-cooperative production variability among farmers was high. This situation led to a major contradiction: to reach farmers effectively one had to work through the powerful chef de canton. Yet "true" participation could never truly be elicited from farmers most under the chief's influence, thus creating a catch-22 situation.

This illustrates that where a dichotomy of interests was maintained between wealthy and poor farmers within a cooperative, project objectives were compromised. To leverage against this, the *process* of promoting ever-more inclusive social structures capable of better steward resources was (and is) therefore as important a *product* as any productivity gain or reversal in environmental degradation per se.

The major challenge in taking a longer term perspective and incrementally promoting consensual and participatory processes to managing resources, is to do so in a way that avoids forcing too much change in too short a period of time onto a stratified social structure unable to absorb such change. Advancing dialogue through providing broad access to key information, and creating as much possibility for a "development perestroika" to occur, step by step, was and must be the objective. This methodology of inducing change in northern Mali could be described, without being normally perceived as such, as an effort in "applied dialectics" with a capital D. But to do so, one must be prepared to work with powerful chiefs in the meantime, whose personal agendas are hardly isomorphic with the ideal objectives of their constituencies.

Somalia. In Somalia I was hired as a socioeconomist by a multinational firm working on a USAID/World Bank contract. My role was to determine what the ideal social organizational bases for grazing associations in Somalia were to be, and assist in forming associations in conjunction with project range ecologists working on the central rangelands development project (CRDP).

Range management planning was to be based on utilization of sound scientifically proven range management principles (Wilkes 1983) based on range condition and trend data as identified by ecologists, and to adapt these principles to the reality of the local situation in three central rangelands districts. In the context of a Somalia in 1983 where "tribes" or "clans" were officially outlawed, where overarching integrative structures were few, and in which family-based (*reer*) decision-making units predominated, how then could decisions be made regarding the sociological basis upon which grazing associations should be formed? From the outset the situation was both ambiguous and contradictory.

Available background materials to assist contextualizing this work included livestock density data, cropping density data, settlement density data, relief and drainage data (Watson 1979). Ethnographic analysis, conducted prior to the banning of clans, on northern Somali pastoral organization was also available (Lewis 1961), along with sociohistorical analysis on the shaping of Somali society (Cassenelli 1982). A data base for livestock ownership by reer and traditional grazing area (*degaan*), along with migratory patterns, was developed through interviews by the project extension and socioeconomic components for most of the central rangelands. So, too, ecological baseline data on palatable and unpalatable species together with soil conditions was assembled by ecologists.

Lewis's structural functional analysis, which focused on northern Somali lineage-based politics, provides a similar sociopolitical context to which central Somali pastoralists function (Lewis 1961). While Lewis identified home wells as a crucial resource management variable for understanding the dynamics of northern Somali pastoralism, Lewis' ethnographic work branded a degree of nomadic mobility on Somali pastoral society wherein "permanent ties to locality" were not seen as significant (Lewis 1961).

Data our project elicited for central Somalia did not wholly corroborate this extreme propensity for mobility which Lewis's ethnographic work in the north highlighted. That is, the ideal typical image of a highly mobile Somali pastoral population, did not reconcile with the reality found in the central rangelands. The importance that agriculture, livestock trade, foreign remittances, and political factors came to have on resource attribution and management decisions in central Somalia during the early 1980s, and particularly on the increasing consolidation of Somali pastoralism centered around degaans was thus a surprising finding (Brown 1984). The extent of actual range degradation found by ecologists in the central rangelands was far more limited than originally anticipated, and the causes for degradation had less to do with pastoral nomadism per se than with agricultural practices of Somali pastoral nomads in one hundred to two hundred millimeters/annual rainfall zones around population settlements (Holt 1986).

Since the project had been designed on the premise of Somali pastoralists being highly mobile, and that the rangelands were in a severe state of degradation, fieldwork findings proved contradictory to many of the assumptions that development experts held.

On the sociological level, project staff thus agreed that since Somali pastoralists of the central rangelands were not so mobile as originally assumed and that since property was in fact not open for all comers but was based on acknowledged rights and obligations among clans and subclans, then a geographic basis for range management could be developed that would be compatible with the traditional range management system. Appropriate social organizations for range management activities in Somalia would be comprised of those reers able to develop and maintain consensus within a degaan regarding the use of rangeland resources.

Given the lack of centralized authority in central Somalia, with decision making regarding clan level issues made on the basis of consensus through meetings of elders (*odayaal*) run generally by degaan leaders (*nabadoon*), the consensual decision making required to actually organize grazing associations of pastoralists on the ground took considerable time and effort. This was in contrast to the organizing of cooperatives in a society such as Bouremboro Songhay, where as mentioned, chiefs having decision-making authority for villages can reach rapid, if not immediate allocative decisions.

A list of retrospective conclusions from my work in the central rangelands that illustrates the kind of ambiguity and contradiction involved in pastoral sector development includes the following:

(1) consensus over range management methodologies required time and confidence building at different structural levels;

(2) fewer management interventions could therefore take place in time and space than planners would have had it;

(3) interventions had a higher probability of being sustained where they in fact did emanate from group consensus;

(4) the key social groups (or rangeland institutions) responsible for stewarding range resources were amalgamations of the very social groups that the government had in fact outlawed (i.e., clans and subclans, and their constituent reers);

(5) a key constraint to reaching consensus regarding range rotation, using a paddock system, were the sanctions which could/would be brought to bear on incursive groups; since occasional use by outside groups to particular degaans in exceptionally dry years was possible, it was essential that all potential user groups be made aware of management plans and sanctions for illicit use (i.e., the mobility that Lewis (1961) had noted for northern Somali pastoralists had to be accommodated for during extreme cases);

(6) this "catch-22"--have everybody on board at the same time-- was an ideal difficult to achieve in practice, but was empirically surmounted in several degaan cases;

(7) the assumption that Somali pastoralism was in any way irrational was contradicted on the basis of (a) pastoralists' overall rangelands' ethnoscientific knowledge, (b) objective range condition and trend data, and (c) the staggering data assembled on the value of "average" livestock holdings in degaans (CRDP 1983). (Clearly the Somali knew very well what they were doing!);

(8) the best that a $40 million project such as the CRDP could hope to achieve was to perhaps enable incremental gains in range and livestock productivity, but at the risk of unbalancing a system that by all productivity indicators was performing extremely well;

(9) it would take at least ten years to truly learn if there was in fact any justification for adapting the range rotation principles the project was promoting, during which time I argued that it was

imperative to address and integrate basic needs into the project's program (i.e., provision of cleaner water, primary health care, and literacy training as a means of rationalizing for pastoralists their continued participation in what otherwise was a highly theoretical exercise of dubious value;

(10) instead of providing high output water resources such as boreholes, as the project had contracted for, which would stimulate range degradation and potentially lead to interclan conflict, it was suggested, unsuccessfuly, that satisfaction of basic needs *as identified by pastoralists* thus become a cornerstone of the project's program in the short term.

While aspects of Western style range management may be beneficial in central Somalia, a project such as the one I worked on can only, in the context of politically turbulent Somalia, render more contradiction and ambiguity than solution to the situation. My attempt to identify the ambiguous and contradictory aspects of the overall and specific approach to range management as Western range managers would have it ideally, and to give the approach a chance to test itself out in an apropriate manner, was seen by decision makers as irrelevant and contradictory to the task at hand. As development anthropologist operating in a politically charged arena where the most partial of truths were orienting a frenzied overall donor/government development agenda, I saw it regardless as my responsibility to identify apparent contradictions and to propose alternative courses of action, especially when both project beneficiaries and staff lives and welfare were significantly at stake.

The conclusions I was drawing, which would impact development planning and implementation, were inevitably based on partial truths and partial understandings. Analogous to Southall's conclusions on Nuer/Dinka cultural divergence falling very much under the category of logical possibility, my recommendations were of a similar order as well, albeit looking into the future. These partial truths were based on the maximum degree of ground-truthing which project management would allow at the time. Unfortunately this did not save the life of the project's chief well driller, who was murdered Christmas eve 1983 over what I contended were unresolved contradictions over land tenure issues pertaining to sub-clan units' perception of grazing rights along the boundary of two adjacent degaans.

Conclusion

The best applied anthropology or development anthropology of the 1990s is anything but academic, and thus stands in contrast to the valid, introspective critique voiced in the early 1970s that anthropology risked dying of irrelevance.

I have argued elsewhere that if anthropologists are to truly impact the development process, they must develop new skills and increasingly assume positions with decision-making authority, in contrast to my own experience in Somalia (Brown 1987; Brown 1990). That this will place anthropologists increasingly in ambiguous, oftentimes contradictory positions is clear. That these positions will be anything but value free is also clear. Because development anthropologists' can neither explain nor predict all contingencies should in no way detract from anthropologists' abilities as optimally objective scientists, interpreters, and communicators of cultural understanding with all accompanying limitations, to attempt not only to study, but to actually better peoples' lives.

References

Asad,T., ed.
1975   *Anthropology and the colonial encounter*. Ithaca: Ithaca Press.

Baier,S.
1980   *An economic history of central Niger*. Oxford: Clarendon Press.

Brown,M.
1984   Social soundness analysis. Livestock marketing and animal health project paper. USAID/Mogadishu.
1986   Activities paysannes first quarterly report. Africare. Dire, Mali.
1987   Development anthropologists, credibility, and project implementation: A strategy for getting anthropologists off the ground. American Anthropological Association Meetings, Chicago.
1990   Non-Governmental organizations (NGOs) and natural resources management (NRM) trends in Africa: New opportunities for anthropologists to adapt and better fit in. Paper presented at American Anthropological Association Meetings in New Orleans, November 28, 1990.

Cassenelli,L.
1982   *The shaping of Somali society*. Philadelphia: University of Pennsylvania Press.

Central Rangelands Development Project (CRDP)
1983   Livestock census forms. Mimeo. Mogadishu.

Clifford,J.
1983   Power and dialogue in ethnography: Marcel Griaule's initiation. In *Observers observed*, edited by G.Stocking. Madison, Wisconsin: University of Wisconsin Press.

Clifford,J., and G.Marcus
1986   *Writing culture*. Berkeley: University of California Press.

de Sardan,O.
1982   *Concepts et conceptions songhay-zarma.*   Paris:
            Nubia.
1984   *Les societes songhay-zarma.* Paris: Karthala.

Evans-Pritchard,E.E.
1940   *The Nuer.* New York; Oxford: Oxford University Press.

Giddens,A.
1983   *Central problems in social theory.*   Berkeley:
            University of California Press.

Gough,K.
1971   Nuer kinship: A reexamination. In *The transition of
            culture: Essays to E. E. Evans-Pritchard,* edited by
            T.O.Beidelman. London: Tavistock Publications.

Kelly,R.C.
1985   *The Nuer conquest: The structure and development
            of an expansionist system.* Ann Arbor: University of
            Michigan Press.

Holt,R.
1986   Personal communication.

Horowitz,M.
1988   Anthropology and the new development agenda. *IDA
            Development anthropology network.* Binghamton
            (Spring).

Howell,P.
1954   *Equatorial Nile project and its effects in the
            Anglo-Egyptian Sudan, being the report of the
            jonglei investigation team,* vol. 2. The Equatorial Nile
            project, its effects and remedies. For the Government of
            Sudan. London: Waterlow and Sons.

Hymes,D.
1972   *Reinventing anthropology.* New York: Pantheon

Lienhardt,G.
1958   The western Dinka. In *Tribes without rulers: Studies
            in African segmentary systems,* edited by J.Middleton
            and D.Tait. London: Routledge Kegan & Paul.

398

1961   *Divinity and experience: The religion of the Dinka.*
            Oxford: Oxford University Press.

Lewis,I.
1961   *A pastoral democracy: A study of pastoralism and
            politics among the northern Somali off the horn of
            Africa.* London: Oxford University Press.

Marcus,G., and M.Fischer, eds.
1986   *Anthropology   as   cultural   critique.*   Chicago:
            University of Chicago Press.

Newcomer,P.
1972   The Nuer are Dinka: An essay on origins and
            environmental determinism. *Man* 7:5-11.

Sahlins,M.
1960   The segmentary lineage: An organization of predatory
            expansion. *American anthropologist* 63:322-345.

Southall,A.W.
1970   Rank and stratification among the Alur and other
            people. In *Social stratification in Africa,* edited by
            A.Tuden and L.Plotnicov. New York: The Free Press.
1976   Nuer and Dinka are people: Ecology, ethnicity, and
            logical possibility. In *Man* 11:463-491.

Watson,M.
1979   Central rangelands development project (CDRP).
            Mogadishu.

Wilkes,K.
1983   Proven or unproven range management principles.
            Mimeo. Central Rangelands Development Project.
            Mogadishu.

Africa, Epistemology, and Praxis:
Aidan Southall's Unique Anthropology

Peter Rigby, Professor
Temple University
United States

The Alur have...shown their independent spirit and ability to fend for themselves in their reaction to the economic pressure to work for cash away from home... Often not a single Alur is recruited in the course of a year (Southall 1956).

Of course, it is not only Africa that is imperiled by the present inequality and injustice, it is ourselves. It is the same weaknesses in our own political economy, with its mad financial heart, its still insatiable military-industrial complex, its greedily excessive consumption and reckless debt, fanned by the modern magic of seductive, hegemonic media, which makes us incapable of dealing with acid rain, ozone depletion, massive waste, excessive wealth and grinding, hopeless poverty, unemployment, racism and the ghetto underclass--the same which in turn makes us incapable either of *allowing* or *enabling* Africa to develop a viable life of its own (Southall 1988c (emphasis added)).

Throughout a long, illustrious, and continuing involvement with Africa and anthropology, Aidan Southall has always been acutely aware of both the rich **content** of African societies and cultures, as well as the **context** of the practice of an anthropology that purports to describe and "analyze" them. In his work, anthropology inhabits a fragile, contingent historical space, in which power plays a major role.

In 1960, I was a political refugee, fleeing from both the wrath of the white racist apartheid regime in South Africa, as well as the more subtle but equally devastating oppression of Roy Wilensky's "Central African Federation," about which I am sure few people today remember very much. As a research fellow of the then Rhodes-Livingtone Institute (now the Zambia Institute for Social Research in Lusaka), I was persecuted by Wilensky's "government" and prevented from carrying out my research (I happened to be a member, first of Harry Nkumbula's African National Congress, then of Kenneth Kaunda's United National Independence Party). In desperation, I contacted Aidan at the then East African Institute of Social Research at Makerere, in Kampala, Uganda. He immediately offered me a temporary assistantship, which I gratefully (and gleefully) took up by driving the two thousand odd miles from Lusaka to Kampala. On the way, I passed through Ugogo in central Tanzania, and was captivated by the people and the cheerful manner in which they went about their lives in an incredibly harsh environment.

In Kampala, I worked for a couple of months on statistical data generated by Southall and Gutkind's studies of the city and its environs and, in the meantime, managed to secure a studentship at King's College at Cambridge University. Not only had Aidan saved my "political neck," he had also provided me with the respite that enabled me to pursue my doctoral studies. When I returned to work among the Wagogo people of central Tanzania in 1961, I was based at EAISR (now the Makerere Institute of Social Research), and once again, Aidan was an intellectual mentor. Thus was cemented a close relationship that (I trust I am accurate in saying) has lasted until the present.

This personal anecdote expresses Aidan's long-standing commitment to the political practice of anthropology as a constantly changing, potentially significant,and exciting practical activity. It is a true devotion to what Marx and Engels called the necessary dialectic between theory and practice, without which any epistemology becomes a sterile exercise in intellectual gymnastics. And herein lies the changing scope and significance of Aidan Southall's enormous contributions to both anthropology and Africa.

As a consequence, it is quite superficial merely to list the incredible diversity of Southall's scholarly work, both theoretically and "ethnographically." Although he may be known for his most extensive and seminal contributions to the "segmentary state" concept and what has rather quaintly come to be known as "Nilotic studies," he is a pioneer in African urban studies and has expanded our knowledge in the theories of language and linguistic change, the study of symbolic and kinship systems, ecology and ethnicity, anthropology and African philosophy, the theory of state formation and power and, now, Marxist anthropology. In this paper, I concentrate upon the latter two components of his work.

I use the word "ethnography" with trepidation, because Southall consistently draws our attention to the fragility and contingency of ethnographic categories in the study of African societies and cultures, beginning with his earliest work among Alur to the most recent essays and reviews (e.g., 1956, 1985, 1988a,b,c, 1989). Hence my earlier remark about his consciousness of the historicity of both "Africanist" anthropology and African cultures *in relation to each other*. The epigraphs to this paper illustrate his consistent awareness of this dialectic (a point to which I return). This dialectic can be the only basis for a truly subversive epistemological foundation and, therefore, for an "authentic" anthropology. But Southall carries out this subversion so politely that many anthropologists fail to notice what's going on; if they did, they might be considerably more disturbed, if not frightened and angered, by the work of this sensitive anthropological revolutionary.

But there is yet another aspect to the dialectic of Southall's anthropology. While constantly being prepared for change in both the theory and practice of his discipline, he has also developed certain themes over the entire period of his work, and he is still developing them. These relate primarily to the seminal notion of the segmentary state and the apprehension of the the ambivalence of power. These concerns have inevitably led him to a confrontation with Marxism and the theory of modes of production and their epistemological implications. I must therefore avoid the temptation to spread myself thinly over his enormous range, in order to concentrate and comment briefly upon the latter aspects of his work. This is a dangerous limitation necessarily enjoined by constraints of space since, as ever, all the threads are connected in his remarkable body of work.

The most economical manner in which I can carry out my limited task is to consider some of Southall's latest publications and their implications for the present and future of anthropology, with particular reference to Africa.

I begin with his review article on Amselle and M'Bokolo's *Au coeur de l'ethnie: Ethnies, tribalisme et Etat en Afrique*, published in *Cahiers d'Etudes africaines* (Southall 1985). While the volume in question is a collection of essays by various authors, the common theme is to demonstrate how the epithets "tribe," "tribalism," and "ethnicity" have been historically constructed (and "de-constructed"), often in the very recent past. This resonates strongly with one of the major subversions of anthropological categories prosecuted by Southall and other (particularly African) scholars (Southall 1970; Mafeje 1971, 1976; and so forth). Southall emphasizes, as do some of the authors in *Au coeurs de l'ethnie*, the political consequences of such constructions, which were based upon their application by colonial administrations and which often resulted in tragedy in postcolonial African states, such as Ruanda and Uganda. These categories allow outsiders to subsume the contemporary politics of class conflict and underdevelopment under the guise of "primal" tribal identities, when the latter are in fact the direct result of the colonial policies and anthropological concepts which created them. (In reporting on the current conflict between competing African political factions in South Africa on 15 August 1990, Tom Brokaw of the National Broadcasting Company actually described the fighting between Buthelezi's government-supported Congress as "tribal warfare"!)

Southall demonstrates clearly through his sympathetic review of Amselle and M'Bokolo's book that anthropologists have political responsibilities, since the categories they helped create in the past can result in death and destruction in the present. Without taking these factors into consideration, any construction of a uniquely anthropological epistemology must be a hollow sham. These epistemological implications are worked out in brilliant detail and at another level in his article "Power, Sanctity, and Symbolism in the Political Ecoonomy of the Nilotes" (1989). This penetrating article demonstrates Southall's propensity for integrating a wealth of detailed historical and ethnographic information within a coherent theoretical framework, dealing with such issues as to why anthropologists begin from a particular "personal" position in their comparisons (1989, 185), why anthropology's "object" must be questioned (1989, 185-186), the fabrication of "tribal" identities by the colonial powers (1989, 186 ff.), and the consequences of these for the theories of rank, class, and state formations.

These are combined with an analysis of the role played by ecology "in the sense of man's place in, reaction with, and appropriation of nature, [as] a major influence in the formation, elaboration, and transformation of these identities, activated by the movement of innumerable groups in the kaleidoscopic fissions, fusions, and recombinations, across the physical landscape in the course of their search for subsistence production and reproduction" (1989, 190). This is a superb historical materialist analysis, without any reduction to ecological determinism. It culminates in a reflection upon the (universal?) ambivalence of political power (1989, 211 ff.) and "the unfolding dialectic of kingship and mode of production" in all precapitalist states (1989, 213). If I may be allowed to "blow my own trumpet" for a moment, I might point out that, although I have not explicitly addressed the idiocy of the term "tribal" as a serious category of analysis, in all my work, from my earliest studies among Wagogo, through work among urban diviners and healers in Kampala, to my Ilparakuyo Maasai studies in Tanzania and Kenya, I have never used the term "tribe." In fact, I have always emphasized that various African peoples' self-definitions usually involve "origins" from, or relations with, "others" (Rigby 1969a, 13, 187; 1985, 9-11, et passim).

I have only two minor quibbles with Southall's masterly presentation. First, Southall remains enmeshed in a conception of "culture" and "political economy" as two separate, interacting "entities" (1989, 201); and second, he adheres to the somewhat shaky "superstructural/infrastructural" model of modes of production in the historical materialist problematic (1989, 203, 214). It could be, and has been, convincingly argued that each of these dichotomies must be approached in a different manner. The notion of dialectic reappears here and demands that such concepts as "culture" and "political economy" be deprived of any essentialist ontology, since they cannot be **defined** except as aspects of each other; but this is not the place to elaborate.

The final effect of the article is to make sense of comparisons of historical conjunctures as diverse as the dominance of kinship groups in Africa to the nature of medieval "feudal" states in Europe and elsewhere. These comparisons are integrated within a particular theoretical problematic dealing primarily with what the author calls "a gradient of state formation processes."

The other articles to which I address myself in order to consolidate the assertions I have made above about the remarkable achievement of Southall's anthropology deal squarely with issues raised in Marxist anthroplogy.

I strongly object to such epithets as "neo-Marxist" and "post-Marxist"; they imply that historical materialist theory is a "body of knowledge" occupying a static (and limited) historical and geographical space, a notion that makes nonsense of Marxian epistemology.

In the first of these (1988a), Southall confronts head-on some of the major contemporary issues in the theoretical construction of the mode of production concept in historical materialism, with particular reference to what he calls the "foraging" and "kinship" modes, and comments upon where such deliberations must lead.

In the second (1988b), he continues his subversive activities by expanding the debate on the segmentary state into direct juxtaposition with "Asiatic" societies, particularly in India, although he wisely avoids the contentious debate surrounding the Asiatic mode of production (Bailey and Llobera 1981). (Southall's discussion here would have been enhanced by some serious consideration of the work of Samir Amin.) Again, the intentions are at once comparative, theoretical, and political as inseparable components in any attempt to give anthropology a distinctive and valid epistemological basis.

In the first article, Southall marshals a formidable set of arguments derived from a critical reading of such diverse figures as Giddens, Althusser, E.P.Thompson, and Habermas. Such an initial procedure **demands** that multiple levels of theoretical and political discourse be conducted simultaneously. And yet all of them are shown to be relevant to, and illuminating for, a wide range of ethnographic and historical information on contemporary gathering and hunting societies, the archaeology of prehistoric foraging social formations, and the global importance of agricultural (and pastoral) societies that fall within the category of the "kinship" or "domestic" mode of production.

Along the way, he deals critically (but sympathetically) with the seminal work of Fried in political anthropology, demolishes Giddens and Service, and uses Habermas selectively and familiarly as an old acquaintance. Most important, this major article establishes the importance of distinguishing between the foraging from the kinship mode of production (*pace* Wolf, Sahlins, etc.), vindicates Marx's reconstruction of "the primal human society" (1988a, 171), and confirms the latter's assumption that the fundamental transition to humanity is based upon **cooperation** and not **aggression**.

Southall confirms that a "reconstructed model of production theory [as] the core of [a] historical materialist approach to long-term change in human society" is indispensable to anthropology (168). But such a reconstruction **cannot** be based solely upon the revisionisms of such western theorists as Giddens, Althusser, Thompson, or Habermas; it must arise from the juxtaposition of these theories with the theory and practice of the societies which are the subjects of anthropological discourse.

In his paper on "The Segmentary State in Asia and Africa," Southall again conducts a multilevel argument. He develops the groundwork established in the previous paper to confront theoretically the segmentary state concept in the context of the understanding of complex Asiatic states. The accompanying political problematic concerns, on the one hand, the demolishing of such anthropological shibboleths as the idea of "chiefdoms" and "tribes," and on the other, to challenge the haughty exclusivity of "Indianists" as students of "great civilizations," which also relegates Africa to the domain of the "primitive" and "tribal."

In achieving the first, he illuminates both the African and Indian materials with new insights. In pursuing the second, he brings anthropology directly into line with the often disregarded, if not denounced, work of such scholars as Cheikh Anta Diop (1974, 1978), W.E.B.Du Bois (1981 et passim), John Hope Franklin (1947) and, more recently, Martin Bernal (1987). As Southall himself concludes (1988b, 82), such comparisons of Africa and Asia:

> break down...the false conceptual barriers dividing regions and cultures studied by separate groups of scholars. It is especially salutary to overcome the intellectual; and analytical isolation of African phenomena and to transcend the arrogance of regarding Indian cultures as *sui generis*.

It is only through the juxtaposition of Marxist theory and anthropological materials in the real conditions of production and reproduction faced by most of the contemporary world, made up largely of impoverished peasantries, that an ongoing dialectic of theory and practice, a reconstructed model of production, can be found. This **enjoins** the marriage of historical materialism and anthropology to create a new epistemological foundation.

In his presidential address to the African Studies Association, from which one of my epigraphs is taken (Southall 1988c), Southall appeals, perhaps a little too tentatively, for a painstaking pragmatism (perhaps a "radical empiricism" is a better term here, as developed in the remarkable work of Michael Jackson (1989 et passim)) and refers appreciatively to a passage from Mao Tse-tung. The citation comes from Mao's brilliant 1937 piece, "On Practice," and bears fuller quotation than that given it by Southall (Mao Tse-tung 1975, 308):

> Discover truth through practice, and again through practice verify and develop the truth. Start from perceptual knowledge and actively develop it into rational knowledge; then start from rational knowledge and actively guide revolutionary practice to change both the subjective and objective world. Practice, knowledge, again practice and again knowledge. This form repeats itself in endless cycles, and with each cycle the content of practice and knowledge rises to a higher level. Such is the dialectical materialist theory of knowledge, and such is the dialectical theory of the unity of knowing and being.

It was inevitable from Southall's earliest work among Alur, to which he brought a penetrating and critical mind, always suspicious of accepted anthropological categories, that he would eventually confront the larger issues of the political economy of the transformations of societies. What was not so obvious was that he would develop a critical political economy of the theory and practice of anthropology itself. In doing this, Aidan Southall has not only been true to the anthropological tradition of meticulous fieldwork and attention to ethnographic detail, he has also raised the discipline of anthropology to a position in contemporary global and "polycentric" discourse (Amin 1989) that it might eventually deserve.

References

Amin,S.
1989   *Eurocentrism*. New York: Monthly review press.

Amselle,J.-L., and E.M'Bokolo, eds.
1985   *Au coeur de l'ethnie: Ethnies, tribalisme et etat en Afrique*.   Paris: Editions La Decouverte.

Bailey,A.M., and J.P.Llobera, eds.
1981   *The Asiatic mode of production: Science and politics*. London: Routledge and Kegan Paul.

Bernal,M.
1987   *Black Athena: The Afroasiatic roots of classical civilization*, vol.I: *The fabrication of ancient Greece*. New Brunswick, N.J: Rutgers University Press.

Diop,C.A.
1974[1955] *The African origin of civilization: Myth or reality.*, Westport, Conn: Lawrence Hill.
1978[1959] *The cultural unity of black Africa*. Chicago: Third World Press.

Du Bois,W.E.B.
1981[1946] *The world and Africa: An inquiry into the part which Africa has played in world history.* New York: International Publishers.

Franklin,J.H.
1947   *From slavery to freedom: A history of American Negroes*. New York: Knopf.

Jackson,M.
1989   *Paths toward a clearing: Radical empiricism and ethnographic inquiry.* Bloomington: University of Indiana Press.

Mafeje,A.
1971Th   The ideology of "tribalism." *Journal of modern African societies* 9:307-333.
1976   The problem of anthropology in historical perspective: An inquiry into the growth of the social sciences," *Canadian journal of African studies* 10:307-333.

410

Mao,T-t.
1975   *Selected works of Mao Tse-tung.* vol. 1, Peking: Foreign Languages Press.

Rigby,P.
1969a   *Cattle and kinship among the Gogo: A semi-pastoral society of central Tanzania.* Ithaca, N.Y: Cornell University Press.
1969b   Pastoralism and prejudice: Ideology and rural development in East Africa. In *Society and social change in eastern Africa*, edited by R.J.Apthorpe and P.Rigby. Nkanga Editions No.4. Kampala: Makerere Institute for Social Research.
1985   *Persistent pastoralists: Nomadic societies in transition.* London: Zed Books.

Southall,A.W.
1956   *Alur society: A study in processes and types of domination.* Cambridge: W.Heffer and Sons for East African Institute of Social Research.
1970   The illusion of tribe. *Journal of Asian and African studies* 5:28-50.
1985   The ethnic heart of anthropology. *Cahiers d'etudes africaines* 100:367-372.
1988a   On mode of production theory: The foraging modes of production and the kinship mode of production. *Dialectical anthropology* 12:165-192.
1988b   The segmentary state in Africa and Asia. *Comparative studies in society and history* 30:52-82.
1988c   "The rain fell on its own": The Alur theory of development and its Western counterparts. *African studies review* 31:1-15.
1989   Power, sanctity, and symbolism in the political economy of the Nilotes. In *Creativity of power: Cosmology and action in African societies*, edited by W.Arens and Ivan Karp. Washington,D.C: Smithsonian Institution Press.

Aidan Southall's Submerged Offering

Onigu Otite, Professor
University of Ibadan, Nigeria

This chapter deals with one of the professional offerings to social anthropology by Aidan Southall, an intellectual giant and mentor, who graciously contributed a paper to my Symposium, A-286, on The Responsibility of the Anthropologist in Africa, at the Eleventh International Congress of Anthropological and Ethnological Sciences in Quebec in 1983. His short paper, titled "Moral Anthropology, Immoral Anthropologists," remains unpublished along with nine others that were prepared. The article is a call on social anthropologists not merely to rewrite their own works, or present critiques on them where necessary, as Gluckman (1961, 11) indicated regarding his Barotse judicial procedures and processes, but more important, to extricate themselves from the label of immorality and enhance moral anthropology. Living second generation anthropologists, that is, the immediate successors of Malinowski and Radcliffe-Brown, could still have some introspective moments to bequeath to their own successors their contributions to Southall's potentially catalytic offering on the immorality of anthropologists. Southall has beaten a new drum for moral anthropology in Africa. The need is obvious for cleansing researched insights, not confessions, into the contradictions and dialectics involving moral anthropology, immoral anthropologists, and the moral wealth of Africans.

Immoral anthropologists earned their tag from their institutionalized complicity in the colonial government exploitation of colonized peoples, and the diversionary management and mobilization of their cultural resources. The distortions and destructions of the social formations, moral values, and cultures of the dominated peoples constituted immoral parts of colonialism, assisted by data produced by immoral anthropologists. As Maquet (1964, 49) points out, the distance between acculturation studies and applied anthropology is quite short, and

> at the request of colonial governments and on their own initiative, anthropologists acted as advisers on proposed or implemented reforms [though urging that such] reforms be as acceptable to the people and as little disruptive of the social fabric as possible.

Although both the colonial government and their colonial anthropologists acknowledged that the indigenous cultures and social organizations were valuable, ostensibly because they constituted cheap instruments of colonial grass-roots government (Indirect Rule), those aspects of their practices and values that were considered repugnant to Western concepts of justice and morality were ruthlessly terminated by legal codes and by the use of force or the possibility of the use of brutal force. As Southall says, "Whose justice and whose morality we need not ask!". Colonized societies had been forced into a peripheral dependency status, degraded, and exploited, as part of the world capitalist system.

As Southall reminds us, "moral anthropology and immoral anthropologists is of special significance for anthropologists because of the prevalent commitment to cultural relativity, which involves an element of moral relativity." Social anthropologists studying **other** cultures have always assumed a high level of objectivity and even morality, seen from their own societal curved lens. It is immoral to help to destroy the moral code and the moral context for the various kinds and spheres of social relations in **other** societies. Equally immoral is what some anthropologists have done in the case of South

Africa, for example, by promoting "the use of scientific knowledge for antisocial ends" (Nadel 1953, 9).

The preoccupation of such anthropologists and other social scientists and historians in serving foreign governments and thereby exacerbating colonial exploitation and its dehumanizing materialism, as well as its distortion of customs and diversion of the precapitalist pattern of development, has also been noted by Morauta and various commentators (1979) in the case of Papua New Guinea.

As Hsu (1964) has noted, immoral colonial anthropologists regarded their cultures and societies as models and as points of reference for others who were referred to as amoral or as without acceptable morals. This position was often worsened when, on the basis of anthropological findings, the very foundation of economic life and societal survival, that is land, was alienated to colonizing Europeans, while the indigenous landowners were forced to settle on special, often infertile areas set apart for them by municipal and colonial authorities, as Southall (1961a, 9) found in the case of Kenya and other countries in central and southern Africa.

We wish Southall's "further guarantee of morality in classical anthropological assumptions [as being] that those we study will study us," were possible. This could have been one way of injecting another form of morality into the lives of dominating societies from which colonial anthropologists were recruited. However, this would still raise the old and plaguing question of ethics and objectivity in social anthropology and the other social sciences. This issue, to use Southall's welcome notion, "may be flogging a horse that never lived" (1965, 116), or a horse that may never be born in the foreseeable future. Nevertheless, this issue brings out Southall's necessity

> to see the immoralities of colonial anthropologists as a
> paradigm of the immorality of men and women in society

and the struggle to achieve a moral anthropology with moral anthropologists as part of the vital struggle to transform society and culture in such a way that global self-destruction can be avoided.

In this connection, we recognize Blyden's (1862) contribution when he pointed out in respect of one colonized region of the world that "Africa will furnish a development of civilization which the world has never yet witnessed. Its great peculiarity will be its moral element."

To change socially recognized relationships "directly by penalizing customary actions and imposing new obligations indirectly by offering new opportunities" (Mair 1961, 11) was morally reprehensible. This self-assumed mandate in anthropological thought, which fueled the equally self-imposed "civilizing mission of Europeans in the Tropics" (Mair 1961, 11), was equally deprecable. Indeed, as Southall has asserted, "once we recognize anthropology as a discipline with colonial and imperial origins, we are bound to see Third World countries as most sinned against." In this respect, and in addition to immoral, psychological, cultural, and inhuman raids by colonialists and their pseudo- and social anthropologists, the colonizing world got more material wealth, while the colonized peoples were left with more social and societal problems.

"Typology makers" or "butterfly collectors" (Southall 1965) in British and Commonwealth tradition in social anthropology, were essentially empiricists with little or no concern for the moral contexts for ongoing observable interactions. Moral codes are largely elusive to "mathematical patterns" and to typologists. The moral content that guides the classifiable actions and relationships of dominated colonized peoples has been forcibly bastardized by colonialism. Being placed under dependency conditions and tagged to capitalism, African societies, for instance, were quite vulnerable to many, but not all, aspects of perversion (Southall 1979, 2).

The essence of the life that has been lost in the process through colonialism with the assistance of immoral anthropologists, is its moral content. This morality has some symbolism around it, in that many kinds of actions or relationships are manifestations of this morality in the economic, political, and religious spheres of life. The moral order prescribes, prohibits, or mediates action, and its various manifestations are, like what Turner (1965, 81-91) has shown in a different context, ways of making visible and tangible beliefs, values, sentiments, and psychological dispositions, which are not otherwise perceivable.

In a similar way, African morality in Southall's anthropology is implicit in many of his works:

> The factor of mutual assistance and also of gratuitous help from older to newer residents was stressed.... The giving of food, or of initial accommodation, lending of money, giving of medicine or of treatment when sick, being in general a kind person especially to foreigners, help in getting a job, loaning a bicycle, and protecting property...

were all mentioned in Southall's (1961b, 218) sample of responses by household heads amongst Ganda, Luo, Nubi, and other ethnic groups. In addition to Southall's observation, there were also "religious representations of moral codes and ideals, for example, of peace and brotherhood, of social solidarity and ritual blessedness" (Turner 1965, 92). These and others, such as reciprocity and redistribution in the economic life of Africans, constitute a general feature of the altruism, and moral core-content of African life which Blyden (1908) described to assert that Africans are "co-operative, not egoistic or individualistic. We, and not I, is the law of African life." Immoral anthropologists were not apparently interested in this moral Africa. Instead, they explained these manifestations of morality away as a cluster of characteristics of uncivilized, undeveloped, backward peoples who were at a low stage in the evolutionary line of Western-type development.

Immoral applied anthropologists were, along with the colonial users of anthropological data, interested in the capitalist and individualistic action-based relationships, and, in the words of Lucy Mair (1961, 23-24), in "the supposed domination of the individual by the group to which he belongs" which is "inconsistent with what we call individualism" and therefore part of the limitations on the disposal of property.

Southall has also been concerned with the immorality of social scientists and political practitioners. In his words,

> Achievement of the goals of the North-South dialogue would relieve us of many embarrassments. It would make the choice of paths of development more genuinely that of the poor countries themselves, and it would save Western countries from the farce of professing the ideals of liberal democracy and political freedom while all the time bolstering the most undemocratic absolutist, corrupt, incompetent and brutally repressive regimes in the Third World as supposed bulwarks against Communism. Such bulwarks always prove to be made of broken reeds, even if resistance to Communism is accepted as a higher priority than world peace, and economic development and social justice... (Southall 1979, 17).

Apart from such questionable priorities, it is immoral to bolster undemocratic systems.

Colonial government regimes were themselves undemocratic, with self-elected, self-imposed mandate to rule. The provision of the supporting anthropological information to enhance the European "civilizing mission" in Africa was unpardonably immoral, despite the argument that anthropologists had no control over the use of their data. Autocratic and dictatorial colonial governments ruined the morality in the lives of the colonized peoples and disorganized the

African well-known form of democracy. Today, after political independence, the erstwhile foreign rulers have turned round without moral qualms to urge Africans to be democratic in politics, government, and development, following their model.

Before and after 1956 when he published his *Alur Society*, Southall overwhelmed the anthropological and social science literature with constructive and challenging insights. These have both enriched and stimulated his colleagues, students, and academic disciples without an indulgence in the glorification of the moral society that Africa has lost. His concern for "moral anthropology and immoral anthropologists" will help shape the present and future course of social anthropology.

Southall's (1979) more recent concerns for rural development, for the rural underprivileged and marginalized peoples, and for small urban centers in their development are, if unintended, means of diluting the immoral concentrates of social anthropologists. In particular, questions concerning the decisions, purposes, funding, and beneficiaries of anthropological research projects will continue to draw attention not only to "moral anthropology and immoral anthropologists" but also to the dangers of anthropological neocolonialism in Africa.

Southall's cordial concern for African societies and values has earned him some of the African "ritual blessedness" that Turner mentioned, for a life well lived, and his youthful retirement will most probably be further enriched as his junior colleagues, students, and successors continue to reflect on "moral anthropology" and "immoral anthropologists."

418

References

Blyden,E.W.
1862   *Liberia's offering*. New York: J.A.Gray.
1908   *African life and customs*. London: C.M.Phillips.

Gluckman,M.
1961   Ethnographic data in British social anthropology. *Sociological review* 9(1):5-17. New series.

Hsu,F.L.K.
1964   Rethinking the concept "primitive." *Current anthropology* 15:169-178.

Maquet,J.J.
1964   Objectivity in anthropology. *Current anthropology* 5(1) (February):47-55.

Mair,L.P.
1961   *Studies in applied anthropology*. London: University of London, The Athlone Press.

Morauta,L.
1979   Indigenous anthropology in Papua New Guinea. *Current anthropology* 20(3) (September):561-576.

Nadel,S.F.
1953   *Anthropology and modern life*, an inaugural lecture. (July 10). Canberra: Australia National University.

Southall,A.W.
1956   *Alur society*. Cambridge: W.Heffer and Sons.
1961a   *Social change in modern Africa*, edited by A.W.Southall. London: Oxford University Press.
1961b   Kinship, friendship, and the net-work of relations in Kisenyi, Kampala. In *Social change in modern Africa*, edited by A.W.Southall, 217-229. London: Oxford University Press.
1965   A critique of the typology of states and political systems. In *Political systems and the distribution of power*, edited by M.Banton. London: Tavistock Publications.
1979   Small urban centers in rural development in Africa. African Studies Program, University of Wisconsin-Madison.

1983   Moral anthropology, immoral anthropologists. Paper
              prepared for Symposium A 286: The Responsibility of
              the Anthropologist in Africa, at the 11th International
              Congress of the Anthropological and Ethnological
              Sciences, in Quebec, Canada.

Turner,V.W.
1965   Ritual symbolism, morality, and social structure among
              the Ndembu. In *African systems of thought*. Preface
              by M.Fortes and G.Dieterlen. London; New York: for
              the International African Institute by the Oxford
              University Press.

Sociologism in Ethnology

George Park, Professor
Memorial University of Newfoundland
Newfoundland

What I have to offer Aidan is an informal essay, meant only to frame an argument not put it to proof, a quick-and-dirty history of our trade. The mix-and-match anthropology in the marketplace has been irking me. I would like to see something friendly done about it. I am not calling for a cull but would applaud a cure.

Forgetting the deathless contributions we all expect to make to the art of riding intellectual waves, what will live after us is our field reports. Those of us in Aidan's generation happen to have lived in a time when sophisticated observation could be done on a good range of human communities still living true to their past. Future generations will envy us that, even while they sit spinning out ingenious explanations of our failures. With such a window on human nature and the human past, how could we coolly leave so much undone? The answer is that nobody much is writing for future generations.

I propose no cure for the overall situation. The world's wisest have decreed that ethnology has little value. But for those of us off at the edge of the woods who do put value on this special kind of study, what is critical is that the work done should not be essentially warped by the presence in it of ourselves, the blindness of our times, and the mindlessness of our institutions. Mary Douglas (1986) does not show that our (academic) institutions do our thinking for us, but has shown that we are strongly inclined to do our thinking for them.

Aidan Southall had the inestimable advantage of spending a long early period of his career at Makerere when that university was basking in the sun of a youthful *kiangazi*. His students and colleagues were in and of the world his ethnology was meant to explore. If anthropologists can't be free of institutional structures, here was one we all could envy, even as in its floruit it stood on the brink of tragedy. If Southall has a tendency to bring the structures he studies to life, part of the reason may be that he was spared having to forge a career in High Academia, whether at Oxbridge or the Multiversity, while formulating his ideas.

To proceed, I shall have to set aside one or two articles of the common faith and professional wisdom of our trade. One is that anthropology forever renews itself, like physics or chemistry. Novel ideas in anthropology are like those in the humanities, which do not accumulate. They can add to our permanent inventory of understandings of the world but not to a coherent *discipline*. Lately, our little tribe has been preoccupied with reflexive understanding, and while this essay is of the times, it is meant to be critical of intellectual fashions that distract us from the main task of ethnology. One such is the essentially neo-Baconian idea that if we find ourselves perplexed the reason must be we have lost our "paradigm"--we ought to be out beating the bushes for another. From the standpoint of the sociology of knowledge, I find it more likely we have lost a sense of mission. Eventually, this should mean we shall be reestablishing the profession on sounder, secular ground. Meanwhile we have entered a period of relatively unstructured (aimless) palaver. If it were just that we had broken down into a series of well-defined "schools" that had stopped talking to each other, it would be cause enough for concern. But is it quite certain we have not broken down into worlds of egocentric play?

My contribution to the palaver will be wondering aloud if we may still get some useful ethnology done. If you grant that the proper audience is yet unborn, you will see you could not possibly write good (yet unborn) science for that crowd today. So reset your priorities to match more nearly the standards of history. I do not argue that ethnology *is* history, as it seems to me that ethnology is essentially comparative where history loves narrative. For ethnology, the nature of human society in general is always at stake but never the issue. General ideas, which must guide the perception of any particular case, are always in a turbulent state. It is this that sets us apart from historians on the one hand and paradigmatic scientists on the other. Turbulence--uncertainty about basics--is normal and normative for us. We do not need to reduce it but to squeeze it for the diversity of perspectives it can suggest on the bits of reality we try to comprehend. But to benefit from this we have to set aims which set limits within which our theoretical minds should be free to roam. In this essay I use some of Aidan Southall's work as a touchstone, asking where the center of our theoretical range ought to be, and where the boundaries.

Intentional institutions

Aidan Southall is one anthropologist who persistently gets at the action without freezing the structure. A shortcoming of the *idea ethnography* now in vogue is that humdrum institutions remain in backdrop and cannot be examined as living features of a community's life. In effect, the anthropologist supplies a script and a troup of actors to interpret it--and we are asked to learn about English kingship from *Lead*. Is there no more direct way to show off a human institution? What we seem to need is a lesson from more recent theater.

I have in mind what is called *collective drama*. Troupes in places as diverse as Norway, Nicaragua, and Newfoundland have restricted themselves to collectives, a quick-frozen version of spontaneous theater. Actors are the playwrights, working up a script interactively on the rehearsal stage. Pen and paper are hardly needed. The accent tends to be neither on plot nor character but milieu. We may suppose the original mystery plays of medieval Europe were got up in about the same fashion. The collective is to *Lear* what Sumner's (1907) "crescive" is to his "enacted" institution. Anthropologists are familiar with crescive institutions but have tended to treat them as Sumner did, as if ossified. They can be treated as intentional. Here is Southall writing on the Mambisa:

> The most remarkable quality of the Mambisa was their success, with their small numbers and loose organization, in establishing and maintaining themselves in the midst of wholly alien populations which had good reasons for hostility towards them. This could hardly have been done except as an expression of the extreme individual self-confidence in the face of cosmic and social forces alike, which was the characteristic basis of Alur supremacy everywhere. This quality was essential to the effectiveness of institutional features such as rainmaking and chiefship. The Mambisa held, as all Alur chiefly groups held, that the innate superiority of themselves as human beings, and of their social arrangements, entitled them to demand certain services of others, or even to exact benefits arbitrarily... In return they offered collective feasting, protection and increasing participation in their society (1954, 226).

In a passage like this we see institutions as the collective product of the actors who take their roles. The book is about one "society," the Alur. The subtitle tells us it is *a study of processes and types of domination*. The chapter cited is called "The Process of Domination" and deals in crushing detail with political traditions and styles of thirty-odd sovereign Alur groups. The region Southall had to deal with was ethnically and linguistically as varied as the region so much more familiar to us from Leach's contemporary *Highland Burma* (1954). But where Leach insisted on the fundamental integrity of Kachin institutions, even inventing a monstrous "oscillating equilibrium" to save this integrity in face of all evidence for cultural pluralism, Southall sees and deals directly with just such pluralism. We cannot doubt local languages permitted him to describe the Alur as a sort of *gumsa* to the non-Alur *gumlao*; Alur marital chauvinism was clearly a match for the mayu-dama doctrine of Kachin; and the expression of structure in ritual was pervasive and quite as unmistakable as in highland Burma. The decisive difference seems to be in the observers and the extent of their commitment to realism. (Yes, when it came to readership within the profession the "idea ethnography" won hands down.)

It should not surprise us that Southall (1976, 1986) was drawn into the extended discussion of Nuer (Nath) ethnology that marked the passing of Evans-Pritchard and Oxonian "British social anthropology" into history. In a recent comment on the "illusion of Nath agnation" given us in *The Nuer*, Southall writes:

> It seems that analyzing Nath society as composed of local cognatic lineage segments might have been much closer to the Naths' own emic model of their society and would have made for a much simpler and far more easily intelligible exegesis. But it would have destroyed the stimulating paradoxical complexity of Evans-Pritchard's account, thereby rendering much subsequent debate redundant. Despite the strongly empirical emphasis of fieldwork in anthropology, the generation of stimulating models attracts more interest than the correct interpretation of empirical data (1986, 2).

And what is the correct procedure for arriving at a correct interpretation? Evidently, it is not the sacrifice of realism in the interest of the model. Models are crucial in comparative work-- Southall's "segmentary state" was much worked over (1954, 1965,

1988)--and perhaps they are always somehow what Leach would have had them, the "organizational ideas" of a society construed in mathematical terms. In an early draft of the 1965 article (which my prying eyes were allowed to see), Southall proposed an elegant feedback model of political change. It was supplanted by the less elegant but better grounded suggestion that system closure (and elegance) is more likely to result from wishful thinking than hard study. "Organizational ideas are only a shorthand for the most significant patterns of social action" that constitute a society, and the link between "organizational ideas and action is indirect and complex" (1965, 114-115). In short, one accepts the rule that the ultimate object of study is not the community's ideas (which always seem to allow some kind of "mathematical" construction yet never can be shown not to overflow it) but action (which always overflows the norms we can infer from it). The real mischief in structuralism derives from the plan of action, which is laid out in *The Savage Mind* (Lévi-Strauss 1966) and which entails "an extreme commitment to the homeostatic model of society, rejected by most people along with the excesses of functionalism" (Southall 1972, 107). By trivializing structure, transactional analysis does escape sociologism. Can you do the same by stuffing your organic model in the attic?

Disciplines and concerns

Generally in ethnological studies the social psychology of the individual hardly surfaces, being submerged partly by time itself, which spirits away evidence, and partly by the observer's focus on structure. Action comes in by way of illustration not the main text. Anthropologists have found remedies, but the problem remains. You can soften structure by reconceptualizing an institution as setting for situated action (social organization) or by denying the importance of institutions and finding the source of order in social categories as such (structuralism). If the one solution is recognizable as a British and the other as a French way of dealing with their common theoretical heritage, Leach was a notable boundary man. In *Highland Burma* he constructed from selected Kachin categories a world whose institutions could be inflated or collapsed by the categorically situated actions of their constituents. These mixed remedies have succeeded in putting the problem of structure on hold. Is there some point in trying to get it back on line?

I am not for giving up the study of institutions. I have elsewhere argued (Park 1972, 1974) that you do not understand them if you do not recognize that the most characteristic and readable human motivation lodges in the roles we play, not in the psyches nature and nurture have given us. But including role motives only complicates, it does not eliminate the problem of reconciling individual freedom with cultural predictability. Suppose Joseph has killed Mary, his estranged wife. Interviewer finds it would not have happened if Joseph had not been psyched up to an act of "manly violence" by friends. The question then becomes why Joseph's action came to be situated in his "one of the boys" role, not that of father, brother, son, church member, good credit-risk, or polite clerk. This calls for a culture-sensitive social psychology. The reigning research strategy at (late) midcentury focused on the institution as an articulation of roles. Motivation could be dealt with by implication ["Little boys soon learn they are privileged over their sisters"] and need not be an explicit concern. So it was *as if* one could do without psychology. Our one preeminent Guru (Radcliffe-Brown) had even gone so far as tacitly to renounce his own major opus (*The Andaman Islanders*) as tainted by psychological thought.

Durkheimian sociologism dates from a publication of 1895. One would have thought the same author's more mature work on "the rise of the religious sentiment in humanity" (1915) would have put the lie to his earlier boast that sociology could be content with "social facts," as though the social world were constituted by the interaction of so many black boxes whose insides we need not speculate about. Open *The Elementary Forms of the Religious Life* almost anywhere and you will find yourself looking at insides:

> If the intermittent failures of the Intichiuma do not shake the confidence of the Australian in his rite, it is because he holds with all the strength of his soul to these practices in which he periodically recreates himself; he could not deny their principle without causing an upheaval of his own being, which resists (1915, 360-361).

But Radcliffe-Brown brought a disguised Durkheimian sociologism back; and it behaved for a time, especially in the 1960s under the general title of "the British school," like the very "paradigm" ethnologists might have been looking for. The finest example of his art is the general essay on African kinship (1950). His scheme worked because it was selectively focused very close to the proper center of concern for ethnology, it relied on observing rather than probing, and it was sociologistic only in a superficial sense. The concern with motivation could remain largely implicit. The concern with *culture* could be transferred from the analytic to the descriptive or even anecdotal mode. It simplified your task in the field, and kept you pointed at the situated actions that are the substance of social structure wherever it is found. The trouble with this "structural-functional" model was its sociologistic mandate. It reduced action to behavior. The universal human motive was--what? Conformity to role prescriptions? Anticipation of diffuse social sanctions? Maintaining boundaries? Social solidarity with an in-group? Life was programmed, ethnologists were sent to the field to reconstruct the programs. In computer jargon this is reverse engineering. The "paradigm" was not one to satisfy the profession for more than a brief generation but was hard to let go because within its limits it worked so well.

The best writers managed to include a rich descriptive text, eye-witness commentary running parallel to the analytical text, the program. Most of us will think first of Raymond Firth and the Tikopia monographs. The blend in his work of description and analysis is unique for the British school, reflecting the looser grip of sociologism on its earlier students--more Malinowski, less Guru. The new fashion did not displace psychology altogether, but tended to push it out of ethnology. Students of older, unregenerate "culture & personality" anthropologists became instead "cross-cultural psychologists" to emulate the greater show of science and system in the British school. Where psychology serves the ends of ethnology, sociologism is in abeyance; the safeguard is gone when ethnology becomes the tool of psychology. Meanwhile the very sterility of "structural-functional analysis" when coupled with the rich experience of extended fieldwork could only generate a need for humanistic strategies. Students of the Guru turned to extended case studies, eye-witness accounts of trouble cases, to bring the barren frame of "social structure" to life. Some of the best ethnology was done this way. A student who fails to read *Schism & Continuity* before taking up *The Forest of Symbols* (Turner 1957, 1967) is doing the equivalent in Ndembu ethnology of learning the calculus before turning to arithmetic.

Scenaristic anthropology is a child of the extended case method, sired by a cameraman. The actual shooting may be done through a glass lens or a pair of organic ones, for an anthropologist converted to his trade by Yanomamö films will see scenarios in the field and write them up as he saw them. Where social structure was pushed out to form a frame (albeit a solid one) for the adventures of Sandombu in Ndembuland (Turner 1957), Yanomamö adventures are framed by a theater in the round. Apart from the possessiveness of men toward their women and children, the open circle of fence, roofposts, and hammocks you would see when the village was empty is the only "structure" you would likely see when it was full. I have no idea what Meyer Fortes would have done in Chagnon's place, but it is intriguing to speculate. What is fairly certain is that a generation come up since *The Fierce People* (Chagnon 1968) has little time for telling Tall Tales.

A lot of this humanistic stuff has been seminal. I for one have been nourished better by Schieffelin's *Sorrow & Burning* (1976) than by the latest paradigmatic (neo-Marxist) anthropology, though individuals working within that frame of theory have realized some wondrous strikes in the least-expected places (I think especially of Sider's Newfoundland (1986)). The trouble I have with an infinite expansion of humanistic styles in anthropology is that ethnology still depends on doing the arithmetic first. In the best work, some of it seeps in; I might cite Read's *High Valley* (1965) or Thomas's *Warrior Herdsmen* (1965). All of us want anthropology to include more than ethnology, but as things are going now I fear the center cannot hold. If all I might ever know about the Kalulu or Gahuku or Dodoth were contained in the three books mentioned, and if what I wanted from them was the kind of basic information that would allow me to compare them in a detailed way with their neighbors, I could hardly rate the sources highly. They contain a kind of anthropology that is great in its way but is not ethnology.

I propose that ethnology centers on institutions and completes its purpose by doing the round of institutions in each culture under study. From a center in social structure, an ethnologist's plan of work fans out in a number of directions, always to some limit which represents the extent of a social scientist's responsibility to the people observed. I close with this rough schema:

Toward psychology. Ethnology wants to understand situated action within the institutional frames that characterize the community. It is no responsibility of the ethnologist to explore implications of any set of field data for a theory of human nature--if you want to do that, put on another anthropological hat. Malinowski's (1927) or Spiro's (1982) comments on the Oedipus complex may or may not survive our time, but the issue will not affect the way we should read their ethnology--and the Trobrianders do not have to care either. There is a social psychology (mainly produced by and taught in sociology departments) not meant to predict behavior but illuminate social interaction, and that is what ethnologists need in their kitbags.

Toward history. Ethnology seeks the meaning of an institution by asking how it came to be what it is, where it is. The main thing to know about context is the other institutions making up the social system. The usual expectation in a traditional society is jigsaw-style "goodness of fit" among its institutions, and often this is seen to be so. Where some history is available, you can see how much movement was needed in Institution A to accommodate changes in Institution B. But the best way to get a sense for the kind of modulations possible with a given set of institutions is to explore the whole set of societies that has a close historical relationship with your target society. Usually this means doing or reading the ethnology of a region, because usually this puts you onto the sets of institutions most similar to your target set. *Alur Society* is such a study. I have found that the political constitutions of southwestern Tanzania are best seen as transforms of each other, and each can be understood better separately than as one in a range. I have also found that when you ask how this could have evolved into that, or that devolved into this, you are not wasting your time. You learn a good deal about what, in principle, "must have happened" (Park 1988) and, especially, why. Ethnologists should not have to do the archaeology of the region, and would usually prefer that trained ethnohistorians did the oral history, but ethnology's responsibility does extend to exploring the range of possible histories and assessing the curve of probabilities within that range, based on the way social institutions work. How likely is it that the Baganda were egalitarians in Msemi's grandfather's day? Egalitarian in what sense? The question will not bear a simple answer. Reading the ethnology affords you a basis of judgment independent of direct informant testimony, putting you in position to read the pertinent oral history critically.

Toward philosophy. Ethnology cannot be content with etic analysis of a culture though it must begin there. A fieldworker has to develop the far more sophisticated techniques of observation required to give an emic account and ultimately square it with the etic. Shall we call the Hehe of Tanzania polygynous? Polygyny got a great boost in the nineteenth century from the numbers of women captured in war. But statistics show a rapid decline, even correcting for Christian converts. Are the main masculine role-models polygynous? How do male and female attitudes compare, and where do they meet? Is there a Hehe culture or must we speak of Hehe *cultures*? Is there still a Hehe culture which reflects what was *before* the wars began? It takes a sophisticated reading of testament, ritual, and manner codes to turn an etic census of plural marriages into a firm ethnological record. But it is no part of the fieldworker's mandate to be pursuing universal truths, and the notion that every new monograph ought to be a contribution to theory bears the implication that ethnology itself (and the future generations who will need it) cannot be important.

References

Chagnon,N.A.
1968   *Yanomamö: the fierce people.* New York: Holt, Rinehart and Winston.

Douglas,M.
1986   *How institutions think.* Syracuse University Press.

Durkheim,É.
1915   *The elementary forms of the religious life,* translated by J.W.Swain. London: George Allen & Unwin.

Leach,E.R.
1954   *Political systems of Highland Burma.* Boston: Beacon Press.

Levi-Strauss,C.
1966   *The savage mind.* Chicago: University of Chicago Press.

Malinowski,B.
1927   *Sex and repression in savage society.* New York: Humanities Press.

Park,G.
1972   The motivational interpretation of institutions. *Canadian review of sociology and anthropology* 9(2):134-149.
1974   *The idea of social structure.* Garden City, New York: Doubleday.
1988   Evolution of a regional culture in East Africa," *Sprache und Geschichte in Afrika* 9:117-204.

Radcliffe-Brown,A.R.
1933   *The Andaman islanders.* Cambridge: Cambridge University Press.
1950   Introduction. In *African systems of kinship and marriage,* edited by A.R.Radcliffe-Brown and D.Forde, 1-85. London: Oxford University Press.

Read,K.E.
1965   *The high valley.* New York: Charles Scribner's Sons.

434

Schieffelin,E.L.
1976 *The sorrow of the lonely and the burning of the dancers.* New York: St. Martin's Press.

Sider,G.M.
1986 *Culture and class in anthropology and history.* Cambridge: Cambridge University Press.

Spiro,M.E.
1982 *Oedipus in the Trobriands.* Chicago: University of Chicago Press.

Southall,A.W.
1954 *Alur society.* Cambridge: W. Heffer & Sons.
1965 A critique of the typology of states & political systems. In *Political systems and the distribution of power,* edited by M.Banton, 113-140. New York: Praeger.
1972 Twinship and symbolic structure. In *The interpretation of ritual,* edited by J.S.LaFontaine, 73-114. London: Tavistock.
1976 Nuer and Dinka are people: Ecology, ethnicity and logical possibility," *Man* 11(4):463-491.
1986 The illusion of Nath agnation. *Ethnology* 25(1):1-20.
1988 The segmentary state in Africa and Asia. *Comparative studies in society and history* 30(1):52-82.

Sumner,W.G.
1907 *Folkways.* Boston: Ginn & Co.

Thomas,E.M.
1965 *Warrior herdsmen.* New York: Random House.

Turner,V.W.
1957 *Schism and continuity in an African society.* Manchester: Manchester University Press.
1967 *The forest of symbols.* Ithaca: Cornell University Press.

On Culture's Direct and Indirect Part in Politics:
Similarities in the Effects of Lecture
Halls and Social Structures

Marc T. Swartz, Professor
University of California-San Diego
United States

In an important recent paper, Southall examines the consequences of "[t]he change of emphasis...from [the study of] power to symbolism and from politics to culture...." (1989, 2) resulting from the currently popular interpretive approach in anthropology. A central topic of his paper is the shift in the work of some anthropologists from an examination of "action" to a preoccupation with meaning and symbolism and a drift away from reports and analysis of empirically grounded, if far from perfect, fieldwork to "interpretation" whose focus in physical reality is not always clear (ibid., 2-6). The aim of this paper is to try to show that an emphasis on culture, far from taking attention away from the study of politics and power, offers weighty advantages for that study. The study of culture's part in politics and social life generally properly includes an examination of the vital influences that are based in culture, but are not themselves cultural. I will argue that the distribution of power can, in some instances at least, only be understood if attention is given to the products of culture and their effects as well as to the direct effects of culture itself.

This interest in culture is not to be taken as an endorsement of the focus on symbolism and hermeneutics that is currently so fashionable in anthropology. I share Southall's concern about a lessening of attention to the real events of political activity, and I agree that the realities of social life are sometimes ignored in favor of interpretive exercises whose significance and verity is sometimes difficult to assess (Southall 1989, 1-3).

The conception of culture I favor is designed to recognize culture as the essential foundation for all human life and to allow the forces involved in it to be examined in all their complexity and with full attention to their role in social life. The position I will adumbrate here holds that political activity, like all other forms of social activity, has its foundation in the culture shared among those involved in it. It is a central contention here that only through a full analysis of culturally based forces at work can political processes be understood. Further, I will argue that it is fruitful to view politics, in the broadest sense, as culture in action, so that in understanding political activity we gain the ability to understand culture's part in social life generally.

This is a development of a view that was first advanced in collaboration with Victor W. Turner (Swartz, Turner, and Tuden 1966) and that had been developing for some time in a series of papers, mainly analyzing data from the Bena of Tanzania, that appeared in the late 1960s and 1970s. More recent developments of this approach have been worked out on data from the Swahili of Mombasa (e.g., Swartz n.d., 1982b, 1983). Although Southall and I have differed in a number of respects (see Swartz 1970 for a discussion directly concerned with differences between our views as they were), my views and his have always agreed on the dynamic character of political and social life and on the importance of empirically grounded discussion. Although we still differ in some respects, the thrust of our interests has become even closer than it once was through developments in what we are both doing. My long-standing admiration of his work has remained and, if possible, has increased during the last decade or so.

A main difference between us is the explicit position accorded the culture concept, and it is well to begin with an examination of that concept. Indisputably, anything can be defined as a user wishes and since Aristotle's "real definitions" were finally set aside, most scholars would, I think, agree that definitions are neither true nor false. Their only measure is that of usefulness. Having said that, we can turn to the part played by what I call "culture" in human affairs as a first step in examining the relationship between culture and politics.

The culture concept

The evolution that produced modern humans results from an interaction between the physical transformations in an erect primate that appeared some millions of years ago and its development of understandings concerning how to deal with its physical and social environment. Although it is likely this interaction began long before then, there is evidence, in the tools our early forebears made and used more than a million years ago, that shows that vital understandings about at least some aspects of the world and how to deal with them were shared among group members. These were transmitted by learning across generations rather than their either being devised anew by individuals each time they were used or by being directly rooted in *Homo sapiens* biologically. These ancient understandings, shared, learned, and socially transmitted, are not significantly different in their general character or social significance from those that serve contemporary humanity as the primary basis for all social activity including political activity.

There is no necessity that these shared, socially transmitted understandings be called "culture." That term could be reserved for contexts, communications channels, webs of meaning, or the material products of social activity. But surely shared understandings themselves, of which most of the things just mentioned are either a subset or a product, should be examined and the processes whereby they operate studied, as they cannot be studied if they are not identified as objects of study. It is, after all, the understandings we share with our fellow group members that, more than anything else, make us what we are. It is quite likely that subsets of these understandings have their own peculiar effects and properties, but we can hardly hope to understand this until we have studied the whole to determine how parts can be separated for investigation. Those understandings shared by two or more members of a social group can be called by any name that is pleasing, but they must be called something and, despite the many different uses of the same word, I will call them "culture" in order to emphasize the fact of their fundamental importance both in the emergence of our species and in every human group.

Since the main component of culture as defined here, as well as in the work of others (e.g., D'Andrade (1987, 195); Goodenough (1971, 22); Keesing (1970, 440); and Spiro (1984, 323)) is "understandings" (i.e., cognitive processes that take place in people's minds), there is a danger that the "idealism" that rightly concerns a number of anthropologists of rather diverse views (e.g., Harris 1968) may distort study and analysis. In fact, although my approach does place a crucial part of culture in the mind, there need be no obscuring of the vital part played in social processes by forces whose origin and locus is not in any individual mind. Indeed, the approach I advocate seeks to make quite explicit just how extra-individual forces operate.

While culture is defined here as made up of understandings in people's minds, all understandings are not parts of culture; only those that are shared are parts of culture. This means that a social process, sharing, is a fundamental part of culture so that, important as cognitive processes are for it, culture is not taken as solely mental. As we will see in the example of "politics" to be considered, the fact that an understanding is shared among a number of people gives it an influence it could not have were it not shared. In the example, the power of Swahili wives will be seen as deriving from the sharing of understandings about men, not just from the understandings themselves. (A much fuller account of the relations between Mombasa Swahili spouses and the sources of wives' power is found in several other publications concerning this community (Swartz n.d., 1982b, 1983).

It should also be made clear that in political processes, as in all others, culture affects behavior both directly and indirectly. The direct effect is the familiar and obvious one whereby people are guided in what they do and believe and in how they make evaluations. The indirect effect is more complex and depends on the part played in social processes by the "products of culture," including but by no means limited to what is often confusingly and self-contradictorily called "material culture."

Cultural products: lecture halls and social relationships

The tools, dwellings, art works, meals, clothing, and such that are produced according to the understandings shared among group members unquestionably influence what people do, believe, and evaluate. This influence is based in the fact that the objects themselves can only be used, or even recognized, as the subjects of understandings concerned with such issues as what they are useful for, how they are employed, who can and cannot use them, what worth they have, and so on. This influence is indisputably a cultural one, but it is not, or need not be, based in the understandings that make the production of the object's possible being. Objects, in other words, produced according to shared understandings, are, and must be if they are to be used, the foci of understandings quite different from those that guided the production of the objects. Thus the shared understandings that produced the objects have the direct effect seen in the production and, also, the indirect effect derived from the objects produced and the understandings that focus on them.

It is quite obvious that these product-centered understandings can affect behavior generally and social processes specifically, quite as much as and sometimes more generally than the understandings directly concerned with how to make or do the things they concern. This effect can take place in exactly the same way understandings about anything else can through indicating the objects' value, use, limitations, dangers, and the proper personnel to be involved with them in various understood ways. This would be hardly worth mentioning were it not for the importance of the processes whereby cultural products affect those who share few, if any, of the understandings about how to make them, use them, or even that they exist. The fact that most of any culture's elements are shared by some members of a group rather than by all of them is broadly accepted among students of behavior. However, the processes whereby understandings affect those who do not share them are little studied and but poorly understood (Swartz 1982a).

These processes include those that stem from what might be called the material consequences of shared understandings. The planners, architects, and administrators who design and decide on the nature of the buildings on academic campuses make their decisions according to understandings they may not share with the students and teachers who use those buildings. Whether or not the designer's understandings that guided them in creating and erecting the buildings are shared by the users, the products of the designers' understandings profoundly affect the users. To take a simple example, the size of lecture rooms affects the style of teaching, the number of teachers, and the kinds of classroom experiences students have, and this is so regardless of the designers' understandings about what kind of buildings should be built and, even, their understandings about what is desirable or not in teaching.

The effects on teaching and learning spring from the deciders' and designers' understandings about such things as construction, land use, building costs, budgets, and student-teacher ratios. Regardless of whether students and instructors share those understandings or not, at least some of the consequences will be the same. It may be that an architect, a chancellor, or a building committee's members understand lectures attended by hundreds of students to be desirable and cost effective or undesirable but unavoidable. If the resulting buildings have many large rooms and few small ones, at least some of the effects on teachers and students will be much the same whether those who planned the building intended them or not and whether they approve of them or not. The buildings are not culture, but they are produced by behavior guided by culture and, in turn, affect behavior without those affected needing to share any of the first set of cultural elements that directed the erection of the buildings. What affects the users of the completed buildings are the understandings about those buildings as these guide behavior involving the buildings.

Cultural products that have effects behavior rooted in the products themselves are not limited to buildings, tools, works of art, and such. They include social relationships since these, too, result from understandings concerning what to do when, where, how, and in what circumstances. Buildings are as they are mainly because of the shared understandings of those involved in constructing them and social relationships are as they are because of the shared understandings guiding the interactions that constitute them. As just seen, the buildings have influences on behavior deriving from their existence and independent of the understandings that directed their construction. The same is true of social relationships.

The influence of social relationships independent of culture has long been studied as "social structure." What is worth pointing out, however, is that although social structure is an independent influence on behavior, it is itself produced by culture. Social relationships are guided by culture, what else could provide the guidance? But their effects are not confined to those of the culture that created them. Indeed, these cultural products have effects, as will appear in a moment, that are not cultural at all.

This is true in all of social life including "politics," whether that be taken broadly as referring to all goal-seeking behavior (Swartz 1968) or whether its reference be limited to the processes involving striving for those goals that are groupwide in their significance. For either usage, the understanding of political activity requires an examination of the culture of those involved in its processes and, of equal importance, an examination of the effect of cultural products, which effect may not itself be cultural.

The case: how the dominated dominate
Or power from social structure

In order to demonstrate the contention that social structural forces are based in culture but are not themselves cultural, I will describe an aspect of Mombasa Swahili society that I presented before

(Swartz 1982b, 1983) but in ways different from that of interest here.

This illustration concerns the relations between husbands and wives in Mombasa Swahili society and the basis for the undoubted fact that wives often get their husbands to buy expensive jewelry and to pay for costly rituals even though the husbands say they do not support these things and do not want to pay for them. What is of particular interest as concerns the ability of cultural products to affect behavior independent of the culture that creates the products is the fact that many Swahili wives have great power in their relations with their husbands despite the fact that Swahili culture is quite unambiguous about their not having such power.

That is, the Mombasa Swahili, as pious Sunni Muslims, believe that God created men to care for and control women. Women are understood to be quite as intelligent as men, but more emotional and less able to plan rationally so that men are better able to allocate resources. These understandings are widely shared by both men and women and, although many men and women agree that wives do, in fact, have the ability to get their husbands to give them what they want, they are uniformly unwilling to agree that wives have power in their dealing with their husbands. There can be little doubt that the understanding about the differences between the sexes in rationality, emotionality, and planning is a substantial resource for men. However, the point is that this cultural element is only one of the resources in the relations between men and women, especially between husbands and wives, and that to stop the analysis of culture's role in male-female relations with the understandings about the power of men and the importance of women not having power in their relations with their husbands would be to truncate analysis. Indeed, on these cultural grounds alone, it is more than difficult to explain the undoubted ability of the majority of wives to get their husbands to spend money as they seem not to wish to spend it.

Still, it is essential for our political analysis to examine a number of dimensions of the culture of the spouse relationship. One of these dimensions is the set of understandings concerning what each spouse wants from the other. These goals are, by definition, central to the politics of the spouse relationship. In regard to these goals, it is important to note that the Swahili, as pious Muslims, share understandings that are reflected in a broad and general separation of the sexes. Men and women who are not married or closely related are not to see or associate with one another and almost never do so. Men spend their days out of their houses save at mealtimes because, in part at least, their presence is understood to make it impossible for other women to visit their wives. Women rarely go beyond their own, their neighbors, and their relatives' houses because it is understood that to do so might bring them into contact with unrelated men. For both men and women, such understandings as those just mentioned, lead to the greater part of each day being spent in the company of others of their own sex and of having a social life outside the immediate family that is entirely limited to members of their sex.

One of the features of women's social lives is that prestige depends on evidence that a woman is loved by her husband. A most serious insult for a woman is to be told by another that no man could love her and the relevant evidence of a husband's love is jewelry, a steady supply of new, high-quality clothing, and the staging of at least one expensive ceremony when a child marries or when a parent dies. In order to have these things, a woman needs money and, given the structure of the Swahili community and of the broader society in which it exists, most women can get money only from their husbands. It is because of this, of course, that having finery and giving ceremonies is taken as a measure of the woman being loved.

Women who have many new and desirable clothes are admired by their fellows, while those without such wardrobes are, women tell me, shamed. Everyone understands that women get their clothing with money controlled by their husbands, so that a woman with few and old dresses is understood to be unloved and, thus, unworthy of respect. The same is true of women with few of the costly twenty-two-carat gold bracelets Mombasa Swahili women wear and of those who have not staged at least one of the highly expensive weddings or funerals.

Husbands are free, all agree, to deny their wives the funds required for the finery and ritual. There are a few solvent men in the community who have denied their wives the substantial sums needed for these purposes, and I could find no evidence that these men suffered any diminution in community standing because of their unwillingness to provide these funds. Further, men derive no direct benefit from spending money on their wives. Unlike the situation, at least as described by Thorsten Veblen, men get little social benefit or prestige from their wives' expenditures. Men do not see one another's wives, and wives, both men and women tell me, do not usually discuss other women's jewelry, clothing, and ceremonies with their husbands. Thus, men cannot realistically hope to impress their male friends and kin by the money spent on their own wives. If men are to benefit from conspicuous consumption, it is through their own consumption. The cars, fine clothing, and prestigious houses that might benefit men are, however, made difficult to buy because the money that would pay for them has gone to the wife.

The conclusion that money spent on wives brings little direct reward is not an inference. A number of men are quite explicit about their belief that the money their wives spend on clothing and such is wasted. Many male informants told me that the greater prosperity of the Indians and Arabs, who live in the same part of Mombasa (Old Town) as the Swahili, is mainly due to the fact that, in these ethnic groups, the wives are not allowed to spend so much money on things of little economic value. "The Indians buy shops," one man told me, "while we buy bangles."

The women's wish to have finery is easy to understand: it brings them prestige with their peers. But why do the great majority of men spend substantial parts of their income on women's goals they do not share? If one asks the men this question, they say they do it because in important respects women react to disappointment in ways similar to those of children. Like children, they say, wives cannot understand that what they want is not practical so that, in the end, the men are faced with the alternative of granting the women their wishes or seeing them become what the men characterize as "unhappy." The understanding that women are more emotional and less rational than men militates against the possibility of explaining to them the dark consequences of granting their wishes and, men say, it is usually useless to try.

Most women agree with this view and react sharply to any suggestion that many women are as rational and able to face disappointment as many men are. Women stress the fact that the Koran says women are emotional and that, because of this, cannot be expected to tailor their desires to what might, in some sense, be taken as pragmatically preferable. When asked why men, who are not understood to be pawns of desire, grant their wives' wishes even when doing so is harmful to family finances, women say it is because of the men's "goodness" and of their love for their wives.

Thus far, nothing has been said about what men want from the spouse relationship. Here the key fact is that this relationship is more distinctive for husbands than it is for wives. For both spouses, only in marriage is sexual activity proper. Sex outside of marriage is a sin and adultery is so serious a sin that in Koranic law it merits death by stoning for both participants. Men are allowed more than one wife, but few Swahili--I know of only one--have more than one acknowledged wife. Some have "secret wives" whose existence is unknown to the main wife and the community generally, but by their nature, these clandestine relationships cannot have the full social and emotional relationship possible in an approved and acknowledged marriage.

For men, the spouse relationship is distinctive in that it is emotionally open. Much of the relationship between husband and wife takes place outside of the purview of all save nuclear family members, and a substantial part is entirely private. In the spouse relationship, men can express themselves freely and can receive emotional support as they cannot properly do in any other relationship. Men's relations with all women other than the wife, including even the relationship with the mother, are restrained by the separation of the sexes. Men's relations with other men, including brothers and friends, are kept within bounds by rivalry and the fear of being shamed. Only with wives are men emotionally free, and the significance of this for the men can be seen in their reactions to their wives' deaths. Many men are devastated by the loss of a wife and lasting depression, and even alcoholism in this pious Muslim community, are not uncommon reactions.

The spouse relationship for women has a quiet significance. It is true that, as for men, sexual expression is only proper within marriage. Unlike the situation for men, however, women are by no means solely dependent on their spouses for emotional expression and support. Women are quite open in their relations with one another.

The fear of shame and rivalry that constrains relations among men are far less potent forces among women. Sisters and neighbors hug one another, weep, laugh, and quarrel freely as men would never do in comparable relationships. Women may well have emotionally significant relationships with their husbands, but this relationship is only one of many such for the women. It is understood that men are independent and strong and that they need no emotional outlet or support so that the absence of these relational features in all relationships save the one with the wife is not understood to be consequential. It is understood that spouses love one another and that they should divorce if they do not, but men are not taken to be dependent on this love for their well being.

The spouse relationship for women is usually the sole source of money. Women who are heiresses, and there are a few in the Swahili community, have money of their own which they can use as they like. The few women who have paying jobs obviously get money from their employers but very few are paid enough to begin to buy the clothing and jewelry all community women want and, even so, wage-earning women ideally and often put the money they earn in their husband's charge. Remembering the significance of having finery in relations among women, getting money from the husband is desirable according to understandings shared among women quite apart from having the money itself.

The spouse relationship, then, is one in which men can get emotional support they cannot get elsewhere and in which women get money whose worth is largely attributable to the fact that their husbands give it to them. The women are not dependent on the men for emotional support because it is available to them in a number of other relationships, while the reverse is not true since emotional expression for men is sharply restricted in all other relationships. It is through the connections between what is unique about the spouse relationship for members of each sex that it is possible to explain wives' ability to bring their husbands to provide money for uses the men say they do to approve and from which they get no obvious advantage outside the spouse relationship. This explanation, however, requires an examination that goes beyond culture and considers the effects of cultural products (i.e., of the social structure and its effect on both men and women).

Analysis

At the beginning of this paper, emphasis was given the role of cultural forces in political activity. It was proposed that culture affects political activity and social life generally, both directly and indirectly. A main source of this indirect effect was said to be through what were called "cultural products." These products, and the first example used was a university building, are, like everything humans do, planned and constructed according to shared understandings. However, their physical character, including the size of the rooms in the building, have an effect that is independent of the cultural elements involved in planning and erecting the building. Nor are cultural products with effects that are not bound to the cultural elements involved in their production limited to physical objects such as buildings.

Anything produced according to shared understandings is a cultural product including social relationships and the social structures resulting from the totality of these relationships and the connections among them. Like other cultural products, these relationships affect what people do independently from the culture that guides the behavior that produces them. The brief account given of the politics of the spouse relationship among the Mombasa Swahili is intended to illustrate the effect cultural products, in the form of relationships and social structure, have on small-scale politics.

What is in many ways the most striking fact about the effect of culture on wives' power in relations with their husbands is that the understandings very widely shared among both men and women hold that there should be no such thing. Men are understood as properly controlling women and this understanding is strengthened by being "celestialized" in that it is taken as part of God's plan as revealed in the Koran. The understandings centering around women's emotionality and inability to plan make it particularly desirable that they not have any considerable ability to affect family finances and this is strengthened further by the understanding that men have a complete right to control the money they earn.

Thus, the culture, the understandings people share, is quite clear about the inappropriateness of wives using funds in ways their husbands do not approve. Yet a substantial majority of wives in this community do just that, spending important sums of money on finery and ceremonies, which their husbands say they do not want to pay for. The husband's power over money has formidable cultural support and, taking that together with the culturally established obstacles to the wife's control of money, it would seem that culture has no part in the actual power most wives have to use money the husband has earned.

There is, however, an indirect cultural source of the wives' power over family money. It derives not from understandings about the desirability of women using the money as many wish to since there are no such understandings. Rather, it derives from the effect of the combination of the nature of the spouse relationship and of the differences in the way the social structure affects men and as compared to women. Men are emotionally free only in their relations with their wives, and it is only from them that they receive warmth and support. The presence of other emotionally free relations is ruled out, not so much by a general understanding proscribing it, but on the basis of the different understandings that guide the course of their different relationships. Thus, men cannot easily be close to their mothers or sisters because of the difficulties in associating freely with members of the opposite sex other than the wife. Closeness with brothers is made difficult by the rivalry in that relationship. The relation with the father is generally considered among the most strife-ridden and tense in the family.

The culture, then, provides a variety of different understandings concerning different relationships which, together, produce a general effect: men are cut off from easy access to emotionally satisfying relations in all relationships save one. This overall effect is probably associated with the specific understanding that men do not need emotional support. The fact, however, that many men actually get such support in relations with their wives indicates that whatever this understanding may do, it does not always guide behavior in every relationship. In fact, it would seem that the specific understandings in particular relationships do that. The overall effect of these is not itself the result of a cultural element. There is no cultural element that holds men as being properly barred from emotionally active relations with mothers, sisters, brothers, and friends. Rather, it results from a common element in the whole array of men's relationships taken together and from the result of this on many men.

At the same time, women's relations outside marriage contain many that are warm and supportive. Women normally do not have relations with men other than their husbands that have this character, but most of their close relations with other women do. As the social structure puts men in the position of having no alternative sources of support other than their spouses, so it gives women many such sources. This makes it relatively painless for wives to behave coldly toward their husbands if they feel displeased, even for rather long periods, but makes it difficult for those husbands who want warmth and support to bear the chill. To avoid it, the men give their wives the things that make them happy, as the men put it, and thereby empower the wives in this regard.

The designers and builders of lecture halls may or may not have understandings about the desirability of large as opposed to small classes. The fact that the buildings built according to the designer's understandings, whatever they may be, have mainly large or mainly small rooms will affect lecturing and learning regardless of what those understandings are. The various relationships outside marriage involving men and those involving women in the Mombasa Swahili community may, but do not seem to, involve understandings about the nature of the spouse relationship. The fact that the understandings that guide their other relationships allow men few or no opportunities for emotional support outside marriage, while providing a number of such for women provides wives with a source of power in their dealings with their husbands that is only indirectly the result of the cultural elements that affect both spouses' relationships with others.

References

D'Andrade,R.G.
1987   Modal responses and cultural expertise. *American Behavioral Scientist* 31(2):194-202.

Goodenough,W.
1971   Culture, language, and society. *McCaleb module in anthropology*. Reading, Massachusetts: Addison-Wesley.

Harris,M.
1968   *The rise of anthropological theory.* New York: Croswell.

Keesing,R.
1970   Toward a model of role analysis. In *A handbook of method in cultural anthropology*, edited by R.Naroll and R.Cohen, 423-453. New York: Natural History Press.

Southall,A.W.
1989   Naked power and fancy dress power. Paper presented at Symposium on Power, Symbolism, and Political Culture, 12th International Congress of the Anthropological and Ethnological Sciences, in Zagreb.

Spiro,M.E.
1984   Some reflections on cultural determinism and relativism with special reference to emotion and reason. In *Cultural theory: Essays on mind, self, and emotion*, edited by R.Shweder and R.LaVine. Cambridge: Cambridge University Press.

Swartz,M.J.
n.d.   *The way the world is: Cultural processes and social relations among the Swahili of Mombasa.* Berkeley; London; and Los Angeles: The University of California Press. In press.
1968   *Local level politics*, edited by M.J.Swartz. Chicago: Aldine.
1970   Area studies, theory, and cross-cultural comparison. *African studies review* 13:63-69.
1978   Religious courts, community and ethnicity among the

454

Mombasa Swahili: An historical study of social boundaries. *Africa* 49:29-41.

1982a   Cultural sharing and cultural theory: Some results of a study of the nuclear family in five societies. *American Anthropologist* 84:314-338.

1982b   The isolation of men and the power of women: Sources of power among the Swahili of Mombasa. *Journal of anthropological research* 38:26-44.

1983   Culture and implicit power: Maneuvers and understandings in Swahili nuclear family relations. In *Yearbook of political anthropology*, edited by M.Aronoff. New Brunswick, New Jersey: Transaction Press.

1990   Aggressive speech, status, and cultural distribution among the Swahili of Mombasa. In *Personality and the cultural constitution of society: Papers in honor of M.E.Spiro*, edited by D.Jordan and M.Swartz. Tuscaloosa, Alabama: University of Alabama Press.

Swartz,M., V.Turner, and A.Tuden, eds.
1966   *Political anthropology.* Chicago: Aldine Publishing Company.

Letter from Nigeria: Humbling
The Ethnographer

Leonard Plotnicov, Professor
University of Pittsburgh
United States

One of the exciting attractions of doing ethnography is the close encounter anthropologists experience with exotic *others*. We enjoy the adventure and romance of spanning cultural gulfs to form friendships based on shared, essential human characteristics and, to the extent possible, experiencing other life ways. It is personally enriching, but not the rationale for our professional duty, to make a detailed and accurate record of the research problem under focus. We like to think that our publications offer worthy theoretical contributions, but wisdom tells us that theories are subject to the whims of fashion and are ephemeral. Good ethnography is everlasting, but it is not achieved simply with lengthy stays in the field. It takes deliberate effort, and obstacles must be overcome.

In addition to bridging cultural barriers, the ethnographer initially must work to diminish disparities of inequality between researcher and informants to develop rapport, as reliable data depend on trust. Surmounting differences of wealth, race, and power stemming from governmental and institutional backing takes charm and impression management (Berreman 1962; Goffman 1959). The anthropologist can literally get down and get dirty to get in and get started. Southall (personal communication) related how, upon settling among the Alur (Southall 1953), he walked up to an unknown farmer tilling his land and commenced working alongside him. In such ways does ethnography begin. Once begun, the manner by which fieldwork commences is familiar to anthropologists. Southall and Gutkind's (1957, 217-218) description of ethnography in their classic study of Kampala is typical:

> a great deal of time has been spent in talking to people, in visiting in their homes and in eating with them. It has also meant that we have had to listen to endless and often trivial complaints, and hence become the emotional buffers for inner conflict and confusion. A permissive attitude on the part of the research worker, particularly vis-a-vis the immigrants is essential if the barriers, not only of race, but also of fear, suspicion and outright antagonism are to be broken down.

As with all social relationships, informants and fieldworkers use (and sometimes exploit) each other. But time in the field sees a wonderful metamorphosis take place with the growth of mutual respect and genuine affection. The resulting relationships have been acknowledged and given tribute in scores of monographs and some symposium volumes (e.g., Casagrande 1960; Freilich 1970).

The bond also creates a moral dilemma at times. The intimacy that comes with mutual trust brings with it a richness of personal or private information that may be quintessentially revealing and instructive on some important aspect of research and the anthropologist must choose between its publication and protecting the source from potential harm or embarrassment. Using fictitious names for people and places is hardly adequate protection and does not resolve the issue.

In my report on Jos (Plotnicov 1967), I tried to emulate the superb ethnographic richness of *Townsmen in the Making* (Southall and Gutkind 1957), and so chose to reveal those characteristics of my informants that they would have preferred remain unmentioned, but which lent the persons credibility for their human foibles. Fortunately, none were injured by these revelations, to my knowledge. Although never resting comfortably with this decision, I justified it in the belief that I had portrayed the variety of men in the new urban setting in depth and accurately. How astonished I was, therefore, to learn recently that I had misjudged some critical aspects of one of my principal informants; the Ijaw man I called Isaac Cookey-Jaja. As neighbors for two years, we became very close. I spent one Christmas at his home town as his guest (Plotnicov 1964) and, as is common with anthropologists, maintained good relations with his family during the past thirty years. I sent them aid during the Biafra conflict. His eldest daughter spent visits with my family while attending her American universities, which I sponsored.

Of all informants, I thought I knew Isaac best. I saw more of him, as he frequently visited during evenings for an interview or just to drink and chat (Plotnicov 1967, 111-112).

> It was Isaac's habit to open up and speak freely once the formal interview had ended for that session. He would sit back in his chair, sip his stout, smack his lips, and commence a long monologue on a topic suggested by something mentioned earlier.

On one occasion "he drank a considerable amount of whiskey 'to ease his cold'" (Plotnicov 1967, 136), which led to a confession of sorts and the embarrassing revelation that his self-portrayal as one of the national elite was pretense and sham. He would like being a Freemason and to have famous Nigerians as his house guests, but that took money and he was broke.

Thus I trusted what he told me and wrote confidently of his having a good marriage and family life, that his interest in the occult was an intellectual justification for his pride in traditional African culture (as expressed in supernatural beliefs), and that his inability to succeed as a civil engineer and contractor in northern Nigeria was due to parochial politics rather than personal inadequacy. When, after the

Biafra war, I learned that he returned to Jos, that he could not revive his business or even support himself, and was described as depressed, I attributed his psychological decline to the insurmountable obstacles of the political climate, and considered him as one of its tragic casualties. Only now, with hindsight, could I have anticipated what a daughter would reveal in the letter reproduced below. For the tone it communicates and for its ethnographic qualities, I present it as it was written, omitting only inessential details and occasionally interjecting editorial remarks for clarification and brevity.

8th December 1989

Dear Leo [the name given me in Jos],

Thank you ever so much for being able to write to me, and to care to find out more about the family you were once very familiar with. It is not common for highly learned people like you to reply or care about people like us. I was very happy just like my sisters, mother and younger brother who were around [residing together in Port Harcourt]. I read out the letter to them and they all asked me to reply to you as soon as possible and send their regards to you and your family.

[She asks about each of my family members.]

I shall now relate to you all that you asked in your letter; beginning with my father.

My father stopped living with us since 1973. He stopped working since 1955. From the year he stopped working, for reasons best known to him, my mother had been the one caring for him and the whole family. However, he has never shown appreciation to her. He does not accept that he has failed in his responsibilities as the family head. When in 1973 my mother told him that she can no longer cope with the family's demands when he is quite capable of working to get us well fed; he became offended and resort to diabolical means.

He was initiated by his "native" doctor friend. These native doctors are wicked, some are said to be wizards. They claim they can control and manipulate people and events on earth.

Our father, by what he admits to us and to many others, reveals that he is the architect of our misfortunes. However, we thank God that upon all these obstacles, we still find ourselves breathing good health and struggling to survive. The misery within the family is not what one can complete narrating in writing within a twinkle of the eye. There are so much confusions in our family now. It is no more a united family. Some are on the side of the mother, some with the father, and some you can't say where they belong to. All these problems have affected all of us greatly--emotionally, physically, socially, morally, etc.

Our father who is supposed to be a renowned civil engineer in Nigeria lost his virtue and fortune to this mysterious world and friends of satanic acts whom he associated himself with. It is an unfortunate situation which he is indirectly regretting. Little did he know that asking his native doctor friend to put us on the negative side would be so harmful to us. He did this to punish my mother. He sometimes said that the best punishment to give to a woman after divorce is to reject the children too, because the man does not gain anything other than the name. He said it is only the woman that gains the fortune of the children. I can't imagine how he thought we would forget him when we have progressed [matured, developed]. But with these things he had done, most of us are bitter with him and we are now used to not living with a father. At times we don't even feel we have a father for we never grew up with him happily.

Constance [I use the names that appear in Plotnicov (1967)] has tried to re-unite the family but it didn't work out. Well, what can we do, than to bear all that came to us. The way has been very rough with most of us excepting our older brother whom my father told us, and in his presence, that he did not include him in all that he did to us, to suffer in this world. That older brother couldn't query him for saying so, rather he is happy about it and both of them are good friends. This very brother of mine was also brought up by our mother. No sooner did he finish his training with the School of Electrical Communication [a pseudonym], than my mother became his enemy. Such is life. Some people don't reap where they sow.

My father did much havoc in our lives. He is now confessing, saying that he thought he was alone; and probably through this frustration gravitated toward a conduct that is abhorrent to him. He does not know how to make amends. We have accepted the situation. We found ourselves believing it to be destiny. But there is still hope: For I know that one's past experiences can keep the person sad, the present may keep him thinking, but the future might terrify him. So I believe there would be changes in our lives. We can't be on the suffering side forever. You might not believe these stories, but I tell you; it's a true to life story. These are just briefings about my father.

My mother is called Cecilia Cookey-Jaja. She was born in 1923. She lost her father when she was a toddler and the mother when she was about three years. She was left to be trained by her maternal uncle who had a cruel wife that didn't like her company in their midst. She became stranded and was later picked up by her older brother of the paternal side. He too had a cruel wife who was also finding fault with my mom. She had been very unfortunate in her up-bringing as she is the only child of her mother. These frustrations pushed her into early marriage. In fact the half-brother was not ready to help her further. So she stopped her education at primary six.

She married my father and she bore 12 children. The first three children died, then Constance [lived] and another after her died also.

Those that died were three girls and a boy. The living ones are six girls and two boys.

She is a hardworking and independent woman. Since I grew up to differentiate good from bad, my mother had been the person feeding and clothing all of us. My father contributed a little but not much. In fact, since 1973, he has not done anything; and it was then he left the family house for Jos. No work at all.

My mother has been the person bearing the whole burden of the family. She is a petty trader and seamstress. She sews school uniforms. She wakes up every night between 2-3 a.m. to cut and sew. Sewing in Nigeria is not made easy as in your country. She is undergoing a difficult task.

She never enjoyed her marriage since her life. In fact there isn't a marriage or rather, it was never a marriage. It was a dangerous union. Nobody told us, but we judged and concluded on our own because we started observing all these happenings right from when we were younger. I don't think there can be reconciliation on this earth between them and even we. We have all grown with bitterness for our dad.

On the whole, my mother has her faults too; but they are not as much as that of my dad. Hers could be endured. Sometimes, I think she is under intense pressure because she sometimes speaks hurtfully to us and when this happens, we feel extremely miserable. Her situation and background is understandable, considering what it entails in raising eight children single-handedly. She is sometimes nervy and over-demanding especially now that she is getting older. At times she tends to be over-protective and sometimes she is short-tempered. We realise they are all due to the mental and physical strain on her. Sometimes we get confused from where the problem is. In any case, when we remember her many good sides, our hearts and thinking become happy. Often times we think and ask ourselves, "What if we were not brought up to the level my mother has kept us"?

At times I think that some of our problems with our mother is as a result of living together with her up till this age. A friend told me that overcrowding adds stress and frustration which often open the gate to anger and outbursts of temper. How much truth is in her idea?

My mother would have been a very happy woman but fate didn't favour her. It is a sad life. No happiness from childhood and none from the husband too. None of us females is married. It is all sadness. But in all, we thank God for making it possible for her to have enough to bring us up to the level we are now.

She likes singing, especially Anthems and Negro spirituals. She has a few music books and she teachers her fellow "Women Christian Association". We learnt her mother too was a famous singer in her days. She was happy to hear from you and she sincerely sent her good wishes to you and members of your family. She too was surprised to hear that you replied to my letter.

[She writes about her siblings, where they live, their jobs, and their children. Her own little boy gives her great joy. She enjoys school-teaching but complains of low wages and the high cost of living. Her ambition is to return to school to study child psychology, but the scholarship required is elusive.]

So far Sir, that's the much I have for you about our family. I hope I have not bored you with my long thesis. With all these troubles, we are still hopeful. God will surely work out his purposes as the year succeeds years. I shall send you pictures next year. I don't have any available one now. Take care of yourself and family. Greetings to all and sundry. From all my sisters and brother, son and nephews, it's best wishes from now and all the time.

Love, Gertrude Cookey-Jaja

Discussion

The letter revealed some inaccuracies in my published data on this family; three infants (not two) died before Constance was born and the dates of birth of Gertrude and Ibelema are off by a year or two. But these details are insignificant and beside the point when compared to the revelations of Isaac's obsession with the supernatural and the family discord his behavior caused.

Are we to believe Gertrude or is this another instance of Rashomon with its multiple perspectives and many truths? Was I misled, simply obtuse, or both? It is possible that my observations were accurate, that Isaac's family life at the time of the research was not under the severe stress it experienced during and after the Biafra period. Even so, could I have been more sensitive to portentous nuances, omens? Surely, they were present. I searched my memory and notes for such indications but could bring forth only two suggestive incidents.

Some weeks after Isaac and I first met, he announced that he had investigated my credentials, and determined that I was who I claimed to be, and not a Soviet or American spy, as some alleged. About a year later, he took me to a "trustworthy" [genuine] soothsayer for a professional session. This, he said, would give me the truth regarding the well-being of my relatives in America. (Spirit messengers were sent to check them out.) Between these events I was able to determine that the same diviner had vouched for my authenticity. But Isaac's faith in the African supernatural was not at all unusual, even among university educated Nigerians. His interest in studying the occult seemed a part of his intellectual curiosity, and not extraordinary. If I could have anticipated what the future held, it would have been more in this domain than in his domestic situation, about which I had far less information.

Seeking to determine where or how I might have improved on my research drew my attention to some remarks on research methods in the Introduction of *Strangers* (Plotnicov 1967, 15-16).

> With each primary informant I attempted to gain an integrated picture of his personal and social life so that a cumulative knowledge derived from all of them might provide an understanding of Jos....
>
> The primary informants were all adult males and heads of families. I concentrated upon them partly in order to use their vantage point as a means to study the family, particularly the family as a system of interaction among component members. My efforts in this regard confirmed my belief that it is not easy to analyze Nigerian urban (or rural) domestic units as micro-social systems; such research would require so intense a focus on the family itself that the observer could undertake little else.

We may be deceiving ourselves if we believe that as strangers and friends (*pace* Powdermaker 1966) ethnographers are privileged to get the most private information. A year or two in the field often results in our developing genuine and enduring friendships but we should not expect that these relationships will disclose the innermost confidences. This does not occur even within our own society and with our most intimate and closest associates. But that should not dissuade us from trying.

References

Berreman,G.D.
1962 *Behind many masks: Ethnography and impression management in a Himalayan village.* Monograph No. 4, Society for Applied Anthropology, Lexington: University of Kentucky.

Casagrande,J.B., ed.
1960 *In the company of man: Twenty portraits of anthropological informants.* New York: Harper & Row.

Freilich,M., ed.
1970 *Marginal natives: Anthropologists at work.* New York: Harper & Row.

Goffman,E.
1959 *The presentation of self in everyday life.* New York: Doubleday.

Plotnicov,L.
1964 Nativism. *Contemporary Nigeria Anthropological Quarterly* 37(3):121-137.
1967 *Strangers to the city: Urban man in Jos, Nigeria.* Pittsburgh: University of Pittsburgh.

Powdermaker,H.
1966 *Stranger and friend: The way of an anthropologist.* New York: Norton.

Southall,A.W.
1953 *Alur society.* Cambridge: W. Heffer and Sons.

Southall,A.W.,and P.C.W.Gutkind
1957 *Townsmen in the making: Kampala and its suburbs.* Kampala: East African Institute of Social Research.

Contribution of Professor Aidan Southall to the Urban Anthropology Studies in China

Ruan Xihu, Professor of Nationalities Studies
Chinese Academy of Social Sciences, and
Executive President
Chinese Association of Global Ethnic Studies
Beijing, People's Republic of China

When we celebrated at the successful conclusion of the First International Urban Anthropology Conference, which was held in Beijing during the winter of 1989-1990, we all knew we had to thank Professor Aidan Southall who, with other foreign scholars and cooperating with Chinese scholars, brought about the holding of the first-ever Urban Anthropology Conference in China. During the conference, Western and Chinese anthropologists interested in urban problems gathered together, theoretically analyzing the origins of cities, their development, and their current situation. The success of the conference not only founded urban anthropology as a branch in Chinese scientific circles but initiated a new aspect for the study of global urban anthropology.

Because of Professor Southall's effort, the conference was scheduled to be held in Beijing, making it easily accessible to Chinese scholars. This made it possible for Chinese and foreign anthropologists to exchange ideas on a broad range of topics. Western scholars know and understand more about China's urban traditions, and Chinese scholars have drawn valuable insights from Western urbanism. The complementarity of learning between foreign and Chinese scholars was the key point of this conference. It can be said that holding the first urban anthropology conference helped to promote a profound and significant transformation of some of the Chinese anthropologists, a move away from research on remote or minority ethnic groups alone, to research on the majority of Han people and to urban ethnicity studies. Since the founding of the People's Republic of China, Chinese anthropologists' main work has been the research of minority ethnic groups in China, studying their origin, religion, culture, and social system from every aspect of the social sciences and the humanities and establishing a quite integrated and scientific understanding. Our research on the Han has hitherto been restricted to studying the relationship between Han and other ethnic groups. Thus, through this urban anthropology conference, China's anthropological research will turn its focal point of ethnic study in rural areas toward ethnic study in cities. In the past, we neglected the fact that people are the principal part of research in anthropology by overfocusing on paleoanthropology. Now we will correct past errors by ensuring that our anthropological research includes Han people, who have the largest population and occupy the most living space in China. This conference thrusts the study of Han people onto the center stage of Chinese anthropology for the first time. This will no doubt greatly enhance the development of China's anthropology.

This profound change in China's anthropology circles is inseparable from Professor Aidan Southall's efforts. But the contributions of Professor Aidan Southall lie far beyond this. From "The Alur Legend of Sir Samuel Baker and the Mukama Kabarega" (1951) to "Power, Sanctity and Symbolism in the Political Economy of the Nilotes" (1989), he has written nearly seventy research articles and nine key publications, reflecting the remarkable achievements of this outstanding anthropologist. Professor Southall is an accomplished scholar on Africa. From his research articles, we can see that he has investigated the peoples of Uganda, Madagascar, Kenya, East Africa, West Africa, and the Nilotes. In our urban anthropology conference, Professor Southall brought us reports entitled "Eras and Patterns of Urbanization in Africa" and "Urban Theory and the Chinese City," which brought to young Chinese urban anthropological circles the study method of urban anthropology and which offered valuable experience and insights to China's anthropologists engaged in urban anthropology research.

It is worth saying that Professor Southall sets a high value on China's urban experience. In his essay "Urban Theory and the Chinese City," he systematically analyzed historic changes in China's cities, pointing out that "the Chinese have been more radical in their experimentation with the relationship of city and society, of town and country, than any other nation."

I was extremely honored to get to know Professor Southall. I feel that he is a scholar of humor and meticulous scholarship. His contribution to global and China's anthropology is great and at the same time, Professor Southall's efforts to bring together Chinese and American anthropologists have opened up bright prospects for future cooperation.

References

Southall,A.W.

1951   The Alur legend of Sir Samuel Baker and the Mukama
            Kabarega.

1989   Power, sanctity and symbolism in the political economy
            of the Nilotes. In *Creativity of power: cosmology
            and action in African societies*, edited by W.Arens
            and I.Karp. Washington, D.C.: Smithsonian Institution
            Press.

1989-90   Eras and patterns of urbanization in Africa. Urban
            Anthropology Conference, Winter 1989-1990, Beijing,
            People's Republic of China.

1989-90   Urban theory and the Chinese city. Urban Anthropology
            Conference, Winter 1989-1990, Beijing, People's
            Republic of China.